Praise for *The Geography of Genius*

"Eric Weiner has single-handedly invented a new nonfiction genre in which a brilliant and hilarious writer leaves his home and family to circle the globe in search of the answer to a timeless question. *The Geography of Genius* is an intellectual odyssey, a traveler's diary, and a comic novel all rolled into one. Smart, original, and utterly delightful, this is Weiner's best book yet."

—Daniel Gilbert, Harvard professor and bestselling author of *Stumbling on Happiness*

"It's rare to read a book that makes you laugh and learn, but Eric Weiner has done it again. This witty, wise explorer offers fascinating insights on how culture has inspired creativity across the ages—ripe for chats at water coolers and cocktail parties—and offers a practical map for how we can all become a bit more inventive."

—Adam Grant, Wharton professor and bestselling author of *Give and Take* and *Originals*

"Weiner is a superb travel guide: funny, knowledgeable, self-deprecating, and always up for sharing a bottle of wine."

—*The Washington Post*

"Weiner is an affable tour guide and a lively, witty writer in the style of Bill Bryson."

—*Booklist*

"There are some writers whose company is worth keeping, whatever the subject . . . and Mr. Weiner is blessed with this gift. He is a prober and questioner, a big-hearted humanist who will always take a colorful, contradictory reality over some unfounded certainty."

—*The Wall Street Journal*

"A witty, entertaining romp. Weiner's vivid descriptions of modern-day life in each locale make the spots feel like must-visit destinations."

—*The New York Times Book Review*

"*The Geography of Genius* is witty, informative, and compulsively readable. Whether you're getting genius tips from Freud in Vienna or hearing the secrets of high-tech powerhouses in Silicon Valley, you'll emerge smarter after reading this delightful travelogue of ingenuity."

—Daniel H. Pink, bestselling author of *To Sell Is Human* and *Drive*

"An entertaining and thought-provoking book. . . . Weiner's wry wit shines through as he drinks sublime tea in China and contemplates a coffin collar in an Edinburgh museum; as he interviews figures such as Jack Ma, a Hangzhou native who founded multibillion dollar company Alibaba; and as he wanders the Ringstrasse of Vienna and the strip malls of Silicon Valley, pondering the conditions that lead to genius."

—*The Christian Science Monitor*

"This witty and fun book has an insight in every paragraph. It's a charming mix of history and wisdom cloaked as a rollicking travelogue filled with colorful characters."

—Walter Isaacson, bestselling author of *The Innovators* and *Steve Jobs*

"Fun and thought provoking."

—*Miami Herald*

"Funny, engaging and wry."

—*Ploughshares*

"A welcome read for lovers of geography . . . travelogues, and the history of science."

—*Library Journal* (starred review)

"Informative and dryly witty, Weiner's odyssey is both an insightful examination of genius and a call to readers to explore their own untapped creative resources."

—*Shelf Awareness* (starred review)

"Well read, thoughtful, and above all curious, Weiner invites the reader to explore a satisfying take on a meaningful topic while also enjoying daily pleasures in cities around the world."

—*BookPage*

THE

GEOGRAPHY
OF GENIUS

Lessons from the World's Most Creative Places

ERIC WEINER

SIMON & SCHUSTER PAPERBACKS

NEW YORK   LONDON   TORONTO   SYDNEY   NEW DELHI

for Sharon

———

Simon & Schuster Paperbacks
An Imprint of Simon & Schuster, Inc.
1230 Avenue of the Americas
New York, NY 10020

For information about special discounts for bulk purchases, please contact Simon & Schuster Special Sales at 1-866-506-1949 or business@simonandschuster.com.

The Simon & Schuster Speakers Bureau can bring authors to your live event. For more information or to book an event, contact the Simon & Schuster Speakers Bureau at 1-866-248-3049 or visit our website at www.simonspeakers.com.

Interior design by Ruth Lee-Mui

10   9   8

Library of Congress Cataloging-in-Publication Data
Weiner, Eric.
  The geography of genius : a search for the world's most creative
places from ancient Athens to Silicon Valley / Eric Weiner. — First
Simon & Schuster hardcover edition.
    pages cm
1. Genius—Miscellanea. 2. Geography—Psychological aspects.
3. Cities and towns. 4. Weiner, Eric—Travel. 5. Voyages and travels. I. Title.
 BF412.W395 2016
  153.9'809—πdc23
                            2015004798

ISBN 978-1-4516-9165-8
ISBN 978-1-4516-9167-2 (pbk)
ISBN 978-1-4516-9168-9 (ebook)

What is honored in a country will be cultivated there.

—PLATO

CONTENTS

CONTENTS

THE

GEOGRAPHY
OF GENIUS

INTRODUCTION: ADVENTURES WITH THE GALTON BOX

PEOPLE BEGAN TO RECOGNIZE MY SPECIALNESS when I was still young. As a ten-year-old, curious about the laws of physics, I wondered what would happen if I tossed a large water balloon off the balcony of my father's fifteenth-floor apartment. So, following in the footsteps of Newton and Darwin and great scientists everywhere, I decided to conduct an experiment.

"Way to go, Einstein," said the clearly impressed owner of the car whose windshield had been thoroughly shattered by the surprisingly robust force of the water balloon. Who knew? Such is the cost of scientific progress, I rationalized at the time. Another incident, years later, involved a fireplace, a closed flue, and the local fire department. I can still hear the firefighter's words: "What are you, some sort of genius?"

Alas, no, I am not. This puts me in what is fast becoming a minority. Today, we suffer from a serious case of genius inflation. The word is tossed around promiscuously. Tennis players and app designers are described as geniuses. There are "fashion geniuses" and "culinary geniuses" and, of course, "political geniuses." Our children are all Little Einsteins and Little Mozarts. If we're having trouble with our latest iProduct, we belly up to Apple's Genius Bar. An avalanche of self-help books, meanwhile, tell us we all have a little genius inside of us (in my case very deep inside), a message we happily imbibe, oblivious to the fact that if everyone is a genius, then nobody is.

I have been watching this evolving—or, rather, devolving—concept of genius for a while now. I am fascinated by the subject of genius in much the way a naked man is fascinated by the subject of clothing. Are we really in a downward genius spiral, or is there hope for us, and even for me?

Genius. The word beguiles, but do I really know what it means? It comes to us from the Latin *genius,* but it meant something very different in Roman times. Back then, a genius was a presiding deity that followed you everywhere, much like a helicopter parent only with supernatural powers. (The word *genie* stems from the same root.) Every person had a genius. Every place, too. Cities, towns, and marketplaces, all possessed their own presiding spirit, a genius loci, that continuously animated them. The current dictionary definition—"extraordinary intellectual power esp. as manifested in creative activity"—is a product of the eighteenth-century Romantics, those brooding poets who suffered, *suffered* for their art and, we'd now say, for their *creativity,* a word that is even more recent; it didn't come along until 1870 and wasn't in widespread use until the 1950s.

Some use *genius* to describe a very smart person—someone with a high IQ—but that is overly narrow, and misleading. Plenty of people with extremely high IQs have accomplished little, and conversely, plenty of people of "average" intelligence have done great things. No, I am speaking of genius in the creative sense—as the highest form of creativity.

My favorite definition of creative genius comes from researcher and artificial-intelligence expert Margaret Boden. The creative genius, she says, is someone with "the ability to come up with ideas that are new, surprising, and valuable." Those also are the criteria the US Patent Office uses when deciding whether an invention deserves a patent.

Consider something as simple as a coffee cup. I might invent one that is painted an unusual shade of fluorescent orange. Yes, it is new, but not especially surprising or all that useful. Now let's say I invent a coffee cup with no bottom. That is certainly new, and definitely surprising, but, again, not particularly useful. No, to qualify for a patent, I would have to invent, say, a self-cleaning coffee cup or a folding one that doubles as a flash drive—something that fulfilled all three criteria: new, surprising, and useful. The toddler steps of incremental innovation don't earn you a patent, or the title of genius. Only a leap does.

The question that intrigues someone such as myself, a creature of geography and a student of history, is not simply what these leaps look like but where, and when, they take place. So I decided to conduct another experiment of sorts, this time minus the water balloon. I embarked on a version of the old Grand Tour, those trips abroad that young English gentry took in the eighteenth and nineteenth centuries in order to broaden their horizons. I am no gentry and, as I said, no genius. College was a blur of cheap beer and unsuitable women. I wish I had paid more attention. This time, I vowed, would be different. This time I would heed the advice of my father-in-law. "Young man," he'd say in his musical, indeterminate accent, "You need to ed-u-cate yourself."

My education begins in London, a city that has produced not only its share of geniuses but also the study of genius itself. If you're like me and fascinated by the so-called science of genius—or like to furtively stick small pins into pieces of felt—then you don't want to miss the Galton Box. You can find it, as I did, at London's University College.

One overcast morning, a spring tease in the air, I hop the tube to King's Cross Station, then walk a few hundred yards to the university's Hogwartsian campus. There, I am greeted by Subhadra Das, keeper of the Box. I like her immediately. Something about her smile and the way she looks me in the eye is reassuring. She leads me down an unassuming corridor to an unassuming room where we find the Box, resting on a table. She dons a pair of latex gloves then, carefully, as if performing neurosurgery on a gerbil, reaches into the Box.

The Galton Box contains the worldly possessions of one Sir Francis Galton. It's an odd collection, befitting an odd but brilliant man. Galton, a nineteenth-century scientist and polymath, a cousin of Charles Darwin's, brought the world statistical analysis and the questionnaire, composite portraiture and forensic fingerprints. He was one of the first meteorologists. He coined the phrase *nature versus nurture*. He had an IQ of nearly 200.

Galton's motto was "Count whenever you can!" To him, anything worth doing was worth doing numerically, and he once confessed that he couldn't fully grasp a problem unless he was first able to "disembarrass it of words." Socially, he was awkward in the extreme, more comfortable with integers than people.

Subhadra extracts a piece of felt and several pins from the Box. She gingerly places them on the table. These, she explains, were Galton's tools for one of his quirkier experiments: an attempt to devise a "beauty map" of Great Britain. He wanted to determine where the most beautiful women of the land lived, then plot the results on a map. This being Victorian times, though, and Galton's being so shy, he couldn't very well hold a beauty contest.

Galton's solution was to stand on street corners in various cities and, with felt and pins tucked discreetly in his overcoat pocket, watch women walk by. If he saw an attractive woman (in his opinion), he stuck four pins into the felt. Less attractive women got three pins, and so on. He traveled across the United Kingdom surreptitiously ranking women's appearances this way, and presumably not raising any eyebrows. He concluded that the most attractive women lived in London, the least attractive in the Scottish city of Aberdeen.

The world did not pay much attention to Galton's beauty map, but it did take notice of his landmark book, *Hereditary Genius*. Published in 1869, it delved deep into the family pedigrees of eminent creators, leaders, and athletes. Galton believed that these people owed their success to genetics, or what he called "natural abilities." For Galton, genetics explained everything. It explained why one family might contain several eminent members and another none. It explained why societies with many immigrants and refugees were often successful, since these newcomers "introduced a valuable strain of blood." It explained why some nations succeeded more than others (elucidated in a chapter with the unfortunate title "The Comparative Worth of Races"). It explained the decline of once-great civilizations—the ancient Greeks, for instance, had begun to intermarry with "lesser" peoples, thus diluting their bloodline. In the end, it explained why every one of his geniuses was a white man, like him, living on a small, gloomy island off the coast of continental Europe. As for women, Galton only mentions them once, in a chapter called "Literary Men."

Galton's book was well received, and no wonder. It articulated, in scientific language, what people had suspected for a long time: geniuses are born, not made.

Subhadra carefully places the pins and felt back into the Galton Box. She confides that she has mixed feelings about the Box, and about Galton, who came from a privileged background yet was blind to the advantages such status bestowed upon him and his friends.

"He thought he was living in a meritocracy," she says. Yet, at the same time, she can't deny that he was brilliant. He was the first to measure things we thought were unmeasurable and, she says, slipping off the gloves, "question things we thought were unquestionable." Galton singlehandedly wrested the subject of creative genius from the hands of the poets and the mystics and placed it squarely in the hands of the scientists.

His notion of hereditary genius, though, was dead wrong. Genius is not passed down like blue eyes or baldness. There is no genius gene; one genius has yet to beget another. Civilizations do not rise and fall because of shifting gene pools. Yes, when it comes to creative genius, genes are part of the mix, but a relatively small part, somewhere between 10 and 20 percent, psychologists estimate.

The geniuses-are-born myth has been supplanted by another myth: geniuses are made. On the face of it, this seems true. It takes hard work, at least ten thousand hours of practice, over ten years, to begin to approach mastery, let alone genius, as one well-known study found. Modern psychology has, in other words, unearthed empirical evidence for Edison's old saw about success being 99 percent perspiration and 1 percent inspiration.

This component, sweat, adds another piece to the picture, an important piece. The picture, though, remains incomplete. Something is missing. But what? That question nags at me, like one of Galton's mathematical puzzles, as I walk briskly across the Victorian campus, the spring tease replaced by a light but persistent rain.

A few months and some seven thousand miles later, I find myself at yet another campus, in the presence of yet another box. This box contains index cards. There must be hundreds of them. On each card, written in tiny but perfectly legible handwriting, is a historic event and the name of an eminent person who lived at the time. The Italian Renaissance and Michelangelo, for instance. The cards are neatly categorized by date and place. It's all so methodical, so Galtonian, I think. The owner of this box, though, is very much alive and kicking. He is standing before me now, shaking my hand vigorously.

Dean Keith Simonton is tan and fit. He's on sabbatical but you wouldn't know it judging by his boundless energy and frenetic schedule. He's wearing jeans and flip-flops and, as he does every day, a T-shirt with an illustration of a genius or leader emblazoned on it. (Today, it is Oscar Wilde.) A mountain bike is propped against the bookshelf. Schubert is playing softly in the background. The California sun streams through the window.

Simonton is a professor of psychology at the University of California–Davis and a self-confessed intellectual spelunker. He loves nothing more than exploring unknown depths, places where others fear to go, owing to the darkness and the loneliness. In that sense, too, he reminds me of Galton. Also, like Galton, Simonton is obsessed with the study of genius and has a serious numbers addiction. ("How are your differential equations?" he asks me at one point. Not so good, how are yours?)

Unlike Galton, though, Simonton does not stick pins into pieces of felt and is perfectly capable of eye contact and other basic social niceties. Unlike Galton, he does not hail from a privileged background. His family was blue-collar, his father a high school dropout. And, crucially, unlike Galton, Simonton does not suffer from an ethnocentric bias. He sees the world clearly, and he is onto something big.

Simonton's obsession, like most, began early. In kindergarten, his family bought a set of the *World Book Encyclopedia*. He was instantly enthralled. He would spend hours gazing at the photos of Einstein and Darwin and other geniuses the way other kids gawk at photos of baseball players and pop stars. Even at that age, he was fascinated not only by the achievements of these godlike men and women, but the way their lives intersected in unexpected ways. Leonardo da Vinci and Michelangelo squabbling on the streets of Florence. Freud and Einstein kibitzing over coffee in Berlin.

In college, Simonton took a course on the history of civilization, but ever the scientist, his papers were peppered with mathematical equations—"fame is directly proportional to the occurrence of name; that is $F = n(N)$"—and references to the laws of thermodynamics. His professor was nonplussed and wrote a stern rebuke: "If you think of the historical process as rigidly as universal laws are conceived of, then you will probably have great difficulty understanding history." Simonton has spent the last fifty years proving that professor wrong. He earned a PhD in psychology and devoted himself to the embryonic field of "geniusology."

It hasn't been easy. Academia, for all its professions of broad-mindedness, doesn't take kindly to troublemakers. This was the 1960s and '70s, a time when creativity and genius were not subjects the academy took seriously, which seems odd, given that universities are supposedly in the business of producing geniuses, but less odd when you consider that, as the author Robert Grudin so astutely observed, "there are two types of subjects that a culture studies little: those which it despises and those which it holds dearest." The subject of genius manages to fit both types. We hold dear the notion of the solitary creator, courageously overcoming the odds, vanquishing the confederacy of dunces allied against her. Yet we secretly (and sometimes not so secretly) despise the know-it-all, especially one with dangerous new ideas.

"When I told people of my plans to study genius, they thought I was nuts," Simonton tells me. "They actually gave me a list of the academic journals that I would *not* be published in." Simonton, by his own account a stubborn man, was determined to prove them wrong.

Over the past half century, he has pioneered the obscure but fascinating field of historiometrics. It's the study of past epochs using the tools of modern social science, mainly statistics. Historiometrics is a kind of psychological autopsy, only the postmortem is performed not on a single individual but on an entire society. It isn't interested in the usual history, though. It cares little for wars and assassinations and sundry disasters. No, the field is interested in the bright spots of history, the epochs that spawned beautiful art and brilliant philosophy and scientific breakthroughs.

Early in his career, Simonton homed in on a phenomenon central to the field of historiometrics: the appearance of genius fluctuates over place and time. Geniuses do not pop up randomly—one in Siberia, another in Bolivia—but in groupings. Genius clusters. Athens in 450 BC. Florence in AD 1500. Certain places, at certain times, produced a bumper crop of brilliant minds and good ideas.

The question is why. We now know it's not genetic. These golden ages come and go much more quickly than gene pools change. So what was it? Climate? Money? Dumb luck?

Typically, these are not the sort of questions we ask about creative genius. We've framed the discussion almost exclusively in terms of something that happens "inside of us." If that were true, though, these genius clusters wouldn't exist. And if creativity were solely an interior process, psychologists would by now have identified a universal "creative personality." They have not, and I doubt they ever will. Geniuses can be sullen introverts such as Michelangelo or happy extroverts such as Titian.

Like Galton, we've been sticking pins in all the wrong places, asking the wrong questions. Rather than asking "What is creativity?" a better question is *"Where* is creativity?" I'm not speaking of trendy metropolises with lots of sushi restaurants and theater. Those are the fruits of a creative city, not its source. I'm not speaking of free food and beanbag chairs but, rather, the underlying conditions, often unexpected, that make a golden age shine. In a word, I'm speaking of culture.

Culture is more than what the dictionary tells us: "a set of shared attitudes, values and goals." Culture is the enormous yet invisible ocean in which we swim. Or, to put it in modern, digital terms, culture is a shared IT network. Yes, it's temperamental and crashes too often for our liking, but without it we can't communicate with one another or accomplish much of anything. Only now, though, are we beginning to fully understand the connection between the cultural milieu and our most creative ideas. Simonton and a handful of other social scientists have quietly been developing a new theory of creativity, one that aims to chart the circumstances of genius.

I've decided to explore this geography of genius, to put flesh and blood on Simonton's numbers. I realize this won't be easy, given that these genius clusters existed not only in a certain place but at a certain time, and that time is not now. I fully acknowledge that, say, Athens of today is not the Athens of Socrates's day. Still, I'm hoping that something of the spirit, of the genius loci, remains.

I tell Simonton of my plans and he nods his approval. As I stand up to leave, though, he throws a name at me: Alphonse de Candolle.

"Never heard of him."

"Precisely," says Simonton. Candolle, he explains, was a Swiss botanist, a contemporary of Galton's. He thought Galton was dead wrong about genius being hereditary and, in 1873, wrote a book saying as much. Candolle laid out a thorough and convincing argument that environment, not genetics, determines genius. Unlike Galton, he even accounted for his own cultural biases. He would only classify, say, a Swiss scientist as a genius if scientists outside Switzerland concurred. His book *Histoire des sciences et des savants depuis deux siècles* was "one of the greatest books ever written on genius," Simonton says.

It sank without a trace. The world did not want to hear what Candolle had to say.

"Just a friendly warning," says Simonton, as I say good-bye, then make my way across the sleepy California campus to a bar where I order a stiff drink and ponder the task ahead.

I've selected six historic places of genius, as well as one current one. Some are huge metropolises, such as Vienna of 1900; others, such as Renaissance Florence, are tiny by modern standards. Some, such as ancient

Athens, are well-known; others such as nineteenth-century Calcutta, less so. Each of these places, though, represented an apex of human achievement.

Nearly all are cities. We may be inspired by nature—a walk in the woods, the sound of a waterfall—but something about an urban setting is especially conducive to creativity. If it takes a village to raise a child, as the African proverb goes, it takes a city to raise a genius.

As I contemplate the quixotic journey that lies ahead, questions flood my mind. Do these genius clusters come in one flavor or many? Clearly, something was in the air in these places, but was it the same something or different somethings? And once the zeitgeist, the spirit of the times, had soured, did the genius of the place evaporate completely, or do trace elements remain?

One question, though, elbows its way to the front of the queue, and it is not a how or a what but a why. Why embark on this journey? The simple answer is that it represents a natural extension of a career spent charting mankind's greatest aspirations, be it the pursuit of happiness or the quest for spiritual fulfillment. Am I hoping that some of the genius I encounter will rub off on me? Sure, but I'm middle-aged, and any hopes of my becoming the next Einstein or Leonardo have long since disappeared, along with my hair. But my daughter—nine years old and brimming with brightness and infinite possibility—is another story. There is still hope for her, and what parent doesn't secretly wish that his or her child might become the next Darwin or Marie Curie? To this end, we tend to focus our energies on *them*—by imparting good study habits or exposing them to a buffet of intellectual possibilities, for instance.

Perhaps we worry about the genes we've passed on to them. In my case, that is not an issue. My daughter is adopted, from Kazakhstan, and therefore spared the curse of my highly neurotic gene pool. My wife and I are providing her nurture, not nature, and that, I believe, is what matters most.

Family has been called variously a clan, a tribe, "one of nature's masterpieces" (George Santayana), "a haven in a heartless world" (Christopher Lasch). It is all of those things but it is also a microculture, one that we shape more directly, and profoundly, than any other. Like all cultures, family culture can either cultivate creativity or squelch it.

This is a big responsibility, if you think about it, which is precisely why, up until now, I've avoided thinking about it. That is about to change. Creativity, like charity, begins at home. As I set out on my journey, one in which I will traverse continents and centuries, I vow to keep this important truth in mind.

ONE

GENIUS IS SIMPLE: ATHENS

THE LIGHT. MAYBE IT WAS THE LIGHT.

The thought shimmies into my sleep-starved brain, strutting with the awkward bravado of a tweedy classicist on crack. Yes, I think, blinking away the hours of stale Boeing air, the light.

Most light doesn't do much for me. It's nice, don't get me wrong. Preferable to darkness, sure, but strictly utilitarian. Not the light in Greece. Greek light is dynamic, alive. It dances across the landscape, flickering here, glowing there, constantly and subtly shifting in intensity and quality. Greek light is sharp and angular. It's the sort of light that makes you pay attention, and as I would soon learn, paying attention is the first step on the road to genius. As I glance out my taxi window, shielding my eyes from the painfully bright morning sun, I can't help but wonder: Have I found a piece of the Greek puzzle?

I hope so, for it is a daunting puzzle, one that has stumped historians and archaeologists, not to mention the Greeks themselves, for centuries. The question that nags is this: Why? Or, more precisely, why *here*? Why did this well-lit but otherwise unremarkable land give rise to a people unlike any other the world had seen, a people, as the great classicist Humphrey Kitto put it, "not very numerous, not very powerful, not very organized, who had a totally new conception of what human life was for, and showed for the first time what the human mind was for"?

This incredible flourishing didn't last long. Yes, "classical Greece" is officially considered a 186-year period, but the apex of that civilization, sandwiched between two wars, only lasted twenty-four years. In human history, that's a lightning flash across the summer sky, the flicker of a votive candle, a tweet. Why so brief?

Ancient Greece. As the taxi slows to a crawl (rush-hour traffic not being something the ancients had to contend with), I ponder those two words. They make me shrink, embarrassed by how much I don't know, bored with the little I do. When I think of the Greeks—if I think of them at all—images of gray men joylessly pondering life's imponderables spring to mind. What can they possibly do for me? I have bills to pay and e-mails to send and deadlines to meet. The ancient Greeks seem about as relevant to my life as the rings of Saturn, or trigonometry.

Not for the first or last time, I am wrong. The truth is, no ancient peoples are more alive, more relevant today, than the Greeks. We are all a little bit Greek, whether we know it or not. If you've ever voted or served on a jury or watched a movie or read a novel or sat around with a group of friends drinking wine and talking about anything from last night's football game to the nature of truth, you can thank the Greeks. If you've ever had a rational thought or asked *Why?* or gazed at the night sky in silent wonder, then you have had a Greek moment. If you've ever spoken English, you can thank the Greeks. So many of our words sprang from their rich language that a Greek prime minister once gave an entire speech, in English, using only Greek-derived words. Yes, the Greeks brought us democracy, science, and philosophy, but we can also thank (or curse) them for written contracts, silver and bronze coins, taxes, writing, schools, commercial loans, technical handbooks, large sailing ships, shared-risk investment, absentee landlordism. Nearly every part of our lives is inspired by the Greeks, including the very notion of inspiration. "We think and feel differently because of the Greeks," concludes historian Edith Hamilton.

My taxi stops in front of a tired three-story building that, except for a small sign that says TONY'S HOTEL, is indistinguishable from all the other tired three-story buildings. I step into the alleged lobby, a white-tiled room that looks more like someone's basement, piled high with rickety chairs, broken coffee machines—possessions you no longer need but, out of sentimentality or inertia, can't bear to part with. Like Greece itself, Tony's Hotel has seen better days.

So has Tony. The Greek sun has etched deep lines on his face; the Greek cuisine has inflated his gut to monumental proportions. Tony is all rough edges and sweetness, a throwback to an older, drachma Greece. Less euro; more endearing. Like many Greeks, Tony is a natural performer. He speaks a little more loudly than necessary and swings his arms in large, theatrical motions, no matter how mundane the topic at hand. It's as if he's auditioning for *Greek Idol*. All the time.

I plop down on my bed and thumb through the small library of books I've packed, a whimsical collection curated from the vast ocean of ink that ancient Greece has spawned. My eyes are drawn to a quirky, little volume called *Daily Life in Athens at the Time of Pericles*. It's a pleasing antidote to the usual history, which is written from a mountaintop and is as dry as a desert. Historians typically track wars and upheavals and sweeping ideological movements like so many weather systems. Most of us, though, don't experience weather that way. We experience it down here, not as a massive low-pressure system but as sheets of rain that slicken our hair, a crack of thunder that rattles our insides, a Mediterranean sun that warms our face. And so it is with history. The story of the world is not the story of coups and revolutions. It is the story of lost keys and burnt coffee and a sleeping child in your arms. History is the untallied sum of a million everyday moments.

Within this quotidian stew genius quietly simmers. Sigmund Freud nibbling on his favorite sponge cake at Vienna's Café Landtmann. Einstein staring out the window of the Swiss patent office in Berne. Leonardo da Vinci wiping the sweat from his forehead at a hot and dusty Florentine workshop. Yes, these geniuses thought big, world-changing thoughts, but they did so in small spaces. Down here. All genius, like all politics, is local.

From this new, terrestrial vantage point, I learn much about the ancient Greeks. I learn that they loved to dance and wonder what exactly transpired during such numbers as "Stealing the Meat" and "The Itch." I learn that, before exercising, young men would swathe their bodies with olive oil, and that "the manly smell of olive oil in the *gymnasium* was considered sweeter than perfume." I learn that the Greeks wore no underwear, that a unibrow was considered a mark of beauty, that they enjoyed grasshoppers both as pets and as appetizers. I learn a lot, but besides these peccadilloes, I learn *what* the Greeks produced, not *how* they produced it, and it is the how that I am determined to nail down.

But first, I need something the ancient Greeks didn't have: coffee. The nectar of the gods shouldn't be imbibed just anywhere, though. Location matters.

For me, cafés are a kind of second home, a prime example of what sociologist Ray Oldenburg calls a "great good place." The food and drink are irrelevant, or nearly so. What matters is the atmosphere—not the tablecloths or the furniture but a more intangible ambience, one that encourages guilt-free lingering and strikes just the right balance of background din and contemplative silence.

I don't know about the ancients, but twenty-first-century Greeks are not exactly early risers. At 8:00 a.m. I have the streets to myself, save the occasional storekeeper coaxing the sleep from his eyes, and a handful of policemen outfitted in full RoboCop riot gear—a reminder that, like its ancient self, modern Athens is a city on edge.

I follow Tony's directions, which he conveyed with wild, swinging arcs, and turn onto a pleasant pedestrian walkway, lined with cafés and small shops, epitomizing the sense of community that characterized ancient Athens. Here I find my great good place. It's called the Bridge. An appropriate name, I decide, since I'm attempting the quixotic task of bridging the centuries.

The Bridge is nothing fancy, just a few outdoor tables facing Draco Street, positioned as if the customers were theatergoers and the street the theater. In cafés like this the Greeks indulge in their national pastime: sitting. The Greeks sit in groups and they sit alone. They sit in the summer sun and they sit in the winter chill. They don't need a chair to do their sitting either. An empty curb or a discarded cardboard box will do nicely. Nobody sits like the Greeks.

I manage a *kalimera*, good morning, and join the other sitters at the Bridge. I order an espresso and warm my hands on the cup. A morning nip lingers in the air, but I can tell, already, that it's shaping up to be another fine Greek day. "We may be bankrupt, but we still have great weather," Tony had announced, triumphantly, as I headed out. He has a point. Not only the sublime light but three hundred days of cloudless skies and little humidity. Might climate explain Athenian genius?

Alas, no. Climate might have sharpened the ancient Greek mind, but it doesn't explain it. For starters, Greece enjoys essentially the same weather today as it did in 450 BC, yet it is no longer a place of genius. Also, plenty of golden ages blossomed in less agreeable climes. The bards of Elizabethan London, for instance, performed their magic under a dreary English sky.

I order a second espresso, and as my brain reboots, I realize that I'm getting ahead of myself. Here I am hot on the trail of genius, but do I really know what it means? As I said, a genius is someone who makes an intellectual or artistic leap, but who decides what qualifies as a leap?

We do. Francis Galton may have gotten much wrong, but his definition of genius, though typically sexist, points to something important: "A genius is a man to whom the world deliberately acknowledges itself largely indebted." Admittance to the club of genius is not up to the genius but to his peers, and society. It is a public verdict, not a private assertion. One theory of genius—let's call it the Fashionista Theory of Genius—states this unequivocally. Admission to the club of genius depends entirely on the whims, the fashion, of the day. "Creativity cannot be separated from its recognition," says psychologist Mihaly Csikszentmihalyi, the main advocate of this theory. Put more bluntly, someone is only a genius if we say so.

At first, this might seem counterintuitive, even blasphemous. Surely, some inviolate aspect of genius must exist separate from public judgment.

No, say the proponents of this theory, it does not. Take Bach, for example. He was not particularly respected during his lifetime. Only about seventy-five years after his death was he declared a "genius." Before that, we assume, he resided in that purgatory "undiscovered genius." But what does that mean? "What—besides unconscious conceit—warrants this belief?" asks Csikszentmihalyi. Saying *we* discovered Bach's genius is tantamount to saying that those who came before us were idiots. And what if, at some future date, Bach is demoted, banished from the pantheon of genius? What does that say about *us*?

Other examples abound. When Stravinsky's ballet *Le Sacre du printemps* premiered in Paris in 1913, the audience nearly rioted; critics called it "perverted." Today, it is considered a classic. When Monet's late work the *Nymphéas* first came out, art critics recognized them for what they were: the result of the artist's deteriorating eyesight. Only later, when abstract expressionism was all the rage, were they declared works of genius.

Greek vases are another good example of the Fashionista Theory of Genius. Today, you can see them displayed in many museums around the world. They sit behind bulletproof glass, armed guards nearby, tourists gawking at these works of art. That's not how the Greeks saw them, though. For them, the vases served a strictly utilitarian purpose. They were everyday objects. Not until the 1970s, when the Metropolitan Museum of Art in New York paid more than $1 million for a single vase, was Greek pottery elevated to high art. So when exactly did these clay pots become works of genius? We like to think they always were, and that only later did we "discover" their genius. That's one way of looking at it. Proponents of the Fashionista Theory of Genius would argue that they became works of genius in the 1970s when the Metropolitan Museum, speaking the language of money, said so.

The relativity of genius is bubbling in my brain as I order another espresso and plan my attack on the Great Greek Mystery. What made this place shine? I've already eliminated climate. Perhaps it was something equally obvious: the rocky terrain, or well-ventilated clothing, or the ubiquitous wine?

Athens is finally beginning to stir, and the Bridge affords a prime viewing spot. I sit back and survey the sea of faces. Are these really the offspring of Plato and Socrates? Many academics have asked that same question. A number of years ago, an Austrian anthropologist posited that modern Greeks were not Plato's heirs but the descendants of Slavs and Albanians who had migrated here centuries later. His theory caused a minor uproar in Greece. People balked at the suggestion that they were anything other than the children of Plato. "I have no doubt that we are the direct descendants of the ancients," asserted one politician. "We have exactly the same vices."

And what vices they were! The ancient Greeks were no Boy Scouts. They held outlandish, weeklong festivals, drank heroic quantities of wine, and never met a sexual act they didn't like. Despite all these antics, or perhaps because of them, Ancient Greece excelled like no other civilization. That much is clear. The rest is as murky as a glass of ouzo. In fact, my investigation into Ancient Greece encounters its first hiccup when I discover there was no such place as Ancient Greece. What did exist were Ancient *Greeces*: hundreds of independent poleis, or city-states, that, while they shared a common language and certain cultural traits, were very different, as different as, say, Canada and South Africa today. Each polis had its own government, its own laws, its own customs—even its own calendar. Sure, they occasionally traded goods, competed in athletics, and fought a few spectacularly bloody wars, but mostly they ignored one another.

Why so many Greeces? The answer lies in the land itself. Hilly and rocky, it formed natural barriers, cutting off the Greek city-states from one another and creating, in effect, islands on the land. No wonder a variety pack of microcultures blossomed.

And thank goodness it did. Nature abhors not only a vacuum but a monopoly, too. During times of fragmentation, humanity made its greatest creative leaps. This tendency, known as Danilevsky's law, states that peoples are more likely to reach their full creative potential when they belong to an independent nation, even if it is tiny. This makes sense. If the world is a laboratory of ideas, then the more petri dishes in the lab, the better.

In Greece, one petri dish flourished like no other: Athens. The city produced more brilliant minds—from Socrates to Aristotle—than any other place the world has seen before or since. (Only Renaissance Florence came close.)

At the time, though, the prospect of such greatness was a long shot, to say the least. For starters, that rocky, hilly land wasn't exactly fertile. "A discarnate skeleton," Plato called it. Also, Athens was a small city, with a population equivalent to that of Wichita, Kansas, today. Other Greek city-states were larger (Syracuse) or wealthier (Corinth) or mightier (Sparta). Yet none flourished the way Athens did. Why? Was Athenian genius simply dumb luck, the convergence of "a happy set of circumstances," as historian Peter Watson puts it, or did the Athenians make their luck? That is, I fear, a riddle that would stump even the Delphic oracle. But, fully caffeinated and armed with the courage of the naive, I soldier on, determined to unlock the mystery. What I need to do first, I decide, is meet the right people.

"Welcome to my office," says Aristotle, with a dramatic, Tony-esque sweep of his hand. It's a line he's clearly used before, but given our vantage point, atop the Acropolis with all of Athens spread below, it is, I concede, a good line.

We had met a few hours earlier, in the lobby of Tony's Hotel. My first impression of Aristotle was that, with his fair skin and unruly, reddish hair that hung across his face like a curtain, he didn't look Greek. A ridiculous observation, I quickly realized. There is no one way of looking Greek any more than there is one way of looking French or American or anything else. The Greeks are not one race; they never were.

My second impression of Aristotle is that he seems distracted. Whether it is the weight of his name, or the stress of the permanent crisis that Greece finds itself in these days, I can't say. But no doubt about it: he is buzzing. As we walk and talk, though, I realize that what I have taken for nervousness is actually intensity—a passion for history that flows through him like an electrical current; 220 volts, I'd say. Possibly more.

As we continue our walk toward the Acropolis, I bide my time, waiting for the right moment to ask about his name. When I first learned that my guide was named Aristotle, I took it as fortuitous. What could be more historically correct, more Greek, than walking in the steps of Aristotle with Aristotle?

As we cross the pedestrian street, now bustling with activity, I dive in, figuring it best to acknowledge the eight-hundred-pound philosopher in the room.

"So, what's with the name, Aristotle?" I ask lamely.

Aristotle shrugs. It's inconvenient, he says, leaving it to me to imagine exactly what form this inconvenience takes. His friends call him Ari, which he hates, though he concedes it does provide some distance from the historical Aristotle and, for that matter, the billionaire shipping magnate Aristotle Onassis, who married Jacqueline Kennedy. With a name such as Aristotle, distance is your friend.

As we dodge tourists and riot police, Aristotle recounts how he fell into the tour-guide business. He wanted to join the Greek army but didn't make the cut. Why exactly, he didn't say, and sensing some still-raw wound, I didn't press. Shut out of the military, he studied archaeology instead and has been looking back ever since. Some twenty-five hundred years back, to be precise. Aristotle's specialty, his passion, is ancient roof tiles. You can learn a lot about a civilization from its roof tiles, he assures me.

"What we're doing right now is very Greek," he says.

"Really? Because all we're doing is walking."

"Exactly. The ancient Greeks walked everywhere, all the time." They were great walkers *and* great thinkers and preferred to do their philosophizing while on the go.

The Greeks, as usual, knew what they were doing. Many a genius has done his or her best thinking while walking. While working on *A Christmas Carol*, Dickens would walk fifteen or twenty miles through the back streets of London, turning over the plot in his mind, as the city slept. Mark Twain walked a lot, too, though he never got anywhere. He paced while he worked, as his daughter recalled: "Some of the time when dictating, Father walked the floor . . . then it always seemed as if a new spirit had flown into the room."

Recently, researchers have begun to investigate scientifically the link between walking and creativity. In a recent study, Stanford University psychologists Marily Oppezzo and Daniel Schwartz divided participants into two groups: walkers and sitters. They then administered something called Guilford's Alternative Uses test, in which participants come up with alternative uses for everyday objects. It's designed to measure "divergent thinking," an important component of creativity. Divergent thinking is when we come up with multiple, unexpected solutions to problems. Divergent thinking is spontaneous and free-flowing. Convergent thinking, by contrast, is more linear and entails a narrowing, rather than an expanding, of your options. Convergent thinkers are trying to find the one correct answer to a question. Divergent thinkers reframe the question.

The results, published in the *Journal of Experimental Psychology*, confirm that the ancient Greeks were onto something. Creativity levels were "consistently and significantly" higher for the walkers versus the sitters. Curiously, it didn't matter whether participants walked outdoors in the fresh air or indoors on a treadmill staring at a blank wall. They still produced twice as many creative responses compared with the sedentary group. It didn't take a lot of walking to boost creativity, either—anywhere from five to sixteen minutes.

The ancient Greeks, living long ago, in an age before the treadmill, did their walking outdoors. They did *everything* outdoors. A house was less a home than a dormitory. They spent only about thirty waking minutes there every day. "Just long enough to do the necessary with their wives," said Aristotle, as we neared the gates of the Acropolis. They spent the rest of their day in the *agora*, the marketplace, working out at the *gymnasium* or the *palaistra*, the wrestling grounds, or perhaps strolling along the rolling hills that surround the city. None of these outings were deemed extracurricular because, unlike us, the Greeks didn't differentiate between physical and mental activity. Plato's famous Academy, progenitor of the modern university, was as much an athletic facility as an intellectual one. The Greeks viewed body and mind as two inseparable parts of a whole. A fit mind not attached to a fit body rendered both somehow incomplete. Picture Rodin's *Thinker* and you have the Greek ideal: a buff man lost in thought.

The Acropolis, at last. Literally "high city," it is not a building but a place, and its location—atop a steep plateau, with natural springs nearby—is no accident. The Greeks had a highly refined sense of place. Socrates, for instance, extolled the benefits of southern exposure two millennia before New York real-estate agents. Buildings were not merely physical entities; they possessed a spirit, that genius loci, or genius of place. Greeks believed that where you were influenced what you thought, and at least one of the best-known schools of philosophy owes its name to an architectural style. The Stoics are so named because of the stoa, or elegant colonnades, under which they did their philosophizing.

We hike a bit more before reaching the peak, where the Parthenon, arguably the most famous structure of the ancient world, resides with all the quiet confidence of a Saudi king or a Supreme Court justice. Tenure will do that. Its status is well deserved, Aristotle assures me. The Parthenon represents an unprecedented engineering feat. For starters, workers had to transport thousands of blocks of marble from the surrounding countryside. The project employed carpenters, molders, bronzesmiths, stonecutters, dyers, painters, embroiderers, embossers, rope makers, weavers, cobblers, road builders, and miners. Amazingly, the Parthenon was completed on time and under budget, marking the first and last time any construction project has accomplished that.

"Take a look at the columns," says Aristotle. "How do they look to you?"

"Beautiful," I say, wondering where he's going with this.

"Do they look straight?"

"Yes."

Aristotle smiles a mischievous smile. "They're not straight at all." He fetches an illustration of the Parthenon from his rucksack.

What looks like the epitome of linear thinking, rational thought frozen in stone, is an illusion. The building has not a single straight line. Each column bends slightly this way or that. Yet when gazing at the Parthenon, as French writer Paul Valéry explains, "no one is aware that the sense of happiness he feels is caused by curves and bends that are almost imperceptible yet immensely powerful. The beholder is unaware that he is responding to a combination of regularity and irregularity the architect had hidden in his work."

When I read those words—"a combination of regularity and irregularity"—they stick with me. I suspect they might explain more than clever engineering. All of ancient Athens displayed that combination of the linear and the bent, the orderly and the chaotic. Within the city walls, you'd find both a clear-cut legal code and a frenzied marketplace, ruler-straight statues and streets that follow no discernible order. We think of the Greeks as reasonable people, the original straight-and-narrow thinkers, and they were, but they also possessed an irrational side, and a sort of "crazy wisdom" prevailed in classical Athens. People were guided by *thambos*, "that reverential terror and awe aroused by the proximity of any supernatural force or being which one discerns," as historian Robert Flacelière explains. The Greeks feared madness but also recognized it as "a gift of the gods."

Disorder is embedded in the Greek creation myth, where in the beginning there was not light but chaos. That wasn't necessarily a bad thing. For the Greeks—and, as I'd later learn, Hindus, too—chaos is the raw material of creativity. Might this explain why Athens's leaders resisted calls to "regularize" the city's unruly layout? Their rationale was partly practical—the winding streets would confuse invaders—but perhaps they also suspected that messiness stimulates creative thought.

None of this means the Greeks were slackers, says Aristotle, comparing them with another extraordinary civilization. "The Egyptians reached what they considered perfection, and they stopped there. The Greeks always wanted to do more. They always wanted to be the best." So all-consuming was this quest for the perfect that Greek artisans devoted as much time and effort to the backs of their statues as they did to the fronts. The Parthenon also represented something else: an overt attempt to stick it to the other city-states. Ictinus, the architect who designed the Parthenon, had seen the Temple of Zeus at Olympia and was determined to outdo it. "It was always this sense of competition that drove them," says Aristotle. Might this competitive zeal explain their genius?

The evolving science of genius has been investigating that very question. In a landmark study, Teresa Amabile, a psychologist at Harvard University, examined what effect a promised reward has on creative thinking. She divided a team of volunteers into two groups. Each group was asked to produce a collage. One group, though, was told that their work would be evaluated by a panel of artists and that those who produced the most creative collages would receive a monetary award. The second group was told, essentially, to have fun.

The results weren't even close. By a wide margin, those who were neither evaluated nor observed produced the most creative collages (as determined by a panel of art teachers). In many follow-up studies, Amabile and her colleagues found similar results. The expectation of a reward or evaluation, *even a positive evaluation*, squelched creativity. She calls this phenomenon the intrinsic theory of motivation. Stated simply: "People will be most creative when they feel motivated primarily by interest, enjoyment, satisfaction, and the challenge of the work itself—not by external pressures." She warns that many schools and corporations, by placing such emphasis on rewards and evaluation, are inadvertently suppressing creativity.

It's a compelling theory, and one that, intuitively, makes sense. Who hasn't felt creatively liberated writing in a private diary or doodling in a notebook, knowing no one will ever see these zany scribbles?

The theory, though, doesn't always jibe with the real world. If we are only motivated by the sheer joy of an activity, why do athletes perform better in the heat of competition rather than during training sessions? Why did Mozart abandon works in progress because his commission was withdrawn? Why does the lure of a Nobel Prize motivate many a scientist? James Watson and Francis Crick, the first scientists to describe the structure of DNA, stated up front that their aim was to win the prestigious prize—and they did, in 1962. And in ancient Athens, this cutthroat nature of life clearly drove some to great heights. "Always excel and be better than others," urged Homer, and if the Greeks obeyed anyone, it was Homer.

Some recent studies cast doubt on the intrinsic theory of motivation.

Jacob Eisenberg, a professor of business at University College Dublin, and William Thompson, a psychologist at Macquarie University, found that experienced musicians improvised more creatively when enticed with cash prizes and publicity. These results appear to fly in the face of the intrinsic theory of motivation. Is the theory flawed or the study?

Neither, actually. What matters, Eisenberg and Thompson suspect, is the type of people involved in the studies. Amabile's participants tended to be novices, with no background in art, while Eisenberg's were veteran musicians, with at least five years' experience. Competition apparently motivates experienced creators but inhibits inexperienced ones.

An evolving theory suggests that some combination of intrinsic and extrinsic motivation is ideal. Some, for instance, might initially be motivated by the promise of an external reward (money, status, etc.), but once immersed in the work they enter a psychological state known as flow. They forget about any external pressure and even lose track of time. That is what Watson and Crick said happened to them. They desperately wanted to win the Nobel, but once they immersed themselves in the research, the prize receded to the back of their minds.

A crucial question is not whether someone is competitive but, rather, for what (or whom) they are competing. In ancient Athens, the answer was clear: the city. The ancient Athenians enjoyed a deeply intimate relationship with their city, the likes of which we can scarcely imagine. The closest term we have to describe this sentiment is *civic duty*, but that carries the weight of obligation and doesn't sound like any fun. What the Athenians practiced was more like *civic joy*. That we find that juxtaposition of words odd speaks volumes about the chasm that separates us and the ancients.

Civic life, though, was not optional, and Aristotle tells me the Athenians had a word for those who refused to participate in public affairs: *idiotes*. It is where we get our word *idiot*. There was no such thing as an aloof, apathetic Athenian, at least not for long. "The man who took no interest in the affairs of state was not a man who minded his own business, but a man who had no business being in Athens at all," said the great historian Thucydides. Ouch. And to think how I whined like a petulant child when I found myself stuck on jury duty for two weeks.

Aristotle and I find a rock and sit down. From here, all of Athens is visible. In every direction, as far as my eye can see, it is unrelentingly urban. An endless sea of low-rise apartments, office buildings, highway cloverleafs, microwave towers. Here I run headlong into a most inconvenient truth: the Athens of today is not the Athens of 450 BC. Modern Athens has indoor plumbing and outdoor demonstrations. Modern Athens has traffic and bankruptcy and iPhones and Xanax and satellite TV and processed meat.

The past, it's been said, is a foreign country. They do things differently there. Yes, they do, and unfortunately this particular foreign country, known as Ancient Greece, has extremely tight border controls. It doesn't take kindly to interlopers such as me. Yet if I'm going to solve the Athenian Mystery, the past is exactly where I need to be. What to do?

"Squint." That was the advice of a friend back home when I'd mentioned my plans to visit Athens. I'd laughed it off, but now I realize it's actually a smart tactic. Sometimes we can see more by narrowing our field of view than by expanding it. The zoom lens reveals as much as the wide angle, and sometimes more.

"Don't squint too much," Aristotle warns. If I could time-travel to Athens circa 450 BC, he says, I'd probably be disappointed. The great Athens, the cradle of Western civilization, the birthplace of science, philosophy, and so much else we hold dear, was a dump. The streets were narrow and dirty. The houses, constructed of wood and sun-dried clay, were so flimsy that robbers gained entry by simply digging. (The ancient Greek word for robber means "one who tunnels through walls.") As a time traveler I would definitely notice the noise—vendors hawking their wares at the agora, a lute screeching off-key—but what would grab my attention and not let go is the stench. People relieved themselves in the courtyard of their own home, or even right in the streets, where the mess would sit until a slave sluiced it away. Conditions were such that, as historian Jacob Burckhardt put it, "no sensible and peaceful person of our day would want to live under them." And he wrote those words in the nineteenth century!

Let's take stock of what we have so far. A small, dirty city, situated on unforgiving land, surrounded by hostile neighbors, and populated by a people "who, when we get down to facts, never cleaned their teeth, never used handkerchiefs, wiped their fingers on their hair, spat everywhere regardless, and died in swarms of malaria or tuberculosis," as historian Robert Flacelière reminds us. Not exactly a recipe for a place of genius. Or is it?

One of the biggest misperceptions about places of genius, I'm discovering, is that they are akin to paradise. They are not. Paradise is antithetical to genius. Paradise makes no demands, and creative genius takes root through meeting demands in new and imaginative ways. "The Athenians matured because they were challenged on all fronts," said Nietzsche, in a variation of his famous "what doesn't kill you will make you stronger" line. Creativity is a response to our environment. Greek painting was a response to the complex light (the Greek painter Apollodoros was the first to develop a technique for creating the illusion of depth), Greek architecture a response to the complex landscape, Greek philosophy a response to the complex, uncertain times.

The problem with paradise is that it is perfect and therefore requires no response. This is why wealthy people and places often stagnate. Athens was both wealthy and not; it was, to turn John Kenneth Galbraith's observation about 1960s America on its head, a place of public opulence and private squalor. The houses of the wealthy were indistinguishable from those of the poor; both were equally shoddy. Athenians were deeply suspicious of private wealth, and the plays of Aeschylus are rife with stories about the misery it causes. Nearly everyone, from craftsman to physician, received the same salary. Laws limited how much money could be spent on funerals and forbade women from carrying more than three dresses on a journey. In ancient Athens, notes the great urbanist Lewis Mumford, "poverty was not an embarrassment: if anything, riches were suspect."

These policies had their downside—forget about that nice water clock you've been eyeing at the agora—but it also meant that Athenians were liberated from the burdens of frantic acquisition and consumption.

"Beauty was cheap and the best goods of this life, above all the city itself, were there for the asking," says Mumford.

When it came to public projects, though, the Athenians spent lavishly and, if they could help it, with other people's money. They paid for the Parthenon, and other glorious projects, using the funds amassed by something called the Delian League. It was the NATO of its day, an alliance formed to fend off a common enemy, the Persians. It worked, and so the Athenians said, in effect, *Thank you very much. We'll take this money and do great things with it.* Nobody ever said places of genius were nice.

Flush with other people's cash, Athens was suddenly the hot spot of the ancient world, explains Aristotle as we circle the Parthenon. "So, if you were an engineer or an architect or a sculptor, or a philosopher, this is where you wanted to be."

This is what I call the Magnetic Theory of Genius. Places such as ancient Athens, or Silicon Valley today, are creative because they attract smart, ambitious people. They are talent magnets. This is true but also a little too convenient, and circular. Creative places are creative because all the creative people move there. Yes, but what was the attraction in the first place? How did the magnet become magnetized?

Timing is important, and Pericles, the great Athenian leader, had exquisite timing. For much of its history Athens was either preparing for war, at war, or recovering from war. But in the window between the Persian and Peloponnesian Wars, from 454 to 430 BC, Athens was at peace, and this is when Pericles doubled down on cultural projects such as the Parthenon. One of the prerequisites for a golden age is peace.

But wait, I hear you say, hasn't wartime generated all sorts of innovations—the jet engine, radar, and much more? Yes, war can spark a few innovations, but they are narrowly focused—a better gun, a faster plane. And while these advances do sometimes spawn civilian applications, the net result of war, concludes Dean Simonton after an exhaustive study, is negative, and "the negative effect holds true for every form of creativity, even for technology."

Aristotle and I are sitting on a stone slab as old as the ages, the Mediterranean sun bearing down on us, the tourists swarming like angry wasps, when I ask point-blank what he thinks. Why Athens? What was in the air?

Aristotle doesn't have a ready answer, no illustration in his backpack to whip out, no clever one-liner. People don't usually ask him that question. Athenian greatness is taken as a given. He thinks for a long while before finally speaking.

"It had to be the political system. First of all, there was freedom of speech and open debate. Something that the other city-states didn't have. In the assembly, you had to stand up at the speaker's platform and address some seven thousand men, forty times a year. No topic was off-limits. If you had any ambitions to become a statesman, you needed the skills of public speaking, and you also had to be educated. Plus, you needed stamina. They would stay there from sunrise to sunset and start with mundane issues, like water or grain supply, then move on to weightier issues.

"So, yes," Aristotle says, the certainty in his voice peaking, "it was democracy."

I'm not so sure. For starters, there is the old chicken-and-egg problem. Was Athens creative because it was democratic, or was it democratic because it was creative? And then there is the voice in my head, that of Dean Simonton, who, again, has crunched the numbers and says no correlation exists between golden ages and democracy. Freedom, not democracy, is what's needed, he had told me. They're not the same thing. "You can have enlightened autocrats. China never had democracy but they had enlightened autocrats." Some psychologists go even further, suggesting that oligarchies may actually foster *more* creativity than democracies since, with less public oversight, they're more willing to engage in risky or "unnecessary" projects. So, as much as I hate to disagree with someone named Aristotle, I don't think democracy alone explains Athenian greatness. I need to keep digging.

We're on the move again, this time, Aristotle assures me, heading to the heart of ancient Athens. It was not, as many people (myself included) assume, the Acropolis. We have left that sacred site far behind. A few minutes later, we enter a gate and spread before us is a collection of ruins, some nearly intact, others little more than stumps of stone. "This is it," says Aristotle with a verbal flourish.

The *agora*. It literally means "place where people gather," but it was much more than that. When Athenians set about rebuilding their city after it was sacked by the Persians, they did not begin with the temples of the Acropolis, as you might expect. They began here, with the true heart of the city.

This messy, chaotic place was replete with the sound of shopkeepers hawking their wares, sophists their oratorical services. It also had an undercurrent of menace. Often, arguments broke out, and sometimes scuffles. Athenians loved their agora, but others didn't see the appeal. The Persian king Cyrus said he had no respect for a people who allocated a special space "where they could come together to cheat each other and tell one another lies under oath."

The Athenian agora was the original everything store. If it existed in the ancient world, you could find it for sale at the agora. As the comic poet Eubulus enumerates, items available included "figs, witnesses to summonses, bunches of grapes, turnips, pears, apples, givers of evidence, roses, porridge, honeycombs, chickpeas, lawsuits, beestings-puddings, myrtle, allotment machines [for random jury selection], irises, lambs, water clocks, laws, indictments." Everything had its place. Separate sections existed for fresh fruit and dried fruit, smoked fish and nonsmoked, spices and perfumes, footwear, and horses. There was even the agora of the *kerkopes*, the thieves' market, where stolen goods were sold.

No one was fonder of the agora than Socrates. He came here to haggle with shopkeepers, catch up on the latest gossip, to discuss the nature of beauty. He is said to have idled away hours at the shop of a cobbler named Simon. No one knows for sure, though. Just when archaeologists think they've found traces of old Socrates—a clay cup, for instance, with the name SIMON etched on it—it turns out to be a false lead. I can hear Socrates laughing across the centuries. "I'm over here; no, over there. Catch me if you can." He was a man who refused to be pinned down—in life and in death.

It's getting late. Aristotle and I are about to say good-bye when he stops and turns. He's been thinking about my geographies of genius, my attempt to nail down a recipe of sorts, and he's not optimistic. "To be honest," he says, strands of auburn hair cascading down his face, his hands uncharacteristically still, "I don't think you will ever find a formula for these places of genius." His words bounce off me and tumble downhill before landing with a thud on the hard and ancient ruins of the agora.

We say good-bye and head in opposite directions. The harsh afternoon sun has softened into a pleasant crimson, and though Tony's Hotel is quite far, I decide to walk, like Socrates.

"Socrates was the Dude."

The words are spoken with great certainty, without a trace of irony. I'm not sure how to respond. By now, I know something of Socrates. I know he is one of the founders of Western philosophy, that he liked to ask lots of questions, and that he was, sadly, executed by the city he loved, charged, unfairly, with impiety and "corrupting the youth." His dudeness, though, comes as news to me. Perhaps I misheard.

"Socrates was the Dude," I hear again, this time with even greater conviction. The words are spoken by Alicia Stallings, poet, longtime Athens resident, and certified genius. She's a recipient of the coveted (and lucrative) MacArthur Fellowship, informally known as a genius grant. If anyone can explain the genius of Athens, surely it is Alicia. At least that's what I'd thought until she started with this dude business.

Earlier, she had suggested we meet at a café in her neighborhood. "It's near the Temple of Zeus," she had told me, as if that were the most natural landmark in the world. That's what I love about Greek directions; they're so much more *interesting* than back home. "Look for the Temple of Zeus" resonates more deeply, is freighted with more history, than "turn left at the Dunkin' Donuts." Athenians aren't being pretentious when they name-drop the gods. They're simply working with what they have. The Temple of Zeus. McDonald's. They're all part of the mix.

And so here I am, wine in hand, trying to wrap my mind around this Socrates-as-dude theory. Alicia is clearly using *dude* in *The Big Lebowski*an sense, which is the best sense, but still, comparing one of history's greatest thinkers to a White Russian–drinking, pot-smoking character in a Coen brothers movie? I don't know. It seems wrong.

Look at the facts, Alicia says, sensing my skepticism. While the world swirled around him, Socrates remained an island of calm. A rock. That's very Dude-like behavior. During his long and fulfilling life, Socrates never wrote a single word. He was too busy being the Dude. And then there is this: at the hour of his execution, just before drinking the hemlock that would still his enormous heart, Socrates implored his followers, "I would ask you to be thinking of the truth and not of Socrates." Not only is that statement admirably Dude-like in its selflessness—it's not about me, it's about the truth—it is also noteworthy in that Socrates spoke of himself in the third person. You don't get any more Dude-like than that.

Yes, Socrates was the Dude, but more than that, he was an Athenian dude. *The* Athenian dude. Never before or since have a man and a city been so perfectly matched. He loved Athens and would never consider living—or dying—anywhere else. He could have avoided execution by fleeing Athens, but rejected that offer out of hand. He had a contract with the city, and he was going to fulfill his end of it.

Eccentric, barefoot, and endearingly stubborn, Socrates occupied that precarious position that all geniuses do—perched between insider and outsider. Far enough outside the mainstream to see the world through fresh eyes, yet close enough so that those fresh insights resonated with others.

Genius is many things, but beautiful is not one of them. Socrates was a profoundly ugly man. "Bearded, hairy, with a flat, spreading nose, prominent, popping eyes, and thick lips," relays the historian Paul Johnson. Socrates, though, was not the least bit troubled by his appearance and often joked about it. In Xenophon's *Symposium*, Socrates challenges Critobulus, a handsome young man, to a beauty contest. Critobulus points to Socrates's elephantine nose as evidence of his ugliness. Not so fast, retorts the great philosopher. "God made the nose for smelling, and your nostrils are turned down while mine are wide and turned up and can receive smells from every direction." As for my outsize lips, Socrates continued, they confer kisses that "are more sweet and luscious than yours."

Whatever Socrates lacked in physical beauty, he made up for with exquisite timing. He was born at a propitious moment in human history, during the time of Pericles, a mere nine years after the Chinese philoso-pher Confucius died. Socrates was twelve years old when the Hebrew priest Ezra left Babylon for Jerusalem, bringing with him a freshly tran-scribed version of the Pentateuch, the first five books of the Torah. Dur-ing this period, known as the Axial Age, old orders were crumbling, and new ones were not yet solidified. Cracks appeared, and as it's been said, the cracks are what let the light in. The genius, too.

Socrates, like all geniuses, benefited from "zeitgeist fit." This doesn't necessarily mean he fit happily with the spirit of his times. What distin-guishes geniuses is not a seamless fit with their times but, rather, what psychologist Keith Sawyer calls "the capacity to be able to exploit an ap-parent misfit." This was certainly the case with Socrates; he pushed the boundaries of acceptable discourse—and got away with it, until he didn't. His ideas resonated even as they riled. That is the way it is with geniuses. They fit in their times the way a pearl fits in an oyster shell. Uncomfort-ably yet essentially. A useful irritant.

Socrates is remembered as a great philosopher, but he was first and foremost a conversationalist. Before Socrates, people talked, but they didn't have conversations. They had alternating monologues, especially if one person was of higher status than the other. Socrates pioneered con-versation as a means of intellectual exploration, of questioning assump-tions, ones so deeply ingrained we don't even know we have them.

Conversation, I realize, is also a vehicle for the sort of group genius I'm probing. Sometimes ideas are the deliberate result of conversation, but just as often they arrive as an unexpected, but no less pleasing, by-product. Henry James recounts how his novel *The Spoils of Poynton* grew from "mere floating particles in the stream of talk." Socrates dipped into that stream often, delighting in how it was never the same stream twice and he was never the same Socrates.

As the waitress brings another bottle of wine, Alicia tells me how she contracted the Greek bug at an early age. "The ancient authors are more modern than what is being written now," she says, delighting in the appar-ent contradiction. "Their writing has an immediacy to it."

I sip my wine and ponder her words. They explain a lot. They explain why Alicia speaks of the ancient Greeks in the present tense. They also explain what distinguishes a good work, even a great one, from a true work of genius. A good poem or painting speaks to people of a certain time. A work of genius, however, transcends those temporal bounds and is rediscovered anew by successive generations. The work is not static. It bends, and is bent by, each new audience that encounters it. As Pablo Picasso said, "There is no past or future in art. If a work of art cannot live always in the present, it must not be considered art at all. The art of the Greeks, of the Egyptians, of the great painters who lived in other times, is not an art of the past, perhaps it is more alive today than it ever was."

If I'm going to understand the Greek mind, Alicia tells me, I need to step back and put myself in their sandals. The Greeks didn't have a word for "create," at least not in the way we mean it. If you asked a Greek poet what he was doing, he would say he was engaged in *poiesis*, literally "to make," a word that applied equally to making a poem or making a fire or making a mess. "They weren't trying to *do* poetry or *be* creative," says Alicia. The Greeks created much of what we now consider art, but, as we saw with the vases, didn't put it on a pedestal. So large did the arts loom in daily life that they were a given. Art was functional. Beauty was a bonus.

This kind of embedded beauty is, I think, the best kind. Today, we go to great lengths to ensure that the rarefied world of art never brushes against our grubby, workaday lives. We have proclaimed art "special" and therefore placed it out of reach.

Alicia knows a thing or two about the intersection of art and life. One day, not that long ago, she was at home with her eight-year-old son. Her husband was at a dentist's appointment. The phone rang.

"Are you alone?" the caller asked.

Alicia thought this was an odd question. "Well, my son is playing in the other room, but other than that, I am alone. Why?"

That's when the caller told her that she had been selected as a MacArthur Fellow. It came with a cash award of $500,000, plus the unofficial title of "genius."

Alicia hung up the phone. That much she remembers. Everything afterward is a blur. If geniuses are the secular world's gods, Alicia was now sitting atop Mount Olympus, peering down at the mortals. The view from up there is nice, but godliness comes not only with benefits but also burdens. For a while she couldn't breathe. Then she could breathe but couldn't sleep. This phase lasted two weeks. She would sit up at night excited, but also worried. Worried about an army of envious poets ambushing her. Worried about the unanticipated consequences of her newfound notoriety. Her sudden genius "has been something to navigate," she says, as if describing a rough patch of white water, or an Athens street during rush hour. "Sometimes I feel like a genius. I mean, the words are flowing. Other times, I write something and think, 'Do I want to publish this? This is not a work of genius. It's a crappy poem.'"

Finally, the hour late, my head fuzzy from the wine, I decide to ask Alicia a time-travel question. If she could transport herself to Athens circa 450 BC, who would she want to share a bottle of wine with? I fully expect her to say Socrates. The Dude.

"Aspasia," says Alicia.

"Who was he?"

"She. Aspasia was the consort of Pericles."

In the classics, we hear little about the women of Athens, and what we do hear is not exactly positive. The best a woman could achieve, it was said, was to be neither seen nor heard.

Such anonymity was not for Aspasia, though. She was seen, and definitely heard. She is rumored to have written some of Pericles's speeches, including his famous Funeral Oration. Aspasia was a feminist about twenty-four hundred years before feminism and the unsung hero of the Athenian flourishing. As I would later discover, these sort of invisible helpers are essential to a golden age. These are people who work behind the scenes, sometimes quite heroically, to make genius happen.

"The people of Athens feared her," says Alicia, her tone of voice belying that, as far as she is concerned, that was a good thing. A very good thing.

The next morning my alarm clock goes off and I curse Plato. He was a brilliant philosopher, one of the greatest thinkers of all time, but he also invented the water clock, an ingenious but diabolical device that utilized water pressure to sound an alarm. Plato's clock was also used to time political meetings; thus the common complaint about long-winded orators who gave speeches that were "nine gallons long."

Plato's water clock represents a rare example of Greek technology. Today we associate innovation almost exclusively with technology, but that was not the case in Ancient Greece. They had slaves to perform menial tasks and so had little incentive to invent time-saving devices. Pursuing new technologies was considered "trivial and unworthy," says Armand D'Angour, a classicist at Oxford University. To be a tinkerer or inventor in ancient Athens was to be relegated to the lowest rung on the social ladder, and to toil anonymously.

The *kleroterion*, for instance, was an ingenious device, used to randomly select jurors, yet nowhere do we find even a mention of the inventor's name, let alone any Steve Jobsian folklore surrounding him. Should a Silicon Valley technokind suddenly materialize in ancient Athens, he would be treated like any other craftsman, with a puny salary, no recognition, and, when his back was turned, a derisive sneer. He was working with his hands, making *things*; he was not a warrior or an athlete or a thinker. An ancient-Greek Steve Jobs would have died penniless and unsung.

I turn off the snooze button—a feature that never occurred to the genius Plato—and scramble downstairs to the Bridge, where I annex a table, order a coffee, and plan my attack du jour on the Great Athenian Mystery. Socrates, I'm beginning to suspect, holds the key. He claimed neither wisdom nor followers. All he did was ask a lot of annoying questions. Just like me, I think, and smile. Yes, a conversation seems fittingly Socratic, but with whom?

Brady. *You must call Brady*. That's what everyone says. If you want to understand Socrates and Athens, ancient or otherwise, Brady is your man, they assure me.

Every city has a Brady. Often the Brady is an expat, but not always. Sometimes the Brady is a local. Either way, the Brady has so absorbed the sinew and marrow of a place, so thoroughly inhaled its essence, that it's impossible to discern where the place ends and the Brady begins. For someone such as myself, trying to grasp a place as complex and confounding as Athens, a Brady is indispensable.

So I call the Brady, who turns out to be a former US diplomat, and a kind of genius, too. He invites me to his apartment, to a symposium. Well, okay, it's a dinner party, but since this particular dinner party is taking place in the storied Plaka district of Athens and not, say, Brooklyn, I prefer to call it a symposium because, let's face it, *symposium* sounds a lot more intriguing than *dinner party*. It certainly sounds more Greek.

The *symposium*—literally "to drink together"—was a centerpiece of life in old Athens, and Socrates was a regular. Food was served, but that was almost beside the point. The main draw was the entertainment, which consisted of "anything from good talk and intellectual puzzle games to music, dancing girls, and similar titillations," notes historian Robert Flacelière. No symposium, though, was complete without wine, and lots of it. The Greeks had some funny ideas about alcohol, as they did about so many things. Aristotle believed that consuming too much wine made you fall on your face, while too much beer landed you on your back, and for reasons not immediately clear, the Greeks always diluted their wine—five parts water to two parts wine, mixed in a large bowl called a krater.

Which brings us to one possible explanation for Athenian genius: the booze. It's not as far-fetched as it sounds. Alcohol and creativity have long been linked in the public imagination, and in the imagination of inebriated writers and artists down through the ages. William Faulkner said he wasn't able to face the blank page without a bottle of Jack Daniel's. Many painters, from van Gogh to Jackson Pollock, liked a swig or four while working. Winston Churchill claims he could not have written *The World Crisis*, his five-volume memoir, without his muse, booze. Indeed, some call this alcohol-fueled productivity the "Churchill gene." There is no evidence such a gene actually exists, but researchers have identified a genetic variation, called the G-variant, which causes alcohol to act more like an opioid drug, such as morphine, in some people. Theoretically (and it is only a theory), this genetic peculiarity lubricates the wheels of creative thinking in some individuals but not others. Or, as Mark Twain put it, "My vices protect me but they would assassinate you!"

You'd think there would be boatloads of research investigating the connection between alcohol and creative genius, given the enormous interest in the subject, not to mention the plethora of willing volunteers, yet I am able to find surprisingly few empirical studies. Nevertheless, a few brave researchers have bellied up to the laboratory.

To understand the significance of the research, we need to step back and examine the four stages of the creative process: preparation, incubation, illumination, and verification. Alcohol affects each of these stages differently. One study, by Swedish psychologist Torsten Norlander, found that alcohol consumption facilitates the incubation stage—that is, when you're not actively trying to solve a problem but, instead, allow it to marinate, letting your unconscious have a crack at it—but impairs the verification stage. In other words, you may come up with brilliant ideas but you won't be able to recognize them.

In another study, psychologists at the University of Illinois served twenty volunteers a moderate amount of alcohol, vodka and cranberry juice. They cut off the volunteers when their blood-alcohol levels reached 0.075 percent, or just below the legal limit for driving. These moderately sloshed volunteers, along with a control group of twenty sober participants, were then given a test that measures divergent thinking—again, an important aspect of creativity.

The results, published in the journal *Consciousness and Cognition*, are enough to make you reach for a drink. The sober men took, on average, 15.4 seconds to come up with a creative response, but the vodka drinkers needed only 11.5 seconds. Later the researchers asked the volunteers (presumably after they sobered up) how they approached the task. The inebriated group tended to describe their approach as "intuitive," while the sober group used words like "analytical." The study provides the first empirical evidence of something we have long suspected: alcohol decreases inhibition and, for some at least, opens creative channels otherwise shuttered.

Two key questions, though, remain unanswered: Which people and how much alcohol? What the researchers didn't do was conduct the same experiment but this time with double, or triple, the amount of alcohol consumed. I'm willing to bet they would get different results, that the creativity boost witnessed at lower levels of alcohol consumption would evaporate.

The ancient Greeks certainly thought so. Not only did they dilute their wine, but they served it in shallow cups, designed to encourage sipping rather than gulping.

Finally, I make my way across the stone streets of the Plaka neighborhood and, after a few wrong turns, find Brady's apartment. It is cozy and well-worn. Troves of books in several languages, living and dead, occupy prime real estate in every room, including the bathroom. Brady is smart. Scary smart. He begins sentences with phrases like "I was just reading Lysias this morning in the original Greek." My sentences do not begin that way. More likely they begin with "I was updating my Facebook status this morning, in the original English."

The guests arrive and our symposium unfolds exactly like an ancient Greek one, only without the dancing girls or the slaves serving food and diluting the wine. That last detail proves crucial, because without someone cutting the wine (or the mojitos or the gin and tonics) a symposium can quickly degenerate into a drunken blur. Indeed, that's precisely what happens. Many profound conversations may have transpired that evening, but I can't recall a single one. Except the light. Someone said, "The light is different here in Athens," and everyone nodded. Also, someone mentioned Socrates. Or was it Plato? Like I said, no one was cutting the wine, so the evening might as well have transpired entirely in ancient Greek.

The next morning, once properly hydrated, I call Brady and he agrees to meet again, this time sans alcohol. Sitting at a café near his house, I am grateful that the sky is unexpectedly overcast, with a light rain falling. Hangovers and severe Athenian light do not mix. I'm also grateful for this second chance with Brady and his smartness. I'm hoping to find answers to questions, or at least better questions, as Socrates would say.

The café, while no Bridge, is pleasant nonetheless. Most of the tables are arranged outdoors under a large awning, the entire ambience infused with an unspoken understanding: *Come, weary traveler. Order a coffee, one will suffice, and sit all day.*

Brady explains how his first love was archaeology. This makes sense. I can tell already that he is naturally shy, more comfortable among ancient ruins than living people. Archaeology is the perfect profession for people like Brady, and Aristotle. Rocks and skeletal remains tell stories, sometimes wondrous stories, but they do not make eye contact or small talk or ask you what you're doing Tuesday evening.

I tell Brady about my search for the circumstances of genius. He takes a sip of his espresso and gazes into the distance, ignoring the tourists on Segways motoring past us, trailing their guide like a flock of helmeted geese.

Does Brady think I'm on track, or a complete idiot—in the modern, not the ancient-Greek, usage? He doesn't say, and his face reveals nothing. Just like Socrates, who was famously poker-faced, and much admired for it.

I reach into my satchel and show Brady a few of the books I'm reading. He nods, neither approving nor censuring, but merely acknowledging that, yes, these are the usual suspects. I show him one book, though, called *The Greeks and the New.* "I haven't heard of that one," he says, and I feel a twinge of victory. I have surprised Brady. I know this because the expression on his face remains completely unchanged.

Brady has lived in Israel, Morocco, and Armenia, picking up languages the way most of us pick up lint. Athens, though, stole his heart. How could it not? In Athens, the past is closer than it is elsewhere, and Brady never tires of that nearness. He still visits the museums occasionally, he says.

I confess that I have a museum problem. I don't like them. Never have. Large and intimidating, they seem designed to invoke feelings of inadequacy: guilt factories disguised as cultural institutions. Brady is sympathetic: "It takes a long time to appreciate museums. First you have to study archaeology for a long time, then you have to forget it for a long time. Then you can go to a museum."

That is, I realize, a very Greek thing to say. The ancients believed that knowledge was good but recognized the dangers of its reckless, indiscriminate accumulation. They possessed a "shiny ignorance," as Alicia called it. None was shinier than that of Socrates. "The only true wisdom is knowing you know nothing," he said.

Some twenty-five hundred years since Socrates uttered those words, social scientists have begun to investigate whether he was onto something. One researcher has focused on a rare neurological disorder known as anosognosia, in which a person who suffers from a disability—paralysis, typically—remains completely unaware of his or her disability. If you put a glass of water in front of the right hand of people with anosognosia and ask them to pick it up, they won't do it. If you ask them why, they'll say they're tired or they're not thirsty. The damage to their brain that caused their paralysis also leaves them unaware of their paralysis.

David Dunning, a psychologist at Cornell University, uses anosognosia as a metaphor to explain the research he's done on ignorance. In a series of studies, he and his colleague Justin Kruger tested a group of undergraduates in such skills as logical reasoning, grammar, and humor. They then showed each participant his results and asked him to estimate how he fared compared to others. The people who did well on the exams estimated their rank accurately. No great surprise there. What is surprising is that those who didn't do well on the exams were convinced they did. They weren't dissembling. They simply were unable to assess their competence, or as Dunning, in an interview with the filmmaker Errol Morris, put it, "We're not very good at knowing what we don't know."

That's because the skills we need to solve a problem are the very skills we need to realize we can't solve it. It's the intellectual equivalent of anosognosia, and this phenomenon, now known as the Dunning-Kruger effect, explains a lot. It explains why most people consider themselves above-average drivers, a statistical impossibility. (*Somebody* has to be below average.) It also explains, I think, why more of us aren't geniuses. The first step in any breakthrough is realizing that a breakthrough is necessary, realizing that your knowledge is imperfect. Those who possess this "thoroughly conscious ignorance," as the Scottish physicist James Clerk

Maxwell put it, are more likely to achieve creative breakthroughs than those who are convinced they have it all figured out.

Brady and I linger at the café, indulging in some world-class sitting and talking, our conversation no more linear than the columns of the Parthenon. And that's fine. Here, unlike back home, there is no mutually understood cutoff point, no unspoken "we should really get going" signals exchanged. This is Athens. It's been around for at least four thousand years and isn't going anywhere. Why should we? All of this past around us, beneath us, makes the present feel a bit less precarious. Maybe that is why the Greeks of today have given up walking and prefer to sit so much. They like the feel of all that reassuring history under their buttocks, steadying them against the cruel present.

We order two more espressos, then lunch, then two beers, and finally two more espressos. "For balance," explains Brady. I understand. My entire time in Greece, it seems, consists of seesawing between alcohol and caffeine, groping for equilibrium. In doing so, I stumbled across a dirty little secret about the Greek notion of "nothing in excess." It's a lie. The ancient Greeks enthusiastically endorsed moderation but seldom practiced it. The Greeks viewed moderation as an end, not a means. Go to enough extremes, they figured, and eventually they cancel each other out and you find yourself in perfect de facto moderation. (That is the theory, at least.) They were closet extremists—"adventurous beyond their power, and daring beyond their judgment," as Thucydides put it. Perhaps every place of genius is equally overzealous. Perhaps that is why they never last long.

Did people, I wonder, appreciate the goldenness of the age? Did they know they were living in special times, or is such a verdict only possible in hindsight? Digging through the ancient texts, I've stumbled across evidence that the Athenians knew they were hot stuff. Witness this bit of swagger from the comic poet Lysippus: "If you haven't seen Athens, you're a fool; if you have seen it and are not struck by it, you're an ass; if you are pleased to go away, you're a packhorse."

That statement is highly revealing. For starters, it tells us that in ancient Athens, the worst thing you could be, the absolute worst, was a packhorse. Second, it exposes a confidence that borders on the arrogant. Pericles laid it on even thicker when he famously called Athens "the school of Greece." Presumably this relegated the Spartans and Corinthians and all the other Greeks to the status of pupil and goes a long way toward explaining why the Athenians were so widely despised. Yet this confidence rarely veered into outright arrogance. Why?

"Hubris," says Brady, who had until now been listening, stone-faced, like Socrates.

Ah, yes, hubris, excessive pride.

"Yes, but be careful with *hubris*," he says, as if speaking of some particularly dangerous species of rodent, or maybe a bad stock pick. "The Greeks didn't mean it the way we do. *Hubris* wasn't only a matter of excessive pride. It was an insult against the gods." And if ancient Greece teaches us anything, it is that we anger the gods at our own peril.

The particular god charged with punishing the hubristic was Nemesis. His name, Brady explains, means literally "going beyond one's allotment." This makes sense. Hubris is a form of greed. You're not content with the lot the gods have given you, so you grab more. That it was a crime against the gods (not a sin, mind you; sin—a Christian concept—wouldn't be invented for another five hundred years) ensured that Greek self-confidence didn't balloon into arrogance, at least not too often.

For the Greeks, Brady explains, virtue and genius were inseparable. You could be the greatest poet or architect in the world, but no one would consider you so if you were an arrogant jerk. I marvel at how that differs from our modern view of genius. Not only are we willing to overlook character flaws if the character in question produces brilliance, we have come to *expect* them from our geniuses. Think of Steve Jobs and his famously peevish personality. Only a true genius, we conclude, could get away with that. That's not how the Greeks saw it. A man was judged not only by the quality of his work but also the content of his character.

Two more Mythos beers arrive, courtesy of the management. These threaten to upset our hard-earned moderation, but we're willing to take that chance. I fear, though, that we're nibbling around the edges of my question, so I blurt it out: "Why Athens? How did a small, dirty, crowded city, surrounded by enemies and swathed in olive oil, manage to change the world?"

The answer, Brady suggests, lies in expertise, or rather the lack of it. Ancient Athens had no professional politicians, or judges or even priests. Everyone did everything. Soldiers wrote poetry. Poets went to battle. It was strictly amateur hour, and that, as far as the Greeks were concerned, was a good thing. They viewed expertise with suspicion, for theirs was the genius of simplicity.

All intellectual breakthroughs, says Brady, from Darwin's theory of evolution to Einstein's general theory of relativity, made the world a little bit simpler. "There is this chaotic mess of seemingly unconnected data out there, and then someone says, 'Wait, here is how it all fits together.' And we like that."

Mathematicians, for instance, speak reverentially of an "elegant proof." An elegant proof is not merely correct but highly streamlined. Nothing extraneous, and nothing missing. An elegant proof is pleasing to the mind the way an elegant design is pleasing to the eye. The Greeks always sought the most elegant solution to any problem. Invariably, that meant finding connections, for, as historian Edith Hamilton put it, "to see anything in relation to other things is to see it simplified."

Brady concedes that, despite his scary smartness, he often falls into the complexity trap. He can't help it. He's an academic at heart, and complexity is what academia encourages and rewards.

When President George H. W. Bush visited Athens, Brady was assigned translation duties. The president was about to address the Greek parliament and thought it would be nice to open his comments with a few words in Greek.

"How do you say 'Long live Greece' in Greek?" President Bush asked Brady.

"Well, Mr. President, there's actually no simple answer to that question because, you see, there are at least two ways of saying 'Long live Greece,' each with a very different connotation. For instance, if you say . . ."

Brady looked up. President Bush was nowhere in sight. He had gone to ask someone else how to say "Long live Greece" in Greek.

I'm digesting that story, my mind a churning whirlpool of caffeine and alcohol, when Brady does something I haven't seen anybody in Athens do before. He looks at his watch. He has to go.

He starts to walk away, but suddenly stops and pivots. "It's all about interlocking feedback loops."

What? Wait, Brady. What does that mean? But it's too late. The Brady is gone, swallowed up by a glistening sea of Greek light, now in its full afternoon glory.

I reach for my fork but it is not there. Nor is my napkin or, most alarming of all, my coffee. Where have they gone? They don't exist yet. Not in the Athens of 450 BC, and that's where I am now. I'm dining at a restaurant called Archeon Gefsis, or Ancient Flavors. It aims to re-create the dining experience of Athens in the time of Socrates. It strikes me as the perfect place to explore the connection between food and creativity, an area littered with romantic notions such as that of the starving artist. That's nonsense, of course. A truly starving artist creates nothing but his own misery. We need food in order to create, but how much and what kind? Did the Greeks eat their way to genius?

The restaurant is tucked away on a small street in a largely immigrant neighborhood, well off the beaten tourist paths. When I had entered, a waiter, dressed in the loose-fitting, togalike clothing of the day, handed me a copy of the *Ancient News*, which doubles as a menu. Cute. The interior is all stone walls and dim lighting and chairs covered in white fabric that looks as if it was cut from the same cloth as the waiter's outfit.

My dining companion is Joanna Kakissis, the National Public Radio correspondent in Athens. Raised in North Dakota, she returned to her ancestral homeland a few years ago. I like Joanna, and besides, in ancient Athens to eat alone was considered barbarous, and I make it a point not to be barbarous.

We sit down and peruse the *Ancient News*. My eyes are drawn to a quote by Epicurus: "The source of all pleasures is the satisfaction of the stomach." A nice sentiment but a misleading one. The Athenians were not foodies. Far from it. Most people, no matter their social stature, were satisfied with a hunk of bread, two onions, and a small handful of olives. The typical Athenian meal consisted of two courses, "the first a kind of porridge, and the second a kind of porridge," quipped the historian Alfred Zimmern. Even the food served during religious festivals was cardboard bland. Clearly, Greek genius did not extend to the kitchen.

Athenians simply didn't care what they ate, or even how much. Their caloric intake was remarkably low. Aristophanes, the satirist, credited the meager Athenian diet with keeping their bodies lean, their minds sharp.

I return to my menu. Some of the items—olives and chickpeas, for instance—sound familiar. Others, such as the stuffed piglet and goat leg, less so. None of the dishes contain potatoes or rice or tomatoes. The ancient Greeks didn't have any of these. They did have wine, thankfully, and the *Ancient News* contains this bit of wisdom from Sophocles: "Drunkenness relieves pain." No argument there. We order a carafe of red, which arrives, I am pleased to report, undiluted.

I order a pomegranate salad and smoked fish. It isn't bad. *Inoffensive* is the word that comes to mind. Joanna feels the same about her lamb shank. And I can vouch that forks are overrated. I manage fine with my knife and spoon.

We try to take our minds off the lackluster food with conversation. Now that I think about it, perhaps that is why the Greeks were so eloquent—it was a coping mechanism, something to take their minds off the god-awful food. As I pick at my salad, I wonder, if ancient Greek cuisine had been better, maybe they wouldn't have invented democracy or philosophy or any of their other accomplishments?

It's not as far-fetched as it sounds. We only have so much creative energy; we can channel it into philosophy or soufflés, sculpture or truffles. Yes, I recognize that cooking can be a creative act, and Julia Child was no doubt a culinary genius, but every activity we pursue comes with an opportunity cost, as the economists remind us. Time spent commuting to work is time not spent with your kids. Time spent debating the relative merits of kale versus arugula is time not spent discussing the nature of beauty and truth. I look down at my plate of bland grub with newfound respect.

I have another reason for meeting Joanna, one that extends beyond the gastronomical. I'm curious how she, a Greek American, feels about the burdens of history. Normally, we think of these burdens in terms of war and sundry calamities, but golden ages can also scar. Future generations feel the sting of comparison, and nowhere is the distance between past glory and current ignominy greater than in Athens.

"People feel they can't live up to the ancients, so why bother?" says Joanna, gnawing at a chewy slab of lamb. That's why so few Athenians visit the Acropolis, she says. It's not the site's familiarity but, rather, its greatness that deters them. *Look at what we once had, at what we once* did. The Acropolis looks down upon modern Athens in more ways than one.

Does this burden of history, though, weigh on all Greeks equally? It's one thing to be a Greek taxidriver or nuclear physicist. Those professions didn't exist in ancient Greece. But philosopher most definitely did. What does it feel like to live and work under that shadow? I take a sip of wine and then explain to Joanna that I'm looking for a Greek philosopher.

"Well, there's Socrates, of course, or Aristotle. Oh, you could try Thales, too, but he was pre-Socratic."

"No, I'm looking for a modern Greek philosopher. A *live* one."

Joanna furrows her brow. This is not a typical request. Most visitors to Greece prefer their philosophers dead. Philosophy is like wine. There are good years and bad years but, in general, the older the better.

"I did know one philosopher . . . Never mind."

"What? I'll take whatever I can get."

"He's dead. He committed suicide."

I stare at my ancient food, silently wondering why, from its inception, philosophy has gone hand in hand with suffering.

"Wait," says Joanna, suddenly perking up. "I know a philosopher. A live one. His name is Plato. He travels a lot, though. Let me check with him and get back to you."

First Aristotle. Now Plato. Any moment now, I think, and I'll be meeting a Socrates.

We nibble a bit more on our food, then, in typically generous Greek fashion, Joanna picks up the tab. She pays by credit card, which the waiter gladly accepts. It's the restaurant's one concession to the twenty-first century.

Plato sends his regrets. He's on a business trip and won't be able to meet with me. Why are these Greek philosophers so difficult to nail down? Joanna is completely out of live philosophers and tries again to foist a dead one on me, but I demur. I make a few queries elsewhere and, sure enough, stumble upon a real live Greek philosopher. His name is Nikos Dimou, and he is a minor celebrity in Greece. Back in the 1970s he wrote an essay called "On the Unhappiness of Being Greek." It hit a nerve when it was first published and continues to hit various Greek nerves as the nation mines ever-deeper reservoirs of unhappiness.

Nikos lives in a far northern suburb of Athens, so he suggests we speak by phone. I call him at the appointed time, pleasantly surprised that Tony's phones work. Nikos is friendly but sounds a bit stressed. Being a son of Socrates isn't all it's cracked up to be, he says. "We're all very proud of our ancestors and we love to say that philosophy and drama were born here, but we haven't actually read any philosophical books or plays. It's terrible—not only to be unable to surpass your father's work, but not to understand it either."

Nikos, though, understands it. As I said, he's a philosopher, and a good one.

"What does it feel like to be a twenty-first-century Greek philosopher?" I ask.

"Hungry. It feels very hungry." He's joking. Sort of. The sophists of ancient Athens may have made a killing, but in today's Athens philosophy doesn't pay well, and meanwhile the ghosts of Plato and Socrates haunt the academic corridors.

Nikos is most acutely aware of "this awful burden," as he calls it, when he attends seminars abroad. "If you say you are Greek, they say,

'Aha, you are coming from the land that created philosophy,' so you better be good. If you are good, it is very good, but if you are not good, it is very bad," he says philosophically.

The philosophers of ancient Athens—unlike, say, the pharmacists of ancient Athens—still have much to teach us. "Each great philosopher is like a monument that stands on its own, and it never gets old," he says. "You can read Plato and he is as alive now as he was two thousand years ago. But, actually, I don't read Plato. I don't like him."

Whoa. Did I hear correctly? You don't like Plato? You are a Greek philosopher and you don't like the philosopher king himself? Isn't that like being a classical musician and not liking Mozart, or a New Yorker and not liking bagels?

Nikos laughs, his voice crackling over the phone line. He's clearly not afraid of Plato's ghost. "Plato was a good writer but not a very good philosopher. He was an aristocrat and he hated democracy. Also, he separated the body and the soul. No, I don't care for Plato."

This is an advantage, one of the few, of being a Greek philosopher in the twenty-first century. You can say things like "I don't like Plato" and get away with it. Heritage has its burdens but its privileges, too.

Before saying good-bye, I'm curious about something. Philosophy is a big tree with many branches. What did Nikos specialize in?

"The Skeptics," he replies. "My PhD dissertation was on the Skeptics."

Of course, I think, hanging up the phone. Of course.

The next morning, I find myself in need of inspiration when I discover that not far from Tony's Hotel is a place called the Hill of the Muses. I like the way this sounds. What writer wouldn't? Most Greeks considered the muses minor deities, but not the poets. For the poets, and other "creative types," the muses were definitely majordomo deities. The muses determined not only when you wrote but also *what* you wrote. Homer was the world's first writer and also, it turns out, the world's first writer with writer's block. He begins *The Odyssey* by thanking the muses. Like all authors, Homer craved legitimacy. Today, that is provided by the likes of the

New York Times Book Review and Goodreads. In Homer's time, it was the muses. The original validators.

We may have outgrown many unfortunate Greek practices, such as slavery, but when it comes to the creative process, we are still very much Greek. We still beckon our muse. We may not believe they are actual beings, but these forces remain just as mysterious, and fickle, as the nymphs who romped on the Hill of the Muses. It's impossible to understand Greek creativity, friends tell me, without understanding these deities. They speak a garbled tongue, though. Best to bring an interpreter.

Mine is Robert Pitt. Robert is an epigraphist. He reads the writing on the walls. On the pottery and statues, too. He comes highly recommended, not only for his command of this ancient language but for his ability to breathe life into it and, in true Greek fashion, simplify it so that even a cretin such as me can understand.

Robert is a trim, lanky man who looks considerably older than his thirtysome years. But nothing about him is the least bit geriatric, mind you. He's just one of those people who was born middle-aged. Like the ancients, Robert believes in the power of place. That's why he lives in Athens, not Oxford or Boston. To truly know the Greeks, he tells me, "you need to know their topography, their mountains, sounds, and smells."

As we hike the winding path that leads to the summit of the Hill of the Muses, Robert tells me how as a young boy growing up in England he fell in love with the ancient Greeks. "I remember reading *The Iliad* and just being blown away by it, by the artistry and the story, and the immediacy of it." A three-thousand-year-old tale with immediacy to it? I realize that for the Roberts and Bradys and Alicias of the world, the past is not such a foreign land. For them, I suspect, it is the present that is alien.

It's still early but already the Mediterranean sun has grown fierce. I suggest we rest for a while. We find two rocks in the shape of benches and sit. "Socrates might have sat here," says Robert matter-of-factly. That's what I love about Athens. The past is always brushing up against you, with such tantalizing what-ifs as "Socrates might have sat here."

I ask Robert about the role that language played in the Greek miracle.

Words mattered to the ancient Greeks, he says, in ways we can hardly imagine. For them, "talk was the breath of life." They had a word for those who didn't speak Greek: *barbaros*. It is where we get the English *barbarian*.

"It was an extraordinarily poetic language, yet at the same time an incredibly precise and subtle one," he says. Not content with simply the active and passive voices, the Greeks invented an intermediate voice, something no other language had.

Always keen to synthesize, the Athenians combined their love of language with their love of drinking. The result was a game where participants tried to outverse one another. Robert has seen this practice preserved on pottery. "We have lots of vases from the symposia where people are scratching out verses and shouting, 'Oh, I thought of a good one.'"

The love of language was instilled at an early age. Children were weaned on a steady diet of Homer—and expected to memorize all twenty-seven thousand lines. It's difficult to overemphasize the influence of Homer on Greeks of this time. Think Shakespeare, Freud, Mark Twain, and John Grisham combined and you get an inkling of how large Homer loomed in the Greek imagination.

More than just the imagination, actually. In a fascinating study, psychologist David McClelland found a direct link between Greek accomplishments and the prominence of "achievement themes" in the literature of the day. The greater the amount of such inspirational literature, the greater their "real-world" achievements. Conversely, when the frequency of inspirational literature diminished, so did their accomplishments.

At first, this might seem odd. Backward. We believe that thought shapes language, and not the other way around. First we have a thought, then we express it. Or do we?

Consider the color blue. In English, we have one word for blue. We can modify it by describing something as light blue or dark blue or sky blue or baby blue. But with the exception of artsy hues such as cobalt and ultramarine, blue is blue. Not so in Russian. That language has two distinct words for blue: *goluboy* for lighter blues, *siniy* for darker blues.

Something interesting happens if you show a group of Russians and

Americans flash cards with colors on them. Not only can the Russians describe more shades of blue, they can actually *see* more shades. In the 1930s, linguists Benjamin Whorf and Edward Sapir advanced a theory first suggested by nineteenth-century thinkers called linguistic relativity. Language, the theory claims, determines not only how we describe the world around us but also how we *perceive* that world. Language doesn't merely reflect our thinking, it shapes it as well. The Greeks used words not only to record greatness but to manufacture it as well.

So perhaps it's not surprising that Robert, a lover of languages, dead or otherwise, chooses Thucydides, "the Shakespeare of his day," as the historical figure he would most want to meet. "He was a genius," Robert says with quiet certitude. "He's literally inventing language. He's a linguist and a psychologist. He's not only describing events, he's looking at why they happened. He's really the first to investigate why people do the things they do and what are the patterns, what are the relationships between words and deeds. He basically invented this entire field and did it in such a way that even today, after being studied for two thousand years, we still see books and articles written about him, and you go, 'Oh, God, absolutely. Here's another whole layer of genius beneath all these other layers.'"

Thucydides, like so many geniuses, was a tragic figure. Exiled from Athens, he died, unsung, his masterpiece, *A History of the Peloponnesian War*, unfinished. It's brilliant nonetheless, Robert assures me, and recommends a translation.

Enough sitting. We resume our trek up the Hill of the Muses, climbing higher and higher. As we finally reach the summit, Robert says slyly, "You wanted to know what made Athens Athens. Well, there it is."

Spread below us like a blanket of blue is the Aegean Sea, glimmering in the bright afternoon light. Some twelve miles away, the waters meet a spit of land. The port of Piraeus.

Without that port, there would be no classical Athens, says Robert, and quotes Pericles: "Because of the greatness of our city, the fruits of the entire earth flow in upon us." Athens was the world's first global city. The Athenians, master shipbuilders and sailors, journeyed to Egypt,

Mesopotamia, and beyond and brought back every good imaginable. Embedded in those goods were some stowaways: ideas. This happens often. Ideas insert themselves into the fiber of merchandise and lie dormant until a careful observer unlocks them. This is why authoritarian regimes that believe they can open their economies but not their politics are fooling themselves. It may take a while, but eventually these subversive ideas, embedded in a can of tomato soup or a pair of Crocs, squirm free.

The Greeks readily "borrowed" these foreign ideas, if you're feeling generous, "stole" them if you're not. Here I find myself staring down an uncomfortable but unavoidable conclusion: The ancient Greeks didn't invent much at all. They were, in fact, tremendous moochers. They borrowed the alphabet from the Phoenicians, medicine and sculpture from the Egyptians, mathematics from the Babylonians, literature from the Sumerians. They felt no shame in their intellectual pilfering. The Athenians, for all their many flaws (see slavery and treatment of women), didn't suffer from the Not Invented Here complex. They recognized that, as Goethe said, "it is unconscious conceit not to admit frankly that one is a plagiarist."

It sounds like a sacrilege, I know. Was Einstein a plagiarist? Bach? Picasso? Yes, in the sense that they borrowed liberally from others. Picasso was largely influenced by Velázquez and van Gogh, as well as African art. Bach by Vivaldi and Lutheran hymns. Of course, they took those borrowed ideas and put their own stamp on them. Athens did, too. Whatever they stole, they then "Athenized," or, as Plato, with more than a touch of hubris, put it, "What the Greeks borrow from foreigners they perfect."

Take pottery. The Corinthians invented the craft but never deviated from their standard animal frieze. Competent work, yes, but static and dull. The Athenians added richer colors and entire narratives: a couple embracing, a child playing a game, men drinking and reciting poetry. Similarly, the Egyptians invented statuary thousands of years earlier. They were stiff and lifeless representations, though. The Athenians animated them, liberating the human form from the block of stone.

This willingness to borrow, steal, and embellish distinguished Athens from its neighbors. Athenians were more open to foreign ideas and, in the final analysis, more open-minded. At the symposia, they enjoyed the poetry of outsiders as much as that of locals. They incorporated many foreign words into their vocabulary and even began wearing foreign clothes. Athens was both Greek *and* foreign, in much the way that New York is an American city and not.

Athens embraced not only foreign goods and ideas. It also welcomed foreigners themselves. They were free to roam the city, even during times of war, an admittedly risky policy since, as Pericles himself acknowledged, "the eyes of an enemy may occasionally profit from our liberality." The Spartans, by comparison, walled themselves off from the outside world, and nothing kills creativity faster than a wall.

These foreigners who lived in Athens were known as *metics* (today, we'd call them resident aliens), and they contributed mightily to the city. Some of the best-known sophists, for instance, were foreign-born. Athens rewarded them with everything from a simple wreath to meals for life at public expense.

On an individual level, psychologists have identified this "openness to experience" as the single most important trait of exceptionally creative people. The same holds true for societies, as Dean Simonton's research shows. He examined a country that has, historically, been among the world's most closed societies: Japan. Looking at a long stretch of time, from 580 until 1939, Simonton compared Japan's "extra cultural influx" (travel abroad, immigration, etc.) and its national achievements in such fields as medicine, philosophy, painting, and literature. He found a consistent correlation: the greater Japan's openness, the greater its achievements, especially in the arts. This hold true, he believes, for all cultures; every leap forward is preceded by an exposure to foreign ideas.

It isn't the ideas themselves, though, that drive innovation. It's that they shine a bright light on that normally invisible sea called culture. People realize the arbitrary nature of their own culture and open their minds to, in effect, the possibility of possibility. Once you realize that there is another way of doing X, or thinking about Y, then all sorts of new channels open up to you. "The awareness of cultural variety helps set the mind free," says Simonton.

Athenians tolerated not only strange foreigners but also homegrown eccentrics, of which there were many. Hippodamus, the father of urban planning, was known for his long hair, expensive jewelry, and cheap clothing, which he never changed, winter or summer. Athenians mocked Hippodamus for his eccentricities, yet they still assigned him the vital job of building their port city, Piraeus. Athens even tolerated characters such as Diogenes, who lived in a wine barrel and regularly ridiculed the famous and powerful. (After Plato described man as a rational animal, a kind of featherless bird, Diogenes plucked a chicken and tossed it over a wall, yelling, "Heads up. Here comes a true man.") Then there was the philosopher Cratylus, who was so determined not to contradict himself that he was reduced to communicating only through simple gestures. Athens welcomed them all.

That evening, back at Tony's Hotel, I heed Robert's advice and curl up with Thucydides. No, that's not right. One does not curl up with Thucydides. One does battle with Thucydides, locks horns with him. There's nothing cuddly about the general. He's all hard edges and cold facts. I'm trying to *get* him, to see what Robert Pitt sees in him, but it's tough going, and I find solace in the words of historian Edith Hamilton, who concluded, "There is no joy in the pages of Thucydides." Amen.

No joy, perhaps, but plenty of insights. Thucydides was the world's first historian and journalist (sorry Herodotus). His chapter on the great plague of 430 BC captures not only the medical details but also the incredible suffering that swept through Athens. Thucydides describes how "people in perfect health suddenly began to have burning feelings in their head; their eyes became red and inflamed . . . next the stomach was affected with stomachaches and with vomiting of every kind of bile that has been given a name by the medical profession." That profession, such as it was at the time, was helpless in the face of the disease and, adds Thucydides, "equally useless were prayers made in the temples, consultation of oracles, and so forth."

That is about all Thucydides has to say about the gods. Zeus, Apollo, Athena, and all the rest do not appear in his pages. This is no coincidence.

He couldn't say the gods didn't exist—that would be impiety and could land him in Socrates-size trouble—so he cleverly chose to simply ignore them. Sometimes what distinguishes a work of genius is not what is included but what is omitted.

I read on and find that, page after page, Thucydides recounts, in great detail, various forms of death and suffering. The ancient Athenians were keenly aware of their mortality, and I realize that this awareness, oddly, contributed to their creative breakthroughs.

Psychologists Christopher Long and Dara Greenwood recently investigated the connection between awareness of death and creativity. They asked a group of undergraduates to write humorous captions for *New Yorker* cartoons. Some of the students, though, were first "primed" with subliminal messages of death. These students produced cartoons judged to be more creative and more humorous.

What might explain this finding? Is it simply a matter of laughing in the face of death? Or is there more to it?

Armand D'Angour, a classicist who was also trained as a psychotherapist, believes that this ability to process grief actually helps explain the Greek miracle. "The inability to acknowledge and mourn loss is apt to lead to a shutdown of vital creative impulses . . . only the resolution of loss allows for a fresh start and renewed access to sources of creativity," he says in his book *The Greeks and the New*. This is a remarkable statement. He's suggesting that mourning, the fully conscious encounter with loss, is not only vital for our mental health but for our creative lives as well.

This dynamic might explain why a disproportionately large number of geniuses, of any era, lost a parent, usually a father, at a young age. A study of some seven hundred historical figures by psychologist J. M. Eisenstadt found that 35 percent lost a parent by age fifteen and nearly half, 45 percent, by age twenty. The list includes Dante, Bach, Darwin, Michelangelo, Dostoyevsky, Mark Twain, and Virginia Woolf. These geniuses possessed not only an ability to rebound from suffering but to transform that suffering into productive, and creative, outlets. Winston Churchill, who also lost his father when he was young, said, "Solitary trees, if they grow at all, grow strong; a boy deprived of a father's care often develops, if he escapes the perils of youth, an independence and vigor of thought which may restore in afterlife the heavy loss of early days."

That's a big *if* though. Psychologist Robert Sternberg reviewed the data and concludes, "The only other groups that suffered approximately the same proportion of childhood trauma caused by loss of a parent were delinquents and suicidal depressives." The question is why some people who lose a parent go on to become geniuses while others become delinquents or suicides. Perhaps, I think, dog-earing Thucydides and reaching for a glass of ouzo, what marks the genius is not *that* they suffered but *how* they suffered. Carl Jung defined neurosis as "a substitute for legitimate suffering." The Greeks were not neurotic. They suffered legitimately, and authentically. They knew that, as John Adams said some two thousand years later, "genius is sorrow's child."

I wake the next morning with a bad Thucydides hangover. Symptoms include headache, dry mouth, and frequent urges to smite a Spartan. What would Socrates do? He would no doubt pepper me with many annoying yet pointed questions, tricking me into examining assumptions that I didn't even know I had made until, eventually, I realized, in a flash of insight, that the truth was right in front of me all along.

Okay, what *else* would Socrates do? He would go for a walk. Yes, that is what he would do, and that is what I will do. I will walk. Like Socrates. Unlike Socrates, mine is not an aimless ramble; I have a destination in mind, and despite my anti-museum bias, it is in fact a museum. Brady had recommended this one, at the agora, assuring me it would induce a minimal amount of guilt, and hinting that important clues to the Great Athenian Mystery are to be found there.

I stumble downstairs and find Tony yelling at his TV. It is not poetry that rouses the modern Greek but soccer. I inform Tony of my plans, and he says he approves of walking, though judging by the size of his expanding paunch, this approval does not extend beyond the realm of the theoretical. Tony's belly says more about the divide between ancient and modern Athens than a library's worth of books. They've gone from a city of walkers and thinkers to one of sitters and worriers.

I climb a steep street near the hotel before reaching a dirt path that circles the Hill of the Muses. Yes, I think, this is good. I can see why the ancient Greeks liked walking so much. It quiets the mind without silencing it completely. With the volume turned down, we can hear ourselves again.

I pass a few hearty runners, huffing and puffing, and a small flock of dog walkers. A short time later, I find myself in another Athens, this one sanitized for your comfort. Tram cars painted like toy trains circle, their occupants snapping photos of ancient relics as if on safari. Now here comes a woman selling balloons, and, yes, one of them is of Mickey Mouse. The transformation is complete. Ancient Athens has been Disneyfied.

I stroll down the Pantheistic Way, the Broadway of its day, before passing under an archway and entering the small Agora Museum. In one room, I find myself staring at a collection of tiny bottles behind the glass of a display case. How cute. What could they be? I squint and read the small placard: "Black glazed medicine bottles perhaps used to hold hemlock—employed in executions." On second thought, maybe not so cute. I move on to a collection of Athenian coins. They are impressive, with detailed, intricate designs that put our quarters and nickels to shame. Once again, I marvel at how the ancients infused beauty into everyday objects. Not us. We segregate form and function. Occasionally, someone comes along and unites the two, and we call him a genius.

I turn a corner and there it is, the clue I've been seeking: several dozen reddish pottery shards. Etched on each is white lettering, still clearly legible after all these centuries. These are no ordinary shards. They're called *ostrakon*, the source for our word *ostracize*. They are ballots. The white letterings are names. This was not a contest you wanted to win, though, as the placard explains: "Each voter scratched or painted on a potsherd the name of the man he thought most undesirable." The "winner" was exiled for ten years. That's a long time. Accounting for inflation and limited longevity, it was even longer back then.

What could get an Athenian citizen voted out? Questioning the existence of the gods could do it. That's what happened to Protagoras, the

Richard Dawkins of his day. So could excessive vanity. Phidias, a painter, was exiled for sneaking a portrait of himself onto a statue of Athena, in what amounted to an early form of photobombing. These cases are understandable. What is more mysterious is why the Athenians also exiled some of their most successful citizens, often on flimsy charges.

We gain some insight by this comment from one Athenian citizen: "Among us no one should be the best; but if anyone is, then let him be elsewhere and among others." In other words, people were expelled for being *too good*. For the Greeks, banishment was a way of keeping the contest fair, a way of providing, as Nietzsche put it, "protection against the genius—a second genius."

When I first read that, I was perplexed. A second genius? What does that mean? And if there is a second genius, who (or what) is the first genius? The answer is Athens itself. As competitive as the Athenians were, they did not, as we've seen, compete for personal glory but, rather, for the glory of Athens. Anyone who lost sight of that imperative risked exile.

Ostracism, though, served another constructive purpose, albeit an unintentional one. Some of those ostracized Athenians did their best work while in exile. Thucydides, for instance, wrote his masterpiece after he was banished, ostensibly for bungling a military campaign. Does rejection spur some people toward greatness?

Sharon Kim, a professor at the Johns Hopkins Carey Business School, conducted a series of experiments designed to investigate the relationship between rejection and creativity. The results were surprising. Those who had been made to feel rejected scored higher on a creative-thinking exam than those who had not. This was especially true for those who had, in a questionnaire, described themselves as "independent." For these people, says Kim, rejection "confirms what they already feel about themselves, that they're not like the others," and that confirmation actually drives them to greater creativity.

The findings raise some intriguing public policy questions. These days, every school district and corporation across the land preaches the importance of inclusion. Should they instead engage in selective rejection? How do we identify those who are likely to benefit from rejection and those who will be harmed by it?

The Greeks didn't have the benefit of studies like these, but they clearly understood the power of rejection, and its close cousin, envy. They believed that man is naturally envious, and that *this is a good thing*. At first blush, this seems absurd. Envy, after all, is one of the seven deadly sins—and, as essayist Joseph Epstein points out, the only one without any redeeming qualities.

For answers, we must, as usual, turn to the gods. In this case, Eris, the goddess of strife. She had two very different sides. "One you would welcome when you came across her, the other is hateful," writes the poet Hesiod. The good Eris, he said, propelled men to great heights by "rousing them to labor" and to outperform their compatriots. This good envy enabled the Greeks to transform competition from a toxic to a productive force. Somehow, they extracted the motivational juice from envy (I want to best my neighbor) without succumbing to its darker side (I want to strangle my neighbor). How did they pull this off? And if they can do it, why can't we?

As I walk back across the Hill of the Muses, past the toy trains and the Mickey Mouse balloons, past the souvenir shops selling philosopher calendars (Socrates is Mr. November), past the runners and the dog walkers, I turn the question over and over in my mind, rotating it like the spits of lamb I see at the ubiquitous souvlaki stands.

I walk and think, think and walk, unconsciously reenacting a ritual as old as this hill. Before I know it, though, I'm walking into the lobby of Tony's Hotel, invigorated by my outing but with no answers, only better questions. *Good*, I hear Socrates say. *Keep asking. The road to wisdom is paved with good questions.*

On my last day in Athens I head to the Bridge for one final espresso and some serious sitting. Ensconced at my favorite table, I reach for my notebook and draw a question mark.

Why Athens? Of all the volumes I've read about these strange and wonderful people, one sentence, from Plato, stands out: "What is honored in a country will be cultivated there." I marvel at its simplicity, how it conveys something both obvious and profound. We get the geniuses that we want and that we deserve.

What did the Athenians honor? They honored nature and the power of walking. They were no gourmands but enjoyed their wine, as long as it was sufficiently diluted. They took their civic responsibilities, if not their personal hygiene, seriously. They loved the arts, though they wouldn't have phrased it that way. They lived simply and simply lived. Often, beauty was thrown in, and when it was, they paid attention. They thrived on competition, but not for personal glory. They didn't shrink from change, or even death. They deployed words precisely and powerfully. They saw the light.

They lived in profoundly insecure times, and rather than retreat behind walls, as the hawkish Spartans did, or under a plush blanket of luxury and gourmet food, as other city-states did, the Athenians bear-hugged that uncertainty, thistles and all, remaining open in every way, even when prudence might dictate otherwise. This openness made Athens Athens. Openness to foreign goods, odd people, strange ideas.

The Athenians got so much right, yet their golden age was, as I said, remarkably brief. What went wrong? In a way, nothing.

In 1944, an anthropologist named Alfred Kroeber published a little-known book called *Configurations of Culture Growth*. Despite the dreadful title, this ambitious and fascinating work aimed to do no less than chart the ebb and flow of human accomplishment. Kroeber believed that culture, not genetics, explained genius clusters such as Athens. He also theorized why these golden ages invariably fizzle. Every culture, he said, is like a chef in the kitchen. The more ingredients at her disposal ("cultural configurations" he called them), the greater the number of possible dishes she can whip up. Eventually, though, even the best-stocked kitchen runs dry. That is what happened to Athens. By the time of Socrates's execution, in 399 BC, the city's cupboard was bare. Its "cultural configurations" had been exhausted; all it could do now was plagiarize itself.

The Athenians hastened their demise, though, by making several missteps, and succumbing to what one historian calls "a creeping vanity."

They practiced democracy at home (for some) but not abroad. Toward the end of his reign, Pericles reversed his open-door policy and shunned foreigners. He also underestimated the resolve of Athens's foe, Sparta, and finally, in a classic case of overreach, Athens (under a new leader) blundered into the Sicilian Expedition, Athens's Vietnam.

The rot came from inside, too. Houses grew larger and more ostentatious. Streets grew wider, the city less intimate. People developed gourmet taste. (If the proliferation of foodies foreshadows the downfall of a civilization, then America's goose is well and truly cooked.) The gap between rich and poor, citizen and noncitizen, grew wider, while the sophists, hawking their verbal acrobatics, grew more influential. Academics became less about pursuing truth and more about parsing it. The once-vibrant urban life degenerated into a circus atmosphere, "with professional freaks, contortionists, and dwarfs usurping the place once occupied by self-respecting citizens," explains Lewis Mumford.

Every place of genius contains the seeds of its own destruction. The Greeks, I think, were aware of this. While they didn't know precisely when their day in the sun would end, surely they knew that just as "human happiness never remains long in the same place," as Herodotus said, neither does human genius.

Sure enough, after the fall of Athens, genius drifted several thousand miles east, where a very different, but no less brilliant, golden age blossomed.

TWO

GENIUS IS NOTHING NEW: HANGZHOU

IS IT POSSIBLE FOR A CUP OF TEA TO RISE TO THE level of genius?

I'm not sure, but this particular tea that I am sipping at a café in Hangzhou, China, comes awfully close. It is served in a glass teapot, with chrysanthemum buds floating in the hot water like lilies in a Vermont pond.

I pour carefully, handling the pot with the sort of hypervigilant care typically reserved for surgical instruments or very small children. Slowly, I take a sip. It tastes like beauty. Genius can adhere to any object, no matter how mundane. Genius—this particular kind of genius—is not a noun or verb but an adjective, a free-floating property waiting for the right host, be it a person, a place, or an especially good cup of tea.

I once met a reformed coffee addict who told me how he was up to six, seven cups a day when something in him snapped and he decided to go cold turkey. No more coffee. Only tea. "Coffee made me think more quickly, but tea made me think more deeply," he said with the conviction of the converted. Now, sitting here holding this perfect cup of tea in this perfect little café in Hangzhou, I realize he may be right and wonder, does that explain the difference between Chinese and Western genius? We in the West go for the quick jolt of caffeine and its rapid-fire flashes of insight, while in the East they imbibe their caffeine more slowly and therefore take the long view. This is, I'd soon learn, one of the many ways in which East and West approach creativity differently.

The café is called Taigu, which means "old place." Not old as in decrepit, inferior to the new, but old as in rooted. Solid. My table feels as if it inhabits its own private universe. With its Tiffany lamps and plush cushions, it reminds me of one of those ornate railway cars from the nineteenth century.

All of this intensifies the pleasure I derive from each sip of my tea. It is, as I said, pure genius, and that is why I have come to Hangzhou. For genius. The West may have invented the word, elevated it to quasi-religious status, but we do not have a monopoly on the concept. There are as many flavors of genius as there are of happiness, or gelato, and I am eager to sample the Chinese variety.

In particular, I've homed in on the Song Dynasty, which spanned from 969 to 1276 AD, a time of great flourishing. The dynastic capital, Hangzhou, was the richest, most populous city in the world. It was also the most innovative. When Europeans were busy picking lice out of their hair and wondering when the Middle Ages would *ever* end, the Chinese were busy inventing, discovering, writing, painting, and, in general, improving the human condition.

This golden age had distinctly Asian characteristics: a group genius marked not by sudden breakthroughs but by gradual developments. An innovative epoch that, in typical Chinese fashion, rested firmly on a bedrock of tradition. A less caffeinated flourishing than found in the West but one no less remarkable. Whatever Hangzhou lacked in terms of Athens's philosophical gravitas, it more than made up for in art and poetry and, especially, technology. Old Hangzhou changed the way we navigate the world, both literally and figuratively.

If you're like me, you probably know that the Chinese invented gunpowder and fireworks. You're probably not aware, though, of the breadth and depth of Chinese accomplishments. The Chinese invented everything from the compass and block printing to mechanical clocks and toilet paper (a genius invention, if ever there was one). Medical advances were made during the golden age as well, and as political scientist Charles Murray points out, "If you were going to be ill in [the twelfth century] and were given the choice of living in Europe or China, there is no question about the right decision."

By almost every measure—wealth, sanitation, education, literacy—China surpassed the West. The Chinese produced the world's finest textiles and porcelain and introduced the world's first paper money. They pioneered advances in nautical technology, too. While Europeans were still deploying tiny galleys powered by muscle, the Chinese were sailing huge, sectioned ships, with as many as four decks, a dozen sails, and up to five hundred men. They also published some of the world's first nautical and astronomical charts, and pioneered the field of archaeology. Meanwhile, using advances in coal and hydraulic machines, they churned out an impressive amount of goods, from plows to Buddhist statues.

The Song Dynasty was also a time of great philosophical and spiritual genius. The blending of Buddhist and Confucianist thought yielded a remarkably tolerant atmosphere. In fact, the technology that fueled China's golden age—woodblock printing—was first perfected in Buddhist monasteries, where some of the world's first books were published. The era also produced a bumper crop of great thinkers, unburdened by the sort of brooding that typically accompanies European philosophy. "Nothing is more foreign to the Chinese genius than metaphysical anguish and anxiety," says historian Jacques Gernet, who has written extensively on the Song Dynasty.

Finally, the period saw an explosion in artistic output, yielding enough poetry and paintings to fill many museums. People were accomplished not only in the fine arts but also in the art of conversation, leading Gernet to conclude that these were "one of the most highly cultured types of human beings that Chinese civilization has ever produced." That any civilization has ever produced. The Song Dynasty was China's Renaissance, Hangzhou its Florence.

That much we know. Beyond lies only fog and questions. What

exactly was in the air back then—and, an even bigger riddle, where did it
go? What is the answer to Needham's Grand Question?

Joseph Needham was a British scientist and sinologist who, in the
early twentieth century, unearthed and chronicled the incredible, and previously unknown, flowering of ancient Chinese science and technology.
His Grand Question was, why did China, at the time light-years ahead
of the West, suddenly lose its lead and fall behind for centuries to come?

Sipping my genius tea, I ponder this Chinese puzzle, but realize I'm
not going to make much progress today. I'm still groggy from the long
flight. I had arrived late at night, and for me nothing is more disorienting
than landing in a strange city in the dead of night. I joined other bleary-
eyed travelers at the taxi stand at Hangzhou's shiny new airport and, on
the drive into the city, was jolted awake by the ultramodern highway and
apartment towers and office complexes, all glass and steel and raw Ayn
Rand ambition. I could hear the voices of friends, the ones who have
spent years studying China. *You won't find the past in China,* they warned.
Chairman Mao wiped it out. You're wasting your time. I worried they might
be right.

My driver exited the highway and we were soon funneled onto a narrow, winding street; we were rounding a bend when the taxi's headlights
briefly illuminated a clutch of late-night revelers emerging from a tavern,
laughing and smiling. Something about their mannerisms, about the puddles of rainwater shimmering in the moonlight, loosened the grip of the
present, and for an instant, a flash, I was transported to Hangzhou circa
1230 AD. This was not merely an intellectual experience. It was more
than that. I could, for a split second, *feel* that era. The past is like that. It
is absent and then suddenly not absent. When this happens, when the
past arrives uninvited, we greet it not with shock but recognition. Yes,
of course, we think. The present doesn't displace the past; it conceals it,
like a blanket of fresh snow. The snow melts and we see what was always
there.

My hotel, abutting a Ferrari dealership in one direction and an Aston
Martin dealership in another, has done a good job of concealing the past,
steadfastly refusing to acknowledge its existence. The lobby of the Crystal

Orange Hotel is sparsely furnished with leather swivel chairs, chrome fix-
tures, and Andy Warhol prints. The staff wear matching black uniforms
and ironic, contemporary expressions. My room features such modern
amenities as automatic blinds and preset lighting configurations labeled
NEW YORK and PARIS (I would never figure out the difference). The only nod
to China's cultural heritage is, oddly, a small goldfish, which I spot doing
laps on top of my minibar. Perhaps it's the temporal dissonance of jet lag,
but sometimes I swear the goldfish is speaking to me. "Don't look at me,
bub," it says. "I have no idea what I'm doing here either."

The next morning, I return to the Taigu Café, order a pot of genius tea, and
assess where I've been, and where I need to go. Athens and Hangzhou. These
two places of genius, separated by fifteen hundred years and some five thousand miles, share no cultural or linguistic roots, yet the deeper I dig, the more
similarities I see. Both cities were blessed with enlightened leaders. Athens
with Pericles, and China with a succession of enlightened leaders known as
emperor-poets. That is, I concede, not a combination you see every day. To
be clear, these leaders were no dilettantes. They didn't write poetry the way
Harry Truman played the piano or Bill Clinton the sax. They were actually
talented. Emperoring was what they did on the side.

Hangzhou, like Athens, was a trading city. In its teeming markets,
you could buy anything: rhinoceros horns from India, ivory from Africa,
as well as pearls, crystal, sandalwood, camphor, cloves, and cardamom.
Hangzhou, like Athens, stood at a crossroads of goods and ideas, a destination for visitors from across China and beyond.

One attraction was the city's "pleasure grounds." (No, it's not what
you're thinking, though there was plenty of that, too, in old Hangzhou.)
These were places where you could learn to play the Chinese transverse
flute, or take an acting class, or simply marvel at the perennial circus unfolding before your eyes: tightrope walkers, jugglers, sword swallowers,
comedians, wrestlers, performing ants. Hangzhou was a city of "constant
pandemonium," writes Gernet, and I'm instantly reminded of the bustling agora in Athens. I'm sensing a pattern here. Places of genius require
a degree of uncertainty, and perhaps even chaos.

Athens and Hangzhou differed in important ways, though. Unlike Athens, Hangzhou embraced new technology. As I said, the pivotal technology was woodblock printing. It was the Internet of the day. Like the Internet, it removed barriers to entry. What had previously been a monopoly controlled by a select few, the scribes and their wealthy customers, was suddenly available to nearly everyone.

Like all successful technologies, block printing came along at the right time and satisfied a need, even if it was one people didn't know they had. In this case, that need was for information. A widening circle of people—members of the burgeoning merchant class—sought to improve themselves by reading the classics, Confucius and Lao-tzu. They gobbled up these works the way we devour histories of the founding fathers. Soon, thousands of titles, on all sorts of topics, were published each year. One library alone, at the Imperial Palace, housed some eighty thousand scrolls.

Not all technological advances caught on, though. Four hundred years before Gutenberg, Chinese craftsmen developed a mechanical printing press. It sank without a trace.

This fact gives lie to one of the greatest myths of innovation: that you can't stop progress. In fact, we stop progress all the time. If we didn't, we would be overwhelmed by a flood of novel technologies—some useful, most not. If we couldn't stop progress, then surely you would know the name Cornelis Drebbel.

Drebbel was a seventeenth-century Dutch inventor, a handsome man with a quiet voice and gentle disposition. He invented telescopes and microscopes, and self-playing instruments. He developed new methods for refrigeration and incubation. His perpetual-motion machines enthralled at least two European monarchs. He was, in many ways, the Thomas Edison of his day.

In 1620, Drebbel completed what he expected to be his greatest invention: a fully functioning submarine. It could hold twelve sailors, who steered the vessel with oars and could stay underwater for long periods, thanks to the pure oxygen Drebbel had bottled and fitted on board. The submarine, successfully tested in the Thames, flopped. It was seen as a curiosity, not a useful innovation. Drebbel's reputation nose-dived. Broke, he spent his later years running a pub. Today, his name hardly merits a mention in the history books. Innovation that doesn't resonate is no innovation at all. Genius, like so much else in life, is all about timing.

Every city has at least one porthole to the past. For Hangzhou, it is Xi Hu, or West Lake, as cherished today as it was in the twelfth century. Before I arrived, Chinese friends raved about the lake, speaking of it in reverential tones, as if it were some sort of celebrity or deity. Over the centuries, some twenty-five thousand poems have been written about the lake. Love songs, all of them. Even Richard Nixon, no romantic he, was smitten. "Beautiful lake, shabby city," he said when he visited Hangzhou in 1972, an observation that, with China just emerging from the Cultural Revolution, wasn't far off the mark.

What connection, I wonder, does the lake have to the genius that was Hangzhou? Genius, as I said, is largely an urban phenomenon, yet creative people clearly derive inspiration from nature. That's why great cities are never fully divorced from the natural world. They always retain visitation rights. New York's Central Park. Vienna's Wienerwald. Tokyo's Imperial Gardens. A city completely detached from nature is a dead place, and not a very creative one.

One of West Lake's early fans was Marco Polo. The Italian explorer visited Hangzhou in the thirteenth century and was clearly enamored—of the lake and of the city. In his diary, later published as *The Travels of Marco Polo*, he devotes some two dozen pages to the wonders of Hangzhou, "without doubt the finest and most splendid in the world." Hangzhou's population was at least 1 million (some estimates place it as high as 2.5 million), making it by far the largest city in the world, and making Marco Polo's beloved Venice, with a population of fifty thousand, look like a hamlet. Indeed, Polo had a difficult time convincing skeptical Europeans that Hangzhou was real and not the result of an overactive imagination.

Polo was a keen observer of everyday life, and he devotes a fair amount of ink lauding the residents' good hygiene. "It is their custom [to bathe] every day, and they will not sit down to a meal without first washing."

Okay, perhaps that is not impressive by modern standards, but for Polo, coming from ragged, diseased Europe, this was the zenith of clean living.

Reading Polo's unfailingly glowing descriptions, though, I can't help but wonder if he had perhaps overindulged in Hangzhou's famous rice wine. How else to explain his sightings of giant pears, "weighing ten pounds apiece," or a hundred-foot-long "hairy fish"?

Keep in mind that Polo was far from home, traveling during an era long ago, before Skype. He was homesick. Then, just when he must have resigned himself to that particular kind of sadness, he comes across a beautiful city on a lake, dotted with canals that people used like streets. He couldn't believe his eyes. Here was a city just like Venice. Here was home.

Much about Hangzhou enthralled Polo, but nothing snared his attention like the women. "Very delicate and angelic things," he writes, noting that they possessed equal parts beauty and cunning. "These ladies are highly proficient and accomplished in the uses of endearments and caresses, with words suited and adapted to every sort of person, so that foreigners who have once enjoyed them remain utterly beside themselves and so captivated by their sweetness and charm that they can never forget them."

I read that and get the distinct impression Polo is speaking from personal experience. Was he familiar with the sexual peccadilloes of the time? Did he know that male masturbation was discouraged but female masturbation strongly encouraged, or that, as historian (and Polo biographer) Laurence Bergreen tells us, "sex toys designed to aid women in reaching orgasm were common [in Hangzhou] and were widely discussed and written about in popular sex manuals"?

No manual was more popular than the classic *The Biography of Emperor Wu of the Han Dynasty*. It was already a thousand years old when Polo arrived in China, but—like *The Joy of Sex*—never went out of fashion. It contains explicit descriptions of sexual positions such as the Turning Dragon, the Fluttering Phoenix, and the intriguing, possibly painful, Overlapping Fish Scales. I'll leave any further details to your imagination;

suffice it to say that the creative spirit of Hangzhou clearly extended deep into the bedroom.

Polo is less complimentary about the men of Hangzhou, whom he regards as almost eunuchlike and "being so cosseted and pampered by their kings . . . have no skill in handling arms and do not keep any in their house." Well, Marco, gunslinging wasn't necessary. Hangzhou, like Athens under Pericles, was largely at peace during its golden age.

For both cities, though, peace came at a price—blood in the case of Athens, treasure in the case of Hangzhou. The Chinese emperors knew they couldn't fend off their powerful enemies militarily, so they bought them off with tribute. Peace was expensive, and therefore valued.

Peacetime should not be confused with dull times. Old Hangzhou was anything but boring. Places of genius never are, as Orson Welles pointed out in his cutting comment about Switzerland: "They had brotherly love, five hundred years of democracy and peace, and what did they produce? The cuckoo clock!" (Actually, not even that. The cuckoo clock is a German invention.)

In his study of golden ages, Dean Simonton found that places riddled with political intrigue, turmoil, and uncertainty thrived creatively. "It is as if the conflicts that plague the political world encourage young developing minds to consider more radical worldviews," he says. That apocryphal Chinese expression "May you live in interesting times" applies to the creative world as well as the political one.

I wake to dark skies and a steady drizzle. I shower, toss the goldfish a smile, then head to the lobby, where I meet Dana. Like many Chinese, she has adopted an anglicized name, ostensibly for the benefit of us foreigners, but I think the Chinese do it for themselves, lest they have to listen to us mangle their names.

I find Dana sitting in a swivel chair beneath an Andy Warhol tomato soup can, looking stiff and out of place with her chunky glasses and sensible bob. I know Dana from previous trips to China, and I'm hoping she can once again help me bridge the great linguistic divide, and perhaps the temporal one, too.

We walk, and a curtain of silence quickly descends. Dana, unlike my gabby friends back home, only speaks when she has something to say. I fill the silence with small talk about the weather.

Crummy day, I say.

No, says Dana. The rain is not bad. In China, a good day is a rainy day. Rain means life.

Well, then, I think, as we splash through ankle-deep puddles, this must be a good day indeed.

I've been in Hangzhou for more than twenty-four hours now and haven't seen the lake yet, Dana informs me, as if this constituted a felony. She insists we go there now, enticing me with the prospect of finding one of Hangzhou's geniuses there, a poet-governor named Su Tungpo.

The lake does not disappoint. Surrounded on three sides by lush green mountains and specked with countless pagodas and temples, it exudes quiet beauty. After a few minutes, we come across a statue. Gold-plated and perfect in every regard, it towers over us. It's Su Tungpo, governor of Hangzhou, poet, painter, travel writer, and engineer. Everyone in today's Hangzhou knows him and loves him. All can recite his poems, recognize his paintings at a glance. There's even a dish named after him, a rich pork concoction smothered in gravy, a delicious irony considering that Su was a vegetarian.

"Many of us are slaves of life, I think," says Dana as we gaze at the statue. "But Su understood life and how to enjoy it."

We cross a small bridge—one of those picture-perfect, little Chinese bridges that I've seen in paintings and Jackie Chan movies but didn't know still exist—and step inside a small museum devoted to the Man. Inside, some of Su's poems are on display, his distinctive calligraphy spread across a few dozen white scrolls, remarkably well preserved. Sometimes he dispensed with the paper and scribbled his poems on trees, rocks, or walls. Such was the spontaneous, almost reckless, nature of his art, and of his times.

If block printing was the Internet of its age, poetry was the Twitter. People communicated in short missives that packed a lot of meaning into only a few characters. Unlike in previous eras, when poetry was limited to divine subjects, Song-era poetry, like today's social media, tackled every topic under the sun, from iron mines to body lice. In Hangzhou, as in Athens, the arts didn't stand apart from everyday life.

It's difficult to overestimate the role that poetry in particular played at the time. People could pay for wine and tea with copies of the most celebrated poems of the day. Regular competitions were held. Even children got involved, such as the seven-year-old prodigy who was summoned to the royal court and asked to compose this poem about the departure of her brothers.

> In the pavilion of separation, the leaves suddenly blew away.
> On the road of farewell, the clouds lifted all of a sudden.
> Ah! How I regret that men are not like wild geese
> Who go on their way together.

Not bad for a seven-year-old. Or a forty-seven-year-old, come to think of it. As I said, everyone wrote poems, but no one wrote more sublimely than Su. One poem in particular, "Traveling at Night and Looking at the Stars," catches my eye:

> Peer at things up close and you may learn their true form,
> but guessed at from afar, they seem like something else.
> Vastness such as this is beyond comprehension—
> all I can do is sigh in endless wonder.

That is a recurring theme in his work, this sense of wonder, which Su, like the Greeks, believed lies at the heart of all scientific inquiry, of life itself. A deep and abiding sense of awe is an indispensable aspect of genius. Many of the greatest physicists—Max Planck, Werner Heisenberg, Hans Bethe—say they found inspiration not in the laboratory but by gazing at the towering Alps or, like Su, a star-filled sky. They all possessed what Max Weber called "the capacity to be amazed." Every genius, no matter his field, has this capacity and knows that, as British philosopher Alan Watts observed, a sense of wonder "distinguishes men from other animals, and intelligent and sensitive people from morons."

Su was also, as I said, a painter, and some of his evocative, impressionistic work is on display here. His method was unorthodox. With a few excited, rapid splashes of ink, he would complete a painting in minutes. "He either succeeds or fails," explains his biographer, "and if he fails, he crumples up the paper, rolls it into a ball, throws it into the wastebasket, and starts all over again."

When art historians use ultraviolet fluorescence technology to examine masterpieces, of any age, they often find layers of previous efforts hidden under the canvas. Geniuses possess a steely determination, a willingness to start over again and again that, while it doesn't fit our Romantic notion of effortless creation, is crucial nonetheless. What distinguishes the genius from the also-ran is not necessarily how many times she succeeds but how many times she starts over.

Music psychologist Gary McPherson conducted a revealing study in which he asked children how long they planned on playing their instruments. He then tallied how much they practiced and evaluated how well they played. He found that the single biggest determinant of their performance was not how much they practiced, or any innate ability, but simply their degree of long-term commitment. Those in it for the long haul played better than those who were not, *even if the short-termers practiced more than the others.* If the long-term committed practiced a lot, they improved *400 percent* more than the short-term committed.

I'm impressed with Su's commitment, and with the sheer number of his paintings. There must be several dozen on display here. "This is nothing," says Dana, and she's right. Some twenty-four hundred of his poems have been preserved as well as countless paintings. Here he shares common ground with the Greeks, and indeed with most geniuses throughout the ages: they were extremely prolific. Bach composed on average twenty pages per day. Picasso produced more than twenty thousand works during his career, Freud some 330 publications. (Van Gogh, in a single man, housed the two traits common to many geniuses, industriousness and insanity. He continued to work up until the day he shot himself.)

In addition to being a poet and a painter, Su was a much-beloved governor and an accomplished engineer. His best-known project was a causeway that traversed West Lake and still does today. Su was a Renaissance man three hundred years before the Renaissance.

As Dana and I step out of the museum, to a brightening sky, I find myself wondering why there aren't more people like that today. Why must we sequester our ambitions? I answer my own question by imagining what would happen if a polymath like Su walked onto a modern college campus.

Is it literature that you're interested in, Mr. Su? Then please see the School of Humanities. Oh, you're a painter? Please drop by the Department of Fine Arts. What's that? It's engineering that piques your interest? We have an excellent school for that, too.

But I want to do it all.

I'm sorry, Mr. Su. We can't help you there. Please return when you've clarified your career objectives. Meanwhile, if you like, I can direct you to Mental Health Services.

We don't often question the rationale for specialization. "Of course there was less specialization back then," a friend said at a dinner party. "The world was less complicated." Yes, it was. But I would argue that the world was less complicated *because* there was less specialization. The specialist is encouraged, rewarded, for parsing his chosen field into smaller and smaller morsels, then building high walls around those tiny bits. A narrow outlook naturally follows.

We mourn the death of the Renaissance man, oblivious to the blindingly obvious fact that we killed him and continue to do so every day on college campuses and in corporate offices across the land.

Writing a book is a creative act. So is reading one. Yet both acts pale in comparison to the resourcefulness required to procure a rare manuscript from ancient China. I am forced to deploy my best groveling skills to get my hands on one book, an important piece of the Chinese puzzle.

It was written by Shen Kuo, an eleventh-century genius who made important contributions to many fields but is perhaps best known for his work on the magnetic compass. Shen was a Chinese Leonardo da Vinci and, like Leonardo, jotted his sundry and brilliant thoughts in notebooks.

Shen's notebooks were lost for centuries, eventually recovered, and only recently translated into English.

Finding a copy, though, has not been easy. At first, this annoys me. We live in a world where anything—certainly any book—is only a click away. Then I take a deep breath and get some perspective. This is not the way it was for most of human history. Books were prized possessions— treasures, metaphorically *and* literally. You had to sweat to get your hands on one, so the moment when your fingers caressed its pages for the first time was that much sweeter.

Shen Kuo's book is called *Brush Talks from Dream Brook*, and I am determined to find a copy, propelled by the tantalizing title and a fierce desire to know this Chinese Leonardo. I plead with friends, and friends of friends, and with complete strangers. My efforts pay off, and a librarian named Norman (at least that is his anglicized name) delivers the goods to my hotel, with all of the furtive intrigue of a drug deal or CIA drop.

The two volumes are heavy in my arms. I stare at them in quiet delight and disbelief, as if they were visitors from another world. I'm eager to dive in, but this is not the sort of text one devours in a pre-caffeinated state, and as much as I have grown fond of the genius tea of Hangzhou, sometimes only coffee will do.

I head to a nearby coffeehouse that had caught my eye. Called Hanyan, it is nestled between a clutch of art galleries and antique shops. Perfect.

I sit down, order my coffee, and am surprised to find Uma Thurman staring at me. She is smoking a cigarette, splayed across a leather sofa, looking oh-so-cool *Pulp Fiction*. Later, in the restroom, I find Robert De Niro, *Taxi Driver* De Niro, checking me out. Electric guitars and traditional Yunnan instruments—guitarlike themselves—hang from the walls, alongside wooden puppets and vinyl LPs. Thankfully, the brash visuals are offset by mellow acoustics—smooth jazz, the faint hum of an espresso machine, the pleasant chortle of incomprehensible Chinese—creating a net effect that is surprisingly tranquil.

So it is here, in this unexpected serenity, where I crack open *Brush Talks from Dream Brook* (vol. 1) for the first time. I hesitate, pausing to ponder the small miracle that is the book. For two hundred years after Shen's death, the lone copy languished somewhere. In 1305, a few copies were printed and fell into the hands of private collectors. The trail then goes cold—for more than six hundred years—until the 1940s, when a renowned book collector, Chen Chengzhong, hand-carried a copy, most likely the only surviving copy, to Hong Kong. There, a bibliophile named Hu Daojing spent his entire career compiling and proofreading the book, rendering it into modern Chinese and, eventually, the English edition I am now holding in my hands.

I open the book, taking time to gauge its heft in my hands, to feel the crook of its knobby spine, the smooth finish of the pages. I turn to an illustration of Shen. He is wearing the traditional silk robes of the time and an angular black hat. He's sporting the requisite chiseled beard and droopy Fu Manchu mustache and is staring off into the distance, as if something incredibly interesting has caught his attention. A faint smile crosses his lips. He looks likable enough, but I can't say I get any real sense of the man. For that, I'll need to dig deeper.

I don't know if they had business cards back then, but if they did, Shen's must have been enormous. He was a mathematician, astronomer, meteorologist, geologist, zoologist, botanist, pharmacologist, agronomist, archaeologist, ethnographer, cartographer, encyclopedist, diplomat, hydraulic engineer, inventor, university chancellor, and finance minister. And those were only his day jobs! In his spare time, he wrote poetry and composed music. He was the first to identify the marine origins of certain rocks and fossils. He produced the world's first topographical map. He was the first to observe the process of sedimentation. He theorized (correctly) that climates shifted gradually over time. Perhaps his greatest contribution was his observation that a magnetic needle will point toward the poles, though not directly. It's always off by a few degrees, with the deviation increasing as you get closer to the north or south pole. Called magnetic declination, it's a discovery that Christopher Columbus wouldn't make for another four hundred years, and one that to this day is crucial for successful navigation. No wonder Joseph Needham called Shen Kuo "perhaps the most interesting character in all of Chinese scientific history."

For much of history, Shen was known (if he was known at all) as a poet. Only later, thanks to Needham, was he recognized for his scientific discoveries. This is not unusual. The reputations of geniuses ebb and flow, moving up and down in relative standing but also in the domain for which we honor them. Goethe was proudest of his scientific work but today is remembered far more as a literary figure. Sir Arthur Conan Doyle thought of himself as a writer of serious historical fiction, yet is remembered for his Sherlock Holmes series.

As a youngster, Shen's big break came when he aced the most difficult exam of the day. Called the *jinshii*, it required mastering a dozen Confucian classics. These exams, today dreaded by Chinese students, actually represented a major advance at the time and help explain the golden age. The aim was to replace a nepotistic system with a meritocracy, and for a while at least, it worked. No longer could you get ahead just because you had a powerful father or uncle. You had to earn your government position.

Competition was fierce. The top candidates, a select few, took the final exam at the Imperial Palace. Elaborate precautions were taken to weed out cheaters. Every entrant was carefully searched before taking the exam, their papers assigned numbers instead of names, and their completed exams copied to prevent judges from recognizing the applicant's calligraphy.

Shen's academics may have been stellar, but his personal life was a mess. He was unhappily married. His wife is said to have beat him. Like many creative geniuses, he channeled his discontent into his work. The year 1075 was his most miserable personally but his most productive professionally, his annus mirabilis, or "year of miracles." That year he made his discovery about the properties of a magnetized needle.

I read more about Shen Kuo and smile, as once again the centuries, and the miles, shrink. Like Thucydides, Shen was exiled, dispatched to a far-flung outpost of the empire, after he misread the political winds and trumped-up charges were leveled against him. As I learned in Athens, rejection can stoke creative genius, at least among the more independent-minded among us.

That's exactly what happened with Shen. Disgraced and forgotten, he settled on his farm in the village of Runzhou. He called the place Dream Brook because it reminded him of the idyllic countryside that had appeared to him in childhood dreams. There, resigned to his solitude, he wrote his masterpiece, *Brush Talks*.

I turn the page and immediately discover that this is a book with no narrative, no story line, no overarching theme. In this sense, it reminds me of Leonardo da Vinci's famous notebook, the *Codex Leicester*, now resting comfortably in Bill Gates's study. (Gates paid $30.8 million for it in 1994.) Like the *Codex*, Shen's book is a collection of random thoughts, observations, ramblings, and digressions, a porthole into the workings of a restless and brilliant mind.

The book is divided into 609 numbered entries, ranging in length from a single sentence to a full page. The titles hint at the breadth of Shen's interests. One is called "Words Used in Tortoise Shell Divination." Another: "A Rich Idiot." Then there is the intriguing "Autopsy via Red Light."

Shen isn't always likable in these pages. He could be a nitpicker—witness the cloying entry called "Errors Found in Books"—but more often he is bighearted and spot-on, as in "Enjoying the Things One Makes for Others" and "The Same Kindness Repaid with Different Outcomes." Plenty of common sense is also in these pages, such as "medical knowledge cannot only be gained from books," as well as the observation that "in this world, things do not often go as we expect." You have no idea, Shen, no idea.

Shen possessed many talents but, ultimately, I think his was the genius of observation. Not any kind of observation, mind you, but the kind that leads to instantaneous insight—what author Robert Grudin calls "the beauty of sudden seeing." His was the kind of observation Charles Darwin had in mind when he warned, "It is a fatal fault to reason whilst observing." Darwin advocated observation unencumbered by assumptions and expectations. *See what is before you, the thing itself. Analyze later.*

Every great discovery, every world-changing invention, every bold theorem, began with this simple act of observation. The genius looks at what everyone else is looking at and sees something different. The world sees another Viennese housewife suffering from hysteria; Freud sees the inklings of something more profound. The world sees two unrelated species of finches; Darwin sees a connection, and a possible explanation for how humans progressed. The grand theories—of the unconscious and of evolution, respectively—would come later, but already their seeds had been planted through simple observation.

Only, of course, it is not so simple. We acclimate to our environment so we no longer see it. Creative people are able to avoid this deadening of perception and "make the familiar strange."

Consider the case of William Harvey. Harvey was a physician living in early seventeenth-century England. People thought then that blood flowed from heart to body in much the same way as the tides surge in and out of the sea. Harvey believed this, too, until one day he observed a fish's heart, still beating after it had been exposed. The beating heart reminded Harvey of a pump he had once seen, and he postulated, correctly, that our hearts also act as pumps. He was able to do this because he had "made the familiar strange," writes inventor and psychologist William Gordon, in the *Journal of Creative Behavior*. It's a skill, he says, that all creative people possess.

For someone who accomplished so much, Shen doesn't get much respect, not even in his homeland. When I mention my interest in him, people either look at me blankly, or wonder why I would bother chasing this relative unknown. I'm not sure why he isn't better known. Perhaps it's because Shen was primarily a scientist during an era best known for its painting and poetry. Perhaps it's because he was not much of a self-promoter.

Shen, though, wouldn't mind his lack of notoriety. A modest man, he lived at a time when that virtue was honored. This deep and abiding humility lies at the heart of Chinese genius, in its ideal form, and explains why some of the most important Chinese classics remain anonymous, as do the greatest inventors. We may not know their names, but, says sinologist F. W. Mote, they live on "in bridges and towers, city walls and tombs, canals with their locks and dams, hulls of sunken ships—in the countless artifacts of ordinary life."

My goldfish is giving me funny looks. That is, if it is my goldfish. I'm not so sure. He seems to have put on a few ounces and has this little mark above one eye that I hadn't noticed before. Does housekeeping change the fish the way they change the sheets? I worry I might be losing my already tenuous grip on reality. Travel can be enlightening but also disorienting. Unsettling. Fortunately, the Crystal Orange provides not only a goldfish for my viewing pleasure but also fourteen channels of television. Ah, yes, I think, the universal narcotic, and reach for the remote. This particular television, though, is not my drug of choice. Every channel, without exception, is tuned to CCTV, the state-run broadcaster.

It's either that or stare at a goldfish with an attitude problem. I tune in to the middle of a heated discussion about Needham's Grand Question or, as it's known today, the "innovation gap." This is the source of much hand-wringing. Everything is made in China but nothing is invented here.

"Why is that?" asks the presenter in perfect, clipped British English. "China has the talent pool, it has the resources." She furrows her brow. "What else does it need?"

There is a long silence from the distinguished panel. *Say something,* I shout at the TV, no doubt startling Gary the Goldfish. (I've decided to give him a name, hoping that might appease him.) Finally, one of the panelists speaks up: "More time." The other panelists harrumph in agreement. Yes, China needs more time. Also, they say, the government needs to get involved. It needs to "build" innovation the way it built bridges and dams and high-speed rail networks. More harrumphing from the panel, with everyone skirting the obvious fact staring them in the face like an oncoming bullet train: mandating innovation is an oxymoron, maybe not as absurd as "scheduling spontaneity," but perilously close.

I click off the TV. The program was less than satisfying. It danced around the unspoken yet urgent question: What happened to all that Song-era ingenuity? And, more pointedly, does modern Chinese culture squelch creativity?

Some evidence certainly suggests that the answer is yes. On tests designed to gauge creative thinking, Chinese participants consistently underperform Western ones. Pressed to explain their findings, psychologists usually point to Confucianism, with its demand for allegiance to tradition and authority, as the culprit. The Chinese, after all, have an expression: "The first bird to fly is the one who gets shot." It's similar to Japan's "The nail that sticks out gets hammered down."

How can someone be creative in an environment like that? Isn't a genius, by definition, the protruding nail, the bird in flight? A few courageous social scientists have tackled the question of culture and creativity head-on. It's a minefield from the get-go.

For starters, there is no one definition of creativity, or even agreement on whether creativity is good or not. Some cultures place no special value on originality. Among the Katanga Chokwe of Africa, "artists work ceaselessly at a repetitive task, like making ceremonial Mwana pwo masks, yet never tire of doing so," writes Arnold Ludwig in the *American Journal of Psychotherapy*. Likewise, the Samoans tolerate repetitive activities without getting bored.

In some cultures, creativity is viewed as something akin to a disease, a dangerous compulsion that must be contained at all costs. The Golan mask makers of western Liberia are presumed to possess supernatural skills but are regarded, writes Ludwig, as "irresponsible, vain, unreliable and untrustworthy." Liberian parents discourage their children from entering the trade, fearful of the shame it will bring the family. Some literally try to beat these artistic propensities out of their children, but many of the wood-carvers persist, driven by a desire that they cannot name, let alone control. "They carve because they must," concludes Ludwig.

We in the West consider creativity—and certainly creative genius—the province of a select few. Yet that is not true of all cultures. Anthropologist Marjorie Shostak interviewed members of the Kalahari Desert's !Kung San tribe, known for their bead weaving, storytelling, and music. When asked who were the most creative members of their tribe, they invariably replied, "Everyone." In primitive societies, most people participate in creative activities. In more "advanced" ones, creativity becomes something special and therefore an option for fewer and fewer people.

Asian cultures—especially Confucian ones such as China and Korea—approach creativity very differently from Western ones. Westerners tend to be concerned solely with the outcome of creativity. The product, as it were. Asians care about process, the journey as much as the destination.

Also, Western cultures equate creativity with novelty; for us to consider something, *anything*, creative it must represent a radical break from tradition. Not so in Confucian countries such as China. The Chinese are less concerned with the novelty of an invention or idea and much more concerned with its utility. Not "Is this innovation new and surprising?" but "Is it useful?" In China, creativity represents not a break from tradition but a continuation of it, a circling back.

Why such different approaches? Our notions of creativity and genius are deeply rooted in our creation myths. These myths are extremely powerful. Even if you're not the least bit religious, chances are you have internalized them. "In the beginning God created heaven and earth." The impact of those words, on the religious and the secular alike, is enormous. In the Judeo-Christian tradition, it is possible—indeed admirable—to create something ex nihilo, from nothing. That is what God did in creating the world, and that is what we humans aim to do, too. In this worldview, the artist (or architect or software engineer) creates something out of the blue, something that did not exist before. The creative act, like time itself, is linear. The creator starts at X and advances—in fits and starts, with plenty of coffee breaks—until he or she reaches Y.

In Chinese cosmology, though, the universe, the Tao, has no beginning nor is there a creator. There has always been *something* and always will be. The creative act, therefore, is not one of invention but of discovery. The Chinese way is *creatio in situ*. Creation in context. Confucius himself said, "I transmit but do not create," and warned people away from the novel and unusual, lest they fall into the trap of "strange doctrines."

It makes some sense, but I find myself resisting this Chinese notion of moving forward by looking back. When the Chinese say, "We can be creative and still honor tradition," is that just some clever wordplay, like saying, "I can eat a dozen glazed doughnuts and still honor my diet"?

Then I read T. S. Eliot. In his brilliant essay "Tradition and the Individual Talent," he argues that the new needs the old; no poet or artist exists in a vacuum. "You cannot value him alone; you must set him, for contrast and comparison, among the dead." A truly creative person, he says, perceives not only "the pastness of the past but also its presence." Tradition is not something that innovative people and places should run from. It is something they should—they *must*—embrace.

That is exactly what the geniuses of Song-era China did. They viewed every potential innovation within a context of tradition. If it represented a natural extension of that tradition, it was adopted. If not, it was dropped. This was not a retreat from the spirit of innovation but, rather, a recognition that, as historian Will Durant would put it some eight hundred years later, "nothing is new but the arranging." The Chinese did not despair, as we might, at the prospect of a lifetime spent reshuffling the stuff of life. They knew that great beauty is to be found in arranging. Genius even.

This helps explain why China's golden age, unlike, say, the Italian Renaissance, was not defined by sudden (and disruptive) leaps, but, rather, gradual and steady progress. Does that make it any less remarkable? I don't think so. All innovation is evolutionary. The difference lies in the marketing. In the West, we are skilled at making even the most minor tweaks *appear* revolutionary. Automakers and computer manufacturers (to name just two culprits) are forever launching *new and improved* models, which are, more often than not, neither. They know it. We know it. Yet we all play along, complicit in promulgating the novelty charade.

All of this would be harmless, amusing even, if we didn't take it so seriously. Yet every day across the United States creativity consultants descend on troubled companies and inform the beleaguered workers that everything that happened until now doesn't matter. The stuffy past is going to be torn down and a new, shiny future erected in its place, one that bears no resemblance to what came before, one that is created ex nihilo, from nothing.

That is not what the ancient Athenians believed. That is not what the Chinese of the Song Dynasty believed. And as I walk along the shores of

West Lake, its waters glistening in the afternoon sun, just as they did during Marco Polo's time, I realize that it is not what I believe either.

I'm beginning to suspect that China's innovation gap is, like so much in this country, an illusion. Are the modern Chinese really less creative than Westerners, or are they simply creative in a different way? I'm hoping that Dana, being both modern and Chinese, might have some answers.

We meet again, this time at one of her favorite coffee shops. Inside is a mélange of rich colors and fabrics. Chinese cozy. I order a coffee, then ask her about the alleged innovation gap. She pauses before answering.

"There might be some truth to this," she says finally. "We have more limits, from our family life and from tradition." It would never occur to her, she says, to disobey her parents about *anything*, and she doesn't understand how American children get away with it.

Young Chinese face another obstacle: language. Written Mandarin consists of thousands of characters, or ideograms. The only way to learn them is by rote memorization. Starting at age six, Chinese children are required to learn five new characters *every day*. With so much cerebral space required to retain all of those characters, perhaps the Chinese simply have fewer neurons freed up for creative thinking. And unlike in, say, English or French, the Chinese language does not lend itself to improvisation or wordplay. The character is the character. Period. How different this is, I realize, from ancient Athens, where language didn't hinder creativity but drove it.

A while later, over lunch, a feast of crunchy tofu, fried fish, and bok choy swimming in garlic sauce, I switch gears and ask Dana about the Chinese sense of humor. Humor can be an important engine of creativity. Studies have found that people who are "primed" with humor, by listening to a stand-up comedian for instance, perform better on creative-thinking exercises than a control group that didn't listen to the comedian.

Humor was much appreciated during the Song Dynasty. Su Tungpo, for instance, possessed an "incorrigible propensity for cracking jokes at the expense of his enemies, friends, and himself," reports his biographer Lin Yutang. I'm not so sure that comedic touch holds sway today, though.

At least one recent study found that the Chinese do not value humor as much as Westerners do, and that they do not equate humor and creativity. I ask Dana about this. Is it true?

"No. That's not true. We value humor." A long pause follows and I can tell by the faraway look in her eyes and the way her chopsticks have frozen in midair, hovering over the tofu, that she has more to say. "But."

"Yes?"

"It must be reasonable humor. *Reasonable* is a very important word for the Chinese."

Reasonable humor? At first, this strikes me as absurd. Isn't humor the opposite of reasonableness? Isn't humor reason on vacation?

Then I remember Arthur Koestler. In his tome *The Act of Creation*, the author and journalist devotes several chapters to the subject of humor and creativity. (It's not easy reading; further evidence that nothing is less funny than the analysis of funny.) Koestler argues that humor and creative thinking utilize the same cognitive muscles, in a process he calls "bisociative shock." We find something funny if it is unexpected yet still logically airtight. As an example, he cites the old joke about capitalism and communism.

"Tell me, Comrade, what is capitalism?"

"The exploitation of man by man."

"And what is communism?"

"The reverse."

Okay, it was probably funnier back in Koestler's day, but the point, he says, is that humor relies on logic. The comedian toys with our rational minds and brings about "a momentary fusion between two habitually incompatible matrices." The punch line comes as a surprise but makes perfect sense. The sudden click of logic makes a joke funny; humor *is* reasonable. Someone without a strongly developed sense of logic is unlikely to have a good sense of humor either.

But not only humor helps boost creativity. A sense of playfulness is also important. Playful kindergarten children, studies have found, perform better on divergent-thinking tasks than children who play less often. This holds true for adults as well, as the geniuses of old Hangzhou knew well. Su Tungpo once described his painting technique as "play with ink" and, according to his biographer, "wielded his [poet's] pen almost as if it were a toy."

In a hopeful sign for the future of creative China, I see evidence that this playful spirit persists today. Such as in the two women I spot near my hotel, one of them wearing a faux-leopard-skin vest, playing a pickup game of badminton on the sidewalk—in the height of rush hour. Or in the arcade game I try one day, called Song Dynasty Sandbag Throwing Game. (It sounds catchier in Chinese, Dana assures me.)

Then there is this tale of playfulness writ large. For a while, a local bus company in Hangzhou ran a route called K155. The combination of letters and numbers looked like *kiss*, and that's what everyone called it. The Kiss Bus. People rode the Kiss Bus even if they weren't going in that direction, a wildly impractical act in an otherwise exceedingly practical nation. Then, one day, they discontinued the line. No more Kiss Bus. People were outraged. They wrote letters to the editors of the major newspapers. Bring back the Kiss Bus! they demanded. There's no happy ending here, I'm afraid. The authorities didn't budge.

I must be the only person in this country of 1.5 billion who can't log on to Facebook, I think, as I pound my keyboard in frustration. I am a victim of the Great Firewall of China, the government's ham-handed, mostly futile attempt to control what people can access online.

We consider these constraints imposed by the Chinese government an impediment to creativity and, if draconian enough, I'm sure they are. Authoritarian regimes can squelch creativity (see North Korea), but they can also foster it, albeit unintentionally. I'm thinking of those resourceful East Germans who cleverly contorted themselves into trunks of cars, or even the transmission, to sneak across the Berlin Wall.

We're told the best way to encourage creativity is to remove all obstacles, but considerable evidence exists to the contrary. In one study, psychologist Ronald Finke asked participants to create an art project. Some people were given a wide range of materials, others little. He found that the most creative work was done by those with the fewest choices. Or consider the difference between Western and Chinese styles of painting. Chinese painting is "vertical." That is, some elements of the painting are mandatory, while others are left to the artist's discretion. Western painting, on the other hand, is "horizontal"; novelty is permissible in all directions. Since Chinese artists work under greater constraints than Western ones, their creativity is channeled into a smaller space.

The same dynamic, the Power of Constraints I call it, occurs in music. Take the electric guitar, an instrument that, as Brian Eno has pointed out, is incredibly stupid. But it can do a few things well, so guitarists channel their creative energy into those few things. The musician is constrained, limited by her instrument, and that makes her not less creative but more.

Robert Frost once likened writing free-verse poetry to playing tennis without a net. Without boundaries, we are lost. That's why the truly creative crave them and, if they don't exist, construct them.

In the 1960s, a French novelist and a mathematician founded an experimental literary movement called Oulipo that took the Power of Constraints to an extreme. Raymond Queneau, the group's cofounder, described Oulipians as "rats who build the labyrinth from which they will try to escape." One member, Georges Perec, wrote a three-hundred-page novel without using the letter *e*.

You might consider that gimmicky or conclude, as critic Andrew Gallix did in the *Guardian* newspaper, that "the Oulipians are into literary bondage." Perhaps, but followers of this odd movement are onto something, I think. They've helped put a dent in one of the greatest myths of creativity: that constraints are something to be avoided. In fact, "we may actually undermine creativity if we make things too easy or too comfortable for individuals of significant creative potential," conclude psychologists Robert Sternberg and Todd Lubart.

This less-is-more phenomenon holds true not only for individuals but for entire nations. A good example is the "oil curse," also known as the paradox of plenty. Nations rich in natural resources, especially oil, tend to stagnate culturally and intellectually, as even a brief visit to Saudi Arabia or Kuwait reveals. The citizens of these nations have everything so they create nothing.

China is very different. People find creative ways to circumvent the Great Firewall, for instance, or to just get through the day. Sometimes that means deploying the most powerful of Chinese weapons. Never mind gunpowder. I'm talking *guanxi*.

The word is usually translated as "connections," but that doesn't convey its full import. "I need to find some *guanxi*," people will say, as if it were a natural resource, like oil, scarce yet absolutely essential. The Chinese are constantly prospecting for new, untapped sources of *guanxi*.

So you can imagine my delight when I, an inept foreigner, stumble onto a veritable gusher of *guanxi*. It turns out that a friend of a friend knows Jack Ma, one of the richest men in China, in the world. Ma made his fortune through an Internet start-up called Alibaba and is often called the "Chinese Steve Jobs." Jack Ma may or may not be a genius, but I bet he has some insights into Chinese creativity, past and present.

One morning, I receive a text message from my *guanxi* supplier. I am to meet Jack in the lobby of the Hyatt Hotel at 5:00 p.m. I am to be on time. I am to come alone. Okay, he didn't actually say that last bit, but it was understood.

I arrive fifteen minutes early and pace the ornate yet uninspiring lobby. Sure enough, at precisely 5:00 p.m., a slight, elfin man walks through the revolving doors. The first thing I notice is that he is wearing sweatpants. Really? Sweatpants? This is one of the perks of $3 billion, I suppose: you can wear sweatpants whenever you feel like it. The only indication that I am shaking hands with one of the wealthiest people in China is the ethereal presence of a young man in a crisp suit and tie who hovers discreetly in the background, ready with a business card or a cell phone or pretty much anything else Jack Ma needs or wants.

We sit down, and I'm instantly aware of eyes on us. Well, to be more accurate, they are on Jack. Born and raised in Hangzhou, he is the local boy made good. A bona fide celebrity. A waitress appears. Jack orders tea, and I follow his lead. Better for deep thinking.

I tell Jack about my quixotic, global search for a geography of genius. But enough about me. I want to hear the story of Jack Ma, local boy turned billionaire. It's an unfair demand on my part, I realize. You'd think it would be enough that he's fabulously, ridiculously wealthy. Maybe it once was, but not anymore. No, these days one must be fabulously, ridiculously wealthy *and* interesting. The public demands it. Every billionaire needs a backstory. Without one, without a tale of Homeric struggle, of overcoming impossible odds, the money is worthless. Well, okay, not *worthless* but worth less.

Jack Ma has a good backstory, I must admit. He grew up poor—not dirt-poor but poor enough. He came of age just as China was opening its doors to the first Western tourists. Young Jack began to hang out in front of the Shangri La Hotel, fascinated by these strange people with their outsize frames and wallets. Jack declared himself a tour guide, offering his services for free in exchange for impromptu English lessons. Jack was a fast learner. Language is never culturally neutral, though. Values embed themselves not only in stuff but also in words. So, alien notions—strange ideas about freedom and opportunity and risk taking—wormed their way into young Jack's brain until, one day, he realized that he was thinking differently. He was still Chinese, but part of him had become American. So when the Internet came to China, Jack was ready. He started Alibaba, and yada yada, he's worth $3 billion.

The story didn't just happen anywhere, though. It happened in fabled Hangzhou, a city that through the centuries has birthed a large litter of geniuses. And it happened—where else?—along the shores of West Lake, the very lake that inspired the likes of Shen Kuo and Su Tungpo all those centuries ago. Ma explains how when Alibaba was in its infancy and had no office space to speak of, the employees used the lake as their conference room, finding a grassy spot along the shores and holding their meetings there.

Jack Ma insists he is "one hundred percent made in China," but his success story is, I think, a hybrid one. Chinese respect for tradition combined with American gumption.

So why aren't there more Jack Mas in China? Is it a fear of taking risks? "No. Just look at the way Chinese behave in casinos, or on the roads. The Chinese are great gamblers." He has a point. The driving, certainly, reveals a willingness to take chances, with their own lives, and others', too.

No, says Jack, it's the education system—and in particular the dreaded, mind-numbing exams—that is squelching Chinese creativity. Those exams, which played such an important role in shaping China's golden age, are now one of the main culprits behind the innovation gap. The exams are a source of endless suffering for Chinese students and, not insignificantly, a creativity killer. Consider this recollection.

"One had to cram all this stuff into one's mind for the examinations, whether one liked it or not. This coercion had such a deterring effect on me that, after I passed the final examination, I found the consideration of any scientific problems distasteful to me for an entire year."

Those are the words not of Jack Ma or an unhappy Chinese student but of Albert Einstein, recalling the deadening effect of similar exams he was subjected to in Germany. Note that it wasn't the material that deterred Einstein, or even the exams per se, but, rather, the *coercion*. Even the most enjoyable of activities becomes a chore if embarked upon under duress, and Chinese schools these days are all about duress.

That partly explains China's current innovation gap, but, says Jack, there is another, more insidious reason. "I would say that China lost its culture, and it has lost its religion."

I nearly spit out my tea. I've spent enough time over the years in China to know that religion is a dangerous subject, one that is broached extremely carefully, if at all. Jack Ma, though, is insulated by a large wad of cash. Modern China offers plenty of freedom of speech, if you can afford it. He continues, "Those religious teachings contain a lot of inspirational ideas, ideas that have very practical applications when it comes to creative thinking."

When I press him for an example, he cites one of China's major religions, Taoism, or "the Way." Between sips of tea, Jack explains that Taoism helped him guide Alibaba to such Olympian heights. "When I compete with eBay, or whoever, I never use the Western way. I always use Taoism."

"Taoism against eBay? What do you mean?"

"When you push me here"—he points to his solar plexus—"I don't push back. Instead, I fight you here, and here. Where you don't expect it. The idea is to use wisdom, fight smart, always keep your balance." The

Western approach, one Jack has come to expect from his competitors, is the way of the boxer. Jack's way is that of the surfer.

His story reminds me of the artist I met a few days earlier. I had asked him about creative destruction. Do the Chinese embrace the concept with the same enthusiasm that we in the West do? He answered my question by drawing a tree, called a *long su*, found in southern China. The roots, rather than being buried underground, hang in the air. When they are long enough, they touch the ground, and sometimes a new tree is born. The new tree doesn't destroy the old one. It grows alongside it. One root can turn into a new tree, yet it is still connected to the old tree. Something new is created yet nothing old is destroyed.

Jack Ma sees no future for Chinese creative genius without a reawakening of this sort of timeless philosophy and culture. Otherwise, "we are just a copy. We copy, we take knowledge, we copy. This approach won't last." But there is hope, he says, and that hope resides in, of all places, the Internet. China, he's convinced, will reconnect with its past through the modern Internet, a technology that allows people to bypass the mind-numbing schools and the government propaganda. "Hopefully in thirty years, if we are lucky, we will have a generation that can combine Confucianism, Taoism, Christianity together. Because of the Internet." How exactly this religious confluence would power another Chinese renaissance is unclear. Ma is wealthy enough now that he needn't fill in the blanks.

After Jack and I say good-bye, I decide to walk back to my hotel and reflect on our conversation. The sun is just setting over West Lake, the light soft and golden.

I'm not sure what to make of his prescription for Chinese creativity. Is it truly a different approach from the Western way, or is this just a bunch of *Karate Kid* mumbo jumbo he serves up to gullible Americans?

As I walk, I recall one study that seems to justify Jack Ma's optimism. Robert Sternberg and fellow psychologist Weihua Niu asked a group of American and Chinese college students to produce artwork, which was then evaluated by a panel of independent judges (from both countries). The American artwork was found to be more creative. Not a surprising result, as we've seen. What is surprising is what happened when researchers repeated the experiment but this time gave explicit instructions to "be creative." The Americans' artwork improved only slightly, while the Chinese showed dramatic progress. Perhaps the reason the Chinese don't think more creatively is because no one has told them they could.

The Chinese are good at playing follow the leader, one academic told me. If their leaders are tyrants, they act tyrannically. If their leaders are poetic, they act poetically. At the time, it struck me as an oversimplification. Now I'm not so sure. If, as the research suggests, creativity is contagious, then it makes sense that in a hierarchal society such as China's "contagion" would necessarily begin at the top and work its way down. The country is unlikely to see a return of the emperor-poet, but might it see enlightened leadership of a different kind?

Definitive answers will have to wait. I'm eager to return to the sanctuary of the Crystal Orange, with its Andy Warhol prints, stacks of books, and a goldfish that is at this very moment no doubt wondering where the hell I've been.

It is easier to explain endings than beginnings. So while the source of China's golden age remains misty, the reasons for its demise are fairly clear. On the scientific front, thinkers such as Shen Kuo, brilliant as they were, failed to stitch together their sundry observations into overarching theories. Hangzhou's emperor-poets, meanwhile, turned out to be better poets than emperors. They made a series of foreign-policy blunders that opened the door to the Mongol invasion of 1279. As I learned in Athens, though, golden ages rarely collapse solely because of outside influences; there is always a rotting from the inside, and that was the case with China. The exam system, once a source of innovation, devolved into a mindless scramble for power and prestige.

"The system's strengths proved to be inseparable from its weaknesses," says Mote, the sinologist. That statement, I realize, could apply to all great places. Eventually, they collapse under the weight of their own greatness.

Did Hangzhou's most famous visitor, Marco Polo, see the end coming? Or was he blinded by the glories of the fabled city? So fantastical were his accounts that skeptics back home labeled his diary *Il Milione*, or "the million." As in a million lies. Yet even on his deathbed, urged by friends to recant and thus rehabilitate his reputation, Polo didn't budge.

"Friends," he said, "I have not written down the half of those things that I saw."

As I pack my bags, I smile at how I am about to perform a reverse Polo. I am heading to the great traveler's homeland, a place that experienced a flourishing even more magnificent, and less likely, than that of Hangzhou. Genius, once again, was on the move, and so am I.

THREE

GENIUS IS EXPENSIVE: FLORENCE

GREAT MINDS DON'T NECESSARILY THINK ALIKE, but they do gravitate to one another, drawn by some powerful, unnamed force. Consider the remarkable gathering that transpired in one room, in Florence, Italy, on January 25, 1504. More than two dozen of the greatest artists of the Renaissance—of any era—were in attendance. Leonardo da Vinci was there, as was a young rising star with the surname of Buonarroti but better known by his first name, Michelangelo. So, too, were Botticelli and Rosselli and Filippino Lippi and Piero di Cosimo, among others. Their collective works could fill a museum, and in fact they do; today, the iconic Uffizi Gallery sits only a few yards from the hall where this gathering took place.

The purpose of the meeting was to choose a location, "convenient and courageous," to display the city's latest masterpiece, Michelangelo's *David*, a work so large, in every sense of the word, that Florentines referred to it simply as the Giant. The seemingly cordial meeting was also palpably rife with rivalries and animosities simmering like a pot of pasta puttanesca. Florence midwifed not only scores of geniuses but also the concept of individual genius, as well as its ugly sidekick, *l'enfant terrible*. In that room, on that day, we would instantly recognize twenty-nine versions of the tempestuous genius. It would be unbearable. And irresistible.

Not since Athens has one city produced so many brilliant minds and good ideas—and in such a brief time. We know what the Renaissance (literally "rebirth") was and have the art to prove it, but *why* it happened at all remains a mystery. Was it the discovery of ancient Greek and Roman texts? The relatively enlightened leadership? Something else?

An even bigger mystery, though, is *where* it happened. Florence was by no means a natural location for such an extraordinary explosion of genius. The city was swampy, malarial, and prone to regular outbreaks of fire, flood, and the bubonic plague. It had no port and was surrounded by spiteful, occasionally bellicose, neighbors. Some of these other city-states were bigger (Venice had a population three times that of Florence) or, such as Milan, stronger militarily. Yet the Renaissance shined brightest not in these places but in Florence. Why? To answer that question, I take a step back, to Plato. *What is honored in a country will be cultivated there.* Athens honored wisdom and got Socrates. Rome honored power and got an empire. What did Florence honor?

An important clue resides in one tiny, circular trinket, about the size of a thumbnail. Of all the art to emerge from Renaissance Florence, this piece soars high above all the rest and helps explain the rest. Without it, these geniuses wouldn't exist, and most likely the Renaissance wouldn't have happened.

Yet chances are you've never contemplated its importance. You probably don't even consider it art. But art it is. Made of pure gold, it contains an engraving of John the Baptist on one side and a lily on the other. It is the florin, the symbol of Florentine wealth and taste and its unique form of reckless pragmatism. Instantly recognized in its day from Cairo to London, it was the world's first international currency. Others tried to imitate it but failed. Some despised it, including one of Florence's own, Dante, who wrote of the "accursed flower" and consigned moneylenders to the seventh circle of hell, where amid murky vapors they would languish for eternity staring at the money bags hanging around their necks.

But without this little gold coin, and all it represented, we would not have Michelangelo's *David* or Leonardo's *Mona Lisa* or Brunelleschi's cupola. And since the Renaissance was not merely an artistic revolution but a philosophical and scientific one as well, it's quite possible that without that "accursed flower" the modern world itself would not exist.

The story of Florence is the story of money and genius. Two words, I concede, not normally uttered in the same sentence. Genius, we think, occupies rarefied air unsullied by the gritty world of cash or transfer payments or, heaven forbid, actuarial tables. Genius is above all that. Genius is pure. Genius certainly can't be bought.

It is a nice idea. It is also wrong. Money and genius are intertwined, as inseparable as two young lovers.

But what exactly is the connection between money and genius? Is it true that, as D. H. Lawrence put it so colorfully, all culture is built on the "deep dung of cash"? In other words, did Florence have a Renaissance because it could afford one? Or is the relationship between money and genius more complicated than that? I am determined to answer that question, and I have a plan. It entails some deep reading, on-the-ground research, and an art historian with a dog.

His name (the art historian's, not the dog's) is Eugene Martinez. Of all the tour guides, art historians, wayward graduate students, and sundry others who earn their living at the teat of Florentine culture, Eugene Martinez got my attention—at first digitally and then in the analog or, as I quaintly like to think of it, real world.

Eugene, fittingly, is a bit of a Renaissance man—tour guide, art expert, gourmand, dog lover. His tour company is called Ars Opulenta, which is Latin for "abundantly luxuriant art." I like the way that sounds, so unapologetically decadent and overflowing with goodness. What really sold me on Eugene, though, was his dog. While the other websites featured somber men and women striking serious art-is-no-laughing-matter poses in front of the Uffizi or the Bargello or some other sober Florentine landmark, the Ars Opulenta site greeted me with a photo of Eugene and a hound of indeterminate breed. Both are smiling, with the red-tiled roof and shiny gold spire of the Duomo barely visible in the distance. The landmark building is almost an afterthought, a backdrop for what Eugene considers the real purpose of all this glorious art: joy. "Enjoying enjoying," Eugene would later tell me. That was the essence of Florence and still is.

Eugene grew up in the shadow of the Cloisters, in a still-scruffy New York, a city of squeegee men and strip clubs and debt. At a young age the visual arts called, and Eugene answered. He majored in art history at NYU, and just in case, by some fluke of fate, that degree proved to be something other than the path to easy riches, he also studied graphic design. His first job was at an ad agency designing advertisements for a bank. Not exactly high art, but it paid the bills. His second job was with *Beaver* magazine, which was even less high art but also paid the bills.

He didn't last long, though. He fell in love with an Italian, then with Italy. He moved there for six months. That was thirty years ago. At first, like all newcomers to Italy, he made a fool of himself. He ordered a cappuccino at 2:00 p.m. and everyone in the café stared at him as if he were a moron, or possibly American. No respectable Italian would ever, *ever*, order a cappuccino after noon. Eugene soon navigated such cultural land mines, learned Italian, and mastered the art of enjoying enjoying.

He launched Ars Opulenta, his tour company, and quickly realized that his dog was good for business. People trust an art historian with a dog. This makes sense. Dogs are comforting, reassuring, while all this art, this *genius*, is intimidating. What if we don't "get" it? What if we say something silly that exposes our ignorance? What if—and this cuts to the heart of our encounter with greatness—we are not worthy? A smiling canine presence puts people at ease.

I am walking to meet Eugene now, a short journey that requires navigating a sea of tourists. I am not Moses and this sea does not part, so I shoulder my way through, inching past the gelaterias and the caricature artists, past the hawkers selling Bob Marley portraits, and past the accordion players before finding the little café where we had agreed to meet.

Eugene has come alone. No dog. I like him anyway. Despite his three decades in Italy, first Rome, then Florence, he has not lost his New Yorker's purposeful gait and endearing bluntness. Not tall, he is carrying a few extra pounds and possesses a fashion sensibility that is more South Bronx than southern Italian.

Eugene orders a coffee the size of a thimble; I, still in the grips of China, opt for a green tea. We find a table and talk.

Eugene is comfortable with what he knows and with what he doesn't. His genius, if I can call it that, is the genius of the outsider. He is a Hispanic American living in Italy, a gay man in a straight world, a straight talker in a field notorious for its obfuscation. Eugene knows his history and his art but feels no compunction to dress them up in the pretentious and largely impenetrable language of the art historian.

During our conversation at the café, I keep tripping over all those slippery Italian names, so Eugene anglicizes them for me. Michelangelo becomes Mike. Leonardo da Vinci becomes Leo; Lorenzo Ghiberti, Larry; Filippo Brunelleschi, Phil. At first, this strikes me as a sacrilege, like referring to Moses as Mo, but I soon warm to the idea. It retrieves these lofty geniuses from the heavens and brings them back down to earth, where they belong. Despite the stubborn mythology, geniuses are not gods, and we do both us and them a huge disservice by pretending they are.

I like the way Eugene says crazy, blasphemous things such as "I don't care for the Renaissance." That strikes me not only as heresy, but also career suicide. Eugene is a tour guide; he earns his living from the Renaissance. It's the equivalent of a meteorologist who doesn't care much for the weather, or a comedian who can't stand the sound of laughter.

"What?" I say. "You don't like the Renaissance?"

"I don't. It's too pretty for me." I'm pondering what he means by that when he says, "Give it a few days. You'll see what I mean."

I promise him I will.

I explain my quixotic search for the geography of genius. Eugene listens intently. He doesn't laugh, which further endears him to me. You'd be surprised how many people do laugh. So deeply ingrained is the myth of lone genius that any other explanation for human greatness strikes many as absurd.

Our plan is to sit and talk, fortify ourselves with caffeine, then cross the Arno River like an invading army of two. This doesn't happen, not today at least. The famous Tuscan sun has gone AWOL, replaced by a steady and cold rain. The café is warm and cozy, a self-contained universe, and Eugene and I have a few hundred years to cover. The world out there, across the Arno, can wait.

Where to begin my dissection of the Renaissance? The obvious starting point is the artists and poets, right?

No, says Eugene. Florence was a city of merchants and bankers. Walk the city's cobblestoned streets to the Mercato Vecchio, the old market, and you'd find industrious men sitting at long wooden tables, changing money, arranging loans, cutting deals. (When a bank went out of business, its table was broken; thus the word *bankrupt* means "broken table.") At the dawn of the Renaissance, Florence boasted nearly eighty banks.

One, though, towered high above the others: the bank of the Medicis. The family held enormous influence over Florence from the twelfth century onward and for a period of about fifty years was its de facto ruler. As their name suggests, the Medicis were originally apothecaries—their coat of arms looked like six pills arranged in a circle—and that is, in a way, the role they played. They revved up the metabolism of Florence, like a dose of caffeine. As with many drugs, the Medici medicine came with side effects, and a real risk of dependency. But theirs was by and large good medicine, and the patient thrived.

The Medicis were great patrons of the arts. But what does that mean? Before arriving in Florence, I had only the vaguest idea. I pictured wealthy socialites, with more money than taste, ordering expensive art the way the rest of us order a pizza. And who can blame me? The very word *patronage* smacks of overweening elitism. Patrons, let's face it, tend to be patronizing.

Not the Medicis, Eugene explains. Theirs was the good kind of patronage, one that aimed not only at satisfying their own private desires for beauty but also the public's. They cared what the average Florentine thought about the artwork they commissioned. Perhaps this was their way of currying favor and thus securing their position as top dog. Who cares? Everyone benefited. In that sense, the art world was more democratic in Renaissance Florence than it is today, where judgment on the quality of art rests in the hands of a few critics and gallery owners. We have cleaved the art world from the world.

Patrons, the good kind, do more than write checks. They inspire. They challenge. The Medicis actively encouraged the city's artists to take risks and placed huge bets that, though they seem wise today, were at the time wildly reckless.

The Medicis didn't merely tolerate innovation. They demanded it, Eugene explains. "These people had more money than God. They wanted the best of the best of the best. And when they already had the best of the best of the best they wanted something else, so they sent people out to develop it." The Medicis were, when it came to taste, no different from other Florentines, only wealthier and, therefore, better able to amass what the humanist Matteo Palmieri called *per bellezza di vita*, "all those things needed to enhance one's life with beauty." Forget *la dolce vita*. In Florence, life was not sweet. It was (and is) beautiful.

The Medicis weren't some clueless art collectors in it for the prestige. They *got* art. Anyone who makes the observation, as the patriarch of the clan, Cosimo de' Medici, did, that "every painter paints himself" is clearly someone with a deep understanding of creativity. A curious relationship, based on intuition, developed between Cosimo and the city's artists. Cosimo didn't need to ask for a certain statue or painting; the artists, such as Donatello, "divined from the slightest indication all that Cosimo desired."

Cosimo was the Bill Gates of his day. He spent the first half of his life making a fortune and the second half giving it away. He found the latter half much more satisfying, once confiding in a friend that his greatest regret was that he did not begin giving away his wealth ten years earlier. Cosimo recognized money for what it is: potential energy, with a limited shelf life. Either spend it or watch it slowly deplete, like yesterday's birthday balloon.

Under a steady drip of Medici patronage, artists were free to pursue their passions without worrying about money. That was especially true of the family's favorites, such as Donatello, who kept his cash in a basket above his studio and told his assistants and friends to help themselves. Not many were tempted. The Renaissance heralded the birth of the starving artist. Michelangelo led an almost monklike existence. Even after achieving extraordinary wealth and fame, he survived on a single crust of bread and jug of wine per day. He rarely washed and often slept in his boots. Forsaking friendship and romantic love, he lived for his art and little else.

"Money, the actual money, possession of money, was meaningless to him," Eugene tells me between sips of what is now his third espresso. "He didn't care about money. When he died, they found a box under his bed with enough cash in it to buy Florence." Michelangelo was the world's first tortured artist. "My delight is in melancholy," he said, a statement that would later become the unofficial rallying cry for countless generations of sullen artists dressed entirely in black.

Actually, when it comes to the relationship between personal genius and personal wealth, the Prayer of Agur provides the best guidance: "Give me neither poverty nor riches." Throughout history, the vast majority of geniuses have come from the middle and upper-middle classes. They had enough money to pursue their passions, but not so much that they lapsed into complacency.

We are at our most innovative when we have something to push against. Creativity does not require perfect conditions. In fact, it thrives in imperfect ones. The block of marble from which Michelangelo carved his masterpiece, the *David*, had been discarded by other artists. They considered it defective, and they were right. But Michelangelo saw that defect as a challenge, not a disqualifier. And while most geniuses grow up not wanting for food or basic necessities, a degree of poverty is helpful; it forces us to flex new mental muscles. Or as the physicist Ernest Rutherford exclaimed, "We have no money so we will have to think!"

Why, though, did the Medicis spend so much of their fortune on art? Were they simply better people than us—or is there another explanation? It's helpful to think of a golden age as a crime scene. It boils down to opportunity and motive. The Medicis certainly had plenty of opportunity: they were loaded. What was their motive?

The answer, once again, resides in that small gold coin, Eugene says. The Florentines idolized the ancient Greeks but found some of their ideas, well, inconvenient. Plato, for instance, disapproved of usury, as did

Aristotle, who argued that money, being a lifeless object, was not meant to breed. Yet that was exactly how the Medicis amassed their fortune. They bred money. No doubt they felt pangs of guilt about this and worried they might spend eternity in hell. Back then, hell was not an abstract fear, a metaphor for a bad situation or an unseasonably warm day. It was a very real place, and not one you wanted to spend a weekend in, let alone eternity. What to do? Thankfully, the Church helped out with a brand-new arrangement: purgatory. Over espresso number four, Eugene explains.

"It is called an indulgence. One day, the Church announces, 'We are selling indulgences. We'll make a deal. Pay for all this beautiful art and architecture and we'll see what we can do about this eternity-in-hell business. We'll start working out the math. Let's see. You built a beautiful altar. By our calculations, we can take eighty thousand years off your term in hell and move you to purgatory.'"

"That sounds like a good deal. Where do I sign?"

"Exactly. So purgatory is one of the reasons these things were built."

To be fair, it wasn't the only reason—as I said, the Medicis genuinely appreciated beauty for its own sake—but you can't ignore the pull of purgatory. The wealthiest family in Italy, if not the world, proved expert at "perfuming a fortune with the breath of art," as historian Will Durant put it so wonderfully. It was art as atonement. The Renaissance, like all great human accomplishments, was propelled in part by that most ancient and powerful of forces: guilt.

The Medici dynasty reached its apex with Cosimo's grandson, Lorenzo, better known as Lorenzo the Magnificent. He actually lived up to his over-the-top name. Lorenzo ran Florence's affairs of state skillfully, but his true loves were art and philosophy. He was a pretty good poet, too, much like the poet-rulers of old Hangzhou. Most of all, though, he was a talent scout bar none.

One day, Lorenzo is observing the craftsmen in the Medici garden, a training ground for new talent, when one young boy, not more than fourteen years old, catches his eye. The boy is sculpting a faun, a Roman god that is half man and half goat.

Lorenzo is stunned by how refined the work is, especially for such a young stonecutter. The boy, working from an ancient model, had created a perfect replica. He even gave the faun a mischievous laugh and opened his mouth to reveal a set of wild teeth.

"You have made this faun very old, and yet left him all his teeth," teases Lorenzo. "Don't you know that old men are always missing some?"

The boy is mortified. How could he have overlooked such an important detail? And to be called on it by the most powerful man in Florence no less. As soon as Lorenzo was out of sight, the boy got to work. He removed an upper tooth, drilling the gum to create the illusion of tooth decay.

Lorenzo returned the next day and laughed with delight. He was impressed—not only with the boy's obvious talent but with his determination to "get it right." Lorenzo invited the boy to live in his residence, to work and learn alongside his own children. This decision, Eugene explains, was nothing short of extraordinary.

"He is a kid, just a kid. A nobody. And Lorenzo says, 'Look, kid, I think you've got it. What do you want to do? Do you want to be a painter? Okay, here is a tablet and here is the stylus. Draw. You want to be a sculptor? Here is a piece of rock. Here is a hammer and chisel. Here is a Roman sculpture to learn from. And here are the best teachers.' It was as if the kid had won *The X Factor*."

Lorenzo's generosity was repaid manyfold. The kid, Michelangelo Buonarroti, was indeed going places.

What does this story tell us about the genius that was Florence? Today, Michelangelo is better known than his benefactor, but perhaps Lorenzo deserves most of the credit. Had he not stopped to examine the work of a young stonecutter, "a nobody," had he not spotted the nascent genius in that boy, and had he not acted boldly to cultivate it, we would not know the name Michelangelo.

We'll never know what would have happened if Lorenzo had chosen some other fourteen-year-old instead of Michelangelo. Genius is like a chemical reaction. Change one molecule and you change everything. What we do know is that the geniuses of Florence did not appear by accident. They were the natural outcome of a system—an informal, sometimes chaotic system but a system nonetheless—that recognized, cultivated, and, yes, honored talent. That system was not confined to wealthy patrons such as the Medicis. It extended deep into the dusty, messy world of a quintessentially Florentine establishment: the *bottega*.

Bottega means, literally, a workshop, but that word doesn't do justice to the role it played in the Renaissance. The *bottega* was where new techniques were tested, new art forms developed, and, crucially, new talent nurtured.

Dozens, if not hundreds, of *bottege* cropped up in Renaissance Florence. None, though, was as remarkable as that run by a pudgy, broad-nosed man named Andrea del Verrocchio. A lackluster artist, Verrocchio was nonetheless a superb mentor and businessman. If anyone knew how to convert money into genius it was Andrea del Verrocchio. His workshop counted the top echelons of Florentine society among its clients, including the Medicis themselves. But competition was fierce, and Verrocchio, whose name means "true eye," was always on the lookout for new techniques and new talent.

Every golden age has its multipliers. These are people whose influence far exceeds their own artistic output. Cézanne influenced scores of Parisian painters, even while his own work remained unloved by the public. Lou Reed is a more contemporary example of a multiplier. The debut album of his band, The Velvet Underground, sold only thirty thousand copies. But, as Brian Eno said, with only slight exaggeration, "everyone who bought one of those thirty thousand albums started a band." Reed's influence on the music scene can't be measured in album sales alone.

Verrocchio was the Lou Reed of the Renaissance. His workshop explains more about this remarkable time than all the artwork in the Uffizi. Inside the workshop's paint-splattered walls, some of Florence's greatest artists cut their teeth, including a promising, young, left-handed misfit from the countryside named Leonardo da Vinci.

I ask Eugene to help me find Verrocchio, or at least the site of his old workshop. I'm hoping something of the essence of the place remains. This proves more difficult than I imagined. Verrocchio's workshop hasn't been converted into a boutique museum. Unlike Michelangelo, he doesn't have a salad or a perfume named after him. Not for the first time, I marvel at how historic cities such as Florence go to such pains to preserve and celebrate the products of their golden ages yet allow the sources of that goldenness to languish, unmarked and unloved.

My map of Florence is useless. Even the great Eugene can't find Verrocchio's workshop. We stop at a pizza shop to ask directions. The young woman behind the counter thinks we're nuts. I can tell by the way her eyes grow big. She's clearly never heard of Verrocchio or his *bottega*, and judging by the way her saucer eyes are now darting about the room, pleading, she clearly wishes we would take our crazy questions elsewhere. She's got pizza to move.

Eugene is out of ideas. We're stuck. Fortunately, a passerby overhears our conversation and, out of altruism or pity, offers to help. Go down that road, then hang a right, he says. That's where you'll find Verrocchio's workshop.

Eugene and I walk down a narrow, cobblestoned street, past vendors selling tripe, a local delicacy, and a clutch of bars and cafés, each more perfect than the next. For once, I do not squint. There is no need. The Florence of today is not all that different from the Florence of Verrocchio's day. Sure, back then it had more green space and fewer tour buses. No coffee or pizza either. Those two staples of modern Italian life had not yet arrived. There were plenty of wine shops and bars, though. Verrocchio and his apprentices were regulars at these establishments, sometimes downing four or five glasses before breakfast. It's a wonder they got any work done.

The directions we were given prove useless. We meander for a while longer, turning down one dead end after another, before finally giving up. In a way, Eugene says, the location of the exact building doesn't matter. Back in the day, Verrocchio's workshop wouldn't have stood out. It was just another gritty shop, nestled between butcher and cobbler. A ground-floor premises, it opened directly to the street and the chaos of children playing, dogs barking, sundry livestock roaming freely. The entrance was narrow, but once inside you'd realize how deep the building was. (To this day, Florentines like to say that their architecture reflects their character—narrow entranceways leading to deep interiors.)

"What was it like inside?" I ask. "What would we see?"

"Can you picture an artist's studio in Paris or New York?" says Eugene.

"Yep. I've got it."

"Good. Now wipe that image from your mind. Verrocchio's workshop was nothing like that. It was a factory."

A factory? I thought these were places of fine art, of genius. Eugene quickly disabuses me of this notion.

The workshops were noisy. The sounds of hammers on wood or on *pietra serena*, the gray stone of Tuscany, mixed with that of clucking chickens, their eggs needed to make the tempera that was used as paint before the advent of oil. The rooms were chockablock with large planks of wood—poplar mainly but also pricey chestnut, for special projects. The wood had to be seasoned so it wouldn't warp and could later be joined. The glue for that task came from rabbits, so add bunnies to the menagerie. And someone had to clean up after all these animals. That unenviable job fell to newcomers, such as a young apprentice named Leonardo da Vinci.

In truth the *bottega* resembled a sweatshop more than an artist's studio. What's worse is that the apprentices were not paid. In fact, they had to pay the *bottega* owners for the privilege of sweating there.

"I can't believe it," I tell Eugene. "Isn't that slave labor?"

"Today, we call them interns." Like a modern internship, says Eugene, the *bottege* provided a career entrée. "If you demonstrated talent, you worked your way up. You go from cleaning out the chicken cages to collecting the eggs, then cracking the eggs open. Then you might become the guy who mixes the colors." Those who worked hard and displayed talent moved up.

Ask Verrocchio, though, if he was in the business of producing geniuses and he would no doubt laugh. Genius? He was in the business of business. Whatever his customers wanted—a death mask or yet another Madonna (the ultimate in Church kitsch)—Verrocchio and his minions would make it. Which is not to say they welcomed every assignment with equal enthusiasm. They much preferred clients with taste, but business was business.

Nothing was taught in Verrocchio's workshop, but much was learned. It was education through osmosis. Total immersion. The young apprentice often lived in the same building as the master, shared his meals, and sometimes even took his name.

Verrocchio's charges didn't learn "creative thinking." No such thing as genius in the abstract exists, any more than love in the abstract exists. These human inclinations require an object for their attention, something to which they can adhere. "Creativity is not a simple result of special types of thinking," writes psychologist Richard Ochse. "It requires thinking about special content—it requires thinking about important questions."

The problem with much of what passes for "creativity training" in corporate retreats these days is that it starts with the assumption that creativity is a free-floating skill that can be taught on its own. It cannot, any more than athletics can be taught. You can teach someone tennis. You can teach them basketball. You cannot teach them athletics.

This is where mentors such as Verrocchio enter the picture. They are an incredibly important component in creativity. Even the most brilliant minds need role models, shoulders of giants on which to stand. In an extensive study of ninety-four Nobel laureates, sociologist Harriet Zuckerman found that most attributed their success to a key mentor in their lives. When asked, though, how exactly they benefited from these relationships, scientific knowledge ranked at the very bottom. So what did they learn from their mentors?

The answer could best be described as thinking styles. Not answers but ways of formulating questions. A sort of applied creativity. Normally we think of creativity strictly in terms of problem solving. We are presented with a difficult puzzle, then we deploy our "creative skills" to solve the assigned problem. That is admirable, but what if we don't know what the problem is we're trying to solve?

Enter "problem finding." Problem solvers answer questions. Problem finders discover new questions, and *then* answer them. It is these new questions, even more than the answers, that distinguish the genius. Which is why Picasso once quipped, "Computers are stupid. They only give you answers."

Perhaps the best example of a problem finder is Darwin. Nobody approached him and said, "Charles, please devise a theory of evolution." He *discovered* the problem—unexplained similarities between different species—then solved it with a unifying theory. All of this took place within his chosen field of biology—not some free-floating creative-thinking exercise.

You don't need to be Darwin to develop problem-finding skills. In a landmark study, psychologist Jacob Getzels and a colleague observed thirty-one art students performing an open-ended task: drawing from a given set of objects. That was it. They were not given any further instructions. Getzels noticed that some of the artists spent more time exploring—manipulating the objects, trying out new configurations. These artists, those engaged in deep problem finding, produced the more creative work. Following up eighteen years later, Getzels discovered that these same artists, the problem finders, enjoyed more success than the problem solvers. The problems we discover on our own are the ones that motivate us the most.

Leonardo da Vinci was a problem finder. Problems also found him. He was an "illegitimate child," born out of wedlock to a notary named Ser Piero. A remarkably large number of Renaissance artists were illegitimate, including Alberti and Ghiberti. For them, as for Leonardo, this was both curse and blessing. Had he been born "legitimately," Leonardo would likely have followed in his father's footsteps and become a notary or lawyer. But those professions' guilds refused entry to illegitimate children. Leonardo couldn't become a doctor or a pharmacist, nor could he attend university. By age thirteen, most doors were already closed to him. Obstacles were placed, and he responded to these. Again, the Power of Constraints in action.

But Leonardo had a few things going for him. He was raised an only child, and research shows clearly that only children are statistically more likely to become geniuses. Psychologists aren't sure why, but suspect it's because parents devote more resources to them and tend to treat them as adults in waiting, not helpless children.

Fortunately, too, Leonardo's father had a few connections in Florence. One of them was Verrocchio. One day, Ser Piero showed him a few of Leonardo's sketches, figuring he had nothing to lose. Verrocchio, the story goes, was speechless and "amazed by promising beginnings and urged Piero to have the lad study the subject," reports Giorgio Vasari, the great biographer of Renaissance artists. And so he did.

Teenaged Leonardo, unproven and of suspect pedigree, no doubt faced his share of obstacles at Verrocchio's workshop. As the newest hire, he was relegated to the thankless tasks of cleaning the chicken cages, sweeping the floors. He must have performed these chores well, for he soon moved up to more challenging assignments such as joining wood or mixing pigments. His climb up the *bottega* ladder didn't stop there.

"Let me show you something," says Eugene. We're now sitting at a café, one of his favorites, sipping wine and enjoying enjoying. He taps on a photo on his iPad, a painting by Verrocchio called *Tobias and the Angel*. This depicts an angel (complete with halo and wings) and a boy named Tobias holding hands, with Tobias gazing admiringly at the angel.

"Very nice," I say, and quickly realize how lame that must sound, not exactly the most nuanced bit of art criticism.

"Yes, but look at the fish."

I hadn't noticed it before but, sure enough, Tobias is carrying a fish, freshly caught and dangling from a string. I take a closer look, and even to my amateur eye, the virtuosity is obvious. The fish is expertly painted; each scale rendered with incredible precision.

"Wow," I say, in another fine display of erudition. "That's good."

"Yes, it is. Too good for Verrocchio."

Perhaps he was having an especially good day, I offer. It's been known to happen. The world's number 300 player upsets Serena Williams. A cliché-prone hack cranks out a passage of Shakespearean prose.

No, says Eugene. The fish looks too good for Verrocchio because it *is* too good. He didn't paint it. It was done by his young assistant Leonardo da Vinci, who was, at the time, all of eighteen years old.

Let's stop and contemplate this for a moment. Verrocchio was a businessman, but he was also an artist, and a proud one, too. Yet he agreed to allow this young, unproven child from a small village to paint an important figure in his painting. Why? Clearly, Verrocchio recognized the talent flowering in young Leonardo. So he put his ego aside and let his protégé contribute to his work—not by holding his brushes or fetching a glass of wine, but by actually putting brush to wood (canvas was still years away).

Let's pause and consider the magnitude of this gesture. Can you imagine Hemingway letting his assistant write a few crisp sentences for *The Old Man and the Sea*? Or Mozart letting his underling compose a few bars of the *Requiem*? Yet such collaborative efforts were common in the workshops of Florence.

The Renaissance was much more of a team effort than we think. Yes, a few stars shone bright, but they were part of a much larger constellation, and a big sky. Art was a collective enterprise; it belonged to everyone. No Florentine artist, not even the self-absorbed Michelangelo, created only for himself. The artists did it for the city or the Church, or for posterity. True genius is never a completely private affair. It is always communal. It is always bigger than itself.

Leonardo and his cohorts would have drawn a blank at terms like *team building*, but that is essentially what they were doing. Unlike in a modern corporate environment, though, the process unfolding at Verrocchio's workshop was entirely organic. Living and working on top of one another, they couldn't help but know one another. They weren't being creative. They were just being.

A workshop position, like a modern internship, wasn't supposed to last forever. Typically, after a few years an apprentice ventured out on his own, assuming he was good enough. Leonardo was clearly good enough, yet he chose to stay at Verrocchio's workshop for an additional ten years. Why? That is one of the great mysteries of the Renaissance. Was he still learning? Were he and Verrocchio lovers, as some historians maintain? Perhaps Leonardo, despite his obvious talent, was no rebel. (Leonardo's contemporaries describe him as a "perfectly docile student.") Perhaps he stayed simply because he was comfortable.

Eugene and I have relocated to one of those perfect trattorias we had spotted earlier, and over a carafe of the house Chianti, he reveals his own theory of why Leonardo stayed at the workshop.

"It was because he was so bright, and scattered. He was all over the place. He didn't finish things. If he had gone off on his own, he would have starved to death. He was a lousy businessman. He didn't know how to get a job, and if he did get a job, he didn't know how to finish it, because he'd be painting and then suddenly he'd be off studying something else. He had Renaissance ADD."

Leonardo's notebooks confirm this diagnosis. They reveal a man prone to distraction and debilitating doubt. "Tell me if anything has ever been achieved; tell me . . . tell me if I have ever done anything that . . . ," he scribbled, again and again, while testing a new pen, or whenever melancholy struck. The workshop provided Leonardo with structure and discipline, qualities he otherwise lacked. In a way, Verrocchio, not his apprentice, was the real Renaissance man. He possessed all the qualities that made the age golden: industriousness, business acumen, artistic flair. He had it all. True, he didn't hit the same high notes as his protégé, but he provided the business skills that Leonardo sorely lacked. He and Leonardo were co-geniuses. For a while.

Important as the mentor is to creativity, it is a thankless role. The mentor is like a catalyst in a chemical reaction. Crucial, yes, but unsung, as any chemist will tell you. Once the molecules have rearranged themselves, not a trace of the catalyst can be detected. So I can't say I was completely surprised to learn that among the thousands of pages of Leonardo da Vinci's notebooks, not once does the name Andrea del Verrocchio appear.

I'm feeling unsatisfied with my progress. Yes, I've made some significant headway. I've learned that mentors are important, as is money (preferably other people's) and constraints. But nagging questions continue to, well, nag. What exactly made this swampy, floodprone, plague-infested city shine like no other? Was it "wealth and freedom," the two ingredients that Voltaire deemed indispensable for any golden age? Or is there some other component, some secret sauce, that I've overlooked?

Eugene thinks for a moment. I can tell he's thinking because he's not talking. With Eugene, those are his only two modes, thinking and talking. Never both. Finally, he says, "*Sprezzatura*. Florence had lots of *sprezzatura*."

"That's too bad. And they didn't have antibiotics back then."

No, Eugene says, with a smile. *Sprezzatura* is a good thing. It means, literally, a "squirt of something extra." *Sprezzatura* is what separates a good meal from one you will remember for the rest of your life. *Sprezzatura* is what separates the number 15–ranked player and Roger Federer. And *sprezzatura* is what separated Florence from Siena and Pisa and Flanders and every other European population center of the time. Yes, money helped, but "without that squirt of something extra the money isn't going to get you anything," Eugene says.

I like this *sprezzatura*. There's something meritocratic about it. We believe geniuses are fundamentally different from the rest of us. Gods who have descended from the heavens to bestow their rare gifts upon us. But maybe that is not true. Maybe all that separates us from them is a lot of hard work, and a little *sprezzatura*. How, though, does an entire city find itself awash in the stuff? Eugene coyly hints that I will find the answers at a place called the Pitti Palace, then pours himself another glass of Chianti.

The palace is a short walk from my hotel. I had passed it several times and wondered, what is that monstrosity? While most buildings in Florence are the epitome of sophisticated understatement, the Pitti Palace is huge and garish. An architectural emoticon.

The palace was built for the banker Luca Pitti, by all accounts an arrogant boor. Pitti had nearly as much money as Cosimo de' Medici but not nearly as much taste. Not surprisingly, the two men despised each other. Cosimo, in a terse letter to his rival, suggested they give each other a wide berth, "like two big dogs, which sniff at one another when they meet, show their teeth, and then go their separate ways." Pitti did not heed Cosimo's advice and continued to attempt to unseat him. Pitti did not succeed.

Yet his palace remains, a monument to excess. I walk up a set of marble staircases, past vaulted ceilings, and step into a room nearly the size of a football field. It is carpeted and completely empty of furniture. Hanging from the ceiling are a dozen or so over-the-top chandeliers; on the walls are enormous friezes of cupids and eagles and lions, randomly intermingled with twenty-foot-high mirrors in gold frames. Walking down a corridor, ogling the *David* knockoffs, past the inlaid tiles and the ornate tapestries, I realize, finally, what Eugene meant when he said that the Renaissance was too pretty for him. He meant pretty in the sense of overwrought, too much.

I also understand what he meant by his even more blasphemous pronouncement that "there was a lot of crap produced during the Renaissance." At the time I protested, but Eugene didn't back down. The era we consider the apex of human creativity also produced a mother lode of bad art and bad ideas.

That's true of many people now celebrated as geniuses. Edison held 1,093 patents, most for completely worthless inventions. Of Picasso's twenty thousand works, most were far from masterpieces. As for literature, W. H. Auden observed, "In the course of his lifetime, the major poet will write more bad poems than the minor."

There's a simple reason for this. The more shots you get at the target, the more likely you'll eventually score a bull's-eye, but the more misses you'll accrue as well. The bull's-eyes end up in museums and on library shelves, not the misses. Which, when you think about it, is a shame. It feeds the myth that geniuses get it right the first time, that they don't make mistakes, when, in fact, they make more mistakes than the rest of us.

What did Aristotle tell me back in Athens? "Archaeologists love mistakes. It reveals process." He's right. A perfectly crafted statue tells the archaeologists nothing about how it was made. Mistakes shine a light on the messy world of creative genius and give the lie to the myth of the immaculate artist: the writer who pounds out a perfect first draft, the painter who, wineglass in one hand, brush in the other, lobs some oil at the canvas and—voilà!—a masterpiece. Lies, all of them.

What the world needs, I decide, is a Museum of Crap. Or, if you prefer something more PG, a Museum of Mistakes. Such an institution would provide a valuable public service. Visitors could see a life preserver from the *Titanic*, the actual sword that Napoléon carried into battle at Waterloo, a genuine can of New Coke, as well as a lovingly restored Betamax. The gift-shop possibilities are endless. T-shirts riddled with typos, eight-track tapes, a complete collection of Michael Bolton albums. Granted, I might be mistaken about the Museum of Mistakes, but my mistaken belief could itself become one of the exhibits. That is the beauty of the Museum of Mistakes. It's all-inclusive.

Until my museum is built, I'll have to settle for the Pitti Palace. It is garish but instructive. I look more closely at the paintings and notice something I hadn't before. The portraits feature people, but also an awful lot of their stuff. I now see the art for what it is: a thinly veiled excuse to show off the owner's possessions. The world's first product placements.

A good example is Crivelli's *The Annunciation with Saint Emidius*. Ostensibly, the painting depicts a religious event, but as art historian Lisa Jardine points out, it's really a celebration of treasured possessions from far-flung locales. "Here is a world which assembles with delight rugs from Istanbul, tapestry hangings from Islamic Spain, porcelain and silk from China, broadcloth from London."

We think of the Renaissance as a lofty era marked by sublime art and deep thought. But it, unlike ancient Athens, was also an incredibly materialistic time. The Renaissance brought us not only the world's first modern geniuses, but also the first modern consumers. These two facts are connected.

Florence was not an empire in the traditional sense—it had no standing army, no naval fleet. It was an "empire of things," to borrow a phrase from Henry James. Beautiful things. "He who has no possessions is regarded as a mere animal" was a common Florentine expression. The Florentines were incredible materialists, but they were not—and this is a crucial distinction—crude materialists. They cherished their possessions in a way we don't. As the philosopher Alan Watts points out, ours is not a genuine age of materialism because "it has no respect for material. And respect is in turn based on wonder."

Florentines saw no conflict between their pursuit of possessions and their pursuit of knowledge and beauty, for they did not subscribe to our wrongheaded notions about the relationship between genius and the material world. We believe that geniuses are necessarily removed from the world around them, the absentminded professor being the personification of this trope. But geniuses are more, not less, attuned to their environment than the rest of us. They notice things the rest of us don't.

Creativity does not happen when we withdraw from the material world but, rather, when we engage with that world, and all its messiness, more authentically and more deeply than we are accustomed. For creative people, it matters not whether their surroundings are good or bad; they derive inspiration from both, taste the salt in all things. Everything is a potential spark.

Florentines did not accumulate objects so much as celebrate them. They are still famously discriminating (or, picky, if you're feeling less generous), possessing a finely tuned sensitivity for the distinctive and the exquisite, and a visceral disdain for the shoddy and the ordinary. Nothing offends their sensibilities more than something that is a little bit off. A Florentine would rather miss by a mile than an inch.

Surely, I think, something must have been in Florentine culture that nurtured their aesthetic sensibility. But what?

I find the answer on the walls. Every room of the Pitti Palace is lined with decorative wallpaper, rich maroons and turquoises imprinted with a subtle floral design. No one notices the wallpaper, and why would they? It's just wallpaper, right?

Wrong. None of this would exist without the wallpaper. None of the luxuriant art packed into this palace, nor any of the other palaces and museums scattered across the city. No Leonardo or Michelangelo either. No Renaissance. Florence's empire of beauty was built on a foundation of wallpaper. To be more precise, it was built on the cloth trade, the source of the city's wealth.

So what? you say. *What difference does it make how Florence got rich? Money is money.*

Actually, it's not. How a nation accumulates wealth matters more

than how much it accumulates. Sierra Leone is rich in diamonds, but
that has turned out to be more curse than blessing. Resource-rich nations aren't innovative for a simple reason: they don't have to be. Florence had no diamonds or oil, or much of anything else, so people had
to rely on their wits and gumption. They had no money so they had to
think.

The cloth trade was not a natural fit for Florence. It needed to import
all of the raw materials—cloth from England, dye from Afghanistan. Florentine merchants traveled far and wide, searching for the finest materials, visiting warehouses and banks. Their travels exposed them to strange
new ideas, and these ideas accompanied them home along with the cloth
and the pigments.

A Tuscan named Leonardo Bonacci, working in the Asia Minor town
of Bugia, was the first to catch wind of Arabic numerals (actually Indian
in origin). Florentines, who, like most Europeans, were still using Roman
numerals, quickly adopted the new system and mastered exact calculations. This passion for precision soon gathered steam. The Italian Renaissance brought the world not only masterpieces of art and literature, but
also double-entry bookkeeping and maritime insurance. These innovations were not historical oddities, divorced from the world of art. They
were as intertwined as the threads on a fine silk scarf.

The Florentines did not segregate the worlds of art and commerce.
Skills acquired in one field spilled over into the other. Even something
as pedestrian as a tax document was expressed in florid prose, with the
auditor describing the rolling hills of a farm or the disagreeable temperament of a surly peasant. Shipping containers were not standardized, so
the Florentine merchant, out of necessity, mastered the art of gauging—
at first, gauging the capacity of a container; later, gauging the realism of
a painting or the proportions of a statue. The bookkeeper's penchant for
accuracy morphed into the artist's precise renderings.

Yet, despite this penchant for precision, Florentines were also great
gamblers. They played games of chance in the street, openly defying both
the Church and the lay authorities. Even the insurance business—not normally the sexiest of enterprises—was brimming with risk and intrigue.

Agents had no statistics or actuarial tables to rely on. It was gambling pure and simple.

This tradition of risk taking spilled over into the world of art. Wealthy patrons placed bets on unlikely horses. A good example is Michelangelo and the Sistine Chapel. Some five hundred years later, he seems like the perfect man for the job. Not at the time, though. Michelangelo was best known as a sculptor, not a painter. Yes, he had done some painting, but primarily small pieces—little in the way of frescoes and nothing on this scale. Yet Pope Julius II chose Michelangelo for the job. The pope was adhering to the Medici philosophy of patronage: choose someone who is clearly talented, then assign him an impossible task—do so even if he seems like a bad fit, *especially* if he seems like a bad fit.

Think of how different that approach is from ours today. We only hire applicants for jobs once we've determined they are a perfect fit. We only assign tasks to those who have already demonstrated they can perform that same exact task. We treat risk not as a noble venture, a dance with the universe, but as something to be avoided at all costs, or at least reduced to a decimal point. And we wonder why we're not living in another Renaissance?

Risk and creative genius are inseparable. Sometimes, the genius risks professional ridicule, and sometimes much more. Marie Curie worked with dangerous levels of radiation up until her death, and she was well aware of the risks. Genius always comes at a price. Some people, and some places, are more willing to pay that price than others.

I'm keen to explore this strange notion of prudent risk taking further, so I've asked Eugene to join me at the Bargello Museum. Soon, we find ourselves lost in a sea of beauty. It is a beauty, he assures me, with a definite purpose. I find this a difficult concept to swallow. Isn't beauty purposeless, and isn't it precisely that purposelessness that we find so compelling?

No, says Eugene. The art of the Renaissance, like that of Athens, was functional. It evolved into something more than that, but in the beginning it was commissioned for a definite purpose: to promote Christianity and, more specifically, the Catholic Church. Okay. Makes sense. The Church was a powerful institution, and like all powerful institutions it secretly worried about its public image. But why art?

"Most people were illiterate, so how could the Church reach them? How could it, for instance, depict the birth of Jesus? Captions won't work. You have to get your message across solely with visual symbols. That is, with paintings, jam-packed with symbolism."

I ponder this, trying to fend off the inevitable, uncomfortable conclusion: Renaissance art—widely hailed as the peak of human accomplishment—began as pure propaganda.

"Um, yeah, of course," says Eugene, as if it were the most obvious thing in the world.

I point out that Soviet art was also propaganda but you don't see anyone standing in long queues to see it.

"That's because it was ugly," says Eugene.

Yes, of course. The genius of the Renaissance had nothing to do with content and everything to do with style, with form. Not a *what* but a *how*. The great artists of fifteenth- and sixteenth-century Florence did not stray from the predictable religious iconography—Saint Francis preaching to the birds, for instance—but they depicted those old standbys in a completely new way.

"They begin to stand and move the way real people do," says Eugene, pointing out how Donatello's *David*, naked and effeminate, strikes a perfectly natural pose, unlike the stiff, inhuman statuary of medieval times. "They still used chunks of rock, but suddenly the chunk of rock moved. It was alive," says Eugene.

This was one of the greatest aesthetic leaps mankind has ever made. But how did it happen? Did sculptors such as Michelangelo suddenly wake up one day with an innate understanding of human anatomy? Mike was extremely talented, with a keen eye for the subtleties of the human form, but he was no superhero. He did not possess X-ray vision. No, there was only one way to understand the human body: by dissecting one. Yet the "mutilation" of corpses was strictly forbidden by the Church. Michelangelo had a problem. But this was Florence, where problems were greeted not as unwelcome visitors but as long-lost friends. Solutions were in the air, provided you knew where to look.

A good place to start, Eugene had suggested, is the Church of Santo Spirito, and the next day I walk there. Located on the "wrong" side of the Arno, away from the main sites, its cream-colored facade exudes quiet simplicity. It is not too pretty.

I heave open a heavy wooden door and stare in awe at the vaulted ceiling, admiring the way it magically magnifies the sunlight streaming in, setting the entire building aglow. Renaissance architecture is, at its core, a giant fuck-you to the oppressive Gothic style that dominated the Middle Ages. Gothic buildings, heavy and dark, diminish us. Renaissance architecture, light and airy, uplifts.

A priest directs me to a small room, the sacristy. On the wall is a large wooden crucifix, nearly life-size. In Italy, crucifixes are as common as gelato, but this one is different. It is—and please forgive my use of a technical term—better. On most crucifixes, Jesus is facing frontward. On this one, though, the body appears to twist and turn, "as if in response to an inner spirit," as one art historian put it.

The crucifix I'm admiring was nearly lost to history. Covered in a crude overcoat of paint, the work of an unknown artist, it languished in storage for decades. Then, in the 1960s, a German art historian named Margit Lisner saw something in the discarded crucifix that others had missed. Lisner realized the work was older than thought, and most likely that of a master. Further tests showed it was carved by the hands of a young Michelangelo.

What's most fascinating about the crucifix is not its artistic merits but its intended purpose. It was a gift, a thank-you note. Young Michelangelo—he couldn't have been more than twenty years old—wanted to express his gratitude to the Santo Spirito Church and, in particular, to its head, a priest named Nicholaio Bichellini. Why?

Cadavers. Michelangelo needed them. Santo Spirito had them. The priest, risking excommunication, or worse, allowed Michelangelo to do his dissections at night. It was unpleasant business. ("Squishy" was how Eugene had described these midnight dissections. "Very squishy.")

Why did the priest allow it? Why would a respected Church official risk so much? Like Florence's fabled merchants, he must have made some calculations. He no doubt knew that Florentines, even in the best of times, practiced a tepid Christianity, and this was not the best of times. He also no doubt factored in the rise of the Humanists. These were secular intellectuals, freethinkers armed with ancient texts and dangerous new ideas.

Being a practical man, Bichellini also knew that Michelangelo was a protégé of Lorenzo de' Medici, the most powerful man in Florence and a benefactor of Santo Spirito's. That surely factored into his calculations. Finally, and perhaps most important, like many Florentines the priest had an eye for talent. He must have noticed something special about the young artist with the surly demeanor. Not necessarily genius, not yet, but something. In the end, he took a risk. A calculated one, yes, but a risk nonetheless.

What does the story of Michelangelo and the cadavers of Santo Spirito tell us about the nature of genius? For starters, it reminds us that genius is messy. You have to be willing to get your hands dirty. There is no substitute for direct observation of nature, and this holds true not only for the beautiful bits but also the squishy ones.

As for Bichellini, he was, like Aspasia of Athens, an invisible helper. Again, these are people who, while not geniuses themselves, facilitate the work of those who are. A socialite who brings people of disparate interests together. An art-gallery owner who takes a chance on a new talent. And a respected priest willing to risk it all to help a young sculptor who was practically oozing *sprezzatura*.

Where there is money, competition is never far away, and Renaissance Florence was no exception. Yes, the artists collaborated on some projects, but amid fierce rivalry. Artists competed with artists, patrons with patrons. Most of all, Florence competed with its neighbors: Milan, Pisa, Siena, and others. Sometimes these rivalries erupted into conventional wars, but more often they expressed themselves off the battlefield. The Italian city-states duked it out for the title of "most cultured," marking one of the few times in human history when a benchmark other than military or economic muscle ruled the day.

One such cultural battle sparked the Renaissance itself. Pisa was outgunning Florence beautywise, and the Florentines were determined to do something about it. The Renaissance, one of the high points of Western civilization, a historic swerve that created all we consider modern and good, began with a world-class pissing contest.

The year was 1401, not a good year for Florence. The city had just emerged from another bout of bubonic plague. Milanese troops, meanwhile, had laid siege to the city and were massed a mere ten miles outside its walls. The city's economy was in the doldrums. All told, you'd think this would be a good time to hunker down and, oh, stock up on canned goods.

But that's not the way Florence rolled. No, they decided it was the perfect time to indulge in some serious art. Specifically, an intricate set of bronze doors on the Baptistery of Santa Maria del Fiore, the city's most important church and a symbol of its cultural aspirations.

The city organized a contest to find the best artist for the job, spelling out the rules in great detail. Contestants were to depict a biblical scene— Abraham's sacrifice of his son Isaac—in bronze and within a quatrefoil, a square frame about the size of a place mat. The winning entry would receive the lucrative contract for the Baptistery doors, as well as the adoration of a grateful city.

Ponder for a moment the sheer moxie this required. Here was a city at its most vulnerable, beaten down by pestilence, threatened by foreign invaders, pummeled economically, and yet its citizens choose this very time to hold a Florence Has Got Talent contest. Not a contest to see who could create the best catapult or plague vaccine, but one whose stated goal was something as outlandishly impractical as beauty.

The contest came down to two finalists, Lorenzo Ghiberti and Filippo Brunelleschi, two young men, both prematurely bald but who otherwise could not be more different in background and disposition. Brunelleschi was the son of a respected civil servant and a certified goldsmith whose early work showed great promise. Ghiberti had absolutely no political connections and virtually no experience as an artist. It should have been a cakewalk for Brunelleschi, but it wasn't.

The judges were split down the middle. So, Solomon-like, they proposed that Brunelleschi and Ghiberti work together on the project. Brunelleschi, in what was likely the world's first case of an uppity artist determined to get his way, wouldn't hear of it. He either worked alone or not at all. Fine, the commission replied, and handed the contract to Ghiberti. Thus began a lifelong rivalry, one that would drive both men to create some of the finest art and architecture the world has ever seen: in the case of Ghiberti, the Gates of Paradise, and for Brunelleschi, the Duomo.

Renaissance Florence was rife with rivalries and feuds. The two giants of the age, Leonardo and Michelangelo, couldn't stand each other. Perhaps it was inevitable. Michelangelo, twenty-three years Leonardo's junior, was a rising star, and in the minds of many Florentines now the superior artist. This new reality surely irked Leonardo.

One day, their simmering animosity boiled over. Leonardo was crossing the Piazza Santa Trinita when a group of men stopped him and asked his opinion of some obscure lines by Dante. Michelangelo happened to walk by. "Here comes Michelangelo," said Leonardo. "He will explain it to you."

The sculptor, thinking he was being mocked, responded angrily, "Explain it yourself, you who made a model of a horse you could never cast in bronze and which you gave up, to your shame." Then he turned and left, but not before hurling one final insult over his shoulder: "And the stupid people of Milan had faith in you?"—a reference to Leonardo's commissions for Florence's rival city.

Michelangelo's taunt surely stung. Leonardo da Vinci, despite his almost godlike reputation today, was a tremendous failure. His plan to render the Arno River navigable failed, as did his attempts to fly. The hours and days he spent working on mathematics and geometry amounted to nothing. He left many works unfinished, including the *Battle of Anghiari*, an important commission for the city of Florence, to which he had devoted three years of his life.

What strikes me most about their squabble is the pettiness, the insecurity uncloaked. Genius, apparently, does not inoculate us from such small-minded emotions. Goethe despised Newton, both as a scientist and as a man. Schopenhauer dismissed the work of fellow philosopher Hegel as "a colossal piece of mystification that will yet provide posterity with an inexhaustible theme for laughter." Ouch. I'm not sure if such mean-spiritedness makes me feel better about history's geniuses or worse. On one hand, it reveals how very human they were. On the other, it reveals how very human they were.

One of the greatest mysteries of the Florentine Renaissance is the role that formal education played—or, rather, the role that it *didn't* play. Florence, unlike, say, Bologna, had no decent university. How can this be? Isn't education an essential ingredient of genius?

Let's examine the evidence. Bill Gates. Steve Jobs. Woody Allen. All college dropouts. (One of the courses Allen flunked at NYU was film-making.) Einstein's PhD dissertation was rejected twice. Fellow physicist Michael Faraday never attended college. Thomas Edison dropped out of school at age fourteen. (He was later tutored by his mother at home. Many geniuses were either homeschooled or self-taught.) While some geniuses—Marie Curie, Sigmund Freud—were stellar students, most were not.

Dean Simonton, in a study of three hundred creative geniuses, found that the majority made it only halfway through what was considered a modern education at the time. Any more, or less, was detrimental. So some education is essential to creative genius, but beyond a certain point, more education does not increase the chances of genius and actually lowers it. The deadening effect of formal education manifests itself surprisingly early. Psychologists have identified the exact year when a child's creative-thinking skills plateau: the fourth grade.

This brings us to a remarkable finding. While the number of degrees conferred and scientific papers published has grown exponentially in the past fifty years, the "rate at which truly creative work emerges has remained relatively constant," says sociologist J. Rogers Hollingsworth, writing in the journal *Nature*. We are experiencing a flood of expertise, and even talent, but no bump in creative breakthroughs.

One culprit, as I said, is specialization. We've carved the world into smaller and smaller bits. Then there is the sheer volume of information that exists in every field today. If genius requires first mastering the body of knowledge in your chosen field and then, and only then, making your own contribution, well, good luck. A physicist or a biologist could spend a lifetime reviewing the work of others and still not make a dent.

Leonardo da Vinci was a poor student. He was well into middle age before he learned passable Latin, the language of the elites and the intellectuals. Leonardo, though, had little patience for conventional wisdom and would no doubt have agreed with psychologist Edwin Boring who, some five hundred years later, said, "It is useful to be ignorant of bad knowledge." In that sense, Florence's lack of a university was a blessing. It saved the city from "a scholastic straitjacket," as urbanist Peter Hall put it.

Which brings us back to Filippo Brunelleschi. Having lost the contest for the Baptistery doors, he decided to indulge his secret passion: architecture. He set off for Rome, with his friend Donatello in tow, to examine ancient ruins. It was not an easy journey, and Rome back then was nothing like the Rome of today. Much smaller than Florence, it was "a city full of huts, thieves, and vermin and wolves prowling the neighborhood of old St. Peter's," writes author Paul Walker.

The locals didn't know what to make of these two young men gazing at arches and columns. "Treasure hunters," they called them, and they were right, though it was a different sort of treasure they sought. The curious Florentines were searching for the booty of ancient knowledge. Brunelleschi painstakingly measured columns and archways. He was especially fascinated by the Pantheon; the dome, at 141 feet wide, was the largest of the ancient world. Inspiration struck. Why not cover the Church of Santa Maria del Fiore in his hometown with a similar dome? It had sat uncovered, exposed to the elements, for centuries. Other city-states were beginning to talk. It was embarrassing.

So that was exactly what Brunelleschi aimed to do. People said it was impossible to build a dome of that size without any external means of

support, but such nay-saying only egged him on, and he succeeded glori-
ously.

One day, I decide to visit the Duomo and see firsthand what all the
fuss is about. Climbing the circular stairs, marveling at the impossible genius of the design, I find myself thinking about the law of unintended
consequences. We usually view unintended consequences negatively.
Some new technology or scientific development doesn't turn out as
planned; it comes back to bite us. Air-conditioned subways raise platform
temperatures by as much as ten degrees. Hospital patients are infected
with microbes during their stay. Computer users develop carpal tunnel
syndrome. "Revenge effects" is what science journalist Edward Tenner
calls these phenomena. The law of unintended consequences cuts both
ways, though. Sometimes, disaster has unexpected benefits, and sometimes what looks like defeat is actually victory in drag.

We can all be grateful that Brunelleschi didn't win the contest for the
Baptistery doors. Victory would have imprisoned him. He would have
spent a lifetime on that project, as Ghiberti in fact did. Brunelleschi would
never have traveled to Rome, would never have built the dome that is, to
this day, Florence's signature landmark. More than that, it inspired countless architects in Europe and beyond. The next time you visit a county
courthouse or an old post office, or gaze in wonder at the majesty of the
US Capitol dome, think of old Filippo Brunelleschi and the law of unintended consequences.

Consider, again, the state of affairs in Florence at the dawn of the Renaissance. The Church was weakened, not only financially but morally as
well. The monks no longer had a monopoly on virtue. Nobody did. All
golden ages, as we've seen in Athens and Hangzhou, contain an element
of free-for-all, a chink in time when the old order has crumbled and a new
one is not yet cemented. It's a jump ball, and that's when creative genius
thrives, when everything is up for grabs. But how do such transitional
times come to be?

Eugene assured me I would find the answer, or at least *an* answer, at
a small museum called the Specola. It's located, literally and figuratively,

in the shadow of the gaudy Pitti Palace. It takes some work to find. I hit a few dead ends—Italian dead ends so they're stylish and interesting—before discovering the museum hiding between a café and a tobacco shop. Forsaken and sad looking, the Specola gets few visitors.

I am greeted by a giant statue of Evangelista Torricelli, inventor of the barometer and a son of Florence. I walk up the staircase, covered in dust, and the burgeoning excitement I feel catches me by surprise. I didn't know they made museums like this anymore. Stuffed animals displayed behind grimy glass cases. Cheetahs and hyenas, walruses and zebras, all with the same frozen expression, a combination of shock and repose, as if they have no idea how they ended up here but are resigned to their fate nonetheless. It's all very nineteenth century. I half expect Charles Darwin to pop up at any moment.

I am not here for the taxidermy, though. After a few detours, and a close encounter with a remarkably lifelike gorilla, I find myself face-to-face with the work of a little-known artist named Gaetano Zumbo. He pioneered the underappreciated art of plastic dioramas. Zumbo's oeuvre includes works with grim-sounding titles such as *Corruption of the Body* and *The Effects of Syphilis*.

One piece, though, stands out. It's titled simply *Le Peste*. The Plague. It's a horrific tableau rendered in great detail: bodies of men, women, and children strewn like fallen timber. A skull rests on the ground like some sort of macabre ornament.

It's hard for us to imagine the horror that was the plague. In months, the disease killed five out of every eight Florentines—as many as two hundred people a day. Corpses were piled high on the streets, and as Boccaccio, a writer living at the time, recalls, "A dead man was then of no more account than a dead goat would be today." The disease is spread by contaminated fleas found on rats or gerbils. They didn't know that then, though, so their attempts at preventative measures—spoonfuls of rose water sweetened with sugar, for instance—now seem pathetically futile. They also prayed, crowding into churches by the hundreds, which only accelerated the spread of the disease.

Horrible times, yes, but what does this have to do with the Renaissance?

Quite a lot. A mere two generations after the Black Death, as the outbreak of 1348 is now known, the Renaissance blossomed in Florence. These two facts are more than coincidence.

The plague, devastating as it was, shook up the established order. Social status was instantly shuffled. Doors previously closed were suddenly open because the person on the other side of the door was now dead. The plague produced one of the essential ingredients for a golden age: instability.

Once again, money rears its shiny head. The plague also created an "inheritance effect." With more than half the population suddenly gone, the city's money was now in fewer hands. People had to do something with that surplus cash. But what? Merchants were understandably reluctant to invest in new ventures. What they did, for reasons that remain something of a mystery, is invest in culture. Suddenly, great art and rare books became "the magic password which admitted a man or a nation to the elite group," writes economic historian Robert Lopez. Culture was now the safe bet. The equivalent of putting your money into treasury notes.

Patrons and artists responded to this new reality by commissioning and creating art that centuries later still takes our breath away. Meanwhile, the Church, unable to prevent the spread of the disease, lost much of its moral legitimacy, creating space for the more secular-minded Humanists to fill. None of which would have happened without the Black Death. Nor would the Athenian golden age have happened had the Persians not first sacked Athens, burning it to the ground, and clearing the way for Pericles's ambitious rebuilding. It is the law of unintended consequences on a grand scale.

The Medicis knew well how to exploit unexpected opportunities. They were skilled and prolific traders of every good imaginable—silk from China, spices from Africa. What they prized most, however, were the ancient manuscripts from Greece and Alexandria. Does the discovery of these lost classics help explain the genius that was Florence?

Places of genius always welcome new information, new ideas.

Florence, though, wasn't the only Italian city-state with access to this information. Others had it, too, yet it didn't inspire them the way it did the Florentines. Why? What did the Florentines see in these yellowed, crumbing scrolls that others did not?

To find answers, I decide to visit the source: the great Laurentian Library built for—who else?—the Medicis.

Designed by Michelangelo, it was, like most of his projects, a headache for all involved. With only one wall completed, he decamped to Rome, leaving it to his underlings to supervise the construction. Yet the building, replete with "boldness and grace," as Vasari put it, is pure Michelangelo.

"It is madness. Nonsense. Art historians go crazy with this," says the art historian, who is waiting for me at the entrance.

"Good crazy or bad crazy?" I ask.

"Both."

Dr. Sheila Barker is, in appearance if not disposition, the exact opposite of Eugene: clothing properly pressed, hair strictly contained, advanced degrees efficiently obtained. (Specifically, a PhD in art history from Columbia University.) She is the Director of the Jane Fortune Research Program on Women Artists at the Medici Archive Project. I found her through a company called Context Travel, one of a handful of firms in Italy that puts experts like Dr. Barker in touch with people like me, thus providing a porthole to that foreign country known as the past.

Like Eugene, Dr. Barker is a history nut, more comfortable in the past than in the present. The morning we meet, she's brimming with excitement. The day before, while rummaging through some archives, she discovered a letter from Galileo. No other human being—besides the man himself and the recipient, a friend—had ever laid eyes on it. *Ever.* The letter was nothing extraordinary—Galileo's telescope was broken, he informed his friend, so he couldn't work that day—but that didn't diminish the electric jolt of joy that had shot through Dr. Barker when she'd stumbled across it. In fact, the ordinariness of the letter, its quotidian content, had rendered its discovery that much more precious. "If I live to be ninety-nine, I'll never forget finding that letter," she says, and I do not doubt her.

We step inside the library, and for a moment I think we're in the wrong place. This looks more like a church. Then I spot the books, floppy manuscripts chained to rows of pews, just as they were in Michelangelo's day.

Today, plenty of us adore books. We give them pride of place in our homes. We consider our books precious, but should we lose one or mistakenly lend one to an unreliable friend, we can always replace it or download it again to our Kindle. That wasn't the case in the fifteenth century. Each book was one of a kind, hand-copied by bleary-eyed monks.

"How many cars do you own?" Dr. Barker asks.

"What? What does that have to do with—"

"How many cars do you own?"

"One. Barely."

"Well, in the fifteenth century a book cost as much as a car does today, in relative terms. So you can imagine what it meant to have a library, a collection of, say, one hundred books. It was like owning one hundred cars today. When someone in the Renaissance had a hundred books, they became known as a scholar."

"Just by owning the books?"

"Just by virtue of owning the books. Because to acquire them, to make that decision of 'Which one should I acquire next?,' you had to know something about the value."

Now I understand why the books were chained. The Humanists believed they contained nothing less than the secret of life, and the arrival of a new manuscript was greeted with the same enthusiasm that we extend to the arrival of the latest version of the iPhone.

Cosimo de' Medici was, if not the world's first book collector, certainly the most ambitious. He modeled his library after the Vatican Library, and when it came to expanding his collection he stopped at nothing. Why go to such trouble and expense?

Dr. Barker answers that question by handing me a sheaf of paper. It's not thick, perhaps five or six sheets. Yet these pages changed the world. It is called *The Oration on the Dignity of Man*. This one document, more than anything else, articulates the underlying idea that drove the Renaissance. It was the era's manifesto.

Written by the philosopher Pico della Mirandola, the *Oration* begins tamely enough. Pico lays out the hierarchy of living creatures. God is at the top, followed by angels. Animals and plants are at the bottom. Angels, being so close to God, have primo access. Pigs and earthworms? Not so much. As for man, Pico continues, God gave him no assigned seat. Theologically speaking, man finds himself in a Southwest Airlines situation: a free-for-all that might result in extra legroom—or the dreaded middle seat.

"Man can either sink to great depths or rise to great heights," says Dr. Barker, channeling Pico. "When he becomes evil, he's really, really evil. But when he becomes magnified in his greatness and in his knowledge and in his purity, he becomes better than the angels and—this is the dangerous part of the text—he can become godlike. Like God."

"I could be mistaken, but isn't that a sacrilege?"

"Yes, it is. This should be burning in your hands."

"Actually, it does feel a bit hot."

Ignoring my lame joke, Dr. Barker continues, "Florence was able to say, 'Now, you know, the son has surpassed the father. We are now taking the place of Rome. We have the power to direct the world, to influence the world, to be the guiding light.'"

Heady stuff. None of which would have come to fruition had the Florentines not seen the value in those musty old books from far away and then multiplied that value.

We're about to leave the library, but something has been nagging at me, something that doesn't quite seem right. The Italians were so innovative, and in so many ways, but not when it came to technology. Sure, they brought us the parachute and increasingly sophisticated means of navigation, but the breakthrough technology of the day, the movable-type printing press, was invented by a German blacksmith, not a Florentine. Why?

The Florentines didn't care for technology for technology's sake, any more than the Athenians did. They saw technology as more ephemeral than art, and therefore less valuable. Any invention, however ingenious, can always be supplanted by something newer and better. The 2.0 version.

I suggest to Dr. Barker—and here I realize I am engaging in my own heresy—that the same might be true of art. Perhaps, I suggest delicately, someone might come along with a newer and better *David*. *David 2.0*.

"That's not possible," retorts Dr. Barker, not angrily but, rather, with the same tone of voice one uses when addressing a fifth grader who just doesn't get it. "Never in the history of art have we seen anything like the *David*. It was the most perfect expression of what it is supposed to be. The Florentines immediately recognized this. They knew that the *David* was the first work of art that had surpassed the ancients, and they saw the ancients as the apex. No, there will never be another *David*."

Maybe that is the best definition of a work of genius: something that renders silly and futile any thought of an upgrade.

Sufficiently chastised, I switch topics and ask Dr. Barker the time-travel question. If she could travel back to Renaissance times, for one hour, whom would she want to meet?

"Not Michelangelo," she says definitively. Brilliant artist but too crotchety. "Maybe Lorenzo." I can see in her eyes that she has departed for the fifteenth century. "I wouldn't turn down Lorenzo." Then silence. "I've got it! Georgius Gemistus."

"Who?"

Georgius Gemistus was a Greek scholar who, at the invitation of the Medicis, traveled to Florence. The Byzantine Empire was crumbling, and suddenly a lot of Greek scholars were out of work (much like today, come to think of it). The Medicis lured the best of them to Florence, in yet another opportunistic move.

They didn't get any better than Gemistus. A bearded, colorful character, he called himself the new Plato. He was, in Dr. Barker's mind, a full-blown expression of the Renaissance notion of pursuing truth at all costs. He did crazy, reckless things. He crashed a meeting of Church leaders and lectured them on the virtues of Plato. Not exactly prudent, but that is precisely what Dr. Barker admires about him.

"He had a kind of fearlessness," she says, further confirmation that risk, more than money, is what was honored at the time. Not so for us, says Dr. Barker. "These days, you don't have risk. Not real risk. You can always file for bankruptcy and start over. Social institutions protect us.

In Renaissance Florence, there was nothing, *nothing*. You could starve to death if you failed. You destroyed yourself, you destroyed your family for generations."

"That doesn't sound so appealing. But what if you succeeded?"

"If you succeeded, your success was said to be legendary. And the ambition was not just to get rich or be happy for one day. The goal was eternal glory, to be in the books with Julius Caesar, with Cicero. With Plato. The Medicis were shooting for eternal glory, in proportions we can't even imagine."

Silently, I wonder what we are shooting for. What do we consider the ultimate manifestation of the human spirit? What would we risk it all for?

As Dr. Barker and I step out of the Laurentian Library and onto the rain-splattered piazza, I am saddened by the answer that springs to mind: the IPO. Surely, I think, reaching for my umbrella, we can do better than that.

One day, toward the end of my stay in Florence, Eugene and I are wandering the halls of yet another museum when I'm overcome with a sort of Renaissance vertigo. So much art, so much *good* art. It's too much. *I'm not worthy*. I feel dizzy.

Breathe, says Eugene, sounding more like a yoga instructor than an art historian. I breathe, and the world rights itself.

A while later, we're admiring one more *David*, or perhaps a *Madonna*, I can't recall, when Eugene mentions, almost as an aside, "the lingering presence of these people." He's right. They do linger. The ghosts of Michelangelo and Leonardo and Botticelli and all the rest hang in the air, like San Francisco fog. You'd think it would have burned off by now, five hundred years later, but it hasn't. The half-life of true genius is inexhaustible.

I wonder what it's like for today's artists of Florence. Do they suffer the same fate as the modern philosophers of Athens? Does all this beauty, all this genius, inspire—or intimidate?

A few days later, I have a chance to ask them myself. I've been invited to a dinner party, and the guests, all artists, have spent years living in

Florence. When I arrive, everyone is already lounging in the small living room, sipping Prosecco, nibbling on antipasti, and in general enjoying enjoying. I mention the tourist season and everyone stiffens, as if they were deer and I had mentioned hunting season. "It's an invasion," says one woman. Everyone nods in silent agreement. More Prosecco is poured.

"So," I say, treading carefully, "what's it like being an artist in Florence?"

"The past," says another woman, "it is like a weight on our shoulders," and as she says this, her shoulders visibly slump. Everyone nods again. Someone bemoans the lack of a single modern art museum in Florence. More nodding. More Prosecco.

"I do not like Michelangelo," says a gray-haired architect, elongating his words, savoring the delicious blasphemy that only a native Florentine could get away with, just as only a Greek philosopher can declare his contempt for Plato.

The consensus is clear. It's no easier being an artist in modern Florence than it is a philosopher in modern Athens. The past can educate and inspire. It can also imprison.

A few days later, I'm talking to a young creative type named Felix. We're walking down via Borgo Ognissanti. It's a brilliant day. The Tuscan sun has finally come out of hiding, and the light is glistening off the Arno. With a sweep of his hand, Felix takes in the tableau and asks, "What do you see?"

"Well, I see some nice architecture, and the Ponte Vecchio and—"

"No. You're looking at a prison. It may not look like it, but that's what Florence is. A very beautiful prison."

Left unsaid, floating in the soft spring air, was the unavoidable conclusion: beautiful prisons are the cruelest of all.

Eugene and I are meeting one last time and have decided to indulge in a pizza. We order one with mozzarella, basil, and extra *sprezzatura*. As we're diving in like famished animals, I realize I've forgotten to ask Eugene my time-travel question. If he could spend an hour talking to someone from Renaissance Florence, who would it be?

"Michelangelo," he says without hesitation. "He was such a nut job.

He couldn't do anything the normal way. That is one of the things I love about the guy. He was sort of a loose cannon."

"You wouldn't want to hang with Leonardo?"

"I'd like to go drinking with Leonardo. He was fun, a real dandy, but I'd love to sit and talk with Mike. I wouldn't party with Mike. He'd be a downer. He'd probably want to punch me in the nose. He was not a very nice person. He was an interesting person."

This makes me wonder, what if we reversed the time-travel experiment? What would Michelangelo say if he came back to the Florence of today?

"He'd say, 'What the hell have you been doing for the past five hundred years? You're making the same art as before.'" Eugene laughs, but of course he's right. The Florentines long ago exhausted Kroeber's "cultural configurations." Their creativity cupboard is bare.

Before digging into another slice, I take a moment to ponder it, to assess it in a Florentine way. It is good, one of the best pizzas I've ever had, but why? Are the ingredients fresher? Perhaps. Is the chef more skilled? Maybe.

The secret, I realize, lies in the proportions. Just the right amount of mozzarella and tomato sauce and basil, no more and no less. Florence, in ways big and small, gets the proportions right, just as Athens did, and this, Eugene suggests between bites, explains not only the beauty of Florence but also the genius. It didn't necessarily possess different ingredients from other places at the time, but it got the proportions right.

"You can't just throw pineapple juice and coconut and rum together and expect to have a good piña colada," says Eugene.

"Although you do need all of those things."

"You do, but if something is a little bit off, it could come out all wrong. Look at genetics. If you are missing one little gene, that changes everything." He's right. The genes of humans and chimpanzees are 99 percent the same. Sometimes 1 percent makes all the difference.

What about the question I set out to answer? Did Florence have a Renaissance because it could afford one? Can money buy genius?

The answer is clearly yes. And no. Money, a certain amount anyway, is indispensable to creativity. Starving people rarely produce great works of art or discover new scientific truths. Also, wealth gives you the chance to fail. Wealth gives you do-overs. That was certainly the case in Renaissance Florence. Failure—sometimes of the spectacular variety—occurred regularly. This did not dissuade people from taking risks; if anything, it encouraged more, as a new artist, or a new generation, aimed to get it *just right*. Like Athens and Hangzhou, Florence was a restless place. It never said, "Good enough." The name Florence (Firenze in Italian) is derived from a word that means "to flower or bloom." It is a verb, not a noun.

So, yes, Voltaire was right. Golden ages require wealth and freedom. But he overlooked a crucial third ingredient: uncertainty. What Thomas Jefferson said about the political world—"a little rebellion now and then is a good thing"—applies to the creative world as well. Tension, a degree of it at least, keeps us on our toes and tests our perseverance. Ghiberti completed the Baptistery doors over twenty-five years, a time marked by incredible political and financial upheavals. Yet his patrons never wavered in their support; they knew instinctively that these tensions would help, not hinder, the young artist. Nothing kills creativity like a sure thing.

Nor do the good times last, though. Sylvia Plath's prophetic statement—"I desire the things that will destroy me in the end"—proved true for Florence as well. The city died the way it lived: at the hands of the Almighty Florin. Its good materialism devolved into crass consumerism. Meanwhile, to pay for Saint Peter's Basilica, Pope Leo X, another Medici, proclaimed a special "indulgence." Much of the money he raised vanished, and the ensuing outrage paved the way for the Reformation. A new world order soon took shape, and the creative energy that was centered in Florence shifted west and north, to a place that, in climate if not disposition, was about as different from the Tuscan city as it was possible to get.

A few months later, back home, I write to Eugene. I have some questions. The next week, I receive a reply. At first, everything seems normal. Wait. This is uncharacteristically brief for Eugene. Where is the rest of the e-mail? I scroll down.

White space.

White space.

Then this:

"Eric. This is Antonio, Eugene's partner. I have horrible news. Eugene is dead."

I stare at the screen for a long time, hoping it is some sort of mistake. A prank perhaps. It is not. Eugene died of a massive heart attack, in mid e-mail. The words that spring to mind are not those of Eugene but of another Florentine expat, E. M. Forster. "The sadness of the incomplete," he once wrote. That phrase lodges itself into my stunned brain, along with the realization that I never had a chance to meet Eugene's dog.

A few seconds later, my mind swerves again, and this time the words of György Faludy materialize. Asked why, at age seven, he decided to become a poet, Faludy replied, "Because I was afraid to die."

All art is, at its core, a stab at immortality. We like to believe that geniuses, by dint of their creations, escape death. They do not. Every life, no matter how well and richly lived, is sadly incomplete. Even Leonardo's. Even Michelangelo's. And, certainly, my friend Eugene's.

Genius offers only the illusion of immortality. Yet we reach for it anyway, the way a drowning man will reach for even the flimsiest of logs.

FOUR

GENIUS IS PRACTICAL:
EDINBURGH

THE FIRST TIME I CATCH A GLIMPSE OF EDINBURGH
Castle, sprouting from the basalt like some giant stone apparition, I am
caught off guard. I'd seen pictures of it, read about it, and so I had modu-
lated my expectations, discounted my reaction, in the language of Wall
Street. Clearly, my calculations were off, for when I turn a corner and it
suddenly materializes, towering over Edinburgh from one of the city's
many extinct volcanoes, I am stunned into an uncharacteristic silence.

Some places are like that. (The Taj Mahal comes to mind.) Having
seen so many images of it, we're certain that we are impervious to any
charms it may possess. Yet when we lay eyes on it, in person, it quickens
our pulse and humbles us. *Oh*, we say, once we can breathe again, *I didn't
know.*

All of Edinburgh is like that. It surprises, and surprise, along with the
attendant phenomena of wonder and awe, lies at the heart of all creative
genius. No matter the amount of preparation and legwork, essential as
they are, every creative breakthrough comes as something of a surprise,
sometimes even to the creator.

Scotland's capital city certainly surprised itself. Like all golden ages, Scotland's moment in the sun was blindingly brief, not even fifty years, yet during that time tiny Edinburgh "ruled the Western intellect," as contemporary author James Buchan put it. Scots made major contributions to—and in many cases invented—the fields of chemistry, geology, engineering, economics, sociology, philosophy, poetry, and painting. Adam Smith brought us the "invisible hand" of capitalism, and James Hutton a radical new understanding of our planet. Down the road, in Glasgow, James Watt was busy perfecting his steam engine, which would soon power the industrial revolution.

A little bit of Scotland is in all of us, whether we know it or not. If you've ever consulted a calendar or the *Encyclopaedia Britannica*, you can thank the Scots. If you've ever flushed a toilet or used a refrigerator or rode a bicycle, thank the Scots. If you've ever received an injection from a hypodermic needle or had surgery and didn't feel a thing, you can thank the Scots. Perhaps the greatest Scottish inventions, though, are the ones you can't touch, for they occupy the realm of the mind. Big ideas such as empathy and morality and common sense. The Scots, though, never let these ideas float off into the heavens, untethered. They grounded them in the here and now. This was the Scottish brand of genius: the melding of deeply philosophical ideas with real-world applications. The bright lights who illuminated old Edinburgh weren't interested in counting angels on a pinhead. They put those angels to work, and the result was the birth of everything from modern economics to sociology to historical fiction.

Good ideas are like toddlers. They can't stay put for long. So the good ideas fermenting in Edinburgh soon reached distant shores. They found receptive audiences across the globe, especially in the American colonies. The Scots taught America's founding fathers how to think about happiness and liberty and, more fundamentally, how to think for themselves. Benjamin Franklin and Thomas Jefferson were tutored by Scottish professors. Franklin, recalling a visit to Edinburgh, described it as "the *densest* happiness" he had ever experienced. Jefferson, writing in 1789, was equally effusive. "No place in the world can pretend to competition with Edinburgh."

Why this sudden burst of genius? It is a mystery that would stump even the great Sherlock Holmes, himself a product of Edinburgh. Sir Arthur Conan Doyle attended the city's renowned medical school. In truth, in the early eighteenth century, nobody saw this golden age coming. Scottish land was rough and stingy, as in Athens, the weather awful, the isolation formidable, the food inedible. Then there was the smell, which, also as in Athens, never failed to make an impression on visitors, such as an English surveyor named Edward Burt: "I was forced to hide my head between the sheets; for the Smell of the Filth, thrown out by the neighbors on the backside of the House, came pouring into the room."

Auld Reekie, or Old Smokey, as the poet Robert Fergusson affectionately called Edinburgh, was a sad sack of a city. "Inconvenient, dirty, old-fashioned, alcoholic, quarrelsome, and poor," says Buchan. The city's inhabitants, a mere forty thousand, weren't exactly a tolerant lot either. They were still hanging witches and blasphemers. As with Florence, Edinburgh suffered a series of catastrophes, some of them self-inflicted, some not. A failed attempt to establish a colony in the Isthmus of Panama depleted much of Scotland's capital. (Why Scotland thought it needed a presence in Panama is beyond me.) Famine struck. Worse, so did the English. They swallowed up little Scotland. In a flash the country lost its king and parliament and army. Scotland had, in effect, been politically castrated.

That a creative flourishing followed soon after makes no sense. (And flies in the face of Danilevsky's law, which, again, states that sovereignty is a prerequisite for creative flourishing.) In one of the many delicious ironies I encounter during my time in Edinburgh, none is tastier than this: The Scottish Enlightenment emphasized the importance of reason—indeed, it is sometimes called the Age of Reason—yet it seemingly defies reason. An explosion of genius that shouldn't have happened, *couldn't* have happened. And yet did.

Don't look to the Scots, either, to explain themselves. All geniuses, no matter how brilliant, share the same blind spot: they are utterly clueless as to the source of their own brilliance. Einstein was at a loss to explain what made him Einstein. Freud, not prone to surrendering intellectually, did just that when asked to explain creativity. "Before creativity, the psychoanalyst must lay down his arms," he sighed.

Likewise, the greatest Scottish minds of the day, such as the philosopher David Hume, were at a loss to explain what made them so brilliant. "Is it not strange that, at a time when we have lost our Princes, our Parliaments, our independent Government, even the Presence of our chief Nobility, are unhappy . . . is it not strange, I say, that, in these Circumstances, we shou'd really be the People most distinguish'd for Literature in Europe?"

For centuries the source of Edinburgh's golden age proved as elusive as the Loch Ness monster—inklings, a few sketchy sightings here and there, but nothing definitive. Recently, though, scholars have unearthed intriguing leads. The Scots, it turns out, have much to teach us on the nature of creative genius, and those lessons, in typical Scottish fashion, are wonderfully odd and unexpected.

As I walk Edinburgh's streets and dive deep into its archives, I soon realize that the Scottish flavor of genius is different from any other I've sampled so far. Scottish genius is quirky and social and informal. Most of all, it is practical.

Practical genius? I admit it's an odd concept. Isn't genius cerebral and lofty, you might ask, the antithesis of practical? That's what I thought, too, but the Scots changed my mind, and they did so the same way they've been changing minds for centuries: with equal doses of persistence and charm—and a few servings of single malt.

Surely, there must be a better way of doing this. That one simple yet sneakily subversive thought is what drove every aspect of the Scottish Enlightenment, from James Watt's steam engine to geologist James Hutton's discovery of "deep time." The Scottish Enlightenment was, at its heart, an Age of Improvement, and the Scots were the world's greatest improvers.

Improvement. You see the word everywhere in Scotland. It's deployed not in the breathless way we Americans use it—*New and improved!*—but in a more somber, almost reverential manner. "Dare to know," Kant said. The Scots agreed wholeheartedly, but found Kant's imperative incomplete. Dare to know and dare to *act* on that knowledge. That was the Scottish way. This combination of the practical and the metaphysical distinguished the Scottish flavor from the others I'd sampled so far in my journey.

Scotland's Age of Improvement started with the land. This makes sense. The land is elemental to our being, even today. Scotland was no Eden. Less than 10 percent of the land was arable. Farming techniques were crude and inefficient. *Surely there must be a better way of doing this,* thought a carpenter named James Small. Small had a big idea, and in the 1760s he invented a radically new plow. That might seem like a minor advance in the scheme of human history, but was in fact a tremendous leap forward—especially if you were a farmer or someone who ate food every now and then. Word of Small's new plow spread quickly, and soon farmers were meeting to discuss other ways to coax a bit more food from the stingy land. From these informal meetings, proper societies and clubs devoted to the embryonic field of agricultural science sprouted like so many flowers in the desert.

The Scots could have stopped with agriculture, I suppose, but that's not the way creativity works. Once launched, it acquires a momentum of its own; breakthroughs in one field inspire breakthroughs in others, and before you know it, you're living in a golden age. Sure enough, the Scottish urge to improve—the Doctrine of Improvability, it might be called—soon spread to other disciplines, including one that, for all of us, is a matter of life and death.

I am staring at this contraption, this thing, puzzling over its intended use. Every golden age, like every family, has its embarrassing artifacts. These odd relics, stashed away in the national attic, prompt incredulity, or worse. I'm thinking of the gladiators' shields from Roman times, the chastity belts of Elizabethan England, the fondue pots of 1970s America. *They sure were a weird bunch back then,* we think.

I've never seen a relic stranger, though, than the one I am staring at right now. Housed behind glass at the National Museum of Scotland, this horseshoe-shaped piece of wood has a metal ring fastened atop. Some sort of torture device, perhaps? That doesn't seem very enlightened of the Scots. No, a small placard informs me, I am looking at a collar. For the dead.

Don't get me wrong; I'm all in favor of accessorizing, but these "coffin collars," as they were known, are not high on my wish list. Why in the world would anyone make a collar for a corpse? I look more closely and see that it appears quite heavy and shacklelike, as if designed to impede egress. Was this some sort of security system against the supernatural?

Alas, no. The coffin collars were designed to thwart grave robbers. The culprits were not ghouls or common thieves. They were, like Michelangelo, students of human anatomy. Legally, only the bodies of executed criminals could be used for dissections, and there simply weren't enough of those to go around. So the medical students, creative and practical, snuck into cemeteries late at night. It was risky, this corpse snatching. Angry mobs had been known to descend upon those caught in the act.

Personally, I'm grateful to these courageous grave robbers for pointing me toward one of the greatest achievements of the Scottish Enlightenment: medicine. Perhaps in no other field did the Scots make so many advances, and so quickly. Some of the greatest names in European medicine were born and worked within a few miles and years of one another in the west of Scotland. The Scottish physician James Lind discovered that eating citrus fruit could prevent scurvy, a disease that was ravaging sailors across the globe. William Buchan, another physician, made the at-the-time radical suggestion that doctors wash their hands before examining patients, and the Scots pioneered the use of surgical anesthesia with chloroform. In the blink of an eye, backwater Edinburgh became the global epicenter of medical education. Graduates fanned out across the world, founding medical schools in, among other places, New York and Philadelphia.

Medical science was hot, the digital technology of its day, and Edinburgh its Silicon Valley. Its heroes were not digerati such as Steve Jobs and Mark Zuckerberg but surgeons such as John Hunter and chemists such as Joseph Black.

But why medicine? And why Edinburgh? Those are the questions on my mind as I climb the stairs of the old Royal Infirmary, a red-sandstone building that reeks of musty secrets, tucked away in a still-functioning wing of the medical school. I walk past consulting rooms and dingy corridors that look as if they haven't changed since the days when Arthur Conan Doyle studied here. I am greeted by a nice woman who, for a few pounds, hands me a ticket to what is officially known as the Surgeons Hall Museum but, unofficially, as the House of Horrors.

Just like those in Silicon Valley, Edinburgh's medical geniuses made their mark with devices and procedures that now, with the gift of hindsight, we find laughingly—and frighteningly—primitive. We eye these contraptions smugly. *Look how far we've come!* In the case of digital technology, it's that poky Commodore 64 that evokes this sort of self-satisfied nostalgia. In the case of medicine, it's devices such as the trephine, one of which is displayed in a glass case here. It looks exactly like a corkscrew, complete with a wooden handle. It was used, the placard optimistically informs me, to relieve pressure on the brain after a skull fracture. Personally, I'd take my chances with the Commodore.

My reaction, I realize, is unfair. At the time, the small medical school was a pioneer. It helped steer the young profession from the regrettable age of the barber-surgeons (history's most unfortunate hyphenation) into what we would (almost) recognize today as modern medicine.

I dive deeper into the building and learn much. I learn that the rationale for building a medical school was made on—what else?—rational grounds. The founder, John Munro, argued that it made economic sense to treat the sick and teach surgeons at home rather than abroad. Money was raised, and soon construction began on the infirmary and an adjacent medical school. When it opened in 1729, the hospital had only six beds. At first, surgeons brought their own instruments, the way plumbers bring their own tools, but the hospital and the school soon grew into world-class institutions. Once again, there was an American connection. Benjamin Franklin served as a conduit between Scotland and the colonies, providing letters of introduction to young Americans wishing to study in Edinburgh. At least one of the medical school's graduates, Benjamin Rush, later signed the Declaration of Independence.

Suddenly, medicine was *the field* to be in, thus launching a long and neurotic tradition of maternal expectations. Scottish mothers wished for nothing more than their sons to become doctors. For many, their wish came true. By 1789, 40 percent of the city's college students were enrolled in the medical school.

Who were these new students? Many were bright and ambitious young men (women wouldn't be permitted to matriculate until 1889) who might otherwise have gone into the clergy, but the Church's popularity was waning, and so they chose medicine, just as today young people who might otherwise have gone into public service are drawn to the money and glamour of Wall Street or Silicon Valley. This dynamic explains why we see spikes in professions at certain times and in certain places. The number of geniuses who appear in any given field at any given time is a function not of the pool of talent available but, rather, the attractiveness of the field. The reason, for instance, we find far fewer brilliant composers of classical music today than in the nineteenth century is not because composers are less talented, or owing to some strange and sudden genetic deficiency, but because far fewer ambitious young people see classical music as the way to make their mark in the world. *What is honored in a country will be cultivated there.*

Medicine provided the perfect vehicle for this uniquely Scottish flavor of genius. It's a practical endeavor, one that leads to tangible improvements in people's lives, yet it also has a theoretical component. Like the modern denizens of Silicon Valley, the medical adventurers of Edinburgh saw themselves as trailblazers. And like Silicon Valley, medical Edinburgh was very much a case of group genius.

I walk upstairs and, on the wall, find an old black-and-white photograph of a dining room. Beside the photograph is a stylish brandy decanter, with fluted lip and removable glass stopper. It's accompanied by a portrait of a rotund, middle-aged man with a kind face. James Young Simpson was an obstetrician and medical maverick—and a classic Scottish success story. The seventh son of a village baker, Simpson showed early academic promise. He was admitted to Edinburgh University at age fourteen.

As with many innovators, Simpson was driven by a fierce desire to solve a puzzle and, in his case, correct an injustice. As a young doctor, barely out of medical school, Simpson had observed a mastectomy performed without anesthesia, an unpleasant experience for all involved, especially the patient. Simpson was determined to do something about that, so he devoted himself to the embryonic field of anesthesia.

One evening, while hosting a dinner party, Simpson filled the brandy decanter with chloroform, a potent chemical about which little was known at the time, and presented it to his guests. You would think they might have balked at their host's unusual brew, but this was Scotland, where no one ever turns down a liquid offered, and so Simpson's friends happily imbibed. Everyone soon grew "ever more cheerful" and giddy, according to a witness.

The following morning, the maid found all of the guests passed out. Simpson was lucky. A higher dose would have killed him and his guests; a lower dose would have discouraged his hunch that chloroform could be used as an anesthetic. He got the proportions right.

Simpson refined the purity of the chloroform, conducted more experiments, and within weeks it was being used in surgery and childbirth across Europe. Some religious leaders, and even a few doctors, opposed its use, arguing that God intended for childbirth to be difficult ("I will make your pains in childbearing very severe"—Genesis 3:16), but when Queen Victoria allowed chloroform to be used during the birth of her son Prince Leopold, the case was settled. James Simpson was fully vindicated, and famous.

It was a classic case of Scottish genius at work: a group effort, conducted in a highly social setting, and carried out methodically yet boldly. Simpson demonstrated a willingness to risk his own life in the name of science, not to mention the lives of his closest friends, and it all started with a hunch.

I climb the stairs and spot an exhibit called "Early Ophthalmology." I look the other way. Ophthalmology, like dentistry, is one of those fields I pretend had no "early." I spot the "Syphilis Exhibit," supposedly a real crowd-pleaser, but give it, as well as the display on parasites, a wide berth and instead stop to look out the window. It's a wonderful view. I can see the hills off in the distance, including Arthur's Seat, the old volcano that sits at the edge of town. I look for a long time, marveling at how the scene before me is virtually unchanged from what a young medical student would have seen nearly three hundred years ago.

I can picture him: scruffy, no doubt, but bright eyed and brimming with energy. What were his dreams? Was he out to save the world—or merely to earn a decent living, make his mother happy? A little bit of both perhaps?

He no doubt shared much with a young coder in Silicon Valley: a tenacious optimism and an unwavering belief in the redemptive powers of technology, not to mention a desire to change the world, to *improve* it.

He did not, however, share the Valley's novelty fetish, its utter disdain for any idea more than five minutes old. The enlightened Scots, in the medical field and beyond, possessed a deep respect for history. The Scots invented history (sorry Thucydides), at least the readable kind. "Conjectural history," they called the genre, and we recognize it today in the works of writers such as David McCullough or any piece of historical fiction. For the Scotts, though, history wasn't merely interesting. It was useful. The Scots studied the past to understand the present, and of course improve it. Like the ancient Greeks and the Chinese, they knew that those who lack a keen awareness of history are destined to "remain forever children in understanding," as Cicero put it. Genius requires not only an accelerator but also a rearview mirror.

Leaving the infirmary, I step outside to a slate-gray sky and stiff breeze. Edinburgh is a compact city, designed for shoes, not cars. I pass a few grubby student bars, with names that could double as 1980s punk bands. Pink Olive, the Blind Poet. A few minutes later, I pass another kind of bar, advertising pole dancing. I'm reminded that the Scots are not saints, never have been. Places of genius always have a seedy underbelly, a by-product, I suspect, of all that tolerance.

I pass a traditional pub. The only poles here are the ones that hold a wooden sign painted with an image of the disgraced man the pub is

named after: William Brodie, better known by the honorific Deacon Brodie. Actually, the pub has two signs, for there were two Deacon Brodies.
By day, he was a successful cabinetmaker and respected member of the
city council. By night, he was an equally successful, and cunning, thief.
He secretly made wax copies of clients' keys, which he then used to pilfer
their belongings. Deacon Brodie stole partly to support his covert gambling habit (as well as two equally covert mistresses) and partly for the
thrill of it.

No one in eighteenth-century Edinburgh suspected good and decent
Deacon Brodie was behind the wave of robberies until, eventually, the
evidence pointing to him was irrefutable. Brodie ran, getting as far as Holland before he was extradited back to Scotland and hanged for his crimes.
Hanged, the story goes, on the very type of gallows he invented.

It's a nice tale, one with a satisfyingly dark and ironic ending. I suspect, though, that Deacon Brodie is more than a historical curiosity, more,
even, than the inspiration for Robert Louis Stevenson's *The Strange Case of
Dr. Jekyll and Mr. Hyde.* But what?

Deacon Brodie, at the very least, helps explain why Edinburgh has
been called a "two-faced" city. The Scots, then and still today, are at odds
with themselves. On the one hand, they possess a reflexive pessimism,
which I witnessed one day when I overheard a couple walking down the
street. The Scottish sun was making a cameo appearance, as it does now
and then, just to mess with people's heads.

"Nice day," said the man.

"Yes," replied his companion, "and we'll pay for it!"

For a Scot, no good deed goes unpunished; every nice day comes at a
price. Yet they also possess a grudging optimism, a belief that anything is
possible, or at least improvable. How else to explain the 1767 decision by
Edinburgh's most revered citizens to entrust the future of their beloved
city to a twenty-two-year-old neophyte architect? Then there is Scotty, of
Star Trek lure. He is an engineer, and therefore naturally cautious. *It can't
be dun, Cap'n,* he says, after Kirk has implored him to squeeze a bit more
warp drive out of the *Enterprise.* No, it can't be done. Then he does it
anyway. Very Scottish.

I return to my hotel and hit the "honor bar." It's located in the sitting room, a lovely common area with a fireplace, Scottish bric-a-brac, and big leather chairs that invite hours of blessed idleness. The bar is generously stocked with wine and beer and, of course, Scotch. You help yourself, then write down what you imbibed and how much. How nice, I think, how trusting of human nature, as I help myself to another glass of twelve-year-old Macallan. And I honor the honor bar. Mostly. Not until the end of my stay do I notice not one but two covert surveillance cameras trained on the honor bar. Practical genius at its finest.

I pivot to coffee and investigate Scotland's two faces. Some two hundred years after Adam Smith and David Hume walked Edinburgh's odorous streets, Harvard Medical School psychiatrist Albert Rothenberg dedicated himself to studying these impossible contradictions that seem to lie at the heart of creativity. He coined a term for it: *Janusian thinking*. It's named after Janus, the Roman god with two faces, which look in opposite directions. Rothenberg defined Janusian thinking as "actively conceiving two or more opposite or antithetical ideas, images or concepts simultaneously." Creative people, Rothenberg found, are particularly adept at this. To be clear: Janusian thinking is not about synthesizing two incompatible ideas but living with their incompatibility. If Hamlet had engaged in Janusian thinking, he would never have deliberated over that pesky question. He would have been content to be *and* not to be.

Rothenberg studied major scientific breakthroughs and concluded that most resulted from Janusian thinking. Einstein, for instance, arrived at his general theory of relativity by realizing that someone who jumped off a building would not find any evidence of a gravitational field in his immediate vicinity, yet that very force caused his plummet. Einstein was able to imagine opposite truths coexisting simultaneously—an object that was both in motion and at rest at the same time—a thought that he later called "the happiest in my life."

Fellow physicist Niels Bohr's hunch that light is both wave *and* particle is pure Janusian thinking. How can something be two very different things at the same time? Simply asking that question, and not necessarily answering it, is the first step to a creative breakthrough, Bohr believed. When you do this, thought is not accelerated but suspended, and Bohr speculated that creative breakthroughs are most likely to occur in this state of suspended cognition.

Janusian thinking not only describes creativity but also cultivates it. In one study, psychologists divided participants into two groups. One was "primed" for Janusian thinking by being presented with paradoxical concepts, while the second group was not. Both groups were then given a test designed to measure creative problem solving. The first group, the one primed for Janusian thinking, exhibited more creative thinking.

I wonder if this love of paradox defines not only creative individuals but creative places, too. Enlightenment Scotland was paradox heaven. *We are British and not British. We are a large nation and a small one. We are cocky. We are insecure. We are practical adventurers. Hopeful pessimists.* No wonder it was a Scottish psychiatrist who penned the seminal work *The Divided Self.* This is a nation of divided selves, of Deacon Brodies.

Everywhere I look in Edinburgh, past and present, I keep bumping up against contradictions. For every one conclusion the opposite also holds true. Unlike Niels Bohr, I find this paradox frustrating, not enlightening.

If anyone can help alleviate my suffering, surely it is David Hume—soulful atheist, social introvert, man of ideas and action. I find him, a statue at least, on the Royal Mile, the main thoroughfare of Old Edinburgh, looking pleased, almost angelic, and dressed in ancient-Greek garb. Of course. The Scots admired the Greeks and to this day like to call Edinburgh "the Athens of the North." (Or as one local wag told me, "Athens was the Edinburgh of the South.")

Hume, even more than Smith, was the quintessential Scottish genius. Simultaneously strong willed and deeply insecure, gregarious and introverted, he was "modernity's first great philosopher," writes historian Arthur Herman.

Hume enrolled at the University of Edinburgh at age twelve—young even by the standards of the day. At first, he studied law, as his family

wished, but the thought of pursuing that profession made him "nau-
seous," and he soon realized that he possessed "an unsurmountable aver-
sion to everything but the pursuits of philosophy and general learning."
So while his family thought he was studying legal textbooks, he was "secretly devouring" the likes of Cicero and Virgil. Nothing fires the intellect
more than forbidden learning.

Hume produced some of his best work while still young. He penned
his *Treatise of Human Nature* while still in his twenties. The book was a
flop, falling "still born from the press," as Hume later recalled. The young
philosopher persisted, though, as all geniuses do, and soon gained notoriety across Britain and beyond. Today, his *Treatise* is considered one of
philosophy's greatest works.

Hume aimed to understand how we understand. Where do we get
knowledge from? After engaging in a series of thought experiments, he
reached the then-radical conclusion that all knowledge comes through
direct experience—through our senses and only our senses. Hume borrowed Isaac Newton's experimental method and applied it to the messy
world of mankind. Hume used himself as a human laboratory, going several days without food, for instance, to gauge the mind's reaction to hunger. He was trying to create what he called "the Science of Man."

This was, he argued, the most important science of all, for how can
we begin to understand our world if we don't understand ourselves? He
conceded that was a difficult, if not impossible, objective, since we can
never fully step outside ourselves, any more than the camera can photograph itself. Knowledge, he concluded, is not universally true but is
"something felt by the mind."

Hume was a skeptic. He questioned everything, including his own
questions. Not surprisingly, he was an unapologetic atheist, a stance that
cost him the support of the Church and two professorships but, crucially,
not his life.

Hume was a rationalist, but not in the cold, robotic sense of the
word. "Indulge your passion for science but let your science be human,"
he urged. "Reason is, and ought to be, the slave of the passions." With
those few words, he upturned centuries of philosophical thought. Most

philosophers, dating back to Aristotle, argued that what distinguished man from other animals was his ability to reason, but "Hume quietly pointed out that human beings are not, and never have been, governed by their rational capacities," writes Herman, the historian. Reason, Hume argued, doesn't determine *what* we want but only *how* we obtain it.

Hume did all of this upending with a smile, for unlike many of his furrowed-brow colleagues, he found genuine joy in philosophy. As he wrote in a letter to a friend, "Reading and sauntering and lownging [*sic*] and dozing, which I call thinking, is my supreme Happiness." Hume would spend weeks holed up in his study, reading and pondering, but then he would emerge again, "absolutely and necessarily determin'd to live, and talk, and act like other people in the common affairs of life." He was a regular in Edinburgh's taverns and at its many clubs.

Hume was not only a social soul but a restless one as well. For a while he lived in London, where he took perverse pleasure in his outsider status. As he wrote to a friend, "Down here some people hate me because I'm a Whig, some people hate me because I'm an Atheist. Everyone hates me because I'm a Scot." He also lived in Paris. *Le bon* David, as he became known, frequented the city's parlor salons, where he jousted with Rousseau and Diderot and other intellectual giants of the day. He even briefly considered becoming a French citizen, but couldn't bring himself to make the leap and returned to Edinburgh.

There, he reveled in the city's democratic stew, the way blacksmith and professor shared the same social space, and often the same bottle of wine. Hume believed this social porousness helped drive Scottish genius, for "the same age which produces great philosophers and politicians, renowned generals and poets, usually abounds with skilled weavers and ship-carpenters."

This is not, Hume believed, mere coincidence, or an act of charity on the part of intellectuals. The philosopher needs the weaver as much as the weaver needs the philosopher. No wonder Adam Smith spent as much time talking to merchants as he did buried in books. He was merely following his friend David Hume's advice: "Be a philosopher. But, amidst all your philosophy, be still a man." I read those words and smile. The wily Scots even converted philosophy into a practical endeavor.

At this latitude, this time of year, mornings are not your friend. The darkness and the chill conspire with your down comforter to immobilize you. On this particular morning I might easily have slept until noon, were it not for the words of Robert Louis Stevenson, mocking me, cajoling me out from under the covers. "The great affair is to move," the Edinburgh native said.

So I move. First to the shower then to breakfast then, boldly, in the spirit of adventurers through the ages, outside. I join a walking path that runs along the city's main canal. It's pleasant and, I'm told, stretches all the way to Glasgow, connecting these antithetical cities in a perfectly Janusian relationship. I am not alone. Others are heeding Stevenson's advice; they are walking and running and cycling, and doing so in attire—T-shirts and shorts—that, to my non-Scottish mind, seems wholly inappropriate given the biting cold.

The word *scrappy* springs to mind. Yes, that is what the Scots are. They are scrappy. I had not previously associated the word with creative genius, but perhaps I should. As I pick up my pace in a futile attempt to stave off hypothermia, it dawns on me how that word, *scrappy*, defines so many of the people and places I've encountered during my journey. Athens rebounding after its sack by the Persians. Florence bouncing back from the plague. Su Tungpo recovering from his two exiles and going on to write some of his most exquisite poetry. *Scrappy*, I decide, deserves a better connotation. *Scrappy* is not mere pluck or stubborn persistence. Scrappy people are resourceful, determined, creative. Scrappy is good.

"It's true," says Alex Renton, a local journalist and a friend of a friend. "We are a scrappy people."

He tells me this over a pint at a little tavern called Kay's. It took some work to find, hidden as it is down an alley. The rotund bartender has the biggest walrus mustache I've ever seen, including on actual walruses. I tell him about my quixotic search for places of genius, and he mentions, without a hint of faux erudition, that he is reading a biography of David

Hume. All of this transpires while he simultaneously, and expertly, pours two pints of ale.

Alex and I find two open stools and quickly appropriate them.

"We are the most myth-ridden country in the bloody world," he proclaims, apropos of nothing, as we order another round from the Walrus. I couldn't help but notice that Alex said "myth-ridden" as if it were a good thing. What does he mean?

"The Scots of the Enlightenment believed in their own myths," he says. "Otherwise, there would have been no Enlightenment."

Now, on the face of it, that sounds delusional. Myths, as we define them today, are falsehoods, misguided beliefs. Lies. They are irrational and to be avoided at all costs. However, another definition of myth, one Joseph Campbell spent a lifetime elucidating, says myths define us. Myths inspire us. Myths are good. Without myths, we wouldn't get out of bed in the morning, let alone create anything worthwhile. The app designer tinkering in his garage in Silicon Valley, the unpublished writer toiling away in her tiny Brooklyn apartment, are driven by the myth of the lone genius. As we've seen, it isn't true, but it is useful.

I ask Alex about another myth of genius—the notion that big things happen in big places. They do not; if anything, genius clings to the small. Ancient Athens had a population of fewer than one hundred thousand people. Florence was even smaller, and Edinburgh smaller still. Yet these cities spawned so much greatness, outshining much larger rivals. How can this be?

"Easy," says Alex as we order our third round, or maybe it's our fourth. "A small nation has to grow big balls."

With those few, colorful words, Alex sums up an entire philosophy of the small. Small places are more intimate than larger ones. Small places, out of necessity, are more likely to direct their eyes outward and are therefore more likely to accumulate the varied stimuli that, research shows, make us more creative. Small places are more likely to ask questions, and questions are the building blocks of genius. Small places try harder.

Small places are also riddled with doubt. This is important. We tend to associate genius with unbridled self-confidence and certainty.

We assume that geniuses know what they are doing. They do not. As Einstein said, "If we knew what we were doing, we wouldn't call it research."

No one exposes this lie more mercilessly than the Scots. They were uncertain about everything, from the worth of their indigenous language, a rascally tongue called Scots, to the fate of their very nation. This endemic doubt, rather than paralyze, empowered, and the Scots, writes historian Richard Sher, "demonstrated their own worth to themselves and others." That's the way doubt works. It either paralyzes or emboldens. Nothing in between.

I ask about Scottish dourness and the distinct gloominess I've detected, both in eighteenth-century Scotland and still today. One day, at the National Library, I saw people queuing to hear a lecture. What was it? Perhaps a local poet reading her collection of inspirational poems, or a professor cataloging Scottish accomplishments? Only when I squeezed past the crowds did I see the poster announcing that the library was pleased to present "Painful Tales: Death and Disease in the British Raj."

As I said, dark. What, I ask Alex, is going on?

"On the one hand," says Alex, between sips, "it's true. We Scots are dark, cruel, and self-abasing." He pauses for a long time, letting me soak up the enormity of that statement, marvel at how it packs so much negativity into such little space.

I'm waiting for the other hand. You can't count on much in this dark, cruel, and self-abasing world, but, in my experience, if there is one hand, then you can count on another to shortly be forthcoming. Yet none is. Alex just stares at his lager, as if hypnotized. I fear he may have dozed off and am not sure what to do.

"On the other hand . . . ," he says finally. I audibly exhale. "On the other hand, we also have a stubborn optimism, a boldness of spirit." Despite all their outward grimness and fatalism, the Scots believe in "man's innate quality of sympathy and benevolence," as one historian put it. All geniuses, I think, share this belief, at least in some form. To create something worthwhile you must possess a grudging faith that your creation will find an appreciative audience. To create is to have faith not only in the moment but in moments yet to come. That's why you don't hear about many nihilists producing creative works.

The Walrus tallies our tab, and Alex and I stumble onto Jamaica Street. The air feels good. I feel good. More than that, I detect a bud of optimism sprouting inside me. It's an unusual sensation, one that, like most unusual sensations, I first mistake for indigestion. But the facts are accumulating faster than our bar tab had. I, too, suffer from bouts of self-doubt and uncertainty. I, too, am a divided self and maintain a sometimes tenuous relationship with reality. Ignorance? I've got boatloads. As Alex and I say good-bye, I happily conclude that I might, just might, have the makings of genius.

As I shimmy back to my hotel, though, doubt creeps into my mind.

"Aha, doubt—another sign of genius!" says one of my divided selves.

"No," says my other self, as I grope for my room key. "You are no genius."

"Perhaps, but I might be Scottish," my unified self decides, and as far as we're concerned, that's nearly as good.

The more I dig, the more I discover that Alex is right: the Scots possessed substantial testicular mass. They weren't satisfied wrestling with the small questions. No, they dove headfirst into the biggest mysteries of their day, of *any* day. Such as, how old is time?

Today, we know (or at least we're pretty sure we know) that the earth is 4.6 billion years old. But in the eighteenth century, conventional wisdom held that the earth was no more than six thousand years old because, well, that's what the Bible said, and absent any compelling evidence to the contrary, that's what people believed.

Most people at least. A soft-spoken polymath named James Hutton wasn't so sure. He began to ask questions, amass evidence. Eventually, with more than a little help from some friends, Hutton synthesized his various findings into a tome ambitiously titled *Theory of the Earth* and presented it to his largely skeptical colleagues at the Royal Society of Edinburgh. That skepticism would erode, during and after Hutton's life-time, and eventually his conclusion that the earth was much, much older than six thousand years would be accepted by the scientific community. A young biologist named Charles Darwin read Hutton's work, channeled through another geologist named Charles Lyell, while on board the HMS *Beagle*, en route to the Galápagos Islands. Darwin's ideas about evolution were profoundly affected by Hutton's findings, and some historians believe that without Hutton there would have been no Darwin.

Despite his stellar achievements, Hutton is a hard man to track down, even in his native Edinburgh. No Royal Mile statue for old James. No museum erected in his honor, no pub named after him. I finally find him sulking on the edge of town. It's called the James Hutton Memorial Garden, but it looks more like a garbage dump. The ground is littered with empty cigarette cartons, tuna tins, candy wrappers. Auditory pollution, too: the thump of jackhammers and the whoosh of cars from a nearby road. Hutton doesn't get many visitors. On this day it's just me and two chain-smoking teenagers, using the great geologist's garden as an ashtray.

Fortunately, the history books have been kinder to Hutton, and in those pages I find a more complete, and sympathetic, portrait of the man who found time. In at least one important aspect, Hutton's childhood resembled that of many geniuses: he lost a parent at a young age. Hutton was only an infant when his father, a merchant, died. David Hume also lost his father as an infant; Adam Smith's father died before Adam was born. I'm beginning to suspect that Sartre may have been right when he quipped that the best gift a father can give a son is to die young.

With his cocked hat and "unaffected simplicity," Hutton was a well-known figure in town. Here is another trait common to geniuses: an utter and complete lack of self-consciousness. Hutton simply didn't care what others thought of him. Few geniuses do. Think of Socrates's nose. Or Einstein's hair. That is not the hair of someone who devoted much of his considerable gray matter to personal grooming. And who can blame him? He didn't want to pay the opportunity cost. Time spent combing your hair is time not spent contemplating the speed of light.

Hutton was a bit of a lost soul. A farmer turned physician turned lawyer, he enjoyed nothing more than digging in the mud and collecting rocks. Those rocks, Hutton believed, contained important clues about the past. The rocks could talk. Yes, geology was Hutton's true passion. There was one slight problem, though: geology didn't exist yet.

So James Hutton did what many geniuses do: he invented a category. "Domain creation" it's called, and it is perhaps the highest form of genius. It's one thing to compose beautiful music; it's another to invent a new musical language, as Gustav Mahler did, or the discipline of evolutionary biology, as Darwin did.

Hutton's genius began with simple observation. He took regular trips to the Scottish Highlands to observe firsthand how subterranean heat created granite. Closer to home, he went on long walks on Arthur's Seat, the mountain on the outskirts of Edinburgh.

I walk the short distance there now. Even with my novice eyes, I can see why Hutton was drawn to it. The mountain is a geological wonderland. Formed 350 million years ago by a volcanic eruption, it has since undergone earthquakes and flooding, was submerged under an ancient sea, and was finally subsumed by an ice-age glacier.

Hutton took meticulous records of altitude and temperature. Arthur's Seat was Hutton's laboratory, one that "offered daily lessons for the philosopher," says Jack Repcheck in his excellent biography of Hutton.

Most of us look. The genius sees. Hutton noted when something wasn't quite right, didn't fit. Rather than dismiss such incongruities or explain them away, he investigated further. He asked questions. Why, for instance, was one layer of rocks, called Salisbury Crags, darker than others in the area? What were fish fossils doing on the summit of a mountain?

Hutton couldn't let these inconsistencies just be. They nagged at him, haunted him. Clearly, he was under the spell of the Zeigarnik effect.

Bluma Zeigarnik was a Russian psychologist. She was at a restaurant one day and noticed how the waiters kept perfect track of orders, but as soon as the plates hit the table, they "deleted" the information. She conducted a series of experiments and determined that we recall information associated with incomplete tasks much more readily than other types of information. Something about an unsolved problem boosts our memory and sharpens our thinking.

Geniuses, I suspect, are more susceptible to the Zeigarnik effect than the rest of us. When faced with an unsolved problem, they persist and can't rest until it is solved. This persistence explains more about creative genius than those apocryphal "aha moments." Asked how he discovered the law of gravitation, Isaac Newton made no mention of falling apples and instead replied, "By thinking on it continually."

James Hutton had lots of time to think. Like many of Edinburgh's geniuses, he was a lifelong bachelor. Hutton's world consisted of his rocks and his friends. The rocks provided the raw material he needed to formulate his theories; the friends provided the guidance he needed to articulate those theories.

The latter proved crucial, for eloquence was not among James Hutton's considerable talents. He was a terrible writer, simply awful. Hutton needed help.

Enter John Playfair, Hutton's close friend, a mathematician with a feel for language. He revived Hutton's parched prose, rendering his papers readable, compelling even.

Articulation of an idea, especially an idea as revolutionary as Hutton's, matters more than we think. It is one thing to be right and quite another to convince others that you are right. You can have all the brilliant ideas in the world, but if no one can understand them, what good are they? The role that Hutton's friend played was more than mere public relations though. The word *articulation* is derived from a root meaning "joining" or "joint." To articulate an idea is to cement it, to cocreate it. The conception of an idea cannot be separated from the voicing of it.

Rarely, though, are both skill sets found in the same person. Thus, the need for what I call compensatory genius. Compensatory genius is when one brilliant mind makes up for the shortcoming of another brilliant one. Compensatory genius can take many forms. Sometimes, as with Hutton and Playfair, one genius actively compensates for the deficiencies of another. At other times, one genius reacts to the work of another. Aristotle responding to Plato, Goethe to Kant, Beethoven to Mozart.

Sometimes compensatory genius takes the form of a support group for those charting unknown intellectual and artistic waters. The French impressionists held weekly meetings, outdoor painting sessions, and other informal gatherings, all aimed at bolstering their spirits in the face of the regular rejection they experienced at the hands of the old guard. Without this compensatory genius, the movement might not have survived.

Sometimes compensatory genius is invisible. Consider the steam engine. Scotland's best-known invention is something of a lie. James Watt didn't invent the steam engine, as is widely believed. He *did* make major improvements to a machine invented fifty years earlier by Thomas Newcomen, transforming it into something more practical. In a way, they *both* invented the steam engine. Paul Valéry, the French poet and essayist, claimed, "It takes two to invent anything." One person constructs a rough idea and a second refines it, compensates for its inadequacies and inconsistencies.

It's getting late. The alleged sunlight is beginning to fade. I trundle down Arthur's Seat, taking in the view of Edinburgh below, not that different from what James Hutton would have seen all those years ago. Back at the memorial garden, the loitering teenagers now gone, I notice a quote, attributed to Hutton, engraved on a small slate of marble: WE FIND NO VESTIGE OF A BEGINNING—NO PROSPECT OF AN END. These few short words sum up his life's work, and perhaps all of human creativity.

I can't help but wonder if Hutton's rare burst of eloquence in reality flowed from the pen of his compensating friend, John Playfair. As I turn onto the street that leads back to my hotel, the sky now a soft crimson, I realize I will likely never know the answer. That's okay. We needn't know the source of a bright light to appreciate its radiance.

Edinburgh, it's been said, is a city built on surprise, a place that reveals its secrets grudgingly, and only to those who work at it. Edinburgh's topography, with its "theatre tricks in the way of scenery," as Robert Louis Stevenson put it, stokes this sense of surprise and its close cousin wonder. "You peep under an arch, you descend stairs that look as if they would land you in a cellar, you turn to the back window of a grimy tenement in a lane—and behold! you are face to face with distant and bright prospects," he wrote.

Stevenson knew more than most that creativity is largely an act of discovery. To dis-cover is to uncover, to unveil and shine a light on what lies beneath. When that happens, you surprise not only others, but yourself. I'm thinking of the writer who stumbles across a passage, marveling at its poetic beauty, its simple eloquence, before realizing that she is staring at her own words, written years ago. When the composer Joseph Haydn heard his masterpiece *The Creation* performed for the first time, he was dumbstruck. "I have not written this," he said, tears welling in his eyes.

I want to explore this connection between surprise and creativity more deeply and would love nothing more than to share a single malt with Robert Louis Stevenson, but he, inconveniently, lives in that foreign land known as the past. So I call Donald Campbell. He knows Edinburgh, past and present, better than anyone else. A playwright and essayist, he penned a lovely little cultural history of Edinburgh that captures the essence of the city. When I read it, I knew I had to meet him.

He wasn't easy to find but I persisted—the Zeigarnik effect in action—and now find myself sitting in his cozy living room in central Edinburgh. It is cold and gray outside, a spring tease having proved to be nothing more than that. I'm sipping my tea slowly, genius-style, as I did in Hangzhou, trying to wrap my mind around what Donald has just told me: Edinburgh is a city that has, for centuries, not only tolerated surprise but thrived on it. What does he mean?

"Well"—he pauses to replenish my tea—"I've lived in Edinburgh for a very long time, yet very often I come across things and places that I didn't know were there before. I just suddenly stumble on them."

The other day, for instance, he was wandering around a neighborhood called the Grass Market when, down an alleyway and up a flight of stairs, he spotted a restaurant, a good restaurant it turns out. "Yet there was absolutely nothing to indicate that it was a restaurant—no sign, nothing. They made absolutely no attempt to advertise. It was like they were hiding."

Then there is his friend, a fellow playwright, who was promoting a new production. "He calls me the other day and says, 'Our play is opening next weekend, but don't tell anyone.'" Campbell laughs at the absurdity of promoting a play by keeping it a secret.

I take a long, slow sip of my tea, hoping the proven therapeutic qualities of the beverage will help me make sense of this. There are two possibilities, I realize. One is that the Scots are nuts, and this whole Enlightenment business was a ruse, an intellectual Nessie. The second possibility is that they are onto something. I'm feeling generous—compensatory, you might say—so I choose the second option. Perhaps the Scots have long known intuitively that we cherish the hidden more than the exposed. That is why God invented wrapping paper and lingerie.

The surprise, and joy, of discovering what had previously been hidden lies at the heart of creativity. Archimedes shouting, "Eureka!" The physicist Richard Feynman upon hearing a single phrase about the possible nature of neutron decay, jumping to his feet and exclaiming, "Then I understand *evvverything!*"

Let's peel the onion some more. We've seen how genius always begins with observation. What distinguishes the creative genius from the merely talented is not knowledge or intelligence but vision. As the German philosopher Arthur Schopenhauer said, "Talent hits a target no one else can hit; genius hits a target no one else can see." The target is hidden, like Donald Campbell's restaurant. Or Robert Louis Stevenson's "theatre tricks." Both are describing a world turned upside down, with incompatible images colliding.

This is what psychiatrist Albert Rothenberg calls "homospatial thinking," conceiving of two or more disparate ideas in the same mental space. To investigate this phenomenon, Rothenberg designed a fascinating experiment. He assembled two groups of artists and writers. One group was shown unusual photographs juxtaposed. For instance, an image of a French four-poster bed superimposed over an image of a platoon of soldiers taking cover behind a tank. A second group was shown the same images, but this time they were not juxtaposed but, rather, presented individually. Both groups were then asked to produce a creative product—a metaphor in the case of the writers, a pastel drawing in the case of the artists. The first group—the one shown juxtaposed images—produced the more creative products. Rothenberg concluded that "creative imagery is excited by sensory input that is random, or at least unusual." And, he might have added, hidden.

Many artists intuitively engage in homospatial thinking, even if they don't know what it's called. The surrealist painter Max Ernst developed a technique he called "frottage." He describes placing a series of random drawings on the floor and how he was "surprised at the sudden intensification of my visionary capacities and by the hallucinatory succession of contradictory images superimposed one upon the other." Creative places such as Enlightenment Edinburgh encourage these sort of improbable juxtapositions.

As Donald Campbell heats another pot of tea, I ponder the implications of this culture of surprise, past and present. You can tell a lot about a place, I realize, by its relationship with surprise. Does it celebrate life's small serendipities or shy away from them? Does it carve out space for the unexpected? In short, are miracles allowed? For "nothing stifles the spirit of discovery more effectively than the assumption that miracles have ceased," observes the writer Robert Grudin.

Perhaps that statement strikes you as odd, absurd even. Perhaps you are highly skeptical of miracles, as am I. But let's not forget that every act of genius, from the invention of the wheel to Mozart's *Requiem* to the Internet, has been infused with hints of the miraculous. Not only is life more interesting in a world where miracles are still possible, but creative breakthroughs are more likely to happen in such a world.

Edinburgh's most impressive miracle is that it exists at all, given the challenges posed by topography and climate. As a stray ray of sunshine pierces the living room like an alien space beam, I ask Donald about this.

It's true, he says. What made, and still makes, Edinburgh so creative is not that it is a nice place but rather that it is difficult. "The great thing about being Scottish is that you've got something to push against. Instead of having to live up to something, you have to push against something. It forces you to make that extra effort." That is, I realize, an apt description not only of Edinburgh but all places of genius.

I decide to walk back to my hotel. Walking, as I learned in Athens, is good for thinking. Besides, Edinburgh makes for an excellent classroom. The divided self exists not only in the Scottish mind but also on the Scottish streets. Edinburgh's two selves are reflected in the two halves of the city, New Town and Old Town, representing, as one historian put it, "elegance and filth, humanity and cruelty."

New Town is indeed pleasant and well planned, the angular layout instantly recognizable to our modern (read rational) sensibilities. I have to confess, though, I prefer the zigzaggy chaos and messiness of Old Town. Here I can picture what life was like in the peak of the Scottish Enlightenment, how these geniuses were living on top of one another, the wealthy and the destitute in the same building.

And here we run headlong into the sticky issue of urban density. The supposition that density is the secret to creative places has, in some quarters, risen to the level of received truth. A group of urbanists, most prominently Richard Florida, has fashioned a cottage industry out of it. At the heart of this industry is a single mantra: "Cities are places where ideas go to have sex." It's a clever line, but is it true?

First, we must, as academics are so fond of saying, unpack it. Behind the density mantra lies a presumed scenario. Take a bunch of smart people, put them in the same densely populated city, add sushi bars and experimental theater and gay-friendly policies, and watch the creative genius happen. It's a nice theory but fuzzy. No one has yet to explain how we get from point A (urban density) to point B (creativity). When pressed, these density theorists point to "interaction opportunities." If all creativity is, in essence, about molecules colliding, then naturally the more interactions the better, since it increases the number of interactions that may result in something brilliant.

I find this explanation less than satisfying. For starters, not all interactions are equally good, any more than all ideas are equally good. Prisons are extremely dense, with lots of interactions, but not a lot of creativity happens there. Slums are dense, too, and while people there may excel in the art of everyday creativity, they do not generally win Nobel Prizes or invent new genres of literature. No, something else besides density must be going on.

I recall what Donald Campbell said when I asked him what he loved about Edinburgh. What keeps him here? He thought about it before

answering with a single word: "Intimacy." It was not a word I was expecting, but when I heard it, something clicked. *Now I understand evvvvery-
thing,* I thought. Places of genius are not only densely populated, they are
also intimate, and intimacy always includes a degree of trust. The Greek
philosophers and poets gathered at a symposium trusted one another, so
a degree of intimacy was established. Verrocchio trusted his craftsmen to
complete their assigned tasks. Today, the cities and companies that excel
creatively are those where trust and intimacy are high.

Yet we continue to focus on density as the pixie dust of creativity.
Why? Because it's easier to measure. Mark off a square mile of a city,
count the number of inhabitants within that zone, and, voilà, you have
measured its density. Intimacy is much more difficult to quantify. We're
like the person looking for his keys in a lit parking lot, rather than the
darkened alleyway where he actually lost them. When asked why, he replies, "Because this is where the light is." If we are going to unravel the
mystery of creative places, we need to spend more time looking in the
dark.

"Why don't we meet at my office?" says the voice on the other end of
the line. He gives me the address of the old medical school. This strikes
me as odd since he is a historian, not a doctor, but it's early, and besides,
after a few weeks in Edinburgh, I've stopped questioning such seeming
incongruities. I'm about to hang up when he adds, "Oh, by the way, I'm
on floor one and a half."

I dutifully jot down that last bit of information. Only later, fully caffeinated, do I take a closer look at the scrap of paper and do a double
take. Floor one and a half? It sounds an awful lot like boarding a train
at platform nine and three-quarters. It's possible. After all, J. K. Rowling
penned the Harry Potter books here. Flat broke, she lugged her laptop
every morning to a local café.

The man on floor one and a half is Tom Devine, historian, rabble-
rouser, and, according to the *Times* of London, the closest thing Scotland
has to a national bard. ("A *living* national bard," he would later clarify.)
Devine imbibes his nation's history the way others imbibe a very old

Scotch, slowly and with a deep appreciation that borders on reverence. In recent years, Tom has devoted much of his considerable intellectual horsepower to solving the riddle that was the Scottish Enlightenment.

Fittingly, the building, heavy and castlelike, looks like something straight out of Hogwarts. I climb the stairs, stopping midway between floors one and two, briefly worrying—irrationally, I know—that I might slip into some strange Scottish tear in the fabric of the space-time continuum. I don't. Instead, I find myself in a perfectly ordinary hallway, illuminated in perfectly normal academic fluorescence, that exists between floors one and two. I am relieved, and a bit disappointed.

Tom Devine is a munchkin of a man, with eyes stuck in a permanent twinkle. Hunched over his desk, he scribbles furiously, not acknowledging my presence. Without looking up, he says, loudly and definitively and with the broadest Scottish brogue I've ever heard, "Did you know that the man who invented Ceylon tea was Scottish?"

"Um, no, Professor Devine, I did not know that."

"Well, he was." The Scots are big on this sort of name-dropping. It is a form of Jewish geography. *Did you know so-and-so was Jewish? Yep, he was.* Both the Jewish and Scottish variants of this game are prone to wildly exaggerated claims, and both, I suspect, stem from a deeply felt tribal insecurity, a need to prove something to the world. *We're a small people, a demographic blip, but we're everywhere, doing miraculous things.*

"It's a riddle," Tom says, speaking now of the Scottish Enlightenment, and I can tell by the way he lingers over the word *riddle*—drawing it out, adding syllables and diphthongs and other linguistic flourishes I can't identify—that he loves, simply *loves*, that such a riddle exists.

One of the University of Edinburgh's more famous graduates, Sir Arthur Conan Doyle, would no doubt enjoy the mystery that was the Scottish Enlightenment. It's not so much a whodunit—we know that—it's more a question of motive and method. Why and how did this tiny city on the edge of the world experience "the most vivacious intellectual shindig in history," as my guidebook puts it, without exaggeration. It is a tough case to crack, and therefore catnip to the likes of Tom Devine.

One of the secret ingredients that made Edinburgh such a hothouse of genius, Tom tells me in that sly way of his, as if divulging state secrets, or the meaning of life, was conversation. Edinburgh, like Socrates's Athens, was a city of gab, and therein lay its genius.

It's a tempting conclusion, one that Socrates would no doubt agree with, but I'm skeptical of this genius recipe. Throw a bunch of smart people together, add food and booze, simmer while stirring occasionally, then stand back and let the brilliant ideas sizzle. Allow to cool and enjoy.

I'm not buying it. Smart people plus conversation do not necessarily add up to genius. It certainly wasn't what emerged from the oven after President John F. Kennedy held a series of closed-door meetings with his closest, and smartest, advisers. No, the result was the ill-conceived 1961 Bay of Pigs invasion of Cuba. Nearly all of the fourteen hundred CIA-trained Cuban exiles were captured or killed. Cuba moved even deeper into the Soviet orbit. It was one of the worst foreign policy blunders in American history. How could it have happened, given the combined intellectual throw weight gathered in that room?

A decade later, a psychologist named Irving Janis investigated the meetings that led to the botched invasion and concluded that the profound error in judgment was due not to stupidity, but rather to a quirk of human nature. When people from similar backgrounds get together, are isolated from dissenting views, and are trying to please a strong leader, the result is consensus around the preferred position, even if it is clearly wrongheaded. Janis coined a term for this tendency: groupthink.

Groupthink is the flip side of group genius. It is the bugaboo in every theory that celebrates the virtues of collective intelligence. Groupthink is collective stupidity, and every culture is susceptible to it. The question is, why does it rear its head at certain times and not others? Why is it that when you get one group of smart people together the result is genius, and with another group of equally smart people the result is groupthink?

That question has no simple answer, but psychologists suspect a lot hinges on a group's willingness to entertain dissenting views. Groups that tolerate dissent generate more ideas, and more good ideas, than groups that don't, studies have found. This holds true *even if those dissenting views turn out to be completely wrong*. The mere presence of dissent—even if wrongheaded—improves creative performance. How we talk matters at least as much as what we're talking about. Conflict isn't only acceptable in a place of genius. It is indispensable.

How did this truth manifest itself during the Scottish Enlightenment? First of all, explains Tom, people didn't talk about just anything. A subject had to be deemed worthy of conversation, "conversable," as Hume put it. Once that happened, anything was possible.

"Even a good bout of flyting."

"Fighting?"

"No, flyting."

"Never heard of it."

Flyting (pronounced "flighting") is, Tom informs me, "ritual humiliation of your opponent by verbal violence."

I shudder. "It sounds vicious."

"Oh, it is." The twinkle in Tom's eyes intensifies. The Scots are great debaters, Tom tells me, his national pride bursting through his academic propriety. If you're looking for verbal violence, Scotland is your place. But—and this bit is crucial—after a good, vicious round of ritual humiliation, the opposing sides headed to the local pub for a few pints. No hard feelings.

For a flyting session to be deemed successful, both aspects are necessary: the ritual humiliation *and* the pints of beer afterward. Without the former, the conversation lapses into tepid banalities. Without the latter, you've got a brawl on your hands.

This sort of tolerance infused life in Enlightenment Scotland, a permissiveness that emerged remarkably soon after the last "witch" was hanged. Writers unleashed broadsides against the Church and politicians and other previously bulletproof targets and suffered no more than "minor inconveniences, pinpricks for their irritating behavior," as one historian put it. Nothing was more celebrated than what the poet Robert Burns called "the man o' independent mind."

Tolerance, though, is one of those words that everyone supports but few define. Tom tells me that tolerance, like genius, comes in different flavors. The most common variant is a passive tolerance; certain transgressions of convention are permitted, though not necessarily encouraged. Edinburgh, for instance, tolerated its eccentrics and its geniuses, who conveniently tended to occupy the same body. Adam Smith, for instance, was often seen on the streets "smiling in rapt conversation with invisible companions," as one contemporary put it. In any other city, someone like that would have been locked up. In Edinburgh, he was celebrated.

But Tom Devine describes another Scottish flavor as an "in-your-face tolerance." That seems like a contradiction to me, but I know better by now than to say so, not here in the land of Deacon Brodie. So I wait and, sure enough, Tom elucidates.

"Take Adam Smith and David Hume." The two philosophers were the best of friends but squabbled frequently, especially over certain subjects, such as religion. "Smith couldn't fathom why Hume made that final leap to outright atheism. Hume couldn't fathom why Smith didn't." The point, says Tom, is that these debates, while heated and laden with colorful vitriol, were never personal. "It was the battle of ideas that mattered."

I love the way Tom Devine talks. I love the way he makes even the most pedestrian of sentences sound like poetry, and the most benign suggestions—"Let's get a cup of coffee"—sound as if he were hatching some dangerous conspiracy and he's inviting you to join him. That is, if you're up to it. If you're man enough. If you're Scotsman enough.

I am, Tom, I am. But, alas, Tom has to run. Something about meeting a TV producer. When you are Scotland's national bard, *living* national bard, everybody wants a piece of you. We're walking out together, down the soulless hallway, down the stairs from floor one and a half to floor one, then through the heavy wooden doors and out into the cold and the gray.

"Come here, come here," he says, his perma-twinkle turned up a few notches. "Look over there. Do you see that black van?"

Um, yes, I do. So?

"Cadavers."

The history department, he explains, is joined at the hip, as it were, with the medical school. They used to bring the cadavers for dissection in hearses, and in the middle of the day no less, and this was freaking out the history students, who were keen to dissect dead ideas, not dead bodies. But the bodies kept coming every Friday, like clockwork. It was a real problem. So Tom asked the medical school to convey the corpses in ordinary vans, not hearses. Judging by the gleeful tone in his voice, Tom never tires of telling this story. Scottish stories, like single malts, improve with age. I'm eager to hear more of Tom's stories, but he is already gone, swallowed up by the gray skies and all that history.

As I've learned, form matters. Not only what we say but how, and where, we say it. During different golden ages, social discourse took different forms. In Periclean Athens, it centered on the symposia, with their diluted wine and clever wordplay. In Belle Époque Paris, intellectual life revolved around the drawing-room salon. In Enlightenment Edinburgh, it was flyting and the favored venue for such verbal jousting: the club.

I want to find out more, so the next day I drop by the refreshingly frumpy Edinburgh Museum, where memorabilia from these clubs are proudly displayed. There's a badge for the Six-Foot High Club. Yes, you had to be at least six feet tall to join, no mean feat back then, when most men measured no more than five feet three inches. The author Sir Walter Scott, a giant in more than the literary sense, refereed the club, overseeing gatherings that featured both "witty conversation" and a "16-pound hammer toss." Presumably, these events did not take place at the same time, but you never know.

I spot a nondescript badge for the mysterious Pitt Club. A small placard informs me, "Detailed information about this club is not known," before going on to speculate, "Perhaps because so many clubs had strict rules, this one made a point of having none." The Scots certainly have a contrarian streak, I think. Is that a mark of genius, or merely stubbornness? My inner Janus whispers that it might be both.

Some clubs specialized, such as the Mirror Club (agriculture), the Rankenian Club (philosophy), and the Corchallan Club (literature). The 7:17 Club met once a week at precisely 7:17 p.m., and the Boar Club supposedly met in a pigsty. Some clubs were not as they appeared. The Poker Club, for instance, was named after the poker used in a fireplace, not the card game. Its members agitated for a Scottish militia and, in general, made trouble. The clubs all had one thing in common: no women were allowed. The one exception was the Jezebel Club, whose members were all prostitutes.

My favorite is the Oyster Club, founded by Adam Smith and his two friends the chemist Joseph Black and the geologist James Hutton. The members met on Fridays at 2:00 p.m. and, as the name suggests, inhaled ridiculous amounts of oysters, washing them down with equally ridiculous amounts of claret.

Some clubs held secret initiation rites and "hid their activities from the general gaze, thus generating an aura of exclusivity and mystery," writes historian Stephen Baxter.

Yet more mystery and secrecy. What is with you people and your mystery fetish? What exactly transpired in those clubs and their "learned suppers," as they called them?

Only about forty miles separate Edinburgh and Glasgow, yet they might as well be on different continents. Glasgow considers Edinburgh aloof and elitist. Edinburgh considers Glasgow boisterous and uncouth. The city's uncouthness, its endearing roughness, fascinated no less of a genius than Adam Smith, who spent hours chatting with merchants and seamen at the city's docks, gathering the threads that he'd eventually weave into his masterpiece, *An Inquiry into the Nature and Causes of the Wealth of Nations*.

I'm en route to Glasgow now to meet Smith's successor, Alexander Broadie. For fifteen years, he occupied the chair at Glasgow University once held by Adam Smith. Surely Broadie knows what transpired behind the closed doors of the Oyster Club and its ilk.

As the train lurches forward, something happens to my mind. Unlike most things that happen to my mind, this something is good. The usual whirlpool of inchoate musings and random associations that pass for rational thought settle, not exactly to a mirror-smooth lake, more like the river in *Deliverance*, but for me that represents progress. Improvement, you might say.

That this unexpected clarity should descend upon me while on a train is no coincidence. Something about train travel—the rocking motion and the passing scenery, there for you to admire or ignore—lends itself to creative breakthroughs. A few great minds did their best thinking on a train, including the Scottish physicist Lord Kelvin and J. K. Rowling, who dreamed up Harry Potter while sitting on board a delayed British Rail.

It's not only trains. Something about motion triggers creative thoughts. Charles Darwin's budding theory of evolution gelled while he was riding in the back of a carriage. "I can remember the very spot on the road . . . when to my joy the solution occurred to me," he later wrote. Lewis Carroll recalled, with equal clarity, the moment when, on a rowboat floating in a pond, listening to "the tinkle of the drops that fell from the oars, as they waved so sleepily to and fro," he dreamed up a magical underground world and a girl named Alice who visits it. Mozart always traveled with scraps of paper tucked into the side pocket of his carriage, "for it is on such occasions that my ideas flow best and most abundantly. *Whence* and *how* they come, I know not; nor can I force them."

Alas, no symphonies or magical underworlds materialize in my mind, but I do think of some brilliant questions for Alexander Broadie. Questions, not answers, but as I learned in Athens, the road to genius is paved with good interrogatives. I want to know how exactly the Scottish penchant for practical genius extended to the clubroom and the tavern. How did these places encourage big ideas, and not (only) drunken rambling?

In our e-mail exchange, Broadie struck me as a person out of time, a throwback to eighteenth-century Scotland, when the country was known as the Republic of Letters.

Dear Eric,

I'll be waiting for you as you emerge from the passenger barrier at the station. Look out for a pale shilpit creature wearing a black jacket, a hat and a shoulder bag. I look forward to our meeting.

Regards,
Alexander

Shilpit? That word befuddled not only me but also my spell-checker, which, in my experience, is not easily rattled. Merriam-Webster came to the rescue, informing me that *shilpit*, an old Scots word, means "pinched and starved in appearance."

As I step off the train, I have no trouble spotting Broadie in the crowd. There he is, as promised, in all his shilpit splendor. He leads me out of the bustling station with the quiet confidence of someone who has bonded with his city, absorbed its essence. As we walk, Broadie explains that while he was originally an "Edinburgh boy," Glasgow and its blue-collar charms have grown on him, and today he wouldn't live anywhere else. "Dynamite wouldn't get me out of this town," he says, and I do not doubt him.

Despite such colorful assertions, Broadie is actually soft-spoken and, I suspect, shy. We stroll through a large public square, past a statue of James Watt, Glasgow's favorite son. A pigeon sits atop his head, and judging by the splotches of white covering the marble, it isn't the first to do so. Poor James Watt, I think. So typically Scottish. No respect.

When Broadie tells me he's chosen an Italian restaurant, I smile and, not for the first time, silently give thanks that Scotland counts among its many discoveries the cuisines of others. We order—I choose a fusilli in olive oil and a Chianti—then dive into the subject at hand. What exactly transpired in these mysterious clubs, and what role did they play in the Scottish Enlightenment?

Broadie doesn't answer my question directly, for that is not the Scottish way. Instead, he says, I need to consider timing. At the dawn of the eighteenth century the Scots suddenly found themselves on the brink of cultural extinction. England had just annexed them. This was demoralizing, but with Scottish politics neutered, intellectuals no longer needed to worry about taking the wrong side, for there were no sides. They were free to wrestle with bigger issues. Sometimes politics can propel a creative movement—as it did in the 1960s—but sometimes nothing is more liberating than a political vacuum.

Gone was the old order and, Broadie tells me as our pastas arrive, "all of a sudden you had to think for yourself." The Scots, though, took that reality and, as usual, twisted it. They thought for themselves *together*, behind the closed doors of the Oyster Club and hundreds more like it.

What made these gatherings special was how they combined the lubricated collegiality of a pub with the intellectual rigor of an academic seminar. Members adhered to a strict drinking protocol. First, the host toasted each guest, then each guest toasted the host, then the guests toasted one another. Do the math and you can see how it quickly adds up to an awful lot of drinking. So it begs the uncomfortable but unavoidable question, were these clubs simply excuses to get well and truly sloshed? Was the Scottish Enlightenment, as some have suggested, really the Scotch Enlightenment?

No, says Broadie. That old accusation—usually leveled by certain troublemakers residing south of Hadrian's Wall—is not only unfair but also untrue.

"Really? How's that?"

"They didn't drink Scotch. They drank claret," he says, as if that made all the difference. Realizing that I find this argument less than convincing, he adds, "Besides, they drank for practical reasons."

Practical drinking? This should be interesting. Do tell.

"The water supply wasn't to be trusted. You'd live longer if you drank claret."

So the Scots, *Homo practicus*, drank boatloads of claret. Merchants drank while conducting business. Judges drank, too, often arriving for their first trial of the day thoroughly soused. At dinner parties, guests were labeled either a two- or three-bottle man, depending on how much wine they were capable of consuming. (Presumably, one-bottle men weren't invited to dinner parties.)

The Scots may have been drunk but they were no fools. Like their heroes, the ancient Greeks, they knew that a little bit of alcohol makes you more creative but a lot makes you fall down. So, like the Greeks, they drank a diluted wine, much weaker than ours today. Besides, Broadie tells me, at these gatherings drinking was merely a detour, albeit a pleasant one, en route to the true destination.

"Which was what?" I ask.

"Mutual cerebral stimulation."

I pause mid-fusilli, intrigued, and more than a little impressed. In a mere three words, Broadie's phrase conveys both erudition and kinkiness. A winning and all-too-rare combination, in my book.

"What exactly did this mutual cerebral stimulation entail?"

"Well, you've got people striking sparks off of each other. One person makes a comment, say a businessman, and then someone from a very different field adds to that, takes it in an entirely different direction."

Pondering this, while simultaneously spearing a stray fusillo, two things come to mind. First, that Broadie and I are not only discussing mutual cerebral stimulation but are *at this very moment* engaging in it. Very meta. The second epiphany is that Edinburgh's golden age—indeed *every* golden age—was interdisciplinary, and all creative breakthroughs the result of what Arthur Koestler calls "mental cross-fertilization between different disciplines." Take James Hutton. Before devoting himself to geology, he studied medicine. His specialty was the circulatory system. He would later apply its principles to a much larger circulatory system: the earth. Again, it's not knowledge or intelligence that makes the genius but, rather, an ability to connect seemingly disparate strands of thought. "Moral philosophers" such as Hume and Smith did this regularly, ranging over a huge swath of intellectual territory: international relations, history, religion, aesthetics, political economy, marriage and the family, ethics—disciplines that, today, hardly talk to one another, and when they do, it's not with their indoor voices.

The geniuses of Edinburgh had no patience for idle banter, Broadie tells me. "We're not talking about conversation as a form of entertainment. We're talking about conversation as the piling up of premises leading to a conclusion. We're talking about conversation that takes an issue forward, conversation as a way of getting somewhere."

"But you don't necessarily know what that destination is, do you?"

"No, you don't. You have to be willing to live with a certain degree of uncertainty. Picasso was asked if he knew what a painting was going to look like when he started it, and he said, 'No, of course not. If I knew, I wouldn't bother doing it.'"

Studies have found that creative people have an especially high tolerance for ambiguity. I suspect this holds true for places of genius as well. Cities such as Athens and Florence and Edinburgh created atmospheres that accepted, and even celebrated, ambiguity.

I am no longer in Glasgow, at least my mind is not. It's back in California, in Dean Simonton's cramped office, with the classical music playing softly in the background, as he tells me about something called blind variation and selective retention. It's a theory of creativity that Simonton has been developing for the past twenty-five years, and it speaks directly to the geniuses of Edinburgh. Creative genius, Simonton believes, involves "superfluity and backtracking." Superfluity is the willingness to pursue hunches that might well turn out to be dead ends. Backtracking is when you return to these supposed dead ends and give them a second look. Geniuses, as we've seen, don't have a higher batting average than the rest of us; if anything, they miss more often, but—and this is key—they are able to recall exactly where they missed and why. Psychologists call these markers "failure indices." They're like mental bookmarks, and geniuses collect them voraciously and methodically.

"Be careful," Broadie says sharply, snapping me back to the present. For a second I think my napkin might be on fire, or worse, but then I realize he is speaking metaphorically. I need to be careful not to confuse the jovial atmosphere of the clubs for docility. "If you had an idea and it was complete rubbish, it would be destroyed. Utterly destroyed," he says, harpooning a strand of linguine as if to underscore his point.

By engaging in this sort of intellectual jousting "we find out not only what others think of our ideas but what we think of them as well," he says. People react to our ideas and we react to their reaction. "They disprove and I improve." Flyting, I realize, is more than a rough sport; it is how the Scots sharpened their ideas.

These intellectual fireworks ignited not only in the tavern and the clubhouse but also, surprisingly, the classroom. As I saw in Florence, formal education and creativity have little to do with each other. If anything, the straitjacket of a curriculum tends to bind the imagination.

Edinburgh was different. The lecture halls were not suffocating but inspiring. Why? What was it about Scottish universities that made them genius factories and not, as I've seen in so many other places, creativity killers?

Perhaps, I wonder aloud, they excelled at imparting knowledge?

Yes, up to a point, says Broadie. But knowledge is not the same as genius and, if anything, impedes it. The geniuses we most admire today were not necessarily the most knowledgeable in their fields. Einstein, for instance, knew less physics than many of his contemporaries. Einstein wasn't a know-it-all. He was a see-it-all. If creative genius is character-ized by the ability to make unexpected and important connections, then clearly breadth, not depth, of knowledge is what matters.

Another way Scottish universities excelled was that the learning flowed in two directions, not only from professor to student but also from student to professor. It was a more formalized and broad-based version of what took place in Verrocchio's workshop. Scottish professors viewed the lecture hall not only as a cash cow (they worked on commission; the more students they attracted to their lectures, the more money they earned) but also as a laboratory. There they test-flew their latest wacky idea. Adam Smith first presented his seminal *Wealth of Nations* as a series of lectures to his students. Their average age? Fourteen.

As we order a couple of espressos—a practical decision, designed to counterbalance all that wine—it dawns on me that these two threads of the Scottish Enlightenment, its dual emphasis on improvement and socia-bility, are connected. All that socializing, all that clubbing—and, yes, all that drinking—had a practical aim: improvement.

I ask Broadie my time-travel question. If he suddenly found himself in the Scotland of 1780, whom would he want to share a glass of claret with? I'm expecting the obvious answer—Adam Smith—but Broadie, in true Scottish fashion, surprises me.

"Adam Ferguson."

Ferguson, arguably the father of sociology, was every bit as brilliant as Smith and Hume. He famously summed up the bittersweet days in which he lived, in which we all live: "Each age hath its sufferings, and its consolations." Ferguson was particularly attuned to the wheels of fate, for he was an ordained minister, a fact which points me in a totally new, and unexpected, direction.

I'm walking along the Royal Mile one day, feeling pleased with my progress, when I spot a church. Called St. Giles, it is impressive with its crown-shaped spire, elegant carvings, intricate stained glass windows, and ceilings that stretch heavenward. It is, though, a church, and in Europe churches are nearly as common as pubs, though if it's elbow room you crave, the church, not the pub, is your best bet. These days, most Europeans have no use for religion.

Usually, neither would someone such as me, hot on the scent of creative genius. In the places I've visited so far, religion had little to do with the flowering of genius. If anything, the religious institutions tended to squelch innovation. This isn't surprising. A basic tension existed. The Church (or mosque or synagogue) was the keeper of tradition; creativity, at least in the Western formulation, represents a break with tradition. It's a recipe for conflict.

Sometimes, the most religion can do is get out of the way. That is what the Catholic Church did, at least partially, during the Renaissance. In Hangzhou, religion was a loose affair, flexible enough to allow for experimentation and "strange doctrines." Before the advent of Islam, the Arab peoples constituted a cultural backwater. With the exception of poetry, they contributed virtually nothing to world civilization, unlike their neighbors—the Egyptians, the Sumerians, the Babylonians, the Persians. Islam changed all that. Shortly after its advent, the Arabs excelled in fields from astronomy to medicine to philosophy. The Muslim golden age stretched from Morocco to Persia and spanned many centuries.

Likewise, the Scottish Presbyterian Church, known as the Kirk, played a major, albeit unintentional role in the Enlightenment. To tell this tale, we need to take a giant step back, to the beginning.

In the beginning, there was the Word. The Word was good, but hardly anyone could read the Word, or *any* word. This was frustrating for all. Being illiterate in the eighteenth century was like having a dial-up connection in the twenty-first. You're awash in a sea of information, but little reaches you, and what does takes a long time to download.

The Scottish Church knew it needed to do something so it launched a major literacy campaign. This succeeded beyond anyone's wildest expectations. Within a century, nearly every parish had a school. Suddenly, Scotland, the poorest nation in Western Europe, boasted the highest literacy rate in the world. People could now read the Word. So far, so good.

What the Church didn't count on, though, was that people could also read other words. This is how new technologies work. Once unleashed, they can't be contained. The Church teaches people to read so they can access the Bible, and next thing you know everyone's reading Milton and Dante. A group of nerdy scientists concoct a computer network so they can share technical data, and next thing you know you're buying underwear online.

The Scots, like the Florentines, fell in love with books but with a significant difference. By now, Gutenberg's printing press was in widespread use. Books were no longer luxury items. Ordinary people could afford them, but these ordinary people didn't read ordinary books. Their taste was considerably more erudite. David Hume's six-volume *History of England*, hardly light reading, was a huge bestseller in Scotland.

How did Scottish Church officials react to this wave of secular reading? They allowed it to crest, and a few ministers jumped in. Not only Adam Ferguson, but also men such as John Home, another minister, who wrote the most popular play of the day. A new kind of genius, simultaneously secular and religious, had blossomed in the hard brown soil of Scotland.

On my final morning in Edinburgh, I go for one last walk along the canal. It's a mostly overcast day or, as the Scots call it, sunny. I know it won't last. The rain is coming, and the wind, and God knows what else. Nothing lasts. That holds true everywhere, but it seems truer, is felt more acutely, here in Scotland. As I walk, pulling my jacket collar up against my face, I am reminded of how, in Athens, this fleeting nature of life stoked genius.

It makes sense. We are at our most creative when confronted with constraints, and time is the ultimate constraint.

The clever Scots, though, devised a work-around for this, too. David Hume, articulating a school of philosophy known as empiricism, famously said that it is a mistake to assume that all men *must* die just because until now all men *have* died. Indeed, when his friend Adam Smith lay on his deathbed, in 1790, he was heard murmuring to those gathered at his side, "I believe we must adjourn this meeting to another place."

So, in an odd way, they did. The Scottish Enlightenment never really ended. It merely relocated. As I said, Scottish ideas reached many distant shores, including the young United States. Nowhere did Scottish ideas flower more magnificently and unexpectedly, though, than on the Indian subcontinent, in a teeming, malarial city that, for a while, lit up the world.

FIVE

GENIUS IS CHAOTIC: CALCUTTA

"THE POSSIBILITY OF COINCIDENCE IS GREATER here than it is elsewhere."

The words loiter in the heavy air, mingling with the sound of clinking glasses, the chortle of laughter coming from a nearby table, and the muted traffic of Sudder Street, before eventually lodging in my brain like an unwanted houseguest. *The possibility—of coincidence—greater here— than elsewhere.* Such nonsense, I think, and if I've learned anything in my travels, it is that one must take such nonsense seriously, for it might just be true.

The speaker of this possibly profound nonsense is a ruddy, cheerful, perpetually broke Irish photographer who goes by T.P. Calcutta is his second home. He keeps coming back, year after year, decade after decade. Calcutta is not an easy city, in any sense of the word, yet that doesn't dissuade T.P. one bit. Coincidence is a precious thing. You take it where you can get it.

We are sitting in the beer garden of the Fairlawn Hotel, itself a product of happenstance. A British officer. An Armenian bride. A city perched on the precipice of a dying empire. All these seemingly random facts converged to manifest the Fairlawn. It's been around since the 1930s, and with the exception of spotty Wi-Fi and temperamental air-conditioning, hasn't changed much since. It is unapologetically postcolonial—or, rather, midcolonial. As far as the Fairlawn is concerned, the Raj never ended. In the lobby—just a few wicker chairs and a table with crumpled newspapers splayed—visitors are greeted by photos of Prince William and Kate, along with other royal bric-a-brac. People don't come here for the nostalgia, though. They come for the beer, and the sylvan garden where it is served. With its cheap plastic tables and pleasantly indifferent waiters, it offers a respite from the madness that lies a few yards away, *out there*.

Like all great places, the Fairlawn is a crossroads, neutral territory where parallel worlds briefly converge: earnest volunteers from Mother Teresa's Home for the Dying, locals decompressing after a long day at the office, relatively well-heeled travelers slumming it, rupee-pinching backpackers on a splurge. Then there are the new arrivals, wide-eyed and tremulous, suffering from the sort of traveler's trauma only India can inflict.

Calcutta, Kipling's "city of dreadful night," is a shock to the system, has always been. That holds true for people visiting India for the first time and for those, such as me, who have made the country a lifelong habit. From a personal and gastrointestinal point of view, these tremors are unfortunate, but for creativity, they are good. Creative breakthroughs almost always require a jolt of some kind, an outside force acting upon our bodies at rest.

Calcutta still manages to jolt T.P. after all these years, he tells me, nursing his Kingfisher and going on about this alleged *possibility of coincidence*. I listen politely but silently wonder if the premonsoon boil that is Calcutta this time of year (the "putrid months," locals call it) is playing tricks with T.P.'s Celtic brain. Isn't coincidence by definition random, and its possibility therefore no more, or less, likely in Calcutta than anywhere else?

When I diplomatically suggest that he might be off his Irish rocker, T.P. responds by showing me a few of his photographs: a dog balancing impossibly atop a stack of tin cans, a simple room where the symbols

of three of India's major religions—Christianity, Islam, and Hinduism—
have miraculously aligned themselves, as if staged by Adam Smith's invisible hand. The photographer's success hinges on his relationship with,
and proximity to, coincidence. As I see in T.P.'s work, these unexpected
juxtapositions, the way the moving parts of time and space momentarily
click into place, imbue a photograph with significance, and with beauty.

The next evening, sitting at the Fairlawn, sipping another Kingfisher,
I ponder the role of coincidence—and its close cousins, randomness and
chaos—and what role they might play not only in photography but in all
creative endeavors. Here I've been searching for a logical, empirical basis
for creative places, a formula of sorts. Might I have overlooked one obvious ingredient: chance?

The English *chance* comes to us, via Old French, from the Latin *cadere*,
which means "to fall," and what is more natural than to fall, like an apple
from a tree, to allow gravity to run its course? Are geniuses simply more
attuned to this truth than the rest of us? Are they, and by extension the
places they inhabit, simply luckier than the rest of us?

It's not as absurd as it sounds. When psychologist Mihaly Csikszentmihalyi asked several hundred highly creative people, including several
Nobel Prize winners, what explained their success, one of the most
frequent answers was that they were lucky. "Being in the right place at
the right time is an almost universal explanation," concludes Csikszentmihalyi. I also recall what Dean Simonton had told me back in California.
Geniuses, he said, are good at "exploiting chance." At the time, this made
about as much sense as T.P.'s possibilities of coincidence, but now I realize
that, as usual, Simonton is onto something.

If any place can illuminate the relationship between chance and genius, it is this "monstrous, bewildering, teeming city," as the great filmmaker Satyajit Ray called his beloved hometown. Calcutta, city of joy, city
of lost causes and second chances, and, for a brief but glorious moment,
city of genius.

I concede that these days the words *genius* and *Calcutta* are not often
uttered in the same breath. If anything, the city is now shorthand for

heartbreaking poverty and inept governance. Third-world misery in a nutshell. Not that long ago, though, it was a very different story.

Between roughly 1840 and 1920, Calcutta was one of the world's great intellectual capitals, the heart of a creative flourishing that spanned the arts, literature, science, and religion. The city gave the world a Nobel Prize winner (Asia's first), an Academy Award winner, a prodigious body of literature neither Eastern nor Western (more books were published in Calcutta than anywhere else in the world, save London), and an entirely new way of conversing (called an *adda*). And that was only the beginning.

The bright lights of Calcutta's golden age included writers such as Bankim Chattopadhyay, a clerk by day and novelist by night, who infused new life into an old culture, and Henry Derozio, who during his "appallingly brief life" not only wrote sublime poetry but also spearheaded an entire intellectual movement called Young Bengal. There was a mystic named Swami Vivekananda, who, in 1893, traveled to Chicago and introduced Americans to a wholly new spiritual tradition; and there was Jagadish Bose, a physicist who advanced the young field of radio technology and, in a remarkably varied career, showed us that the line between living and nonliving matter is not as sharply defined as we thought. There were women, too, such as Rassundari Devi; illiterate until her twenties, she went on to write the first autobiography in the Bengali language and inspire women everywhere.

At the time, people sensed they were living in a special time but didn't have a name for it. Now we do: the Bengal Renaissance. Named after the main ethnic group in Calcutta, the Indian awakening, like its Italian cousin, rose unexpectedly from the embers of catastrophe: not the bubonic plague, but the British. Again. As you recall, Scotland also thrived shortly after the English barged into their country. Everywhere the English go, it seems, they bring nothing but trouble and genius. "Without the West this awakening would not have happened," says Subrata Dasgupta, a Calcutta native and chronicler of his city's glory days. "Without the West there would not have been a Renaissance."

Which is not to say that the Bengal Renaissance was simply a British

export—like the Beatles or warm beer—and that Indians simply swallowed this swill wholesale. The Bengal Renaissance was much more than
that. But as one Calcuttan scholar told me, using appropriately colorful
language, the British "inseminated Indian thought with Western ideas,"
and these ideas then took on a life of their own. Again, a jolt to the system. Only this time it was more than a jolt. It was an earthquake.

The fault lines of that quake run through a small, unremarkable church
called Saint John's. I arrive early. The gate isn't yet open, so I wait, baking in the already fierce sun, until the *chowkidar*, the guard, takes pity on
me and waves me inside. I walk down a narrow brick pathway, across the
manicured grounds, and after about a hundred yards spot a white marble
monument. It honors Job Charnock, a seventeenth-century English sea
captain, and father of Calcutta. The original inseminator. Etched on the
stone is HE WAS A WANDERER, WHO AFTER SOJOURNING FOR A LONG TIME IN A LAND
NOT HIS OWN, RETURNED TO HIS ETERNAL HOME.

Touching, but only partially true. While this may have been a "land
not his own," Charnock made it so. He took an Indian wife (saving her
from the now outlawed practice of suttee, in which Indian widows committed suicide by throwing themselves onto their husband's funeral
pyre) and fathered four children. He wore loose, baggy kurtas, smoked a
hookah, or water pipe, and drank the local libation, a potent moonshine
called arrack. Job Charnock, founder of Calcutta, son of English aristo-
crats, proud servant of the queen, went native.

That might come as a surprise given our image of the British and
their attempts to rule India without interacting with India—witness
the creation of Calcuttan neighborhoods called White Town and Black
Town, and exclusive redoubts such as the Bengal Club where the only
natives allowed were the ones who washed the dishes and served the tea.
And while some, perhaps even most, of the British colonialists agreed
with Lord Macaulay, a senior official in the Raj, who infamously said
that "a single shelf of a good European library was worth the whole native literature of India and Arabia," there were exceptions. Some of the
British recognized something old and wise in what others saw only as

backwardness; and, likewise, more than a few Indians saw wisdom in
these pasty-skinned, uptight people with funny ideas about sex and God.
These exceptional people, Indian and British, together planted the seeds
of the Bengal Renaissance.

The British were not the first, only the latest, to think they could
change India. Before them came the Buddhists and the Mughals, among
others. The history of India is the history of acculturation without assimilation, of responding to a foreign influence by neither rejecting it nor
blindly absorbing it, but, rather, "Indianizing" it. Indians performed this
magic with everything from the Buddha (miraculously transforming him
into an avatar of Lord Vishnu) to McDonald's (the Maharaja Mac contains no beef, in keeping with Hindu custom). The resulting hybrid culture confounds many Westerners, like British economist Joan Robinson,
who famously observed that "whatever you can rightly say about India,
the opposite is also true."

We've already seen how places of genius occupy the center of various cultural currents. Recall the great sailing ships of ancient Athens, or
the traveling merchants of Renaissance Florence. The creative cultures
that emerged from this intermingling were necessarily hybrid, mongrel
cultures. "There is nothing less pure than culture," one Indian academic
tells me, and I realize he's right. I also realize that the term *pure genius* is an
oxymoron. Nothing about genius is pure. The genius borrows and steals
and, yes, adds his own ingredients to the mix, but at no point does purity
enter the picture.

What distinguished Calcutta's mélange is that it was not accidental.
It sprang from "a marriage of folk genius and Western sensibility," as one
historian put it. An arranged marriage, no less, for Calcutta represents the
world's first (and possibly only) case of premeditated genius. "Nowhere
else in the modern world has a new culture emerged from the deliberate
intermingling of two older ones," said Sudhin Datta, a poet who lived at
the tail end of the Bengal Renaissance.

One day, I'm walking—in the hypervigilant state that India demands,
eyes darting about, braced for menace, or coincidence—when I'm struck
with a sharp pang of déjà vu, even though I've never visited Calcutta

before. Oh, no, I think, am I having one of those "India moments," a past-life regression perhaps? It happens here, and more often than you'd think. People go off the rails and never get back on. Then I realize that, no, the reason Calcutta seems so familiar is that it looks an awful lot like London. The British "created a hotter version of home," as one regular at the Fairlawn tells me.

As the capital of the Raj, Calcutta also served as a sort of laboratory, a proving ground for promising but untested ideas. The use of finger-prints in criminal investigations was first tested here, a product, as you recall, of our old friend Francis Galton. Calcutta had a sewage system and gas lamps before Manchester. The city has always had creativity coursing through its veins, even if it was, at first, an induced creativity.

The rains wreak blessed havoc on Calcutta. People welcome the relief from the heat, but it comes at a cost: streets flood, lights flicker, traffic snarls. That's the case today, and that was the case one early June day in 1842. Water pooled in the streets, carriages kicked up mud, splattering passersby. The unpleasant conditions, though, didn't deter a crowd of several hun-dred, mostly Indian, from attending a funeral. Heads bowed, hearts heavy, they walked alongside the casket of David Hare, a Scottish watchmaker turned educator and philanthropist. Emotions were raw. "People wept and sobbed for him like orphans after his death," reported one witness. One speaker praised Hare as a "champion of the cause of modern education, a harbinger of the dawn of the 'Age of Reason' in a country floundering in the filthy swamp of superstitions, a valiant fighter for the cause of liberty, truth and justice . . . the friend of a friendless people."

Like Job Charnock, David Hare died a long way from home. We don't know why he left his native Scotland for the unknown, malarial shores of Calcutta. Back then, one embarked on such a journey knowing it was most likely one-way. Perhaps, like any good Scot, he was seeking adven-ture, or a chance to begin anew through the redemptive power of travel. Whatever the reason, once on Indian soil, Hare never looked back. He studied Bengali culture, but, with his being Scottish, the urge to tinker, to improve, soon took hold.

Hare sold his business, turning his attention from the mechanical working of watches to the workings of the human mind. Hare was the exact opposite of the disinterested colonial overlord. A generous man, he paid the tuition of those who couldn't afford it and took a real interest in his students' well-being, to the point where, as a friend recalled, "their sorrow was his sorrow—their rejoicing was his rejoicing." He established the Hindu College, the first Western-style university in India, thus introducing to the subcontinent the very Scottish notion of better living through education. Indeed, Calcutta's flourishing is a clear example of one golden age begetting another. The genius of Adam Smith and other Scottish greats was transmitted to Calcutta via zealous messengers such as David Hare.

I spend hours, days, sequestered in the dusty archives of the Asiatic Society, excavating the past. The deeper I dig, the more connections I unearth. Both peoples like their libations and are the only two nations in the world to name their national drink after themselves—Scotch for the Scottish and Bangla for Bengal. Both places suffer pangs of insecurity. Calcutta, says the writer Amit Chaudhuri, is "in conflict with itself." That's very Scottish, very Deacon Brodie–esque. Both peoples, too, were marginalized. So how did they manage to produce so much genius?

Again, timing is crucial. David Hare arrived in Calcutta when competing currents swirled around the city. "Hare watched with keen interest these clashes of rival ideologies, and exerted all his might to evolve a synthesis out of it, where East and West could meet, could give and take," says his biographer Peary Mittra.

Hare's superiors supported his efforts, not out of altruistic motives but because they needed an educated, and literate, workforce. Little did they know. Just as Scottish Church officials spread literacy thinking they would get a nation of Bible readers, British colonialists spread literacy in India thinking they would get a city of clerks. Instead, they got a city of poets.

The hotel guard swings open the gate and I step onto Sudder Street. It's no wider than an alley but packs in more life than a small city. I walk past the backpacker hotels, forlorn buildings where you can rent a room for less than the cost of a beer at the Fairlawn; past the Blue Sky Café, which serves Indian, Chinese, Thai, and Italian food (and does all of it surprisingly well); and past the little shops that somehow squeeze a Costco's worth of goods into a space no larger than a studio apartment. I'm taking this all in when a taxi, driving on the wrong side of the road, whizzes by and nearly hits me. Clearly, traffic signs are taken as mere suggestions. A red light means you might want to consider stopping. Or not. Oh, and the one-way streets change directions once a day. (That's a very *interesting* time of day.) As for lanes? *Bffft.* Those are for other, less creative drivers. There is no place on earth more creative than a Calcutta intersection.

Let me be blunt: Calcutta is an ugly city. It is, though, a lovable ugliness. It is the ugliness of the platypus or the armadillo, or a toothless old lady who melts your heart. It is an ugliness, as writer and film critic Chitralekha Basu says, "that draws one in, inscrutably."

This sort of ugliness has its advantages. Just ask the Rolling Stones. In a 2003 interview, guitarist Ron Wood said of fellow band member Keith Richards, "Keith brings the air of raggedness, which we'd be lost without." Nothing sticks to a smooth surface. A certain roughness, and ugliness even, is required in our creative lives.

I enter New Market, a teeming bazaar, and find workers, still sleeping, splayed across the pavement, a clutch of boys playing a pickup game of cricket, chai wallahs heating the morning's tea over open fires, a billboard advertising a cream that promises fairer underarms, smiling children, pigs gorging on a trash pile, baskets of squawking chickens. On the streets of Calcutta, food is sold, cooked, consumed, and evacuated. Life is on public display all the time. People brush their teeth, urinate, and do all the things that, elsewhere in the world, take place behind closed doors.

I realize I've seen this before. The agora of Athens, the lakefront of Hangzhou, the piazzas of Florence, the streets of Old Edinburgh. Life lived so publicly increases the amount and variety of stimulation we're exposed to. Think of a packed commuter train versus the backseat of a limousine. If creativity is about connecting the dots, then the more dots at our disposal, the better. Private spaces hoard dots. Public spaces are awash in them, and they're free for the taking.

Creativity also requires kinetic energy. Calcutta has plenty, even if the energy is mostly circular, an "undying, directionless motion," as one local writer puts it. Nothing much happens in Calcutta, and it doesn't happen at great speed. That's fine. The destination matters less than the velocity. *The great affair is to move.* As we've seen, motion primes creative thinking—witness the walking philosophers of ancient Athens or Mark Twain pacing in his study. They didn't get anywhere physically but traveled far in their minds.

I walk another twenty yards, in heightened alertness, then spot a small statue nestled between a travel agency and a tea stall. The man depicted is bearded, and sagelike, with a garland of marigolds looped around his neck.

Every Renaissance needs a Renaissance man. Florence had Leonardo. Edinburgh had David Hume. Calcutta had Rabindranath Tagore. Poet, essayist, dramatist, activist, Nobel Prize winner, he embodied the full flowering of the Bengal Renaissance. Though he wore so many hats, toward the end of his life he summed up his existence in four short words: "I am a poet." For Tagore, everything else was derivative. This points to an obvious but nonetheless important aspect of people who lead creative lives: they see themselves as people leading creative lives, and they're not afraid to say so. "I am a mathematician," shouted Norbert Wiener in the title of his autobiography. Gertrude Stein went a step further, boldly declaring, "I am a genius!"

Today, Tagore is not so much read in Calcutta as worshipped. His image—always with long, flowing beard and wise, crinkly eyes—is everywhere. His songs blare from speakers at traffic crossings. Bookstores devote entire sections to his work. *You must read Tagore,* people tell me, and they quote Yeats, who famously said that to read one line of Tagore "is to forget all the trouble in the world." There are two types of geniuses: those who help us understand the world and those who help us forget it. Tagore managed to do both.

Tagore's work possessed the timeless quality that distinguishes all genius. There is nothing yesterday about him. One day, I walk into a music store and am shocked. Shocked that a functioning music store still exists somewhere on the planet, and shocked that the world's last music store contains so much Tagore. Entire aisles are devoted to his music. This would be like finding Gershwin occupying prime real estate in US music stores, if we had music stores, that is. If genius is defined by staying power, then Tagore is clearly a genius. As a popular musician tells me one day over coffee, "Tagore is the most modern form of music ever. He is the most modern because even now you go to the toilet and you can sing his song. You get onto a bus and you can sing his song. And people do it."

A golden age is like a supermarket. It offers boatloads of choice. What you do with that choice is up to you. Shopping at a supermarket doesn't guarantee a delicious meal, but it does make one *possible*. By the time Tagore came of age, the foundations of the Bengal Renaissance had already been laid. The supermarket was open for business. He was a regular and creative customer there. Tagore, like many geniuses, eschewed parochialism. He took inspiration where he could get it—Buddhism, classical Sanskrit, English literature, Sufism, and from the Bauls, itinerant singers who wandered from village to village, delighting in the moment. The genius of Tagore was the genius of synthesis.

I want to learn more about Tagore, so I decide to visit his ancestral home, called Jorasanko. I'm pleased to discover that not a lot of squinting is required. The red sandstone compound is a bit worn, but it doesn't look all that different from in Tagore's day.

I step inside, removing my shoes, as instructed—this is holy ground—and am greeted by a smiley woman named Indrani Ghose, keeper of the house of Tagore. She is a large woman, with a smile to match her girth and, on her forehead, a bright red bindi. Her office looks as if it hasn't changed since the nineteenth century either. Old filing cabinets, an underpowered and noisy ceiling fan, chairs with torn rattan, all lit by that particularly pallid brand of fluorescent light found in the offices of Indian bureaucrats and Scottish academics.

Not surprisingly, she is a fan of Tagore's: "I don't know if there are gods or goddesses or not but there was Tagore. He is like a god to me." We sit for a moment in silence. "You want to find the heartbeat of the city, of Tagore, right?"

Yes, I say, exactly.

She assures me I've come to the right place. This is where young Tagore came of age. Growing up, he experienced both intense loneliness and relentless stimulation. The youngest of fifteen children, Tagore was constantly surrounded by chaos and culture, both on the streets and inside his home. The Tagore children roamed the grounds barefoot and unfettered. It was a heady, tumultuous time and, years later, Tagore would write: "Looking back at my childhood I feel the thought that recurred most often was that I was surrounded by mystery." That mystery, and its accompanying chaos, infuriated and inspired him, in more or less equal measure.

Chaos. The word is often used, incorrectly, as a synonym for *anarchy.* "It's chaos in here," we say when confronted with our teenage daughter's room, or our emotional lives. Chaos, we believe, is bad and must be avoided at all costs.

What if we are wrong? What if chaos is not toxic? What if it is actually the stuff of creative breakthroughs?

At first, I concede, it doesn't make sense. Aren't creative people constantly searching for ways to contain chaos, to "find a form that accommodates the mess," as Samuel Beckett said? Yes, they are, but they also periodically crave chaos, and if it doesn't present itself naturally, they produce it. Beethoven's notoriously messy desk. Einstein's messy love life. Self-induced chaos, I call it. Creative people know that randomness is too important to be left to chance.

This thirst for chaos, as well as order, is deep-seated, and evidence suggests it has a neurological basis. A number of years ago, neurologist Walter Freeman conducted a fascinating experiment into how the brain reacts when confronted with new odors. He attached electrodes to the brains of rabbits, then exposed them to a variety of odors, some familiar, others not. When confronted with a new odor, one that did not correspond to any other odor in their "databases," the rabbit's brain entered what Freeman calls an "I don't know state." This "chaotic well" enables the brain "to avoid all of its previously learned activities and to produce a new one."

Freeman concludes that our brains need chaotic states to process new information—in this case, new odors. "Without chaotic behavior the neural system cannot add a new odor to its repertoire of learned odors," he writes.

Freeman's conclusions are incredibly profound. Far from being an impediment to creativity, he says, chaos is an essential ingredient. Our brains not only make order out of chaos, they also make chaos out of order. The creative person doesn't view chaos as an abyss but, rather, as a mother lode of information. True, it's information that doesn't make sense to us, yet, but eventually it might, so best to pay attention.

The creative person collaborates with chaos, but collaboration is not the same as capitulation. Perennial chaos is hardly conducive to creativity any more than perfect order is, "yet somewhere between the two, there is a magical meeting of overview and surprise, which creativity builds upon. Within it, exists all possibilities," notes Belgian chemist and Nobel laureate Ilya Prigogine. Creative people are forever dancing in this space, on the edge of chaos.

Recent research illustrates just what a powerful dance this is. In one experiment, subjects were given shapes and forms—lines, circles, triangles, rings, hooks, etc.—from which they had to create objects with recognizable functions, a piece of furniture, for instance, or a utensil or toy. The products were then evaluated by judges for their creativity. Participants were given a choice. They could either select the materials and category in which they created or let them be randomly selected for them.

The results were as clear as they were unexpected. The less choice people had—the more random both the objects they had to work with and the type of products they could create—the more creative the outcome. That result might surprise you since we live in a culture that worships choice (or at least the illusion of choice), but randomness is the more potent elixir for creativity. Why? Constraints, again, explains Dean Simonton. "By beginning with the totally unexpected, the participants in these experiments were forced to stretch their creativity to the highest degree," he concludes. (There are limits. Too much random stimulation produces anxiety, not genius.)

We thrive in "chaotic," stimulating environments. This is true physiologically as well as psychologically. Rats raised in stimulus-rich environments develop more cortical neurons, the brain cells that enable thought, perception, and voluntary movement. Their brains weigh more and contain higher levels of important chemical compounds compared to rats deprived of stimulation. Our bodies, and our minds, crave not only stimuli but complex, varied stimuli.

A number of years ago, prominent cardiologist Ary Goldberger discovered something unexpected about the human heart: a healthy heartbeat is not regular and rhythmic but chaotic and irregular. Goldberger showed empirically that extreme regularity, not irregularity, predicts imminent cardiac arrest. Another example is to be found in epilepsy patients. Epileptic seizures were once thought to be the result of chaotic brain activity, but the opposite is true. "In seizures, the EEG becomes regular and periodic, and it is the normal EEG that is irregular," notes medical professor Alan Garfinkel of UCLA.

A city such as Calcutta supplied this sort of randomness in spades and still does. No two street corners are exactly alike, no two days either. When a young musician named Arka tells me what he loves about Calcutta is how "the chaos and madness has its own rhythm," he is uttering not only a poetic truth but a scientific one as well. A chaotic system has boundaries, and its own sort of order. It is not the same as anarchy, which is a complete absence of rules or purpose. The difference between chaos and anarchy is like the difference between a dance troupe and a melee. Chaos is order dancing.

No wonder Calcuttans find chaos inspiring and actively seek it out. They dance lustily with chance, flirt openly with coincidence, and would no doubt agree wholeheartedly with the words of Erik Johan Stagnelius, a nineteenth-century Swedish poet: "Chaos is the Neighbor of God."

The Tagores knew this neighborhood well. Their rambling home resembled a performing-arts center, with dramas and concerts staged regularly. "We wrote, we sang, we acted, we poured ourselves out on every side," Tagore recalled.

Loneliness pervaded the large compound as well. Tagore's father, a landlord and merchant, traveled often. When he was at home, he remained steadfastly aloof. Geniuses almost always have one parent who withholds love, and sometimes both do. The genius grows up lacking emotional comfort, and so he compensates, in good ways and bad. As Gore Vidal once said, "Hatred of one parent or the other can make an Ivan the Terrible or a Hemingway; the protective love, however, of two devoted parents can absolutely destroy an artist."

I step into a room, the marble floors cool under my bare feet, and find myself in the presence of Tagore's paintings. Some are almost childlike in their simplicity, others complex and disturbing. There are many portraits of veiled women with distant, haunted eyes. Tagore never set out to paint. It happened accidentally, by coincidence, and how this transpired says much about the nature of creativity.

It began, as all things did, with his poems. They were not nearly as spontaneous as they seem. A lot of sweat went into each stanza. A compulsive revisionist, he would cross out words and lines, entire pages. As he searched for just the right words, he'd turn these markings into doodles, some quite elaborate.

One day, he showed these doodles to his friend Victoria de Campo, who glanced at them and said, "Why don't you paint?"

So he did. At the age of sixty-seven, with no formal training in art, he painted. And painted. Over the next thirteen years, Tagore produced some three thousand paintings.

That story reminds me of the jazz drummer described by Oliver Sacks in his book *The Man Who Mistook His Wife for a Hat*. The drummer suffered from Tourette's syndrome and experienced sudden, uncontrollable twitches, creating unintentional, and unexpected, sounds in his drumming. Sometimes when a "mistake" occurred, he'd use it as a seed for an improvisation that wouldn't otherwise have occurred to him. Someone listening to the drummer wouldn't hear a mistake but a riff.

The drummer, like Tagore with his doodles, surprised himself, provided his own jolt. From a chaos-theory perspective, the stray sound represented a random occurrence, but one that the drummer ingeniously transformed into a "bifurcation point." Think of a rushing river, where the water strikes a boulder, then splits into two streams. The boulder is the bifurcation point; that is, a junction where a turbulent, chaotic system splits into new orders. Bifurcation points look like obstacles but are actually opportunities since they enable us to "switch tracks." All geniuses possess this capacity to transform a random event—and, yes, even a mistake—into a chance to veer into an entirely new and unexpected direction. It takes cognitive flexibility, a psychologist would say. I'd use another word to describe the drummer, and others like him: *courageous*.

In the adjoining room, I spot a black-and-white photograph of Tagore, with his feral gray hair and beard, standing shoulder to shoulder with an equally hirsute man. Tagore is staring intensely straight ahead. The second man looks more at ease and appears to be suppressing a smirk. It's Albert Einstein.

These two intellectual giants met several times, first in Berlin in 1926 and later in New York. What a strange pair they made. Tagore, "the poet with the head of a thinker," and Einstein, "the thinker with the head of a poet," as Dimitri Marianoff, a relative of Einstein's, said. An awful lot of gray matter was in that room, "as though two planets were engaged in a chat," Marianoff recalled.

They were like planets in separate orbits, since these two geniuses didn't see eye to eye. Their meetings, quipped the philosopher Isaiah Berlin, amounted to "a complete nonmeeting of minds."

In a discussion about the nature of reality, Tagore expressed his belief in a "relative world," one that does not exist without our conscious awareness of it.

Einstein retorted: "If there were no human beings anymore, the Apollo Belvedere no longer would be beautiful?"

"No. This world is a human world."

"I agree with regard to this conception of beauty, but not with regard to truth."

"Why not?" parried Tagore. "Truth is realized through men."

After a long pause, Einstein, the hard-nosed scientist, said in a barely audible whisper, "I cannot prove my conception is right, but that is my religion."

Should we be surprised that they didn't see eye to eye? I don't think so. Recall how Michelangelo and Leonardo sniped at each other like petulant teenagers. Contrary to the hoary cliché, great minds do not think alike. If they did, civilization would never progress.

The fact that Tagore met Einstein while traveling overseas comes as no surprise. Tagore was a restless soul, and once said the reason he traveled so much was in order to "see properly." Yet time and again he returned to Calcutta.

This makes sense. Creative people thrive on ambiguity, and you don't get any more ambiguous than a city such as Calcutta in a country such as India. Tagore didn't dodge this ambiguity. He embraced it. He delighted in the contradictory and the unexpected and most of all, notes the writer Amit Chaudhuri, was "mesmerized by coincidence."

I read that, and T.P.'s "possibility of coincidence" springs to mind. What exactly did he mean? And what does coincidence have to do with genius?

Try this experiment. Spill some water onto a highly polished tray and watch how it beads into complex, often beautiful forms. This happens because a variety of forces, including gravity and surface tension, often working at odds with one another, act upon the water. (Gravity wants to spread the water across the tray in a thin film, while surface tension wants to consolidate the water into compact globules.) Repeat the experiment and you'll get a different result each time. That's not because the process is random—it is not—but because it's extremely difficult to discern the subtle variations in play. "Tiny accidents of history—infinitesimal dust motes, and invisible irregularities in the surface of the tray—get magnified by the positive feedback into major differences in the outcome," explains M. Mitchell Waldrop in his book *Complexity*.

The tray of water is an example of a complex, not complicated, phenomenon. I realize most dictionaries define these two words synonymously. They are, in fact, very different. Complicated things can be explained by examining their individual parts. Complex ones cannot. They

are always greater than the sum of their parts. This dynamic has nothing
to do with the number of parts or, say, the cost of the object. A jet engine
is complicated. Mayonnaise is complex. You can easily replace a part in
a jet engine and not alter its fundamental nature. It's still a jet engine,
though possibly inoperable. With mayonnaise, if you change one ingredient, you run the risk of altering the essence of its mayonnaise-ness. What
matters is not the components alone but how they interact with one another. (Speaking of interactions, people tend to describe themselves as
complex and their spouse as complicated.)

Complex systems are more likely to produce what scientists call an
emergent phenomenon. A simple example of emergence is wetness.
What does it mean, from a molecular point of view, to say that something is wet? You can examine individual molecules of water yet not detect anything resembling wetness. Only when enough molecules coalesce
does the quality we call wetness emerge. An emergent phenomenon represents a new kind of order created from an old system.

Genius clusters, such as that of Calcutta, are emergent phenomenon,
which is why they are so difficult to predict. British and Indian cultures
collided, but they did so in complex (not complicated) ways. Alter one
variable and you no longer have a golden age.

As we saw in China, creativity is inextricably tied to a culture's ancient
creation myths. The West's notion of creation ex nihilo, "from nothing,"
is only one way of thinking about creativity. There is also an Indian way,
and I suspect this, too, explains the creative flourishing.

In 1971, Ralph Hallman, a professor of philosophy at Pasadena City
College, wrote an obscure academic paper called "Toward a Hindu Theory of Creativity." Hallman concedes right off the bat that such a theory
requires a good deal of guesswork. Nowhere in the Hindu texts is the creative act described explicitly. But consistent threads and themes are found
in this ancient literature, and Hallman pieces it together for us.

The Hindu cosmology in some ways resembles the Chinese one. As
you recall, the Chinese adhere to a cyclical conception of time and history.
There is nothing to invent, only old truths to rediscover and combine in

imaginative ways. "Since man cannot create out of nothing, he can only bring existing materials into new relationships," says Hallman, noting how this contrasts with the Western view, with its emphasis on novelty.

So ingrained is our fixation on novelty that we can hardly imagine a concept of creativity where it doesn't feature prominently. If the creative person isn't actually creating something new, what is she doing? The answer, says Hallman, lies in "substituting *intensity* for *originality*." For Hindus, the genius is like a lightbulb illuminating a room. The room has always been there and always will. The genius does not create or even discover the room. She illuminates it. This is not insignificant. Without that illumination, we remain ignorant of the room's existence, and of the wonders that lie inside.

Different faiths emphasize different senses as pathways to the divine. For Hindus, it is vision. When a Hindu goes to a temple, he doesn't go to "worship" but for *darsan*, to see the image of a deity. Seeing isn't part of worship, it *is* worship. Seeing, when done properly, is an act not only of devotion but of creation. In the Judeo-Christian tradition, Yahweh speaks and the world is created. In Hindu cosmology, Brahma sees that the world is already there. Likewise, the creative person sees what others do not. "He has a capacity for noting things, for allowing them to fill his full field of vision," says Hallman. It is vision as a form of knowledge.

This elevation of vision, above all the other senses, explains a lot. When I look at, say, an Indian bookstore, I see only chaos, with everything from Tagore to Grisham stacked floor to ceiling. The clerk, though, *sees* a hidden order, and when, one day, I request a particular title (a historical novel called *Those Days*), he expertly retrieves it in seconds.

I realize all of Calcutta, then and now, is like this. Hidden order is everywhere—the way the chai wallah prepares each cup of tea in precisely the same manner, the way the rickshaw wallah expertly weaves through traffic. John Chadwick, who helped decipher the ancient Linear B code, once said that it is "the power of seeing order in apparent confusion that has marked the work of all great men." So, too, does it mark the work of all great places, for in these places good ideas are easier to see. They pop.

Looking at creativity this way changes everything. It's no longer about knowing but about seeing. Steve Jobs was no Hindu and may or may not have been a genius, but he clearly recognized the importance of vision. "When you ask creative people how they did something, they feel a little guilty," he said in a rare moment of humility, "because they didn't really do it, they just *saw* something. It seemed obvious to them after a while."

The college that David Hare founded all those years ago (now called Presidency University) has, like so much of this city, seen better days. Everywhere the paint is peeling and chipped. The words *faded* and *decaying* spring to mind. If I try, though, I can picture life back in the day: the crush of students, the sense of infinite possibilities, that feeling that you were, if not creating a new world, certainly re-creating one.

I stroll among the stolid red-sandstone buildings, with their significant archways and important columns. I spot the requisite painting of Tagore in fulsome white beard and black robes, along with busts of revered professors from the golden days. All very interesting, but not whom I have come to see.

Finally, I spot a small sign that directs me toward the physics department. On the wall, someone has scrawled a piece of highbrow graffiti: "Space and time would have evolved in a better way without us." It strikes me as a very Bengali thing to say: cerebral, in an inscrutable way, and mildly subversive.

The large office I step into now requires no squinting. It hasn't changed at all since the nineteenth century. Inside, I find an elegant silver samovar, a blackboard, a wooden "grievance box," giant steel filing cabinets, an old Parisian clock, a photo of Einstein, and in one corner a jumble of rusting laboratory equipment.

The office once belonged to Jagadish Bose. He was the Bengal Renaissance's scientist extraordinaire, the first Indian to break into the until-then closed club that was Western science. Bose invented one of the first semiconductors, for which he reluctantly accepted India's first patent. (For years, Bose had resisted, arguing that scientific breakthroughs belonged to the world.) He also conducted experiments involving radio waves and, according to some accounts, invented the radio itself years before Marconi.

Bose had much in common with his friend Rabindranath Tagore. Like Tagore, he borrowed heavily from the West but was by no means simply a product of the West. His scientific approach, like Tagore's poetry, was also deeply informed by his Indian worldview. For Bose, poet and scientist share a common goal: "to find a unity in the bewildering diversity." Bose and Tagore were monists. That is, they believed that the universe, though it may appear incredibly diverse, is one thing, and nothing can exist outside of that thing.

Bose's career trajectory was buffeted by personal tragedy or, in the language of chaos theory, bifurcation points. Forks in the road. He was enrolled in medical school in London, en route to what would most likely have been a successful but unremarkable career as a physician, when he contracted a mysterious illness. His condition was exacerbated by the odors present in the dissecting room. It was unbearable. Reluctantly, Bose dropped out of medical school. He then took the short train ride to Cambridge, where he studied physics, chemistry, and biology. Much to his delight, he discovered that he had stumbled across his true calling: pure scientific research.

After completing his studies, Bose returned to India in 1885 and, over the objections of a few British officials, was appointed professor of physics at Hindu College. It was the most prestigious university in India but, still, by Western standards, rough and underequipped. Bose was forced to improvise and act as "technician, instrument maker, experimentalist all rolled into one," writes Subrata Dasgupta.

Bose's big break came in August of 1900, when he traveled to the International Physics Conference in Paris to deliver a paper. Though he didn't know it at the time, this paper would alter the course of his career. He was nervous as he took the podium. Back in Calcutta, he had no colleagues with whom to discuss his unconventional findings, which he was now about to share with the world's most renowned physicists.

Bose clenched his jaw, swallowed hard, and delivered his paper. He explained how, when conducting experiments into radio waves, his instruments experienced a sort of "fatigue" remarkably similar to that experienced by human muscle. After a period of "rest," his instruments regained their old sensitivity, leading Bose to the remarkable conclusion that inert matter is, in a way, alive. "It is difficult to draw a line and say, 'Here the physical phenomenon ends and the physiological begins,' or 'That is a phenomenon of dead matter and this is a vital phenomenon peculiar to the living,'" he told his colleagues.

His paper was greeted with the stunned silence and incredulity that is always the fate of radically new ideas. Bose was constantly bumping up against obstacles. First, those erected by British racism and later the more formidable barrier: scientific parochialism. As a physicist conducting experiments on plant life (his latest interest), he was stepping on other specialists' turf, with predictable reactions: *What does a physicist know about botany?* Yet it was precisely his outsider status, and perspective, that enabled Bose to conduct what Darwin called "fools' experiments." Who else would think to administer a dose of chloroform to a hunk of platinum, as Bose did in one of his experiments?

Bose colored outside the lines. It came naturally to him. If you believe in monism—unity in diversity—then boundaries don't mean much to you. Fences are an illusion. Bose watched the increasing specialization of science with alarm, worried that the discipline was "losing sight of the fundamental fact that there can be one truth, one science which includes all branches of knowledge," he wrote. One of his books opened with an epigraph from the Rig Veda, a Hindu holy text: "The real is one; wise men call it variously."

In Indian science, the divine is never far away. "An equation for me has no meaning unless it represents a thought of God," the great Indian mathematician Srinivasa Ramanujan said. Bose, too, openly acknowledged an "unconscious theological bias" in his work, something I can't imagine many Western scientists doing. Yet, Bose explained, when one approaches the world with this attitude, discoveries such as his didn't seem so unbelievable, "for every step of science has been made by the inclusion of what seemed contradictory or capricious in a new and harmonious simplicity."

I read that, and Brady's words come rushing back like a monsoon cloud burst. "There is this chaotic mess of seemingly unconnected data out there, and then someone says, 'Wait, here is how it all fits together.' And we like that." All genius makes the world a bit simpler. Dots are connected. Relationships uncovered. Toward the end of his career, Bose wrote that he took great pleasure in connecting "many phenomena which at first sight do not seem to have anything in common." Not only does that sum up Bose's work, it is also a pretty good definition of creative genius.

Would Bose have made these discoveries without the presence of the West? Clearly, the answer is no. He would have lived out his days in his village, never attending school in Calcutta, for without the British there would be no school, no Calcutta. Yet he probably wouldn't have made his discoveries had he been born in London and steeped in English culture. Bose was, in the words of Subrata Dasgupta, "another extraordinary example of the cross-cultural mind that characterized the Bengal Renaissance." The "Indo-Western mind," as he calls it, displays an extraordinary ability to "move between two worlds."

I would argue, though, that the genius of the Indo-Western mind lies not in the Indian or the Western lobes but in the spaces between. What emerged in Calcutta in the late nineteenth century was an interstitial genius. The genius of the hyphen. Sunreta Gupta, novelist and professor of theoretical epidemiology, puts it this way: "Calcutta taught me that the best state to be poised in is in between two cultures and their productive discourse."

Toward the end of his career, Bose established a research institute that bears his name. It's still around today, and one day, in the midst of a ferocious monsoon downpour, I visit it. I step inside the main lecture hall and gaze at the domed ceiling and religious iconography. I feel as if I have entered not a research institute but a temple. This is precisely the reaction that Bose intended. In inaugurating the institute, he honored the role of science, but added, "There are other truths which will remain beyond even the supersensitive methods known to science. For these we require faith, tested not in a few years but by an entire life."

Bose's career was, appropriately, nonlinear. He suffered many setbacks, taking them in stride, for he had come to realize "that some defeat may be greater than victory." Toward the end of his career, he became focused—obsessed, some might say—on his hypothesis that plants possess a "latent consciousness." He could never prove this and died "a lapsed scientist and half-forgotten mystic," claims the scholar Ashis Nandy.

That strikes me as unduly harsh. I prefer to remember Bose by this entry from the *Encyclopaedia Britannica*, written shortly after his death. Bose's work, it said, "was so much in advance of his time that precise evaluation is not possible."

Bose's career was the product of many things, but especially coincidence. He wasn't looking for the "Boseian thesis," as his work into the responsiveness of nonliving matter is now known. He stumbled across it while conducting experiments in an entirely different subject, radio waves. His instruments were acting odd and he could have overlooked this anomaly, written it off as faulty equipment, but he didn't. He investigated.

Fast-forward thirty years to the summer of 1928 and a laboratory in London. A young microbiologist named Alexander Fleming is growing staphylococci bacteria in petri dishes, part of research into influenza he was conducting at Saint Mary's Hospital. One day, he notices something unusual: a clear area where there shouldn't be one.

Many biologists, perhaps most, would have thought nothing of it. But Fleming was curious. He discovered that a bit of mold had fallen into the dish when it was briefly left uncovered. The mold, belonging to the genus *Penicillium*, had killed the bacteria, thus the clear area in the petri dish. Fleming named this antibacterial agent penicillin. The world's first antibiotic was born.

Later, Fleming reflected on the odds of making such a discovery: "There are thousands of different molds and there are thousands of different bacteria, and that chance put that mold in the right spot at the right time was like winning the Irish sweepstakes."

Perhaps, but Fleming had a few things going for him. Having grown up on a Scottish hill farm, he was reflexively thrifty, a hoarder. He wouldn't discard anything until he was sure he had wrung every bit of usefulness from it. So he picks up a dish of staphylococci, which he has been hoarding for days, and sees something unusual. He recognized the importance of this anomaly for, as Louis Pasteur famously said, "Chance favors the prepared mind."

Over the centuries, scores of such accidental discoveries have occurred, including Archimedes's principle, Newton's law of universal gravitation, dynamite, the Dead Sea Scrolls, and Teflon. We have a word for this kind of unexpected goodness: *serendipity*.

Serendipity is an invented word, more than most. It was coined by the British writer and politician Horace Walpole. Writing to a friend in 1754, Walpole conveyed how thrilled he was to have discovered an old book with the Capello coat of arms, which was just what he needed to adorn the frame of a cherished painting. Walpole attributes his good fortune to his uncanny ability to find "everything I wanted *à point nommé* [at the right place at the right time] when I dip for it."

Continuing his letter, he mentions how he's just read a remarkable book called *The Three Princes of Serendip*. (Serendip is an ancient name for the island of Sri Lanka.) The princes "were always making discoveries, by accidents and sagacity, of things which they were not in quest of," wrote Walpole.

The key word—and one that is often overlooked—is *sagacity*. Yes, serendipitous discoveries are stumbled upon, but not by just anyone. Alexander Fleming had been studying microbiology for years when he noticed something amiss in that petri dish. Alfred Noble had long been experimenting with different forms of the highly volatile chemical nitroglycerin when he discovered a way to stabilize it, in what is now known as dynamite. Muhammed edh-Dhib, a young bedouin shepherd, was no archaeologist, but he knew something "wasn't right" when, in 1946, he tossed a stone into a cave near Jerusalem and heard a strange sound. He had stumbled across the Dead Sea Scrolls. *Chance favors the prepared mind*.

The observant mind, too, for that is essential to a serendipitous discovery. Some fifty years earlier, notes the *Encyclopedia of Creativity*, another scientist also spotted an unexplained patch of dead bacteria cells in a petri dish but didn't consider it worth pursuing. Doing so would have taken him off track. The scientist skilled at exploiting chance is willing to be derailed. She is more sensitive to small variations in her environment, and especially to anomalies. Taking note of, *noticing*, what others explain away is crucial to exploiting chance.

Serendipity also demands a certain restlessness. When the Princes of Serendip stumbled upon their happy accidents, they were not reclining in a La-Z-Boy. They were on the move, interacting with a varied swath of their environment. It's known as the Kettering principle. Charles Kettering, a renowned automotive engineer, urged his employees to keep moving, for "I have never heard of anyone stumbling on something sitting down."

A Spanish Gypsy proverb expresses the same idea this way: "The dog that trots about finds a bone." Sure, it's possible to move too quickly and miss important clues that whiz by—the dog that gallops finds no bone either—but, in general, velocity is creativity's friend.

Calcutta may once have shone bright, but do any embers still burn? One day, I meet a local journalist and writer, Anisha Bhaduri, who I hope can help answer that question. She suggests we meet near her office at the *Calcutta Statesman*.

We're at a coffee shop inside one of the god-awful malls that Indians mistake for progress. Anisha is young with bright eyes and a quick wit. She's telling me about her book collection, some two thousand titles (modest by Calcuttan standards, she assures me), and how as a girl she was weaned on a steady diet of Tagore, and how she's just completed a novel herself. Though I know she's saying all this, I'm having trouble focusing on her words, owing to a loud banging noise from nearby. It's driving me nuts. It doesn't seem to bother Anisha, though.

"Don't you hear that noise?" I ask. "When is it going to stop?"

"It's not going to stop," she says with quiet certainty.

"Shouldn't we say something, *do* something?"

"There's nothing we can do." Her voice betrays not frustration but quiet resignation.

She possesses, I realize, the natural Calcuttan ability to block out anything that is either annoying or out of her control, which, now that I think about it, includes most things in Calcutta. Her ears register the audio just as mine but she does not hear it.

William James once said that the essence of genius "is to know what to overlook." Bengalis are expert overlookers. One day I was walking along the banks of the Hooghly River when I spotted a group of men bathing in the filthy water. Later, I asked my friend Bomti, how could they bathe in such dirty water? "They don't see the dirt," he said. It's not, he explained, that they see the dirt and decide to ignore it; they actually don't see it. I have not yet developed this skill, this art of nonseeing and nonhearing. I am, in fact, so distracted, *infuriated*, now by the incessant banging that I nearly forget what I want to ask Anisha. Oh, yes, I wonder if, like Florence and Athens, Calcutta also suffers from a golden-age hangover. Does any of the old creative fire still smolder?

Yes, she says, it does. There's still a thriving literary scene—witness the many bookstores. Packed along College Street, as far as the eye can see, they are typically no larger than an SUV but still manage to stock an impressive number of titles. And this is one of the few places in the world, along with Paris and certain precincts of Brooklyn, where you can declare yourself a "public intellectual" and not get laughed out of town.

All true, she assures me, but Calcutta these days is mainly "functionally creative."

"'Functionally creative'? What do you mean?"

"Look"—her voice rises above the noise—"nothing in this city works—*nothing*. No two days are the same. What worked yesterday may not work today. So you learn to improvise."

This is what psychologists call small-*c* creativity. It's the sort of quotidian creativity that we all possess in varying degrees. Small-*c* creativity might mean jury-rigging a finicky lawn mower rather than buying a new one, or rearranging your living room furniture rather than building an extension.

Small-*c* creativity is important. Not only does it help us get through the day, it also limber us up for big-*C* creativity, in much the same way that bodybuilders progress to heavier and heavier weights. Creativity is like a muscle, one that Calcuttans are, out of necessity, constantly exercising. To be clear, I'm not suggesting that rearranging your furniture is an accomplishment on a par with Einstein's general theory of relativity, but it does get the creative juices flowing, and who knows where that might lead.

There are no straight lines in Calcutta. Everything is circuitous, even the conversation. The Bengalis, word lovers that they are, have invented one for this sort of nonlinear conversation. It's called an *adda*, and it played an important role in shaping the Bengal Renaissance.

What is an *adda* exactly? It's something like the Greek symposium, only without the watered-down wine and flute girls, or anything resembling an agenda. "An agenda would absolutely kill an *adda*," one person tells me, clearly horrified at the prospect. That's why professional comedians and compulsive philanthropists are among those barred from an *adda*, for "if it cannot be enjoyable for its own sake then its existence becomes meaningless," observes the writer Buddhadeva Bose.

An *adda* is a conversation with no point, but it is not—and this is a key distinction—a pointless conversation. An *adda* might sound like a simple bull session. Bengalis assure me it is more than that and proudly point out that the tradition (some version of it anyway) has survived to this day, despite the decline of Calcutta and the rise of social media.

An *adda* is something like a book club, only instead of talking about a book, participants can talk about anything—the train journey they're about to take, the latest cricket game, politics. Sometimes an *adda* takes place at set times in someone's house, or one might break out spontaneously at a coffee shop or tea stand. The type of location matters less than the feel of the place. It must be just right. "In the wrong place, the people, too, seem all wrong. And the right note is never struck," explains one contemporary *adda*-goer.

We've seen how conversation plays an important role in any creative milieu—the philosophical musing at the symposia of Athens, the give-and-take at the Florentine workshops, the verbal violence of Scottish flyting—but Calcuttans took the art of conversation to a whole new level and sanctified it with not only a name but an entire mythology.

As my days in Calcutta unfold, my fascination with the *adda* grows exponentially. I read everything I can get my hands on. Reading about an *adda*, though, is like perusing a cookbook or sex guide. Helpful, yes, but no substitute for actual experience.

I make a few inquiries and, sure enough, find myself invited to an *adda*. I'm excited. Here's an opportunity to actually travel to that foreign country, the past, rather than read about it.

The *adda* is held at the home of Ruchir Joshi, journalist, novelist, and bon vivant. He's invited a few of his friends, fellow Calcuttans who, like Ruchir, left the city for a while but boomeranged back. Over *aloo tikka* and rum-and-Cokes, the conversation meanders. We veer from the serious (Indian cinema) to the silly (Indian politics). There is no logical progression. To demonstrate a point about Calcuttan geography, Ruchir deploys saltshakers and other household implements.

Despite the lively conversation, I can't help but detect a sadness in the air, a feeling that while the city had a good run, its best days lie behind it.

"I was born on the rump end of a great historical freak-out," says Ruchir. "By the end of the sixties it was over and we didn't know it." With golden ages, there is always a lag, and it might take decades for people to realize that the glory days are over.

"It was a cocktail, an alchemy," adds Swaminathan, a slight man who, from the moment he arrived, has rolled one joint after another. "For one hundred and fifty years, nothing could challenge Calcutta, *nothing*, from Tokyo to Cairo." His voice trails off, mingling with the streams of white smoke swirling about him like a low-pressure system.

Several rum-and-Cokes later, Ruchir declares, "The city is a great teacher, a cruel teacher."

We all nod, though I'm not sure exactly what he means.

"What about feeling good?" I ask. "Where does that enter the picture?"

"Feeling good is not a service we provide in Calcutta," he says sharply. "If you're looking for the easy path, you're in the wrong place."

Places of genius are never easy. The Bengal Renaissance didn't happen because Calcutta was a nice place to live. It happened because it *wasn't* a nice place to live. The creative flourishing was, as it always is, a reaction to a challenge.

A few more rum-and-Cokes and I'm beginning to understand the nonlinear beauty of an *adda*. Topics require no transitions. They arrive unannounced, and sometimes with great ferocity, like the monsoon rains.

"There is a stubbornness to this city," someone says, apropos of nothing, and that rings true. Great places, like great people, tend to be stubborn, though they prefer to call it persistence.

When I ask, point-blank, how I can unlock the mystery of Calcutta, Ruchir replies, "Everyone enters Calcutta through the back door," but fails to mention where I might find that door.

An *adda*, I realize, is a great forum for asking questions. Rarely does it yield definitive answers, but as I learned in Athens, it's the questions that matter.

Finally, Ruchir declares the *adda* over. We've exhausted topics of conversation. Plus, we've run out of rum and Coke.

As we stand to leave, Swaminathan, barely visible through the cloud of smoke now engulfing him, offers me this parting advice: "Walk. Get up early, at dawn, and just start walking. Don't take a lot of money, don't have a destination in mind. Just walk. Don't stop walking. You might have an epiphany."

I promise him I will.

A few days later, walking purposelessly, as Swaminathan had suggested, heeding no GPS, and guided only by the words of Robert Louis Stevenson, "the great affair is to move," I find myself unexpectedly enjoying the nonlinear quality of the exercise and of the city.

As I meander, I meet a Canadian priest named Gaston Roberge. He has lived in Calcutta for the past forty years and counted Mother Teresa and Satyajit Ray among his close friends. He recently compiled a list of seventeen things he loves about Calcutta. "O Kolkata, *mon amour*," he calls it, using the Bengali (and now official) spelling of the city's name. I chuckle at No. 2 ("You can urinate anywhere as per need") and No. 12 ("Traffic lights are to be obeyed only if a policeman is standing nearby"), but No. 16 nails the place. "Kolkatans have created a unique human configuration: individualism combined with gregariousness. Each one does what he / she wants while enjoying being in a group."

In one sentence, he has summed up not only the genius of Calcutta but of all great places. In these places, one is alone together. Sometimes this happens by design. Sometimes by coincidence. The beautiful thing is that it doesn't really matter.

Today, Calcutta's greatness is spoken of in the past tense. Yes, as I said, a few embers continue to glow, but the creative fires that burned so brightly have largely been extinguished. Calcutta's biggest export these days is a persistent and especially melancholic strain of nostalgia. This is the sad fate of most places of genius. They only get one shot at greatness.

Most places, but not all. One city managed to defy the odds and produce a delicious double dip of genius the likes of which the world had not seen before, or since.

SIX

GENIUS IS UNINTENTIONAL: VIENNA PITCH-PERFECT

EVEN BEFORE I COLLECT MY LUGGAGE AT VIENNA'S übermodern, Euro-smooth airport, before I hop on the whisper-quiet train that will magically transport me with nary a bump (lest I spill my espresso) to the heart of this most seamless of cities, I see him. He is in profile, a black silhouette against a stark white background, his considerable nose practically bursting off the serving plates and T-shirts and chocolate bonbons, careening across the centuries and announcing to all who care to listen, and even those who don't, *Genius coming through. Get out of my way.*

A few minutes later, while walking to my hotel, I spot Vienna's other iconic personage, splayed across a poster, bearded and inscrutable, cigar in hand, silently imploring me to talk about it.

Mozart and Freud. The two faces of Viennese genius. Two men, separated by a century, but who shared a love for their adopted city and who, crucially, were shaped by it in ways neither fully understood.

Vienna's golden age was longer, and deeper, than any other. It was, in fact, two distinct golden ages. First, in roughly 1800, a musical flourishing brought us Beethoven, Haydn, Schubert, and the wunderkind Mozart. Then, a century later, a much broader explosion of genius touched every field imaginable—science, psychology, art, literature, architecture, philosophy, and, once again, music. Freud, with his eclectic interests and confessional couch, epitomized this second Viennese golden age; Mozart, with his laserlike focus and discreet sycophancy, the first. That is where we begin, with the music.

Vienna's musical flourishing is the story of how enlightened, if sometimes overzealous, leadership can help spark a golden age. It is the story of helicopter parents and arrogant youth colliding. It is the story of how a stimulating environment can spark genius, and also extinguish it. Most of all, it is the story of artist and audience collaborating to produce a work of genius.

Normally, we don't consider the audience in the genius equation. We assume that they are merely the passive recipients of the gifts that the genius bestows. They are much more than that, though. They are the appreciators of genius, and as art critic Clive Bell said, "The essential characteristic of a highly civilized society is not that it is creative but that it is appreciative." By that measure, Vienna was the most highly civilized society to grace the planet.

Mozart didn't compose for an audience but for *audiences.* One audience was the wealthy patrons—nobles, typically, including the emperor himself. Another audience was the city's finicky music critics. A third was the public at large, middle-class concertgoers or dust-caked street sweepers attending an open-air, and free, performance. Musical Vienna was not a solo performance. It was a symphony, often harmonious, occasionally discordant, never dull. Mozart was no freak of nature. He was part of a milieu, a musical ecosystem so rich and varied it practically guaranteed that, eventually, a genius like him would come along.

Arriving in Vienna in 1781 from sleepy Salzburg, Mozart was ecstatic. He was twenty-five years old and at the top of his game. So was Vienna. His timing could not have been better. A new emperor, Joseph II, was on the throne, and determined not to be outdone by London or Paris in culture, he was willing to spend cash toward that end. He was more than Vienna's musical sugar daddy, though. He appreciated music, *got* music. He played the violin himself, practicing an hour each day. He was, in that sense, much like the poet-emperors of old Hangzhou and Lorenzo the Magnificent. He led by example.

The new emperor and the young composer were, in a way, doppelgängers. Both struggled to escape the shadow of a strong, domineering parent and succeed on his own terms. Joseph could not have been more different from his mother, Maria Theresa, a wholly imperious leader, and so anti-Semitic that on those rare occasions she met with Jews, she had a partition installed so she didn't have to look at them. Joseph, on the other hand, saw himself as a *Volkskaiser*, a people's emperor. "I am not a sacred relic," he snapped at a subject who tried to kiss his hand.

Soon after he ascended to the throne, he fired most of the palace staff and stripped his personal office of all ornamentation. He drove through the streets in an inconspicuous green carriage or traveled by foot— something unheard of for an emperor. He often socialized with those several rungs down the social ladder and took an active interest in the nitty-gritty of Viennese affairs. Sometimes he'd rush to the scene of a fire, help extinguish the flames, then chastise the firefighters for not responding more quickly.

At times he got carried away. He banned the ringing of bells during thunderstorms (a harmless local superstition) and the baking of honey cakes because they supposedly caused indigestion. If they had had Big Gulps in the eighteenth century, he would no doubt have banned them, too. Kaiser Joseph was the Michael Bloomberg of the Austro-Hungarian Empire, a well-meaning but occasionally tone-deaf technocrat determined to improve people's quality of life. One way to do that, he believed, was through music, and he put the full weight of his office (and his wallet) behind Vienna's push to musical prominence.

He didn't have far to push; Vienna already stood on a solid musical foundation, one that dated back to Roman times. By the sixteenth century, some two hundred years before Mozart, Italian opera had arrived, and the Viennese embraced it like a long-lost relative. Music was in the air. Private orchestras popped up like flash mobs, competing with one another for the title *best*. As in Renaissance Florence, the musicians of Vienna were responding to a demand, not only for "good" music but for new and innovative compositions.

Music was not reserved for the elites either. All of Vienna had the bug. Hundreds of organ-grinders, dragging their instruments through the streets, provided the soundtrack for the city. Open-air concerts in city squares were held regularly. Almost everyone played an instrument. In tightly packed apartment buildings, tenants coordinated practice hours so as not to drown one another out.

Music was more than mere entertainment. It provided a means of venting political sentiments. "What cannot be said in our times is sung," wrote one newspaper critic. And it was sung in a variety of languages, for Vienna—like so many places of genius—was an international crossroads. Slavs, Hungarians, Spaniards, Italians, French, Flemish—they all converged on the city. "The number of foreigners in the city is so great that one feels simultaneously foreigner and native citizen," remarked Baron de Montesquieu, betraying hints of both pride and regret. While such diverse cultures might have clashed anywhere else in the world, they did not in Vienna. "It was the peculiar genius of Vienna, the city of music, to resolve all these contrasts harmoniously in something new and unique," writes Viennese author Stefan Zweig, who I turn to again and again for insights into the city. "For the genius of Vienna, a specifically musical genius, has always been that it harmonized all national and linguistic opposites in itself." Like Athens, Vienna didn't reject the foreign nor did it import it unquestioningly. It absorbed and synthesized and, in doing so, created something both familiar and alien. Something new.

The Vienna of today may be spotless, an urban neat freak, but in the late eighteenth century it was a dirty, crowded city of two hundred thousand. Carriages careened through the streets, kicking up grime and dust. Workers sprayed the streets twice a day in a futile attempt at sanitation. Vienna was also noisy, the sound of horse hooves clattering against cobblestone a constant intrusion. Genius blossoms not in the desert but, like the lotus plant, in the muck and the messiness.

Mozart didn't work in a studio or some trendy "incubator space" but at home. I'm curious to see that home, to walk on its aging floors, to breathe its air. Only one problem: my GPS, befuddled by the twisting, nonsensical streets, keeps leading me astray. I find this annoying but oddly gratifying, too, and as I'm dispatched down yet another dead end, I can't help but smile. A small victory for Old Europe. A triumph for analog.

Finally, I find it, down a cobblestoned street that my iPhone swears does not exist. No. 5 Domgasse is a handsome building but not extravagant. No Pitti Palace this. It fits the city. The scale is right, the proportions just so. A Florentine would approve.

I walk up to the third floor, just as Mozart did, a voice in my head tells me. I've been hearing voices for a while now. No, not *those* kinds of voices—the kind that museums plant in your minds, thanks to audio guides. Usually, I despise these gizmos. They're ungainly. Holding one to your ear like a 1980s cell phone feels unnatural, and the narrators always sound vaguely condescending.

Only this voice is not like that at all. It is lightly accented, authoritative yet friendly. I like it, and I wish the Voice could stay in my head forever, gently enlightening me about what I am seeing and where I am heading next.

The apartment is airy and expansive. I have no musical ear, or any other musical body parts, but something about the way the light fills the rooms, the way the sound ricochets off the walls, makes me feel that even someone as harmonically challenged as myself could compose a few notes here.

Mozart only lived here a few years, though, the Voice informs me. He moved often, a dozen times in a decade. Why such restlessness? Sometimes Mozart moved for the usual reasons: he could afford a nicer place or needed more space for his growing family. Other times he had no choice. The neighbors complained about the racket, not necessarily the music but the late-night billiards games and marathon parties. Mozart, like so many geniuses, had his diversions. One of them was billiards. He loved to play and, by the time he moved to this apartment, could afford his own table.

Life at No. 5 Domgasse was hectic, to put it mildly. Children scampered underfoot, dogs barked, pet birds squawked (one, a starling, could sing Mozart's piano concertos), houseguests milled about, friends shouted at one another in the heat of a high-stakes billiards game.

This was the way Mozart liked it and is one reason why he considered Vienna "the best place in the world for my profession." Something about Vienna brought out the best in him. The city tolerated his vices—gambling and scatological humor among them—in a way that sleepy Salzburg did not. More than that, Vienna provided the sort of happy collisions, possibilities of coincidence, that spawn creativity.

Maybe, I think, it's no coincidence that billiards was his preferred game. It reflected life in Vienna. The various composers ricocheted off one another, these collisions altering their speed and trajectory, often in unpredictable ways. The result of all this ricocheting and vectoring lies before my eyes: leatherbound books, a sizable collection that occupies an entire shelf of Mozart's study.

His complete works, the Voice tells me. An impressive oeuvre for someone who died at the absurdly young age of thirty-five. Mozart, like Shen Kuo or Picasso, was incredibly prolific, often completing six sheets of music in a single day. He worked constantly, and with no set hours. Sometimes his wife would find him at the piano at midnight, or at the crack of dawn. He worked to the very end, composing the *Requiem* on his deathbed, singing the alto parts himself.

What others view as distraction, geniuses such as Mozart see as fodder. In a letter to his sister, Mozart reports from Milan, where he's studying in an especially lively conservatory: "Above us is a violinist, below us another one, next to us a singing teacher giving lessons, in the room across from ours there is an oboist. That is amusing to compose by! Gives one lots of ideas." Personally, it would give me lots of headaches. But not Mozart. For geniuses such as him, the environment, pleasant or not, was always a source of inspiration.

In fact, Mozart sometimes composed in the thick of the commotion. He'd be sitting in the middle of a card game or a dinner party, there but not there. To an outsider, he appeared spacey, but he was in fact composing, thinking in music. Only later would he commit the notes to paper. This explains why Mozart's scores are so clean, with none of the cross-outs and markups so common in other composers' works. It's not that Mozart didn't write rough drafts. He did. He wrote them in his mind.

One of Mozart's most important audiences was his wife, Constanze. She was his invisible helper and influenced his music tremendously, and sometimes unintentionally. One of Mozart's string quartets (part of the "Haydn" Quartets, named in honor of his mentor) stands apart from the others. It's less melodic, more piquant. "Much too strongly seasoned," sniffed one critic at the time. Italian musicians, upon receipt of the quartet, returned it to Vienna, due to "printing errors," not realizing those were the notes Mozart intended. Musicologists long puzzled over this incongruous piece, this outlier.

There is a reason, though, why it sounds the way it does. Mozart wrote the piece on the night when Constanze was giving birth to their first child. Not before or after her labor, mind you, but *during*. (Thoughtfully, Mozart first summoned a midwife before sitting down at the piano.) Constanze later confirmed that the quartet contained several passages that reflected her distress, especially the minuet. Mozart, like all creative geniuses, did not distinguish between inspirational moments and ordinary ones. For Mozart, everything was material, even a moment that most of us would consider exactly the least inspiring for a musical composition, or much of anything else for that matter. Here was the ultimate in commotion, an event that would, for me at least, kill any creative impulses I might have, and what did Mozart do? He composed!

What might explain Wolfgang's ability to thrive in such a frenetic environment? Recent research points toward something called the disinhibition hypothesis, developed by the late Colin Martindale. A psychologist at the University of Maine, he spent his career investigating the neuroscience of creativity. His tools were not surveys and word-association tests but fMRI brain scans and EEGs. Martindale zeroed in on "cortical arousal." When we concentrate intensely, neurotransmitters such as norepinephrine and serotonin are released, and this leads to increased heart rate, quickened breathing, and heightened vigilance. Martindale suspected that cortical arousal might be related to creative thinking, but he wasn't sure exactly how.

To find out, he hooked up a group of people—some highly creative and others less so—to EEG machines, then gave them a series of tests that measure creative thinking. The results were surprising: the more creatively inclined subjects showed lower cortical arousal while taking the test than did the noncreative subjects.

The heightened concentration of cortical arousal is helpful when balancing your checkbook or evading a tiger, concluded Martindale, but not when trying to compose an opera or write a novel or come up with the Next Big Internet Thing. For that, we need to enter a state that Martindale called defocused, or diffused, attention. Someone in this state of mind is not scattered, at least not as we normally think of the word. Like Buddhists, they have mastered the art of "detached attachment." They are both focused and unfocused at the same time.

But why, Martindale wondered, are some people able to benefit from this diffused attention while others are not? Creative people are no more capable of controlling their cortical arousal levels than noncreative people. Creative achievements, he concluded, are based not on self-control "but rather on unintentional inspiration."

Unintentional inspiration? What can that mean? Martindale, who passed away in 2008, never said, but I can't help but wonder if this phenomenon explains why creative people are often restless. By changing locations, they are unconsciously attempting to lower their levels of cortical arousal, defocus their attention.

Whatever Mozart did, it clearly worked. With astonishing regularity, he performed musical miracles, writing entire symphonies in the time it takes most of us to do our taxes. He is said to have written the overture to his opera *Don Giovanni* the night before its premiere. But—and this is crucial—he always performed these miracles when someone, a patron usually, demanded it. "Once he was moved to compose, inspiration took over but the inspiration for that inspiration was likely a commission he had just received, a performance that required a new composition, a gift to an appreciative friend," writes Mozart biographer Peter Gay. Mozart didn't work "on spec." Rarely did he write a single note without knowing precisely when and where it would be performed. Like Leonardo da Vinci, Mozart didn't finish everything he started. He left behind some one hundred musical fragments—unfinished compositions that he either lost interest in or, more typically, for which the commissions were withdrawn.

Mozart liked money. He earned a lot but spent even more—on fancy clothes, gourmet food, and, most of all, gambling. Mozart, alas, was a better composer than a billiards player, and he soon found himself some fifteen hundred florins in debt—more than a year's comfortable salary at the time. These debts were a source of great misery—he was always pleading for money—but they also drove him to write more scores. In a way, we have Mozart's gambling habit and spendthrift ways to thank for much of his sublime music. Had he been a better billiards player, or a thriftier shopper, we wouldn't have as much of his music to enjoy.

Mozart was both extrinsically motivated—some outside force demanded something of him—and also intrinsically motivated; once immersed in a work, he was soon lost in the psychological state known as flow; time became inconsequential and he soon forgot about the demands of the world "out there." As we've seen with other geniuses, this combination of intrinsic and extrinsic motivation brought out the best in him.

Which is not to say that Mozart was a perfectly balanced individual. Far from it. Read a few of his letters and you'd be forgiven for thinking that Baudelaire was right when he said, "The beautiful is always strange," for Mozart had one strange, overtly scatological sense of humor. "Oh, my ass burns like fire!" begins one of his milder descriptions. Yet the Hollywood image of Mozart as some sort of emotionally stunted man-child is dead wrong. No man-child could write music as emotionally nuanced as that of Mozart. And as much as we like to think of Mozart as a genius who transcended time and space, that is not the case. He was very much a man of his times. In a way, he was *more* of his times than others, and that is precisely what made him so brilliant. His music, especially his opera scores, required "a keen sensitivity to the society on which its success or failure depended," writes biographer Volkmar Braunbehrens.

Mozart loved Vienna. He loved not only its musicality but also its tolerance and its seemingly bottomless reservoir of possibility. Most of all, I think, he loved its high standards. The Viennese, like the Florentines, were a picky bunch, "and even the most unassuming citizen demanded good music from the wind band just as he demanded good value from the landlord," observes Stefan Zweig in his memoir, adding, "This awareness of being under constant and pitiless observation forced every artist in the city to do his best." The city brought out the best in its musicians because it accepted no less.

Mozart wanted to reach a broad audience, yet not everyone has the same "musical intelligence." What to do? Dumbing down his music was not an option; he was too much the virtuoso for that. So Mozart happened upon a solution that was way ahead of his time. He constructed his symphonies the way Pixar constructs movies: designed to appeal to two distinct audiences at the same time. In the case of Pixar, those audiences are children and their parents. Much of the humor soars over the kids' heads, but the parents get it and appreciate it. Mozart also had two distinct target audiences. He explains his approach in a letter to his father, dated December 28, 1782: "There are passages here and there from which connoisseurs alone can derive satisfaction, but these passages are written in such a way that the less learned cannot fail to be pleased, though without knowing why." Perhaps all works of genius—from *The Magic Flute* to *The Incredibles*—are like that. They operate on several levels simultaneously. Like the Parthenon, their linear appearance is an illusion; all great works contain hidden curves.

It's been said that originality is the art of concealing your sources. There is more than a little truth to that, and Mozart borrowed heavily from his fellow composers, living and dead. He was deeply influenced by the Italian operatic tradition, by his teachers Padre Martini and Joseph Haydn, by the music of Bach and Handel. He copied these masters' scores by hand, as if the mechanical act might enable him to channel their greatness. Mozart's first four piano concertos, written when he was only eleven years old, were skillfully crafted but not exactly original. He simply pieced them together from the works of other composers. He wouldn't write a truly original piano concerto until he was seventeen years old—still young, of course, but not freakishly so.

The child prodigy is a fiction. Sure, some young musicians play exceptionally well, but rarely, if ever, do they produce anything innovative at a young age. One study of twenty-five exceptional pianists found that, while they all had support and encouragement from their parents, most didn't truly distinguish themselves until much later in their careers. Yes, young children sometimes display remarkable skill, but not creative genius. That takes time.

Why then does the myth of the child prodigy persist? Because it, like all myths, serves a purpose. Sometimes myths inspire, like those of Horatio Alger. *If a poor kid from the wrong side of the tracks can make it big, then maybe I can, too!* Sometimes myths serve as pacifiers: they let us off the hook. *Mozart was a one-off, a freak of nature. I could never compose music like him so there's no sense trying. Now where did I put the remote?*

Mozart adored his teachers, but as a student of Italy he was no doubt aware of Leonardo da Vinci's observation that "the pupil who does not surpass his master is mediocre." Mozart absorbed his teachers' knowledge and techniques, but then developed a style wholly his own. That could not have happened anyplace but Vienna, a giant laboratory for musical experimentation.

The musicality of the city was only one reason Mozart loved Vienna. He also went there for the same reason young people through the ages have moved to the big city: to make a name for themselves, to test themselves in the big leagues, and most of all to escape the suffocating embrace of a parent.

Overbearing in the extreme, Leopold Mozart was the original helicopter parent. An accomplished but unremarkable musician himself, he was determined to avenge slights, real and perceived, through his genius son. It was a recipe for disaster.

Sure enough, when Mozart set out on his own, their relationship began to show signs of strain. In one letter, from September 1781, Wolfgang sounds remarkably like any young man bristling to demonstrate his independence.

From the way in which you have taken my last letter—as if I were an arch-scoundrel or a blockhead—or both—I am sorry to see that you rely more on the gossip and scribbling of other people than you do on me—and that in fact you have no trust in me whatever. . . . Please trust me always, for indeed I deserve it. I have trouble and worry enough here to support myself, and the last thing I need is to read unpleasant letters.

The greatest asset a city provides the aspiring genius, I realize, is not necessarily colleagues or opportunities but distance. A buffer between our old selves and our new.

Much separated Mozart and Beethoven. Fifteen years. A few hundred miles (Beethoven was born in Bonn, Mozart in Salzburg). Musical styles. Temperament. Body type. Sense of humor. Fashion sensibility. Hair. These two musical giants crossed paths only once, in 1787. Beethoven, a mere sixteen years old but already cocky, was visiting Vienna. He listened to Mozart play the piano, then pronounced his style *zerhackt*, choppy. Did the two meet privately? Here the historical record is less clear, but some evidence suggests they did.

Oh, to be at that meeting! The current and future king, side by side. According to biographer Otto Jahn, Beethoven played a short piece for Mozart, who, assuming it was a "showpiece prepared for the occasion, praised it in rather a cool manner." Beethoven knew he had to make a stronger impression and pleaded with Mozart to give him a theme for improvisation. Mozart did, and this time Beethoven nailed it. Mozart, the story goes, walked silently to his friends sitting in an adjoining room and said, "Keep your eyes on him; someday he will give the world something to talk about."

Mozart died before he could see his prophecy realized. Yet the ghost of Mozart haunted Beethoven throughout his life. He assiduously avoided even a hint of imitation, conscious or otherwise.

Places crowded with genius are a mixed blessing. While inspiration is everywhere you turn, there is always the danger of mimicry, even if unintentional. That fear shadowed Beethoven throughout his career but also propelled him down new, less taken roads.

A century later, the Viennese novelist Robert Musil captured this dynamic beautifully: "Each thing exists only by virtue of its limitations, in other words, by virtue of a more or less hostile act against its environment: without the Pope there would be no Luther, and without the heathens, no Pope, and so it cannot be denied that man's most deeply felt association with his fellow-men consists in dissociation from them." Mozart reacted to Haydn, and Beethoven to Mozart. Billiard balls, ricocheting off one another, sending each other in new and wonderful directions.

Five years after his brief meeting with Mozart, Beethoven moved permanently to Vienna, more accomplished and even more cocky. The city and its suburbs, writes biographer Edmund Morris, "were to enfold him more and more, until he became as unbudgeable as a hermit crab."

I walk past the iconic Burgtheater and the nearly equally iconic Café Landtmann, Freud's favorite, then hike up five flights of stairs to a small, stiflingly hot apartment. It is shabby and worn, unpolished, like its former tenant.

Beethoven lived here. That, though, is a statement that could be said of many places in Vienna. Beethoven made Mozart look like a homebody. He moved constantly—anywhere from twenty-five to eighty times during his thirty-six years in Vienna, depending on which account you believe.

If you could time-travel to the Vienna of, say, 1808, you'd certainly want Ludwig van Beethoven as a drinking partner, and a fun-loving, if unreliable, friend. You would not want to have him as a tenant. He was a landlord's nightmare. Visitors (often attractive young women) came and went at all hours. His apartments were littered with rough drafts— Beethoven, unlike Mozart, was constantly revising his scores and always worked on more than one piece at a time. His bathing methods were . . . unconventional. Sometimes, in the throes of composing, loath to interrupt his muse, he'd simply douse himself right there in the living room. It gets worse. Here is a distinguished French visitor describing what he saw when he called upon the young genius:

> Picture the dirtiest, most disorderly place imaginable—blotches of moisture covered the ceiling; an oldish grand piano, on which dust disputed the place with various pieces of printed and manuscript music; under the piano (I do not exaggerate) an unemptied *pot de nuit* [chamber pot]; beside it . . . a quantity of pens encrusted with ink . . . then more music. The chairs were covered with plates bearing the remains of last night's supper, and with clothing, etc.

Might Beethoven's slovenly ways help explain his musical genius? Many of us certainly hope so. After all, what slob hasn't been heartened by that famous *Life* magazine photograph of Einstein's desk, with papers strewn everywhere?

Psychologists at the University of Minnesota recently conducted a series of experiments aimed at shedding some light on that age-old question, is my pigsty of a desk the mark of genius or simply of piggishness? In one study, participants were divided into two groups and asked to fill out a questionnaire in an office setting. They were then asked to come up with creative uses for Ping-Pong balls. Some were assigned a tidy room, while others completed the task in a messy one, cluttered with papers and supplies. Both groups generated the same number of ideas, but those produced by the messy-room folks were rated more "interesting and creative" by a panel of judges.

Why? Kathleen Vohs, the lead researcher, suspects that a messy setting "stimulates a release from conventionality." You see disorder around you, everything is off-kilter, so your mind follows this vector into unknown territory. Vohs and her colleagues have begun to investigate the role of messiness in the digital world. Preliminary findings suggest a similar mechanism at work: "clean" websites cultivate less creative thinking than "messy" ones. Beethoven didn't have the benefit of these studies, but I can't help but wonder if his messy ways represented a subconscious effort to stir his creative pot, a sort of self-induced chaos.

Any sign of Beethoven's slovenly manners has studiously been erased from his apartment. *You clean up real good, Ludwig.* But to call it a Beethoven museum is to do both the institution and the man an injustice. So halfhearted, so pathetically cursory, is the effort that I can't help but like it. The past feels closest when unadorned. No billiards tables or leatherbound editions here. No lovingly curated displays. No wise Voice to guide me. Just a few mementos—some handwritten (sloppily, of course) scores, a printed invitation to his overture "Coriolan," and in one otherwise empty room Beethoven's piano. It's much smaller than I expected. It looks as if it belonged to a child, not a musical giant.

Yet here Beethoven wrote his first, and only, opera, *Fidelio,* and a sweet little bagatelle called "Für Elise." The piano, a sign informs me, dates back to Beethoven's "last creative period." That strikes me as unduly harsh. Did Beethoven think of it that way? Sure, he knew he was going deaf and agonized over the loss of the one sense that "ought to have been more perfect than in all others." Yet his deafness never disrupted his creative output.

Many geniuses suffered from illness and disability. Edison was partially deaf, Aldous Huxley partially blind. Alexander Graham Bell and Picasso were dyslexic. Michelangelo, Titian, Goya, and Monet all suffered from various illnesses that actually improved their artwork. Michelangelo, for instance, was in great agony as he painted the Sistine Chapel, twisting his body and bending backward to paint the enormous ceiling. As the project progressed, his personal discomfort was reflected in the figures he painted; they, too, began to take on a twisted form. Later, this became the artist's hallmark and ushered the way for mannerism, the next great art style. What doesn't kill you will not only make you stronger but also more creative. The Power of Constraints manifesting itself on a personal level.

Is that what happened, I wonder, with Beethoven? The sign doesn't say. Where is the Voice when I need it?

Throughout his life, Beethoven couldn't seem to shake restlessness, evidenced not only in the frequent changes of address, but also the fast-paced walks across town, his beaver hat flapping in the wind, and the frequent trips to coffeehouses. All this movement, I suspect, represented

Beethoven's attempt to diffuse his attention, trigger something inside him. It didn't take much. "Any change of scene, whether from town to country or just out onto the street, was enough to stimulate his creativity," writes Edmund Morris in his biography of the composer.

That old stereotype of the "sensitive artist" is truer than we think. Creative people, research shows, are *physiologically* more sensitive to stimuli. In experiments, they consistently rate various stimuli—electric shocks and loud noises—more intensely than less creative people.

This helps explain why creative people periodically retreat from the world. Proust in his cork-lined bedroom. Dickens, who, when deep into a manuscript, avoided any social events, for the "mere consciousness of an engagement will sometimes worry a whole day." Psychologist Colin Martindale speculates that creative types engage in a feast-and-famine dynamic. They deprive themselves of novelty, for a while, so they will crave it, and appreciate it, later. Hunger is the best spice.

Vienna provided composers such as Mozart and Beethoven with both stimulation and isolation, allowing them to live simultaneously in the world and apart from it. A perfect balance.

"Would you like to go on a musical adventure?" asks Friederike over the phone.

"Sure," I reply, not sure what I'm getting myself into, especially since I have never met Friederike.

She is the friend of a friend, host of a popular classical-music program on Austrian radio, and, I'm told, is good at explaining music to neophytes such as myself. She knows music *and* she knows Vienna. Surely, then, she must know something about genius.

She says she'll pick me up Friday morning and asks the name of my hotel.

"The Adagio."

"Oh, like the music."

"Um, yes," I say, "like the music."

I have absolutely no idea what she's talking about. We hang up, and I immediately google the word. It had not occurred to me that Adagio was anything other than a pleasantly Euro-sounding name concocted by the hotel chain the way pharmaceutical companies invent names for their drugs. Soothing. Reassuring. But meaningless. Professor Google sets me straight. *Adagio* is indeed a musical term. It means "slowly." This explains a lot, I think. It explains the five-foot-high clefs painted on the walls of my room. It explains the slow service; the staff is merely keeping perfect time.

Friederike pulls up in a tired-looking Peugeot, which, I soon discover, she converses with. I find this a bit off-putting. Plus, it's a French car but she speaks to it in German, further confusing me. I don't understand a word she's saying, but it sounds affectionate. I'm happy they have such a good relationship. Really, I am.

She hands me a map. It instantly comes apart in my hands. It's an old map, she explains, from Cold War times, when Vienna was a hotbed of espionage, but she likes the relief it shows, the contours of the hills just outside Vienna. Is that where we're heading? I ask.

Friederike doesn't hear me. She's talking to the Peugeot, offering what sounds like words of encouragement. Now she's back, telling me one theory—a fantastical-sounding one, I confess—about why Vienna is such a creative place. The Alps begin here, she says. Vienna is like the head of a snake, and snakes have magical powers. It's the sort of fuzzy-headed, New Age explanation for genius clusters I have so far avoided.

I try to make small talk by pointing out what a nice day it is—warm, with a slight breeze, and aren't those trees blooming?

Yes, says Friederike. Chestnut trees. She concedes it is indeed a nice day but quickly adds that rain is coming from the north. Soon, it will turn bitterly cold and wet. She says this with an air of dark inevitability, and I'm reminded of the Scots. The good never lasts long in Vienna, either. One moment it's sunny, the next moment you're drenched. One moment you're living in a vibrant capital city, the seat of an empire, and next thing you know you're living in a second-rate, provincial town. Don't be fooled by the apparent solidity of the stone buildings and the beefy palaces. It is all subject to the cruel whims of history.

Now Friederike is running through the roster of composers, rattling off names with the same quiet fervor of a die-hard sports fan. Haydn was the adult in the room, less flamboyant and so today less appreciated. Schubert was the native son; unlike the rest he was actually born in Vienna. Beethoven was like Prometheus, "stealing fire from the gods." She loves Beethoven. She calls his music "a box within a box within a box." There's always another box to discover. She's been listening to him all her life and she's still discovering boxes. As for Mozart, she says simply, "He was the God of all. His music is like paradise."

Einstein also adored Mozart, once calling his music "so pure that it seemed to have been ever-present in the universe, waiting to be discovered by the master." It's actually a very Chinese observation. Again, in the Eastern view of creativity, all discoveries are actually rediscoveries, all inventions reinventions. There is nothing new under the sun, but the old is plenty wonderful and, like Mozart's music, just waiting to be uncovered.

We've left the city center far behind and are now entering uncharted territory. We pass a young woman with a large musical instrument strapped to her back. The case looks as if it has melded with her body, making it difficult to distinguish where instrument ends and woman begins. I'm reminded of one of those lumbering giant tortoises that live forever and don't seem to have a care in the world.

I point out the woman to Friederike and mention how I've heard that every Austrian child plays an instrument. Is it true?

Yes, Friederike says, but quickly disabuses me of any *Sound of Music* fantasies I might be harboring. Austrian children are *forced* to play the piano or the violin at a young age, "and they hate it, just like kids everywhere," she says as we round a bend.

Now we're climbing and climbing, Friederike coaxing the little Peugeot. *Auf geht's, mein Kleiner. Du schaffst das!* "Let's go my little one. You can do it!"

What is the name of this mountain? I ask, trying to steer the conversation from the automotive to the human realm.

"Not a mountain," she chides. "A hill."

I forgot. We're in Austria. We pass a terraced hillside where something is growing, though what exactly I can't say.

"It's a vineyard," says Friederike, reading my mind. Vienna has some seventy, more than any other city in the world. I had no idea. Does this, perhaps, explain why Beethoven escaped to these mount—er, hills?

Yes, she says, he liked his wine, but more than that, he liked his nature. Beethoven desperately wanted to flee the heat and dust and stench of Vienna. So he did. Every chance he got, he'd hop a carriage to the Wienerwald, the rolling green hills just outside town. Away from the suffocating fans and the finicky critics and the pesky landlords, away from his audience, he was finally at peace. He would walk and think, often staying out past dusk. The notes came to him while he walked, he once said, and I think, yes, the way the questions came to Socrates, or the words to Dickens.

Friederike parks the Peugeot, congratulating it on a job well done.

"Can you still hike in these woods?" I ask.

"*One* can hike," she says, before citing a Japanese proverb. "'A tough man climbs the mountain. A wise man sits in the water.'"

So, okay, no hiking. I'm good with that.

We walk a few yards (walking and hiking constituting two distinct activities) before reaching an overlook.

"Look at the hills," says Friederike. "So soft and silky."

I imagine Beethoven standing on this very spot, two hundred years ago, his hearing fading but his mind as sharp as ever. What did he see? What did these excursions do for him? We get some inkling from his writings. He once called nature "a glorious school for the heart," adding, "Here I shall learn wisdom, the only wisdom that is free from disgust."

This side of Beethoven surprises me. I had pictured a gruff man, a mercurial womanizer and bon vivant, not a tree hugger. But he was. Literally. Down there, near the so-called Eroica House, where he lived while writing the eponymous symphony, a large linden tree grows. Beethoven, legend has it, would regularly wrap his beefy arms around it for inspiration. One day, I did the same, hoping some of that magic might rub off. So far, I have detected no sudden spike in musical ability, but it's still early days.

Friederike tells me how Beethoven always had a picture in mind when he composed. "Painting with music," Friederike calls it.

What she is describing, albeit metaphorically, is synesthesia. That's the condition where a person's sensory "wiring" is crossed. People with synesthesia hear colors or smell sounds. All creative people, I think, have a touch of synesthesia, in the sense that they don't limit their source of inspiration to a single sense. A painter might find inspiration in a piece of music, a writer in a distinctive scent. Friedrich Schiller, the poet and philosopher, always kept a carton of rotten apples under his desk when he wrote. He said it reminded him of the countryside. Picasso claimed to suffer from an "indigestion of greenness" after walking in the woods. "I must empty this sensation into a picture," he said.

We're back in the Peugeot, and Friederike has returned to her composers' scorecard. Gustav Mahler's music is the most Viennese, she says. "It is some kind of happiness never fulfilled. An aching heart. So sad. That is life." Music, she says, *good* music, is about "exporting sadness." I like that. It gives me a whole new perspective not only on music but on all art forms. Artists are in the import/export business. They are, as we've seen, more sensitive than the rest of us, importing the suffering of an imperfect world; then they process this suffering, remake it into art, and export it, thus lessening their sadness and increasing our pleasure. A perfectly symbiotic arrangement.

My use of a term borrowed from biology is no coincidence. The field provides a whole new way of thinking about creative environments. "An ecology of human creativity," psychologist David Harrington calls it. What does this mean?

For starters, it means viewing genius from a more holistic perspective, realizing that all the parts are connected. Biologists studying ecosystems know that it's impossible to tinker with one part of that system without fundamentally altering the whole. Creatologists, Harrington argues, need to think about creative genius in the same way. For instance, take the concept of "selective migration." That's when organisms flock to a certain environment not because they have been displaced by some natural disaster, or because their inner GPS dictates such a move, but because they have identified that environment as beneficial. They know they will thrive there. This is precisely what Beethoven, Mozart, and Haydn did. They moved to Vienna because the habitat met their particular needs and they knew they'd flourish there.

Another term that Harrington borrows from biology is *biochemical demand*. We know that organisms place certain demands on the ecosystems that they inhabit. Plants, for instance, consume sunlight and water. If the ecosystem can meet those demands, then the organisms will survive; if not, they will perish. It's that simple. Likewise, Harrington argues, creative people place certain "psychosocial demands" on their ecosystem—"demands that must be met if the creative processes are to flourish." These demands include time, workspace, communication channels, and access to audiences.

Harrington, again borrowing from biology, emphasizes the importance of "organism-environment fit." Ultimately, whether an organism survives depends not on the organism itself but on its relationship with its environment. Likewise, creative people must be a good "fit" with their environment if they are to realize their potential. For instance, some people thrive in an environment that encourages risk taking while others do not. A "good" cultural fit, though, isn't necessarily a frictionless one. Socrates is the best, and most tragic, example of this.

Finally, as any biologist knows, environments don't only shape organisms, they are shaped *by* them. These organisms deplete resources, yes, but also give something back. Plants suck up carbon dioxide but also emit much-needed oxygen into the atmosphere. Similarly, creative geniuses drain the cultural resources of a city—money, space, time—but deliver something in return. One look at the Parthenon or the Duomo tells you that.

So, what happens when we view the musical geniuses of Vienna from this new, ecological perspective? We see the "organisms"—Mozart, Beethoven, Haydn—engaging in selective migration, moving to the ecosystem where they are most likely to thrive, Vienna. We see them depleting resources—their patrons' money, their audiences' time, their landlords' patience. We see them shaping their environment, changing it for centuries to come. Haydn inspired Mozart, and Mozart inspired other composers: Chopin, Tchaikovsky, Schumann, and Brahms. We see how these musical organisms fit in the ecosystem but not too well. They push back.

Einstein's secretary once said that if Einstein were born among the polar bears, he would still be Einstein. But unless the polar bears were well versed in theoretical physics, that is not true. Einstein would not be Einstein. Which is not to take anything away from Einstein, or the polar bears, but simply to point out that he was part of a creative ecology, and trying to isolate him from it is not only silly but futile. If Einstein had been born fifty years earlier, chances are we would never have heard of him. The field of physics was not open to new ideas at that time, and without that receptivity Einstein's brilliant theories would have died on the vine. More likely, a bright young scientist like him would never have gone into physics but, rather, chosen a field where the big questions were still in play.

Just as it is too simplistic to think of genius as solely an internal phenomenon, so, too, is it a mistake to think of it as a direct result of a particular time and place. Vienna didn't "produce" Mozart the way Toyota produces a new car. The relationship between place and genius is more complex (not complicated) than that, more intertwined. More *intimate*.

"Food," says Friederike.

"Yes," I reply. "What about it?"

"In order to understand Vienna and its music, you need to understand food."

I flash back to my unfortunate experience with the cuisine of ancient Greece.

We park and find a little restaurant. We decide to sit outside, it being such a glorious day, the air so warm and soft. Yes, Friederike agrees, but not for long, she reminds me. The cold and the rain are coming, and everything will change.

I silently stare at my menu, afraid to contradict her. I'm starting to learn my lesson: never interfere with Viennese fatalism. It's like taking food away from them.

I'm struggling to unscramble the menu when Friederike comes to my rescue and orders us fish soup and salad accompanied by a sort of wine spritzer that she assures me is good, even though I've never had a positive experience with any beverage in the spritzer family.

The sun feels warm on my face. The air caresses my skin. I know it won't last long, though, that a cold rain is coming, so I plow ahead with my questions. Vienna had a bounty of musical talent at the time, but was that enough to make the leap into the realm of genius?

No, she says, talent alone was not enough. "You also need marketing. Beethoven wouldn't be known as a genius if he wasn't good at marketing. Mozart had a built-in marketing machine with his father." The notion of the lone genius, she agrees, is a folktale, a story we like to tell ourselves.

"If you don't have the possibility to sell yourself, to be known, you won't be a genius. You cannot just sit under a chestnut tree and write or paint or whatever. I know five painters who are real geniuses, but no one has discovered them. You can be as good as Rembrandt, but if no one discovers you, you will only be a genius in theory." She leaves unsaid the inevitable conclusion: a genius in theory is no genius at all.

And here, she says between sips of spritzer, Mozart was a true virtuoso, navigating the treacherous waters of palace politics, biding his time until he could break out on his own. Soon after arriving in the city, he nuzzled up to one Countess Thun. A woman with "a most unselfish heart," as one English visitor put it, she loved nothing more than to connect people. She opened doors for Mozart, and he didn't hesitate to walk through. He resented nobility, though, and occasionally his disdain boiled over. "Stupidity oozes out of his eyes," he said of Archduke Maximilian, the emperor's brother.

Mozart could get away with this sort of insubordination partly because he was so talented and partly because the times were changing. The age of the freelance musician was beginning to stir. This must have been liberating—and terrifying. Uncertainty defined the freelance life (still does), and Mozart was the first musician to experience this. It caused him endless grief and might even have hastened his death, but it also kept him on his toes. Comfort is the enemy of genius, and thank goodness, Mozart never got too comfortable.

Circumstances matter. Not only when and where you're born, but which gender. Mozart's sister Maria Anna—better known by her nickname Nannerl—was also an extremely talented musician, "but she was a woman, and it was her fate to bear children," says Friederike. "It was the same with Mendelssohn and his sister. Women geniuses are always forgotten." She says this without any audible bitterness but as if stating a simple law of nature, such as "plants need water."

Later, I would dig deeper into the life of Nannerl Mozart, curious to find out more about this genius in theory. She was an accomplished pianist and harpsichordist. Five years older than her brother, she was very much a role model in his early years. Three-year-old Wolfgang would look over her shoulder during lessons and, later, tried playing exercises from her notebook. They were close outside the music studio, too, even inventing a secret language and the imaginary Kingdom of Back.

When Mozart wrote his first symphony, at age eight, it was Nannerl who actually put pen to paper, transcribing the notes her brother intended. Was she more than a stenographer? Was that symphony her own? No one knows. We do know, though, that Nannerl's musical career was cut short when she married and had children.

Today Wolfgang's music is held up as a pinnacle of human achievement. And Nannerl? She has an Austrian liqueur named after her. Apricot schnapps. I hear it is very good.

Why is history so bereft of women geniuses? The reason is simple: until recently, most of the world wouldn't allow it. We get exactly the geniuses that we want and that we deserve. If anything underscores the importance of environment to the making of creative genius, it is the glaring paucity of women in the pantheon. Historically, women were denied the resources required for creative excellence: access to mentors, rewards (intrinsic and extrinsic), patronage, an audience. At the age when most geniuses produce their first notable works, their twenties, women were burdened with child care and housekeeping. They couldn't very well lock themselves in cork-lined studios like Proust or only open the door for someone bearing food, as Voltaire did.

The Romans had a saying, *libri aut liberi*, "books or children." For most of history, that was a choice women were not permitted to make. Yes, there were exceptions, Marie Curie being the most notable, but the two-time Nobel Prize winner is, unfortunately, the exception that proves the rule.

If women were given a chance, it was inevitably because of extraordinary circumstances. Rosalyn Yalow, a medical physicist and Nobel Prize winner, recalls that when she was accepted into the graduate program at the University of Illinois in 1941, just as the United States entered World War II, she was only the second woman allowed to matriculate. (The previous one had enrolled in 1917.) "They had to make a war so that I could go to graduate school," she said, only half joking.

Our food arrives, and I take the opportunity to shift gears. I'm curious about Friederike's radio show. Her listeners, she explains, are not connoisseurs, but "normal people." Her job, she says, is to "seduce them into listening to music." I notice she says *music*, not *classical music*. This is no accident. Put the modifier *classical* or *classic* in front of a work—of music, of art, of anything—and you suck the life out of it, kill it. Friederike would never do that to a piece of music. Besides, Mozart and Beethoven did not write a single note of classical music. They wrote contemporary music that we now classify as classical. There is a big difference.

We finish our meal, and I have to admit the spritzer was not bad. Back in the Peugeot, I tell Friederike about my plans to see a performance of Schubert and how I worry I might not "get it." In this regard, I am a strict Freudian. The good doctor was a brilliant psychologist but also famously tone-deaf. Me, too. Sure, I played the trombone in grade school. For a while. But complaints from family members, neighbors, and the local branch of the ASPCA quickly, and mercifully, put an end to my musical career. So how am I supposed to appreciate the musical subtleties of a Schubert performance?

"Listen for five minutes," she says.

"And what if I still don't get it?"

"Listen for another five minutes."

"What if it still doesn't resonate?"

"Then leave." I feel a rush of relief until she adds, "But be aware that by doing so you are losing an entire cosmos, a world, that you won't ever find again."

I don't know what to say. I've misplaced many things in my life—car keys, wallets, modifiers—but never an entire cosmos. I'm not about to start now. I promise to heed her advice.

We pull up to the Adagio. We say good-bye, then slowly, adagio, I step out of the Peugeot. As Friederike pulls away, I can hear her saying something to her car. I can't understand a word, but, to my ears, it sounds like music.

Golden ages need their wild ones, their enfants terribles, but they also need their grown-ups. In the case of Vienna, that would be Franz Joseph Haydn. He is best described by what he was not. He was not prone to scatological humor. He did not embark on gambling benders. He did not have wild affairs. He did not fit our image of the difficult genius, and so these days Papa Haydn, as he was known, ranks lower in the musical pantheon. That doesn't seem right. Not only was Haydn a brilliant composer, he was also a teacher and mentor to both Mozart and Beethoven. He spanned the entire golden age and was, in many ways, the glue that held it together. Haydn was composing before Mozart was born, and by the time Papa died, in 1809, at the impressively old age of seventy-seven, Beethoven was already a well-established composer and Schubert was an up-and-coming member of the Vienna Boys' Choir.

Sadly, Papa gets few visitors these days. One morning I decide to do something about it—not merely out of pity, mind you. Papa Haydn, I bet, holds important clues to the musical genius that was Vienna.

Haydn is not easy to find. Unlike Mozart's and Beethoven's apartments, Haydn House is located far from the city center, as if old Papa were hiding. I hop on the subway, which, like everything else in this city, runs flawlessly, and, before I know it, emerge aboveground in a different world, one of leafy streets and vegetable vendors, and no tourists. In Haydn's day, this neighborhood, called Windmühle, was a summer retreat for nobility and the well-to-do. It took an hour by carriage to get downtown, a journey Haydn avoided if at all possible. He preferred life among the apple orchards and vineyards.

I walk for a while, past boutiques and coffeehouses, before spotting Haydngasse, a small, especially pleasant street with kids playing and flowers blooming. Haydn House is a compact, cream-colored building, handsome but not the least bit flashy, much like its former inhabitant. Haydn lived here for the last twelve years of his life. They were, by all accounts, happy years. He was finally a free man, no longer under the musical thumb of his patrons, the Esterházys. "How sweet is the taste of a certain freedom," he wrote to a friend upon learning of Prince Esterházy's death.

The man at the ticket counter looks surprised to see me. On this day I am the only visitor, save for a British couple, genuine aficionados on a musical pilgrimage, judging by their fluent use of terms such as *libretto* and *counterpoint*.

I enter the house and find myself eye to eye with a not-handsome but dignified man. No wild Beethoven hair or Mozart dandyism but, judging by the kind and steady eyes depicted in the watercolor, a man of character. A musical mensch.

On another wall, Haydn's daily routine. The man lived by the clock. An early breakfast, then seated at the piano and composing by 8:00 a.m. At 11:30, he went for a walk and received visitors. Lunch was served promptly at 2:00 p.m. At 4:00 p.m., he sat down at the piano again. At 9:00 p.m. he read. Dinner at 10:00 p.m. Bed at 11:30 p.m. This was not merely the routine of a fastidious man; Haydn was tracking the trajectory of his muse, discerning the optimal rhythm for his workday. Inconveniently, for many a genius this means an early start. Victor Hugo was up by 6:00 a.m., ate breakfast, then started writing. Milton made them all look like slackers. During the summer months, he was working by 4:00 a.m. Pavlov, the Russian behaviorist with the salivating dog, was particular about his working hours; he considered 8:30 to 9:50 a.m. his most productive time.

Inspiration, it's been said, is for amateurs. True creativity requires showing up at the desk, or the piano, even when you don't feel like it. That's what Haydn did. He stuck to his schedule whether he was in the mood or not. He called his morning sessions "fantasizing." These were rough sketches. Refining would come later, after his walk. Haydn never put anything down on paper unless he was "quite sure it was the right thing," says Rosamond Harding, a music historian.

That happened often enough. In these rooms, he penned some of his finest work, including such masterpieces as *The Creation* and *The Seasons*. He was incredibly prolific and produced some of his finest works later in life. Unlike Mozart, he thrived in quietude, not chaos. Unlike Mozart, Haydn was unhappily married. He and his wife, Maria Anna, gave each other a wide berth. An unpleasant woman, "reputedly the most tyrannical wife since Xantippe," as Morris put it, referring to Socrates's brutish spouse, she took little interest in his music.

Haydn, like his student Beethoven, found comfort and companionship in nature. He collected tropical birds and paid top florin for them— once spending 1,415 florins (a typical year's salary) for an especially rare breed. It was a ridiculous, impractical hobby, especially for an older, dignified man such as Haydn, but I find it oddly reassuring. Haydn was not an automaton, no musical robot. He had his peccadilloes. Geniuses do.

Haydn taught both Mozart and Beethoven so it's tempting to pigeonhole him as a mentor, the Verrocchio of Vienna, but that would be unfair. Haydn was a master composer in his own right. One of his fortes was the string quartet. He did for that genre, says historian Peter Gay, with only slight exaggeration, "what Caesar Augustus did for Rome: he found it brick and left it marble."

Haydn transmitted his passion for the quartet to Mozart, who picked it up quickly. Haydn, like Verrocchio, knew talent when he saw it and was humble enough to call Mozart "the greatest composer I have ever known by person or by name." The two men got along famously well. I can't help but wonder if Mozart, far from home, saw in Haydn a surrogate father, a kinder, less autocratic version of Leopold. Mozart felt deeply indebted to Haydn and spent three years working on what are now known as his "Haydn" Quartets, dedicating them to the "celebrated Man and dearest Friend," as he enthused in a letter. It was one of the few times Mozart wrote anything for free.

I walk upstairs and spot, on the wall, some three dozen canons, framed and yellowing, that Haydn wrote but refused to publish. Why? I wonder. Why did you not send them out into the world, Joseph? Were they not good enough? Or perhaps they were too good and you, a resolutely pious man, feared they'd be seen as trespassing on God's turf? It's possible. Other artists have spoken of creating a work so precious that they prefer to keep it private, lest it be tainted by criticism or, worse, praise. Sometimes, the greatest applause is silence.

In an adjoining room, various medals are on display. "Objects of honor," the placard calls them. Haydn had another name for them: "The toys of old men." Haydn was paid handsomely but, like many creative geniuses, didn't care much for money. "When I sit at my old worm-eaten piano, there is no King in the World whose good fortune I envy," he wrote.

I spot, behind glass, a draft of one of Haydn's more romantic and radical works, a prelude called "The Representation of Chaos." (An ironic title given his preference for order.) Musicologists suspect the work was influenced by his student Beethoven. Like Verrocchio and Leonardo, the relationship between Haydn and Beethoven, mentor and acolyte, flowed in both directions. Student as teacher, teacher as student.

Theirs, too, was a complicated relationship. They first met in Bonn. Haydn was passing through town, and Beethoven, only twenty years old but not lacking in confidence, took the opportunity to show Haydn a cantata he had written. Haydn was impressed and, in effect, told the young composer to keep at it. Two years later, in July of 1792, Beethoven's benefactor, one Count Waldstein, dispatched him to Vienna to study with Haydn. On the eve of his departure, the count wrote a letter of encouragement that, in a few short words, captures the musical shamanism that animated Vienna at the time: "By means of assiduous labor you will receive the spirit of Mozart from the hands of Haydn."

Alas, the transmission didn't go quite that smoothly. The two men couldn't be more different. Haydn, formal and impeccably dressed; Beethoven, rough and unkempt. Beethoven was also impatient; he wanted a crash course in the musical technique known as counterpoint and soon realized he was not going to get that from Papa Haydn. Haydn's teaching style was too methodical, too rigid, for Beethoven. Haydn, for his part, found the young composer headstrong and arrogant. "The Great Mogul," he teasingly called him.

As the lessons continued, Beethoven grew increasingly exasperated. He couldn't simply quit though. That would amount to career suicide. So Beethoven, in essence, two-timed. He continued to show up for lessons with the master Haydn, but his real teacher was a lesser-known composer named Johann Schenk. They kept that arrangement a secret. At Schenk's urging, Beethoven copied the exercises in his own handwriting so that Haydn wouldn't suspect anything was amiss.

Beethoven eventually made his peace with Haydn and even learned a thing or two from him. One cold March day, in 1808, Haydn made what would be his last public appearance. He had just turned seventy-six, and was in failing health; everyone knew the end was near. The piece was Haydn's *The Creation*. Beethoven was in the audience, sitting in the front row. After the performance, the Great Mogul knelt down and, tears welling in his eyes, kissed the hand of his mentor and friend.

Finally, the day arrives when I can stop contemplating the role of audience and join one. I had purchased my ticket a few days earlier from a ponytailed, tattooed, young man who, from behind the counter, nodded his approval when I told him I wanted to hear Schubert. This would not happen back home. Young, ponytailed, tattooed men do not, as a rule, get excited about Schubert. But this is Vienna, where culture is utterly devoid of elitism. The ticket cost only seven euros. It was so cheap for a reason, and that reason, I'd learn, says much about the musical genius that was, and is, Vienna.

On the day of the performance, I walk across town to the Musikverein, perhaps the finest concert hall in Vienna. When I arrive, I find Mozart waiting for me outside. He is wearing his trademark frilly shirt and powdered-white wig and talking on a cell phone. Everywhere I look I see Mozarts, each dressed identically and each hawking tickets. The city's Mozarts, I'd later learn, are actually resourceful Albanians, hoping to make a quick euro off Wolfgang. I can hear old Leopold Mozart protesting the misappropriation of his son's persona, but secretly smiling at his international acclaim and enduring brand recognition.

I arrive early, as the ponytailed ticket guy had suggested. I show the usher my ticket, for the *Stehplatz* section, and he directs me upstairs. So far, so good. I walk up an ornate, marble staircase. A young woman in jeans whizzes by me, practically knocking me over. Clearly, she, too, holds a *Stehplatz* ticket.

Stehplatz, you see, means "standing room," as in no seat, and competition for space is fierce. I'm lucky. I snatch one of the last prime seats—er, spots. Located up front, near the railing, it affords a clear, if distant, view of the stage. I marvel at the chandeliers, the gold-leaf inlay, the frescoes of angels dancing on the ceiling. Staring in awe, I realize what I am looking at: a secular cathedral.

I had requested a *Stehplatz* seat for a reason, and not because I am cheap, not that only. I wanted to experience culture at its least highfalutin, and you don't get any less falutin than standing perfectly still for two solid hours.

My fellow *Stehplatz*-ers are diverse. Young and old. Well dressed and shabby (Euro-shabby, that is, which isn't really shabby at all). Standing next to me is a young Japanese guy. He explains that he's studying violin in Vienna. The city may have lost much of its past glory, but in certain districts of Tokyo and Hong Kong it still looms large as a musical promised land.

A buzzer sounds, and the chattering instantly evaporates, as if someone had pushed a giant mute button. The anticipation is thick. I'm on the edge of my space. Finally, the orchestra walks onto the stage and everyone applauds wildly, as if greeting a rock star.

Then the pianist, a large man dressed in coat and tails walks onto the stage and the applause crescendos. The Viennese care deeply about their music; you mess with it at your peril. A century ago, in this very concert hall, Arnold Schoenberg's unorthodox piece Chamber Symphony No. 1 was performed for the first time. The audience didn't care for it and showed its displeasure by rioting and practically torching the concert hall. A riot over classical music? Really? But standing here now, feeling the passions, my disbelief fades. We are more "civilized" today—the worst sanction a composer risks is a bad review in the *New York Times*—but I wonder if, in our attempt to tame culture, we have lost some of its essence.

The virtuoso pianist Yefim Bronfman begins to play. It does nothing for me. I was afraid of this. I'm also starting to regret those two whiskey sours I had before the concert. My legs are tired. My head is spinning. I begin to sway, and not to the music. I hope nobody notices. I'm tempted to cut my losses and relinquish my primo space, but I hear Friederike's words: *Wait five minutes. Then another five.*

The music stops. I do nothing, recalling an unfortunate incident when I thought the performance had ended and broke into applause. It had not. It was merely a break in the score—an adagio section, perhaps—and everyone looked at me as if I were a cretin. So now I wait. As if on cue, the audience erupts into wild applause. Then, suddenly, all jump to their feet. All, that is, except for us in the *Stehplatz* section. We are already on our feet. Chalk up another one for the cheap "seats."

I find myself wondering whether their applause is sincere or reflexive, a reaction more to Bronfman's reputation, his Mozartian marketing, than to his music. Is that unfair? I don't think so. Rarely do we experience anything today—a piece of writing or music or the latest blockbuster movie—unmediated. Curation is necessary, given the deluge of cultural choices available, but it also means we always have someone else in our head telling us what we like and don't like. Something about this audience's reaction, though, strikes me as immediate and raw. It's not their knowledge of music that explains this, I think, but their receptivity, their openness.

Bronfman plays again. My swaying has subsided, and so, too, does my restlessness. No new cosmos reveals itself, but I do experience *something*. A pleasant sensation, not unlike the one elicited by the whiskey sours but with a sharpness and clarity that the sours lack. Goethe's observation that music is "liquid architecture" comes to mind, and, yes, I know what he means. I can hear the archways and the porticoes, sloshing and swirling inside my head. This musical epiphany doesn't last long, perhaps ten or fifteen minutes, but that is okay. What distinguishes an epiphany is not its duration but its intensity.

When I eventually turn to leave, it is not so much because I have tired of the sonatas but because my legs and back have begun to ache. The downside of *Stehplatz*. I relinquish my space and a crowd instantly fills it, like compressed air rushing into a vacuum.

Walking back to my hotel, past the Albanian Mozarts and the organ players and the edgy graffiti, a deep appreciation washes over me. Yes, an appreciation for the music, a two-hundred-year-old piece that sounded as fresh as yesterday, but also an appreciation for the city that nurtured it. No wonder Mozart and Beethoven and the rest thrived here. They had an entire city cheering for them. More than cheering. The audiences of that time, like the one I was part of this evening, were not mere spectators. They egged on their musicians, prodding them, pushing them to ever greater heights. An audience, a *good* audience, is a sort of co-genius. They disapprove and the genius improves. When the musician gets it "right," nothing is sweeter than the heartfelt applause of a discerning audience.

Mozart's Vienna had one other kind of audience, perhaps the most important of all. Here, I'm reminded of what W. H. Auden said about poets: "The ideal audience the poet imagines consists of the beautiful who go to bed with him, the powerful who invite him to dinner and tell him secrets of state, and his fellow poets. The actual audience he gets consists of myopic school teachers, pimply young men who eat in cafeterias, and his fellow-poets. This means, in fact, that he writes for his fellow poets."

So the musical greats of Vienna wrote for one another. Mozart wrote for Haydn, his mentor and surrogate father. Haydn taught Beethoven and was in turn influenced by him. Beethoven wrote for a dead Mozart, going to such pains not to imitate him that this avoidance constituted a kind of imitation.

This realization hits me over the head like one of those rare, and expensive, therapeutic breakthroughs. Which is fitting, because nowhere else was the web of creative genius woven more tightly, and productively, than in the Vienna of Sigmund Freud.

SEVEN

GENIUS IS CONTAGIOUS:
VIENNA ON THE COUCH

MOZART WOULD HARDLY RECOGNIZE THIS VIENNA.
The year was now 1900. A century had passed, and the city had grown
tenfold. It had experienced a short-lived revolution, a cholera outbreak,
a financial collapse, but not a lot of genius. Yes, there was Brahms, but
one genius does not a golden age make, and the half century following
Beethoven's death in 1827 had produced few bright lights. It seemed as if
Vienna were heading down the same one-way street that Athens and Florence and most other places of genius had, but then it suddenly reversed
course and accelerated again. Appropriately, this U-turn was prompted by
the construction of a shiny new boulevard.

The Ringstrasse was the most ambitious urban project since the re-
construction of Paris, a physical manifestation of the sense of inexorable
progress that was in the air. The new emperor, Franz Joseph, ordered the
old, medieval walls razed to make way for this "nineteenth-century version of Disney World," as one historian calls it. The new road projected
all the syrupy optimism of Tomorrowland. "When one walks out into

the new Ringstrasse," said a streetcar operator at the time, "one thinks of the future."

And what a future it was! Freud is the best-known name to emerge from this intellectual stew, but he had plenty of company: the philosopher Ludwig Wittgenstein, the artist Gustav Klimt, the writers Arthur Schnitzler and Stefan Zweig, physicist Ernst Mach, composer Gustav Mahler, to name just a few. If any place can lay claim to the title of Birthplace of the Modern World, it is Vienna.

The genius of fin de siècle Vienna resided not in any one discipline but in an intellectual and artistic energy that infused every nook and cranny of the city. This energy spread with the speed and ferocity of a California wildfire. Vienna offers proof positive that creativity is contagious, that genius begets more genius. Everything that we consider good and modern, from architecture to fashion, technology to economics, can trace its roots to the elegant, twisted, teeming streets of turn-of-the-century Vienna.

Driving this unexpected Renaissance was an equally unlikely, marginalized group of immigrants. They came from the far corners of the Austro-Hungarian Empire, bringing with them raw ambition and fresh insights; Vienna's story, and the story of its Jews, are as inseparable as a composer and her piano. How, I wonder, did these outsiders, these Others, come to play such a crucial role in shaping the second act of Vienna's golden age?

That is the question on my mind as I enter the Café Sperl, a short walk from the Ringstrasse. To step into the Sperl is to step back in time. The owners, bless them, have studiously resisted the temptation to gentrify. No track lighting, no Wi-Fi, no baristas. Only simple wooden booths and grumpy waiters. A billiards table sits in one corner, newspapers, mounted on long wooden poles, resting atop it like the fresh catch of the day.

Yes, I am here for the caffeine, I confess, but not just that. The story of Viennese genius is incomplete without the story of the coffeehouse. The city's history is written on its cigarette-stained tables, and on the faces of its surly but endearing waiters. Within its walls, and on its terraces, much of Vienna's genius unfolded. At the Café Sperl, Gustav Klimt and his merry band of artists declared the Viennese Secession, thus launching

Vienna's own modern-art movement, a break from the past encapsulated by Klimt's famous words: "To each age its art, to art its freedom."

Like the concert hall, the Viennese coffeehouse was (and is) a secular cathedral, an idea incubator, an intellectual crossroads—in short, an institution as much a part of the city's fiber as the Opera House or apple strudel. It also provides an important piece of the genius puzzle, for some of the city's best ideas (and a few of its worst) first took flight in the smoke-filled air of the coffeehouse. What exactly made the Viennese coffeehouse so special? How, I wonder, can an establishment that serves caffeinated beverages ignite a golden age that changed not only the world but the way we think about the world?

Vienna didn't invent the coffeehouse. The world's first sprang up in Constantinople (now Istanbul) in 1554, the first Western European one nearly a century later when an enterprising young man named Jacob opened a shop in Oxford, England, that served the "bitter black beverage." From the outset, coffee was considered dangerous. It was known as the "revolutionary drink," the stimulus of the masses. When people drank coffee, they got agitated, and who knew where that agitation might lead. Soon after Jacob's coffeehouse opened, King Charles II issued a decree limiting their numbers. And no wonder. The whiff of democracy was in the air. Europe's first coffeehouses were called levelers, as were the people who frequented them. Inside their walls, no one is better than anyone else.

That was certainly true in the Viennese coffeehouse. It was "a sort of democratic club, and anyone could join it for the price of a cheap cup of coffee," writes Stefan Zweig in his wonderful memoir, *The World of Yesterday*. What exactly did that admission price get you? For starters, a warm room. At the time, the population of Vienna was exploding; so severe was the housing shortage that some people squatted in the zoo. For those lucky enough to get apartments, they were small, drafty, and often unheated.

The admission price also got you information. Lots of it. Any coffeehouse worthy of the name supplied the day's newspapers, carefully mounted on long wooden poles, as they still are today. This is where you went to find out what was happening around the corner, or halfway around the world. As we saw in Florence, access to new information is crucial. Alone it is not enough to spark a golden age, but one rarely ignites without it.

Not only information but opinions circulated in the coffeehouse. These were the currency of the day, hotly traded, and always in demand, explains Stefan Zweig. "We sat for hours every day, and nothing escaped us, for thanks to our collective interests we pursued the *orbis pictus* of artistic events not with just one pair of eyes but with twenty or so; if one of us missed something, another would point it out to him, since with a childish wish to show off, we were always vying with each other, showing an almost sporting ambition to know the newest, very latest thing. We were engaged in constant competition for new sensations."

Most of all, the admission price got you conversation and companionship. Fellow travelers. The denizens of the coffeehouse were of a particular type, that strange combination of introvert and extrovert that defines most geniuses or, as Alfred Polgar puts it in his brilliant 1927 essay, "Theory of the Café Central," "people whose hatred of their fellow human beings is as fierce as their longing for people, who want to be alone but need companionship for it." I love that line. Whenever I read it, I imagine an archipelago of lonely souls. Islands, yes, but arranged in proximity to one another, and that proximity makes all the difference.

The Viennese coffeehouse is a classic example of a third place. Third places, as opposed to home and office (first and second places), are informal, neutral meeting grounds. Think of the bar in *Cheers*, or any British pub. Other establishments—barbershops, bookstores, beer gardens, diners, general stores—can also be third places. What they have in common is that they are all sanctuaries, "temporary worlds within the ordinary world," says Johan Huizinga, a scholar of play.

The chatter that filled the coffeehouse amounted to a kind of improvisation, like that practiced by musicians and comedy troupes. That form of conversation was far more conducive to generating good ideas than that staple of creativity consultants everywhere: brainstorming. Brainstorming sounds like a great idea, but it doesn't work. Dozens of studies have demonstrated this conclusively. People produce more good ideas—twice as many—alone than they do together.

One problem with brainstorming is that it has an agenda, even if it is unspoken: we're going to sit around this table until we come up with a REALLY BIG IDEA. That creates a lot of pressure; brainstorming relies almost exclusively on extrinsic motivation. Not good. At the coffeehouse, there was no agenda. The conversation unfolded completely nonlinearly, like a Calcuttan *adda*. "Purposelessness sanctifies the stay," as Polgar put it.

Which is not to say that good ideas didn't emerge from the coffeehouse. They did. But the key word is *from*. The ideas gelled afterward, once the cigarette smoke had cleared, the caffeine exited, and the rush of new information settled. We collect our dots in the company of others. We connect them by ourselves.

Sometimes the most obvious explanations are the best, so perhaps what made the Viennese coffeehouse so special was the coffee. The evidence, alas, is disheartening for coffee addicts such as me. Yes, caffeine does increase alertness, but that's not the same as creativity; increased alertness means our attention is less diffuse, and therefore we're less likely to make the sort of unexpected connections that are the hallmark of creative thinking. Also, caffeine disrupts both the quantity and the quality of sleep, and studies have found that people who experience deep REM sleep perform better on creative tasks than those who don't.

So, if not the coffee, then what else might explain the fecundity of the coffeehouse? I perk up my ears. The whoosh of the espresso machine, the hum of improvised conversation, the ruffling of newspapers turning. When we think of the ideal place for contemplation, we tend to imagine quiet ones, a belief drilled into us by forced readings of Thoreau's *Walden* and legions of shushing librarians, but quiet, it turns out, isn't always best.

A team of researchers, led by Ravi Mehta of the University of Illinois at Urbana-Champaign, found that those exposed to moderate noise levels (seventy decibels) performed better on a creative-thinking exam than those exposed to either high levels of noise or complete silence. Moderate noise, Mehta believes, allows us to enter "a state of distracted, or diffused, focus." Again, the ideal state for creative breakthroughs.

At Viennese coffeehouses, the regulars have their *Stammtisch*, their usual place. I don't know Dardis McNamee's *Stammtisch* so I'm at a loss. Where is she? The problem, I realize, is that I'm looking for an American, and Dardis has long ago shed her American mannerisms. She has become Viennese. No wonder I can't find her.

A New Yorker like Eugene Martinez, Dardis McNamee came to Vienna eighteen years ago and instantly fell in love with the place. She learned German at an age when the brain supposedly can't absorb a new language. She is both insider and outsider. In other words, the Brady of Vienna.

Finally, after a few false starts, I spot her. In her sixties, she carries herself with the quiet insouciance of someone who no longer has anything to prove. She orders for us, in perfect Viennese German. The dialect is softer, more musical, than standard German, a source of great pride for the Austrians. I tell Dardis how I always thought of the Austrians as just like the Swiss, only less fun.

No, she says, it's the other way around. "In fact, the Austrians think the Swiss are completely deadly dull." One reason Vienna is infinitely more interesting than any Swiss city, she says, is because it is international, a crossroads of cultures, and has always been.

In the nineteenth century, immigrants from far and wide flooded into Vienna. They came from Galicia and Budapest and Moravia and Bohemia and Turkey and Spain and Russia. By 1913, less than half of Vienna's population was native born. Vienna took this sort of ethnic diversity in stride "for the genius of Vienna, a specifically musical genius, has always been that it harmonized all national and linguistic opposites in itself," writes Zweig. Freud's Vienna was every bit as musical as Mozart's—*more* musical, perhaps, in the way it reconciled competing ideas, as well as melodies.

Ethnic diversity can jump-start creativity. Dean Simonton demonstrated how this happens on a national level, with a country such as Japan. What about in smaller groups, such as corporate boardrooms or coffeehouses?

Psychologists at the University of Iowa designed an experiment that aimed to find out. They divided 135 students into two types of groups: ones consisting entirely of Anglo-Americans and others more ethnically diverse. All of these groups were then given an exercise called the Tourist Problem. They had fifteen minutes in which to generate as many ideas as possible for convincing more foreign tourists to visit the United States.

By a clear margin, the ideas generated by the ethnically diverse groups were judged more creative and "significantly more feasible" than those produced by the ethnically homogenous ones. "Group genius can only happen if the brains in the team don't contain all the same stuff," says psychologist Keith Sawyer.

Researchers, though, also stumbled across a downside to ethnic diversity. While these diverse groups did perform better than homogenous ones, they also produced more "negative affective reactions"—or, in English, bad vibes. Members of the ethnically diverse groups didn't feel as comfortable as members of ethnically homogenous ones, yet they produced better ideas.

So it was at the coffeehouses of Vienna. They provided a supportive atmosphere but also a highly critical one, in the best sense of the word. Says Zweig, "We criticized one another with a severity, artistic expertise and attention to detail greater than any of the official literary pundits of our great daily papers applied to the classical masterpieces." The coffeehouse was not a "nice place." Places of genius never are.

Vienna was multiethnic but the lingua franca was German. That's important. As I discovered in China, language not only reflects thought; it shapes it. The Chinese language, with its thousands of characters, all set in stone, discourages wordplay. Not so German, Dardis tells me, as our coffees arrive.

"People accuse the Germans of not being creative, but their language is fabulously flexible. English speakers don't get it. I mean, the Germans are inventing words constantly. The language was designed for inventing words."

Language helps explain something that has nagged at me for a long time: Why are there so many German-speaking philosophers? From

Schopenhauer to Nietzsche, Kant to Goethe, the list is long. I had always chalked it up to dreary winters and a brooding disposition. That's part of it, Dardis concedes, but a bigger part is the German language itself. It lends itself to philosophical thought. In German, for instance, it's possible to attach all sorts of qualifiers and ancillary ideas to a sentence without bogging it down, as would happen in English. Also, she continues, "In English, we think in terms of action. Actors and active verbs, and things acted upon. We say, 'I went *there*. I did *this*. I came, I saw, I conquered. In German, you often have a situation that affects the speaker, or the agent, indirectly. But the situation exists in and of itself, so for example, in English, we say, 'I am cold.' In German, you say, 'It is cold to me.'"

"That sounds like a fairly subtle difference."

"I know, but it's actually a pretty big difference because the fact that you are experiencing the cold is not the most important thing. The cold—the fact that it is cold—is more important, and then, secondarily, that you are the person experiencing it. So you get to emphasize the quality of the experience."

"Okay, but how does that translate into creative thought, into philosophy?"

"Well, it means that it's not all about action. It's about the idea behind the action. And it wouldn't have occurred to me to think about this as anything other than the way life is until I had to learn this other language, where the meaning falls in a different place in the sentence." Place matters, even in sentences.

Dardis and I talk for hours. She doesn't seem to be in a hurry to leave, have any urgent business to conduct. I gently ask about this.

"The business of Austria or Vienna has *never*, ever, been business."

"What is the business of Vienna?"

"Life. Life is the business of Vienna."

Vienna, she says, practices a "gentle kind of hedonism." Nobody works past 2:00 p.m. on Friday afternoon. "You can know people in Vienna for years—and this is still true—and you don't really know what they do for a living."

"You don't ask?"

"No, it's not that you don't ask. It's just not what people are talking about. They're talking about where they went on their last holiday; they're talking about what they saw in the theater; or the movie they went to; or something they read; or some lecture they heard; or this conversation or, I don't know, some new restaurant they found. It's only with your really, really close friends that you really know what they're doing for a living." The same social dynamic was at work in early twentieth-century Vienna.

Dardis tells me a story, one that has over the years risen to the level of coffeehouse legend. One day in 1905, a diplomat announces to his dinner guests that there is going to be a revolution in Russia. One guest expresses his skepticism. "Sure, and who is going to foment this revolution? Herr Bronstein down at the Café Central?" Everyone laughed. Lev Bronstein, though, the disheveled, chess-playing regular at the Café Central, would soon change his name. His new name? Leon Trotsky. And he would foment a revolution in Russia. No one, I suppose, asked him what he did for a living.

Dardis must have told this tale a hundred times, but it still tickles her. It says much about Vienna, about how the tumult and the genius of the city were hidden—under "a coating of waltzes and whipped cream," as one historian put it. As in Edinburgh, I'm reminded that every city has two faces: the visible and the not-yet visible.

Dardis and I say good-bye, and I reluctantly leave the Café Sperl. Viennese coffeehouses have that effect on people. Once inside, you want to stay forever. Back in the day, that's what people did. They conducted business at the coffeehouse; a few even had their mail delivered there. Writer Hugo von Hofmannsthal, a regular at Café Central, once said, "Two attitudes seem modern in our time: analyzing life and escaping from it." In the coffeehouse, you could do both simultaneously, and for only a few shillings. It was pure genius.

I have an appointment with Dr. Freud, and I want to keep it. No, that's not the whole truth. Part of me wants to go but another part resists. This defiance no doubt stems from some deeply submerged childhood trauma, quite possibly involving my mother, but there is no time now for this sort of psychic excavation. I mustn't keep the good doctor waiting, not with his profound psychological insights and strict cancellation policy. Besides, if any one person encapsulates the intellectual hothouse that was Vienna, it is Sigmund Freud. He had a complex relationship with the city, one replete with all of the competing motives and unconscious wish fulfillment that the good doctor traded in.

I step softly, lightly, out of the Hotel Adagio and onto the Ring-strasse, with its grand buildings and elegant cafés, virtually unchanged since Freud's time. Freud loved the Ringstrasse and every day at precisely 2:00 p.m., rain or shine, circled it, walking at a brisk, almost frenetic pace. Clearly, he was sublimating.

The day is gray and drizzly, but I don't mind. I take quiet pleasure in each step, savoring the delicious fact that Freud walked here, too. *On this very ground.* What was he thinking as he marched so determinedly around the Ringstrasse? Was he fuming about having been passed over, yet again, for promotion to full professor? Was he furious that *The Interpretation of Dreams*, now a classic, had sold a measly three hundred copies in its first printing? Perhaps he was in a more upbeat mood, relishing his latest archaeological acquisition, plotting a home for it among the growing collection of statues and other artifacts that threatened to subsume his study. Perhaps Freud wasn't thinking about anything at all as he placed one foot in front of the other, but was simply *being*, in a Buddhist way, but that strikes me as highly unlikely. Freud was always turning over *something* in his mind, trying to solve an old problem, or discover a new one.

Freud was neither born in Vienna nor did he die here, yet the city shaped him, molded him, in ways large and small. Vienna midwifed his radical ideas about the human mind—ideas that could, I'm sure, only have taken flight in the Vienna of 1900. They would certainly have gained little altitude in his hometown of Freiberg, Moravia (now located in the Czech Republic). Population forty-five hundred, it was myopic and rabidly anti-Semitic, "an excellent place for his family to leave," writes Freud biographer Janine Burke. And leave they did, when Sigmund was only four years old. Had they not, we would not recognize the name Sigmund Freud.

Vienna became home, and home is always complicated. The more I learn about Freud's thorny, troubled relationship with Vienna, the more I am reminded of Mozart's equally hot-and-cold rapport with the city. Infuriated by slights, real and imagined, the composer regularly threatened to decamp to Paris or London, but could never bring himself to leave his beloved Vienna. Like Mozart, Freud was alternately ignored, loved, and despised, his reputation ebbing and flowing like the Danube in a storm. Like Mozart, Freud vacillated wildly. Sometimes, he spoke fondly of "my Vienna," but more often chose considerably harsher words for his adopted home. He once described the City of Dreams (so named, ironically, because of Freud's dream theory, which was at first roundly mocked) as "almost physically repulsive." Its inhabitants had "grotesque and animal-like faces . . . deformed skulls and potato noses." Such mutual enmity is one reason why Freud enjoyed a better reputation abroad than he did at home, the fate of many a genius.

As much as Vienna infuriated him ("I could beat my Viennese with a stick"), it also inspired him. Sometimes we find more inspiration in the places (and people) that annoy us than in those that please us. Freud needed Vienna, and Vienna needed Freud, though neither could bring themselves to admit it. What exactly was it about Vienna that, despite Freud's objections, goaded him toward greatness? Did he flourish here despite his troubled relationship with the city, or because of it?

When asked about the secret to a happy life, Freud famously answered, *"Liebe und Arbeit."* Love and work. He engaged in both activities wholeheartedly, unapologetically, at the same address: Berggasse 19. The Victorian building served as home office, meeting room, smoking lounge, library, and archaeological museum. Surely, I think, as I veer off the Ringstrasse and onto a side street, Freud's old address contains valuable clues into the greatness that was fin de siècle Vienna. But where is it? Once again, my GPS has failed me.

Then I turn a corner and—wham!—Freud hits me in the face like a therapeutic breakthrough. A bright red banner emblazoned with the letters F-R-E-U-D practically screams across the decades, demanding my attention. There's nothing subliminal or *un* about the sign. It is pure id.

Freud would not approve. He regarded the obvious with the same contempt most of us reserve for wine spritzers.

Berggasse 19, the solidly middle-class address where Freud overturned centuries of thinking about the human mind, today sits directly across the street from a thrift shop and an upmarket day spa offering hot-stone massages and mani-pedis. What does that *mean*? I wonder. I find myself asking that question a lot lately. It's inevitable, I suppose, when following in the smoke rings of the founder of psychoanalysis. I need to be careful, I remind myself, and silently vow to remain vigilant against this sort of overreach, to remember that sometimes a cigar is just a cigar, that not every sign is a SIGN.

I enter Berggasse 19 just as Freud did, through a set of heavy wooden doors and up a wide, marble staircase that exudes solidity. Everything about the building does. Did Freud's patients find that sturdiness reassuring? Did it alleviate concerns about placing their health, mental *and* physical, in the hands of a quack, a madman (Jewish no less) who traded in fairy tales? Did they know that, as they climbed these solid stairs, as I am now, they were embarking on a journey into uncharted depths of the human psyche? Did some, I wonder, turn back at the last minute? Or did they soldier on, reassured by Freud's credentials, or perhaps the recommendation of a friend who had been cured by the Moravian doctor? It was, I suspect, naked desperation that propelled these troubled souls, Vienna's worried wealthy, up the stairs and across the threshold into the pleasantly cluttered office of Herr Doktor.

"Welcome to Berggasse nineteen," I hear. The Voice is back. This time, appropriately, it has acquired a compassionate yet clinical tone. I feel reassured. All is well. Almost immediately, though, the Voice disappoints, as voices are wont to do. "If you are expecting to see the famous couch here, I have some bad news." Alas, explains the Voice, the couch is in London, where in 1938 Freud, one step ahead of the Nazis, fled to safety.

Okay, no couch. I can live with that. It's only a couch, I tell myself, and besides, a photo of it is on display here. Swollen with pillows and covered with a Persian rug, a colorful Qashqai, I have to admit, it looks inviting. Give me a few minutes on it, and I'd open up, too.

I step inside the entrance hall, and the century separating Freud and me instantly evaporates. The small space sits frozen in time, as if the good doctor had stepped out for a moment, perhaps for his afternoon constitutional around the Ringstrasse, and will return any minute now. There's his hat and walking stick, his traveling trunk, his leather doctor's bag, chunky and reassuring, a tartan blanket and a small pocket flask that Freud carried with him on his daily walks. Freud, a man of habit, kept the same furniture all his life. I'm reminded of Florence's good materialists. If ever there was a man of lofty ideas, it was Sigmund Freud, yet he also felt compelled to ground himself in the tactile world, lest he drift away into a permanent dream state.

The doorplate is the original and reads PROF. DR. FREUD. The doctor part came relatively easily, but not the professor title. Time and again, Freud was passed over for a full professorship, in favor of lesser candidates. His interest in the controversial topic of human sexuality surely didn't help his case, nor did his Jewishness. He persevered and eventually got that promotion, though only after two well-connected patients lobbied on his behalf.

Nearby, in the waiting room, I see a deck of tarock cards. He loved to play the local game, as he did most things Viennese. Whatever he said about the city, Freud was, in habit if not disposition, typically Viennese. Every morning he'd sit down with the *Neue Freie Presse*, the popular, devoutly liberal, and largely Jewish daily. At his favorite coffeehouse, the Landtmann, he sipped *einen kleinen Braunen* (a short black coffee) and, when hiking in the Alps, wore lederhosen and a feathered hat. Like many Jewish immigrants, Freud strived to be *überwienerisch*, more Viennese than the Viennese. Assimilation was the goal or, as Steven Beller puts it in his history of Viennese Jewry, "to become an invisible Jew." Alas, that proved impossible. In Austria at that time, there was no such thing as an invisible Jew. Vienna accepted outsiders into the fold, but only up to a point.

During Freud's day, a severe minimalism was in vogue, a movement spearheaded by the controversial architect Adolf Loos, but you wouldn't know it glancing around Freud's apartment. His taste, while not quite Beethovenian, favored Victorian coziness. "Cluttered plentitude" is how

Freud biographer Peter Gay describes it. Every inch of space was covered with *something*: Oriental carpets, photographs of friends, etchings, and, of course, books.

I walk into what was his old consulting room and see black-and-white photos of the Freuds. A young Sigmund, no older than six, standing next to his father, Jacob, a struggling and hapless wool merchant ("unheroic" in Freud's mind). They had recently arrived in Vienna, the Voice tells me.

As an immigrant, Freud was well positioned for greatness. A disproportionately large number of geniuses, from Victor Hugo to Frédéric Chopin, were geographically displaced, voluntarily or otherwise. One survey of twentieth-century geniuses found that one-fifth were first- or second-generation immigrants. That dynamic holds true today. Foreign-born immigrants account for only 13 percent of the US population but have nearly a third of all US patents granted and are 25 percent of all US Nobel laureates. Being an immigrant is one of the two most common life experiences of geniuses, along with "familial unpredictability," a redundancy if ever there was one.

Why are immigrants more likely to achieve genius status? The conventional explanation is that they belong to a closely knit group that is fiercely motivated. Immigrants have something to prove. I find that explanation accurate but incomplete. Sure, immigrant status might explain their economic rise, but what about their creative edge? Why would being born in another country make your ideas richer, your art more sublime?

Researchers believe the answer lies in "diversifying experiences," which Dutch psychologist Simone Ritter defines as "*highly unusual* and *unexpected* events or situations that are actively experienced and that push individuals outside the realm of 'normality.'" When this happens, we develop greater "cognitive flexibility"; that is, we see the world around us with fresh eyes.

Simply knowing of another way of looking at the world opens up possibilities and enhances cognitive flexibility, and the immigrant is, by dint of his life experience, exposed to these alternative viewpoints. Immigrants have more ingredients to work with than nonimmigrants, and that *can* lead to greater creativity. I say *can* because simply being exposed to a foreign culture will have zero impact on your creativity if you remain closed to new ways of thinking. Our minds don't automatically expand when confronted with something unusual. The opposite may happen. We may shrink, retreat psychologically, when confronted with the Other. So why do some people respond to a multicultural environment by becoming more open, and others by shutting down, or retreating to bigotry?

Psychologists aren't sure but suspect it comes down to obstacles. Immigrants face all sorts of obstacles and constraints, and constraints—or, more precisely, *our reactions* to these constraints—are the fuel that feeds the fires of creativity. For instance, as a young man Freud wanted to join the military, but that profession was closed to him as a Jew. He briefly considered a career as a lawyer, but one day he heard a lecture in which Goethe's essay "On Nature" was read, which said, "Nature! She hides under a thousand names and phrases and is always the same." Freud was mesmerized by those words and vowed to become a research scientist. Alas, practical matters—money—intervened. Research didn't pay well enough for him to start a family, so he pivoted, settled on a career in medicine. Had he not, he would never have seen those "hysterical" patients and might never have stumbled upon his theory of the unconscious.

Freud may be a household name today, but in the Vienna of 1900 he was known (if he was known at all) as a "dogged and awkward loner . . . an inconvenient outsider," recalled his friend Stefan Zweig. Freud's now-celebrated theories were greeted with a yawn, and a sneer, as a bunch of "fairy tales." That's not surprising. All genuinely creative ideas are initially met with rejection, since they necessarily threaten the status quo. An enthusiastic reception for a new idea is a sure sign that it is not original.

This rejection burned at Freud, infuriated him—and hardened his resolve. "Freud's intellectual originality and professional isolation fed off one another," writes Carl Schorske in his history of fin de siècle Vienna. As we saw in Athens, some people are devastated by rejection while others are motivated by it. Why such different reactions? As you recall, researchers at Johns Hopkins University found that rejection boosts creativity most markedly in those who consider themselves "independent minded";

that is, those who stand apart from the world, who rejoice in their Otherness. Freud, a self-proclaimed "conquistador," certainly fit the bill.

Freud was doubly marginalized. As a Jew, he existed on the fringes of Viennese society, belonging to "an alien race," as he once put it. He also resided on the periphery of his chosen profession, psychology. That is often the case with geniuses, as Thomas Kuhn points out in his landmark work, *The Structure of Scientific Revolutions*. He explains that newcomers to a discipline are less committed to traditional rules and "are particularly likely to see the rules no longer define a playable game and to conceive another set that can replace them." Geniuses are always marginalized to one degree or another. Someone wholly invested in the status quo is unlikely to disrupt it.

A glance at some of history's greatest discoveries and inventions demonstrates the power of the outsider. Michael Ventris was a professional architect who, in his spare time, deciphered Linear B, Europe's earliest writing, a language that had stumped classicists for centuries. Ventris succeeded not despite his lack of expertise in the classics but because of it. He wasn't burdened by bad knowledge. Nor was Luis Alvarez. A nuclear physicist by training, he, not a paleontologist, determined that a huge asteroid striking the earth led to the extinction of the dinosaurs. The paleontologists were fixated on terrestrial explanations: climate change or perhaps competition for food with early mammals. Alvarez looked skyward for answers, and that is where he found one.

So it was with Sigmund Freud. Medicine at the time could not explain why Freud's patients—young, otherwise healthy women, for the most part—were suffering from "hysteria" or other neurological conditions. The discipline of psychology proved inadequate to the task, so Freud, in true genius fashion, invented an entirely new field and called it psychoanalysis. Freud was what Harvard psychologist Howard Gardner calls a "Maker," or what I like to think of as a Master Builder, someone whose genius lies not in their contributions to an existing discipline but in constructing an entirely new one. This is, I think, the highest form of genius.

"Freud's passions included traveling, smoking, and collecting," the Voice tells me. One of these would kill him. The other two would inspire.

Freud's passion for collecting was a very Viennese thing, though his was of a specific kind. An amateur archaeologist, he greedily scooped up ancient statues and other artifacts.

Evidence of this passion lies before my eyes now. I hardly know where to focus first. Over here is the wooden figure of a bird-headed deity from ancient Egypt that Freud kept next to his chair during analysis sessions. Over there, an Egyptian tombstone in bas-relief. Here a plaster cast of an antique relief, *Gradiva*, and there, a cabinet filled with ancient artifacts, and a picture of the Sphinx at Giza.

When Freud feared losing the entire collection to the Nazis, he arranged to have two pieces smuggled out: a nineteenth-century Chinese jade screen and a tiny statue of Athena, the Greek goddess of wisdom. Scarred and pitted, the statue occupied pride of place on Freud's desk. This is no coincidence. Athena represents not only wisdom but reason, and Freud aimed to understand, rationally, the deeply irrational psychic forces that drive us in peculiar, unhealthy directions. The statue, always within sight, served as a constant reminder of the primacy of reason, even in seemingly irrational times.

Freud had the good fortune of living during the heyday of archaeology. New sites were being discovered almost every week, it seemed, ancient wonders unearthed. Many of these ended up in Vienna's numerous museums and the curio shops frequented by Freud. Nor was there a shortage of experts willing to talk about these miraculous findings. Freud's heroes were almost all archaeologists; the one he admired most was Heinrich Schliemann, who, in 1871, discovered the ancient site of Troy. Freud also struck up a friendship with Emanuel Lowy, a professor of archaeology. "He keeps me up to three o'clock in the morning," Freud wrote. "He tells me about Rome."

Freud was no dilettante. He had a deep understanding of these ancient cultures and applied this to his psychological theories. He once likened himself to a sort of excavator of the human psyche since, as he told one patient, he "must uncover layer after layer of the patient's psyche, before coming to the deepest, most valuable treasures."

Freud placed his artifacts strategically so that no matter where he looked as he sat in his upholstered consulting chair, his eyes fell on something old and significant. They were there when he treated patients, and they were there when he sat down in his study, often late at night, to write.

Creative people do this. They surround themselves with visual and auditory, and even olfactory, prompts. Why? So that even when they are not thinking about a problem, they are thinking about it. Incubating. Creative geniuses spend a lot less time with furrowed brows than the rest of us.

The artifacts that crowded Freud's office affected not only him but also his patients, some of whom described the consulting room in almost religious terms. "There was always a feeling of sacred peace and quiet," recalls Sergei Pankejeff, a wealthy Russian aristocrat whom Freud nicknamed the Wolf Man because he dreamed of trees filled with white wolves. "Here was all kinds of statuettes and other unusual objects, which even the layman recognized as archaeological finds of ancient Egypt," he recalled.

Freud, not an outwardly demonstrative man, spoke effusively of his collection. "I must always have an object to love," he once told his colleague, and later rival, Carl Jung. Freud collected until his last days, believing that "a collection to which there are no new additions is really dead."

Freud's interest in supposedly dead civilizations (I say *supposedly* because ancient Greek and Roman ideas live on inside all of us) underscores something I've encountered ever since I landed in Athens: the past matters. We can't innovate without building on the past, and we can't build on the past unless we know it. No one understood this better than Sigmund Freud.

Archaeology was Freud's hobby, and here he joins hands with many geniuses. Darwin gobbled up novels. Einstein played the violin, and played it well. "Life without playing music for me is inconceivable," he once said. A recent study found that Nobel laureates in the sciences are more involved in the arts than less eminent scientists.

These outside interests serve several purposes. First of all, they diffuse attention and allow problems to marinate. They exercise different mental muscles. Einstein, for instance, took brief music breaks *while* working on particularly thorny physics problems. "Music helps him when he is thinking about his theories," his wife, Elsa, said. "He goes to his study, comes back, strikes a few chords on the piano, jots something down, returns to his study." Recalled Einstein's eldest son, Hans Albert, "Whenever he felt he had come to the end of the road or into a difficult situation in his work, he would take refuge in his music. That would usually resolve all his difficulties."

Sometimes, these diversions have a more direct impact on the genius's work. Galileo was able to discern the moons of Jupiter partly because of his training in the visual arts, specifically a technique known as chiaroscuro, used to depict light and shadow. Archaeology played a similar role for Freud. It directly informed his psychological theories, such as the Oedipus complex.

Vienna, a crossroads of cultures and ideas, encouraged this sort of intellectual synthesis. Yes, there were boxes, academic and professional constraints, as there are everywhere, but people moved more freely from one box to another. The novelist Robert Musil was trained as an engineer. His fellow writer Arthur Schnitzler was a physician. The physicist Ernst Mach was also a renowned philosopher.

Freud kept the city's literati at arm's length, but he couldn't help but benefit from the billiards table that was Vienna. He ricocheted off some of the other creative geniuses of the day. The composer Gustav Mahler was briefly a patient of his, seeing Freud for help with impotency. An etching hanging on a wall here suggests another collision. It is of a bushy-haired Einstein. The two men met once, in 1927, in a suburb of Berlin. Over coffee and cake, they chatted for some two hours. Afterward, Freud described Einstein as "cheerful, agreeable, and sure of himself," adding, "He understands about as much about psychoanalysis as I do about physics so we had a very pleasant talk."

They had more in common, though, than that. Reading Einstein's journals, I am struck by how, like Freud, he saw himself as an outcast, one man against the world: "I am truly a 'lone traveler' and have never belonged to my country, my home, my friends, or even my immediate family with my whole heart." Those words could just as easily have been written by Freud or Michelangelo or any number of other geniuses.

Vienna afforded a young and curious physician such as Sigmund Freud all sorts of opportunities for experimentation—some fruitful and others not. A glass container on display here, the size and shape of a mayonnaise jar, tells the tale of one such ill-fated experiment. Purchased from the Merck Company, the jar contained packs of cocaine. At the time, in the late nineteenth century, cocaine was a new and little-understood drug. Some doctors, including Freud, believed it might be used to treat all sorts of ailments, from heart disease to nervous exhaustion.

Freud tested the drug on himself and, in 1887, reported, "I have taken the drug myself for several months without any desire for continued use of cocaine." Clearly, he wasn't using it properly, I think, before digging deeper into Freud's cocaine habit. The drug led to an incident he would regret for the rest of his life and that would haunt his dreams. He prescribed cocaine to a sick friend, only worsening his suffering by adding addiction to his other maladies. Cocaine did have a therapeutic benefit, as an anesthetic for eye surgery, but Freud overlooked that breakthrough, and instead credit went to his friend Carl Koller (dubbed "Coca Koller" by Freud).

In other words, Freud failed. Here again we bump up against one of the most misunderstood aspects of genius: failure. Usually, when the topic comes up, so, too, does the old bromide about how successful people "embrace failure." Which is true. They do. Except it is also true that failures embrace failure. If anything, they embrace it more tightly. So, what is the difference between failure that leads to innovation and failure that leads to . . . more failure?

The answer, researchers now believe, lies not in the failure itself but how we recall it or, more precisely, how we store it. Successful failures are those people who remember exactly where and how they failed, so when they encounter the same problem again, even if in a different guise, they are able to retrieve these "failure indices" quickly and efficiently. "When the critical information is found, the partial picture suddenly becomes complete and the solution is found," explains one psychologist. In other words, "successful failures" reach an impasse like everyone else but are better at remembering the exact "location" of that impasse. They are willing to backtrack.

The implications of this are tremendous. For starters, it suggests that knowledge by itself is less important than how we store that knowledge, and how readily we can access it. Also, the advice we were given as children when confronted with failure, "forget it and move on," is dead wrong. "*Remember* it and move on" is the way of the genius.

I step into Freud's private study gingerly, as if entering sacred ground. There is the gold-rimmed mirror that hung over his desk. How often, I wonder, did he gaze into it and see the effects of all those surgeries, attempts to stem the cancer that was eating away at his jaw, the result of all those cigars? Freud was in great pain but kept smoking right up until the end. If he couldn't smoke, he said, he couldn't write. He worked constantly, seeing patients from early in the morning, meeting with colleagues and friends in the evening, and then reading and writing until late at night. Just like Mozart.

One of Freud's most loved objects, still here, was his desk chair. It was designed by a friend to accommodate Freud's unusual sitting position. He sat diagonally, with one leg thrown over the chair's arm, his head unsupported and a book held high in the air. Later, I'd try to replicate this position myself and couldn't maintain it for more than a few seconds before various body parts began to cramp. Why in the world would Freud sit that way? Did he actually find it comfortable? Was it simple masochism? What did it *mean*?

Perhaps he was trying (unconsciously of course) to create a "schema violation." A schema violation is when our world is turned upside down. Temporal or spatial cues are off. Something is wrong. Beethoven's pigsty of an apartment or Einstein's messy desk are a kind of schema violation. A few psychologists have tried to induce a schema violation in the laboratory. For instance, they would ask some participants to make breakfast in the "wrong" order, and others to make breakfast in the conventional way. Those in the first group—the ones engaged in a schema violation—subsequently demonstrated more "cognitive flexibility." You don't have to actually participate in a schema violation to benefit from it. Watching others do it (provided you can relate to them) is enough to do the trick. For creativity, watching people do weird things is nearly the same as doing those weird things ourselves.

This explains a lot. It explains why in a creative place such as Vienna breakthroughs in one field led to breakthroughs in entirely different fields. As Howard Gardner puts it, "The very knowledge that there *could* be a new painting raised the likelihood of a new dance or poetry or politics." Schema violations explain how Freud was influenced by the cultural scene of Vienna even though he didn't engage in it directly. Novelty was in the air. Genius begets more genius.

What's more, new ideas such as Freud's had a better shot at recognition in a city such as Vienna because, as Mihaly Csikszentmihalyi puts it, "creativity is more likely in places where new ideas require less effort to be perceived." Places accustomed to new ideas, new ways of thinking, are more attuned to their arrival, and genius and the recognition of genius are inseparable. You can't have one without the other.

Vienna also provided Freud with the raw materials he needed to forge his theories. A seemingly endless flow of the worried wealthy washed up on Freud's overstuffed couch, for the City of Dreams was also the City of Lies. Here was a city where everyone was having sex but nobody talked about it. Here was a city that invented a word, *Wienerschmäh*, for the art of telling beautiful lies. The city had become, in the words of journalist Karl Kraus, a "moral sewer called Vienna, where nothing and no one was honest, where everything was a charade."

Consider the case of Felix Salten, a young writer best known as the author of *Bambi: A Life in the Woods*, the inspiration for the Disney movie. Salten is also the author of *Josephine Mutzenbacher: Memoirs of a Viennese Prostitute*. Here is a snippet from the very first paragraph: "I became a whore at an early age and experienced everything a woman can—in bed, on chairs, across tables, over benches, standing against walls, lying on the grass, in dark hallways, in private bedchambers, on railroad cars, in lodging houses, in jail; in fact, in every conceivable place where it was possible—but I have no regrets." Let's examine exactly what we're dealing with here. The creator of *Bambi*—*Bambi!*—was secretly writing pornographic novels on the side. This single fact tells you everything you need to know about life in turn-of-the-century Vienna, and why it was the perfect place for Sigmund Freud and his far-fetched theories about the human psyche. "It is difficult to envision [Freud's] own scholarly career and output having taken place in a radically different environment," concludes Gardner.

Yet Freud's ideas were not bound by place and time. That is the way brilliant ideas work. They sprout only under certain specific circumstances yet are universally relevant. Ideas are like bananas. That bananas grow only in tropical regions doesn't make them any less delicious in Scandinavia.

Freud saw himself as "an adventurer . . . with all the inquisitiveness, daring and tenacity of such a man." If Freud was Don Quixote, then he needed a Sancho Panza. Every genius does. Picasso had Georges Braque; Martha Graham had Louis Horst; Stravinsky, Sergey Diaghilev. Who was Freud's Sancho?

I find myself staring at a faded photograph of two bearded men. One is Freud, not the professorial and stooped Freud of later years but a young and feral Freud, with a linebacker build, fulsome beard, and a glint of recklessness in his eyes. The man standing next to him is slighter in stature. Both are staring into the distance, as if they see something that has piqued their interest.

The second man is Wilhelm Fliess, a brilliant but eccentric physician and numerologist. The two men, both adrift in their otherness, met at a conference and became fast friends, corresponding for a decade. "I am pretty much alone here with the clearing up of the neurosis," Freud wrote to Fliess in 1894, shortly after they met. "They pretty much consider me a monomaniac."

Fliess read Freud's manuscripts, offering critiques and suggestions, and Freud provided an audience for Fliess's strange ideas. They seemed like a natural fit. A classic case of compensatory genius. Here were two "highly trained professional physicians working at, or beyond, the frontiers of acceptable medical inquiry," as Peter Gay writes. What's more, they were both Jewish and therefore "propelled into intimacy with the ease of brothers in a persecuted tribe."

Fliess had some *very* odd ideas. He believed that all health problems, especially sexual ones, could be traced to the nose. He recommended cocaine for treatment of this "nasal reflex neurosis" and, failing that, surgery. He performed such surgery on several patients, including his new friend Sigmund Freud. We don't know if Freud believed any of Fliess's wild ideas, but Fliess "was precisely the intimate he needed: audience, confidant, stimulus, cheerleader, fellow speculator shocked at nothing," says Gay. In one letter, writing in the full bloom of their bromance, Freud says to Fliess, "You are the only Other." Freud's choice of words is telling. What did the great Sigmund Freud see in this Other, this strange little man with a nasal fixation?

We have to keep in mind that at the time Fliess's ideas were no more outlandish than Freud's. Both men teetered on the edge of respectability, so they propped up each other. "You have taught me," a grateful Freud wrote, "that a bit of truth lurks behind every popular lunacy."

Sometimes, though, what lurks behind lunacy is more lunacy, and Freud eventually reached that sad but unavoidable conclusion about Fliess. They began to argue constantly. By the summer of 1901, Freud informed his erstwhile friend that "you have reached the limits of your perspicacity." The bromance was over.

Today, while Freud's ideas may be out of fashion, he still stands alongside history's greatest minds, while Wilhelm Fliess is a forgotten crank with some strange ideas about the nose. But would Freud have succeeded, overcome his isolation, without Fliess, his Sancho Panza, by his side? Remember: exposure to dissenting views boosts creative thinking *even if those dissenting views are dead wrong.* Freud needed Fliess. He needed him as a sounding board, for his ear, not his nose. In their correspondence (only Freud's letters survived), you can hear the good doctor wrestling with despair ("Gloomy times, unbelievably gloomy"), and testing his newfangled ideas on a receptive, yet also critical, friend.

The case of Wilhelm Fliess reminds us that places of genius are not only magnets but also colanders. They separate the wacky but brilliant ideas from the plain wacky. Vienna rejected Fliess's ideas but, eventually, accepted Freud's. That is the genius of the colander.

Freud may have dumped Fliess, but he remained a conquistador, one in need of fellow travelers. This time, though, he wouldn't put all his eggs in one crazy basket.

I'm staring at another photograph. The half dozen or so men depicted are posing stiffly, even by the stiff standards of the day. Staring into the camera intently, as if thinking deeply, or perhaps constipated, a few manage a quarter smile. Not Freud. He is seated in the middle, signaling his primacy, his beard now sufficiently tamed, hat resting on his knee, his expression revealing nothing, à la Socrates. I look more closely and see that all the men, including Freud, are wearing identical gold rings. These are the founding members of the Wednesday Circle. Begun in the fall of 1902, its members included young physicians "with the declared intention of learning, practicing, and disseminating psychoanalysis."

The Wednesday Circle met at Freud's house at 8:30 p.m. after dinner. The meetings followed a strict routine, as one of the founding members, Max Graf, recounts: "First, one of the members would present a paper. Then, black coffee and cakes were served; cigars and cigarettes were on the table and were consumed in great quantities. After a social quarter of an hour, the discussion would begin. The last and the decisive word was always spoken by Freud himself."

It was a heady time. All in that room sensed that they were present at the creation of something akin to a new religion. "We were like pioneers in a newly discovered land, and Freud was the leader," recalled Wilhelm Stekel, another founding member. "A spark seemed to jump from one mind to another, and every evening was like a revelation."

Freud needed the Wednesday Circle. He was in uncharted waters. His theories about human sexuality were radical and subversive. He needed not only collaboration but also confirmation of his sanity, lest he suffer the fate of many a budding genius: a nervous breakdown. Howard Gardner believes that support is needed on the verge of a creative breakthrough "more so than at any time in life since early infancy." He says the budding genius most of all needs conversation, "often inarticulate and struggling," but which "represents a way for the creator to test that he or she is still sane, still understandable to a sympathetic member of the species."

I am about to leave Freud's office, but I'm curious about something. Whatever happened to Freud's beloved artifacts? By the end of his life, the collection had mushroomed to some three thousand items, occupying every spare inch of space of Berggasse 19. Most of them accompanied Freud when, in 1938, he fled Vienna, an escape engineered by Marie Bonaparte, his most faithful, and powerful, disciple. He settled in London, where, surrounded by his beloved artifacts, he told a visitor, "I'm home again, as you see."

Home among his objects but not his city. To the very end, Freud was ambivalent about Vienna. Should we be surprised? Not really. That's the way it is with geniuses and their cities; the fit is never perfect; there's always an element of friction, of discord. Socrates loved Athens like a brother, and the city repaid him with a death sentence. Su Tungpo's beloved Hangzhou sent him into exile, not once but twice. Leonardo blossomed in Florence, but when rivals circled, and the Duke of Milan beckoned, he decamped. Freud and Vienna were not always a happy fit, but they were a *productive* fit. They brought out the best in each other. Perhaps, I think, as I linger in Freud's study, that explains the geography of genius. Yes, I feel that I'm on the verge of a breakthrough, some deep insight into not only the nature of creative genius but also my own lifelong search for fulfillment. Yes, it's all coming together. All that's missing is . . .

"I'm sorry but that's all the time we have today," the Voice informs me.

Typical, I think, stepping out onto the street and finding a slate-gray sky. As I walk east, toward the Ringstrasse and the Hotel Adagio, I can't help but smile. Even in death, Freud continues to illuminate and frustrate, in more or less equal measure.

As I walk back to my hotel, it occurs to me that while Freud may have been an outlier, a self-proclaimed conquistador and philistine, he shared at least one obvious trait with the literati of Vienna: his Jewishness. This was one of the defining characteristics of Vienna's golden age. While Jews constituted only 10 percent of Vienna's population, they accounted for more than half of its doctors and lawyers, and nearly two-thirds of its journalists, as well as a disproportionately high number of the city's creative geniuses, from the writer Arthur Schnitzler to the composer Arnold Schoenberg to the philosopher Ludwig Wittgenstein. It is, writes Steven Beller in *Vienna and the Jews*, a number "so large it cannot be ignored."

Why were so many of the city's greatest minds Jewish? Does the answer lie in genetics—did Jews, as Francis Galton would have it, "introduce a valuable strain of blood"? Of course not. The explanation is cultural. For starters, Jews enjoyed a centuries-old tradition of literacy, one they maintained even when sequestered in the shtetlach of Europe. By studying the Talmud and other religious texts, Jews kept their minds sharp, nurtured their love of ideas, and reveled in that particularly Jewish pastime: the joy of argumentation.

This studiousness explains some, but not all, of their success. Jewish ambition was bridled for so long that, when it was finally unleashed in the "emancipation of 1867," the result was dramatic. Thousands of Jews flocked from the countryside to Vienna, which had become "the prime escape route from the ghetto," says Beller.

These new arrivals settled in the neighborhood of Leopoldstadt, on the northern bank of the Danube Canal. Today, in the wake of the Holocaust, it is home to a much smaller Jewish community, and I have come here looking for answers.

I step into the Georgian café that my lunch partner had recommended and quickly spot him, in glasses and a sweater, looking relaxed and writerly. Doron Rabinovici, a novelist, is a longtime resident of Vienna and an expert on the city's Jewish past.

We order lunch, and soon after I dive into my questions. Why were so many of the geniuses of fin de siècle Vienna Jewish?

Pent-up demand, he says. Certain professions, such as the military and most government jobs, remained closed to Jews, so they channeled their energies into those that were open: law, medicine, and journalism.

"Okay, this might explain why Jews succeeded in these fields," I reply, "but success is not the same as creative genius. How did the Jewishness of a Freud or a Karl Kraus explain the creative leaps they made?"

"Let's look at Freud. As a Jew, he was an outsider from the beginning.

So he was not so afraid to be an outsider with his ideas. He had nothing to lose."

I have an aha moment, right there in a Georgian café in the Jewish quarter of Vienna. If you were an insider—say, a member of the ruling Hapsburg family—you're not about to rock the boat. But if you are a Jew in Vienna in 1900, the boat is already rocking, so why not make a few more waves? It's the blessing of the outsider, and it explains not only why Jews excelled in Vienna but why other marginalized peoples do as well. In the United States, for instance, Unitarians, per capita, account for a hundred times more notable scientists than do Methodists, Baptists, and Roman Catholics. Geniuses are also statistically more likely to come from religiously mixed marriages. Marie Curie's father was an atheist, her mother a Catholic. (Marie grew up in devoutly Catholic Poland.)

For the Jews of Vienna, it wasn't their religious beliefs that propelled them to greatness (most were secular), but their marginality, the precarious station they occupied. In a big city such as Vienna, continues Doron, "everybody had their place, except for the Jews, and therefore some of them developed really interesting new and avant-garde ideas."

"And one of them is Freud's theory of the unconscious?"

"Yes," says Doron, and that is no coincidence. A Jewish thinker such as Freud was perfectly positioned to come up with a theory of the irrational because he faced an irrational situation every day. "If you wanted to be an Austrian, you were told, okay, then you have to assimilate. And if you assimilated, they would say you never will really succeed because in your inner, inner soul you are still a Jew. I mean, if you are a Jew in Vienna, irrationality is on your mind because it is irrational how they behave towards you."

This makes sense. As we've seen, creative people have an especially higher tolerance for ambiguity, and nothing was more ambiguous than the life of a Jew in the Vienna of 1900. You were simultaneously an insider and an outsider, one of us and one of them, accepted and shunned. This is not a comfortable position—the psychic equivalent of Freud splayed across his reading chair—but it is, I think, the perfect configuration for creative genius. As outsiders, Jews were able to see the world around them with fresh eyes; as insiders, they were able to propagate these fresh insights, to make the invisible visible. For a while. The precarious position they occupied didn't last long and ended disastrously.

Everything about the Vienna Academy of Fine Arts reeks of solidity and permanence. It feels as if it could withstand a nuclear strike. It takes all my strength to pull open a heavy wooden door, the same door that a young artist tried, and failed, to breach in 1904. He applied twice and was rejected twice. The young artist grew increasingly despondent and bitter and, soon, angry as well. Eventually, he abandoned art and entered politics. As I step through the door, I can't help but wonder how history might have been different had the academy seen fit to accept this young artist named Adolf Hitler.

Here I find Martin Guttmann, in black T-shirt and jeans, looking considerably younger than his fifty-odd years. Guttmann, an Israeli-born physicist, is ostensibly teaching a photography class. He considers it philosophy, though. All art is philosophy, he tells me. No wonder he feels at home in Vienna, I think. This city, historically at least, tolerated hybrid thinkers like Martin Guttmann.

We walk the short distance to the Café Sperl, just as the artist Gustav Klimt did many times, and find a table outside. Martin lights up immediately. Everyone around us is puffing away, too. This is the tame Viennese's last rebellious act. *We no longer lead the world culturally or intellectually or in any other way, but we smoke like a global power!*

I tell Martin about my quest, about what I've learned so far in Vienna, and what I haven't yet. One question foremost on my mind is population. Unlike Athens or Florence or Edinburgh, Vienna was an enormous city, with more than 2 million people crowded onto its streets by 1900. What role did this play in its flourishing?

"Have you heard of phase transition?"

"No."

"Okay, let's say you have a bunch of molecules, and without even heating them, you put them in a smaller space or you put them in a bigger space. By doing that, you can turn the molecules from gas to liquid or liquid to solid, and these things have completely different observable properties. If you pressure water, just by putting it in a smaller volume, it becomes ice."

"Just by changing the space?"

"Yes. That is what is called phase transition. By changing the external environment you can create new properties that are completely different, a different regime. And you see it happening again and again."

The Vienna of 1900 was experiencing a sort of phase transition, except instead of more and more molecules squeezed into a small space, it was people. It's the urban-density theory again, but with a twist. What matters, says Martin, is not only the degree of density but the *rate* at which it occurs.

"From the 1880s to before the First World War, Vienna quadrupled or quintupled in population. Now try to imagine what it means to be in a city that quadruples in three decades, from say the 1980s until today. It means that you go out on the street and all of a sudden you become engulfed. It is cumulative. But you can feel it yourself. If you live on the same street and the population quadruples or quintuples, all of a sudden you begin to see the regime of chaos. And if the question is, 'How does a place like Vienna help geniuses?' I would say in the 1890s people were more open to revolutionary thinking because from their own experience they saw that things were changing qualitatively."

I like Martin and his mind and could sit here all day, sipping beer, inhaling secondhand smoke and thirdhand ideas. As we range over topics from physics to sex, I get a taste of what it must have been like to live in the Vienna of 1900. A spring afternoon. A cold beer. No agenda, and no silos. People from wildly divergent fields actually speaking to one another, and in language unburdened by jargon. "You pick up a book from a physicist in the 1890s, and it is written in a way that people can understand. They had to defend their theories to a wide audience," Martin tells me. How different from today, I think, when an academic is considered successful when no one can understand a word he says.

Martin has developed his own "taxonomy of genius," as he calls it. He sees only two kinds of geniuses: unifiers and revolutionaries.

Revolutionaries, the more recognizable kind of genius, turn conventional wisdom on its head. Unifiers "take a lot of distinct, unconnected ideas and put them all together in a way that is completely unopposable. Completely defensible." Unifiers connect the dots. Revolutionaries create new dots.

One type of genius isn't better than the other, says Martin, just different. We may value revolutionaries more today—our age worships at the feet of creative destruction—but unifiers, such as Bach and Kant and Newton, can change the world every bit as much as revolutionaries, and sometimes more. Bach, for instance, took a lot of disparate musical traditions and integrated them in a way no one had done before.

The milieu matters much more for revolutionaries than for unifiers. "You can be a unifier anywhere," Martin says. "But if you are a revolutionary, you need a special environment."

"What sort of environment?"

"An environment that dramatizes a predicament."

"So they can revolt against something?"

"No, so they can feel the break is in the air."

"What do you mean?"

"In the Vienna of 1900, everybody felt a break was in the air. And the break was everywhere. You see a break in music, and a break in physics. So people said, 'What about my field? Maybe there is a break there, too?'"

I sip my beer and recall those "schema violations," as well as Dean Simonton's research. He reviewed the historical records and found that whenever new, and often competing, schools of philosophy emerged, other *completely unrelated* fields also thrived. The break was in the air.

The Vienna of 1900 had "so many breaks in the air that you felt like the entire world was breaking up," says Martin. That's why the contemporary journalist and raconteur Karl Kraus described turn-of-the-century Vienna as "a laboratory for world endings." People knew they were living in a dying empire, that an explosion was coming; it was only a question of when. This sense of impending collapse was, oddly, liberating. The old rules no longer applied, so why not think about problems differently? That is, says Martin, exactly what Freud did.

"He started hearing more and more stories from women who were coming to him saying they were abused, and he said it couldn't be true that they were all abused. And then he started saying, 'Well, they have this kind of fantasy life,' and that is really where psychology starts. At some point he had to say, 'They couldn't all be true.' In other words, it is a break from the most simple explanation. And that is something that one needs a certain mentality for. When would you ever go in this direction?"

"It takes guts, doesn't it?"

"It takes guts, but you also have to be open to this kind of tsunami idea that is completely opposed to common sense. And how do you get there? When you see it happening elsewhere."

Toward the end of my time in Vienna, I find myself standing in front of the Loos House, the groundbreaking work of architect Adolf Loos. It sits directly across a small square from the Hofburg Palace, the former seat of power and, at the turn of the century, home to the ruler Franz Joseph. Perhaps fifty yards separates the two. Fifty yards and about five centuries, for one represents the old world and the other the new. The palace is ornate in the extreme, fronted with classic domes and statues of Greek gods. It looks like something out of a children's fairy tale gone horribly awry.

The Loos House, on the other hand, is austere and minimalist. "The house with no eyebrows," people called it, because it had no blinds. Loos's choice of location was no accident, for his work was a reaction to the frilliness of the Hapsburgs. In his essay "Ornament and Crime," Loos lays out his architectural philosophy: "The evolution of culture marches with the elimination of ornament from useful objects." Excessive ornamentation, he believed, causes objects to go out of style and become obsolete. Ornamentation was wasteful and "degenerate," and no society that indulged in it could rightfully call itself modern. If, as Brady had told me back in Athens, genius always makes the world a little bit simpler, then, Loos argued, ornamentation does the opposite. He said, "You can measure the culture of a country by the extent to which its lavatory walls are scribbled." I read that and sigh; this does not bode well for us.

The intellectual dynamism of a Freud or a Wittgenstein constituted a reaction to this ornamentation; an attempt to hack through all that frilliness and arrive at the truth. Vienna was a teacher, but one of object lessons as much as anything else. Places of genius challenge us. They are difficult. They do not earn their place in history with ethnic restaurants or street festivals, but by provoking us, making *demands* of us. Crazy, unrealistic, beautiful demands.

Emperor Franz Joseph was progressive in some ways, but not when it came to architecture. He despised the Loos House. He considered it an abomination, an affront to a centuries-old tradition of frilliness. No surprise there. What is surprising, though, is what he did about it—or, rather, what he *didn't* do. He did not have Loos noosed or even arrested. Surely he could have. He was emperor after all, and if history has taught us anything, it is that emperors can do as they damn well please. No, Franz Joseph took more of a housekeeping approach. He ordered the palace blinds drawn so he wouldn't have to see the Loos House. It was a practical, and tolerant, reaction. Perfectly Viennese.

So, too, was the reaction to the poster I'm staring at now, smack in the middle of the Ringstrasse. It's a painting of a woman. She is looking to one side, avoiding my gaze. She is well toned, muscular even. She is wearing a pair of bright orange boots, and the mildly annoyed expression of a runway model. Nothing else. A triangle of black hair is clearly visible between her legs. You can't help but look. The artist, Gustav Klimt, surely intended it that way. The painting is arresting even today. I can only imagine what kind of reaction it elicited a century ago. In his career, Klimt ran into obstacles—a work commissioned by the University of Vienna was deemed too controversial—but by and large he was free to pursue his art unmolested. Likewise, Freud published his scandalous treatises on human sexuality without fear of censorship.

As I stroll along the Danube Canal, walk Vienna's streets, ride its silky-smooth streetcars, a word pops into mind: nice. Vienna today is nice. A pleasant curio shop of past glories, like your grandfather's attic, only with better coffee. The Vienna of 1900, though, wasn't nice. It was a city of dirty politics and brothels and a palpable sense of impending disaster. Tension is a necessary ingredient for a place of genius. Tension in the larger world of politics, and tension in the smaller worlds of writers' conclaves and board meetings. Tension, not necessity, is the mother of invention.

It starts to rain, at first a pleasant drizzle, then a not-so-pleasant downpour. I seek shelter at the Café Sperl, this time alone. I ensconce in a corner booth, with its plush, soft-green velour padding, faded, and practically oozing *Gemütlichkeit*, a particular kind of coziness. This is another side of the Viennese coffeehouse, one not of conversation but of contemplation. From my perch, I defocus my attention and watch the world go by. It does not go by quickly. Time passes differently in a Viennese coffeehouse. Less presto, more adagio.

Darkness has settled. I order cheese, and some herring, and wonder, if I sit in a Viennese coffeehouse long enough and drink enough turbocharged espresso, might I, too, become a genius? Might I develop a theory of the unconscious or a radically new school of art, or atonal music? Or might I just get the jitters? Tough to say. But the world now seems, as Loos imagined it, vast and intimate at the same time. The more I ponder that formula, the more I realize it may hold the key to the genius that was Vienna. To create, we need both elements: vastness to open our minds to the Other, intimacy to consolidate our insights.

A woman sits at the piano and begins to play. This being Vienna, she plays well. As I nibble on my herring and take in the music, not so much listening as imbibing, it dawns on me that Vienna's double dip of genius was an illusion. It was, in fact, one continuous golden age, with an interlude, a gap, that allowed the orchestra to catch its breath before playing again, this time with even more passion and virtuosity.

Most golden ages fizzle. Vienna's ended with a bang. Literally. On June 28, 1914, in Sarajevo, a young Serbian assassin named Gavrilo Princip shot and killed Archduke Franz Ferdinand, the heir presumptive to the Austrian throne, sparking World War I. Vienna's reign as a cultural and scientific juggernaut came crashing to an end. After the war, other European capitals enjoyed their moments in the sun, Paris and Berlin in the

1920s, for instance, but the mantle of genius soon sailed West, across the Atlantic and to the New World. These American places of genius were different: less eclectic, more specialized. Think of New Orleans and jazz; Detroit and cars; Hollywood and film; New York and modern art.

The ultimate example of this new monochrome golden age took root not in a big city, but in the rolling farmland and suburban sprawl of Northern California. In 1971, a young journalist writing in a trade journal called *Electronic News* gave the place a name: Silicon Valley. It stuck; a catchy moniker for what is perhaps the least likely yet most far-reaching genius cluster. As I board the plane that will take me there, I wonder, is it the last great place?

EIGHT

GENIUS IS WEAK:
SILICON VALLEY

I AM IN A BOOKSTORE WITH MY NINE-YEAR-OLD daughter. Having successfully steered her away from Harry Potter land and nimbly skirted Rick Riordan world, we find ourselves in the nonfiction section. I'm trying to get her interested in history, and in genius.

I spot a display that seems to satisfy both wishes: minibiographies of famous historical figures: *Who Was Benjamin Franklin? Who Was Albert Einstein?* And there, sandwiched between Thomas Jefferson and Theodore Roosevelt, is Steve Jobs.

Really? Steve Jobs? Sharing the same lofty cerebral space with Jefferson and Franklin—and Einstein?

While I was researching this book, people always asked me, "How do you define *genius*?" I answer their question with a question: Was Steve Jobs a genius? The responses are invariably passionate, and split right down the middle.

"Yes, absolutely he was a genius," some people argue, whipping out their iPhone to underscore their point. "Look at this thing, man. It's awesome. Steve Jobs changed the world. Of course he was a genius."

"No, he wasn't," others argue just as passionately. "He didn't invent anything. He stole other people's ideas." Okay, they concede, "Perhaps he was a marketing genius or a design genius." They say this knowing full well that true genius never requires a modifier. We don't describe Einstein as a "scientific genius" or Mozart as a "musical genius." Both of these men transcended their particular fields, as genius always does.

So who was Steve Jobs? Genius or not? The Fashionista Theory of Genius tells us that, yes, Jobs was a genius because we (or at least many of us) believe he was. Genius is a social verdict, and the people have tweeted. That we are even asking the question of Jobs and not of, say, Thomas Adès, speaks gigabytes. Never heard of him? He's one of the greatest classical composers of our time. We get the geniuses that we want and that we deserve.

A more important question, for my purposes, is not whether Jobs was a genius but whether the place that nurtured him is. Does Silicon Valley deserve pride of place alongside classical Athens, Renaissance Florence, Song Dynasty China? Again, some of you will shout a loud "Nay!" You'd point out that while past greats such as Thucydides proudly proclaimed that they aimed to create "a possession for all time," the same cannot be said of the coders and other technokinds residing in the Valley. Your new iPhone, gleaming and magical, will be obsolete before you can even *say* Thucydides. You might also point out that these past golden ages sparked in many different directions—art, science, literature—while Silicon Valley plays basically one note, albeit in different keys. Complicating matters is that, unlike the stories of Athens and Florence, Silicon Valley's story isn't told in the past tense. It's still unfolding.

Clearly, though, the Valley meets at least one important criterion for genius: impact. We live differently today from how we did twenty-five years ago, thanks largely to the products and ideas that have been perfected, if not invented, in Silicon Valley. These innovations have changed not only how we talk to one another but what we say, for, as Stanford University historian Leslie Berlin points out, "by changing the means, you change the content."

What is honored in a country will be cultivated there. Clearly, we honor what the Valley is selling. We honor it every time we stand in line for the latest Apple iteration, and every time we log on to Facebook or Twitter.

Silicon Valley is different in other ways, too. For starters, it is not a city. It is suburban sprawl, which all the California sunshine and digital pixie dust can't hide. Silicon Valley is also more familiar than Athens or Florence. I may not own any Greek statuary or Renaissance paintings, but I do own an iPhone. I may not write Chinese poetry or produce Indian art, but I google regularly. I don't know any ancient Greek philosophers, nor have I hobnobbed with a Medici, but I do know people who reside in the Valley. I briefly lived there myself a while ago. Heck, I've even binge-watched the eponymously named HBO series. So, yes, I know Silicon Valley.

Or do I? Silicon Valley, I realize, is a lot like my iPhone. It does wondrous things. I can't live without it. But I have no idea how it works or what's inside. Apple warns me not to open the back; bad things will happen if I do. I have obediently complied, content to buy into the shiny slab of mythology resting so perfectly, so ergonomically, in the palm of my hand. That is about to change. Screwdriver please.

Good, Socrates says. *Recognizing your ignorance is the beginning of all wisdom.* Freud, student of the ancients, concurs, adding that my overconfidence is clearly masking some deep-seated insecurity and probably has something to do with my mother. David Hume echoes both Socrates and Freud, adding that I will never know Silicon Valley, or any place for that matter, unless I know its history. Otherwise, I will remain forever a child. It's time to grow up.

Arriving in Palo Alto, it quickly becomes apparent that Silicon Valley, unlike say, Florence, doesn't wear its history on its streets. Walking down the city's tony University Avenue, with its pricey eateries and designer-bike shops, the $100,000 Teslas silently gliding by, the past is nowhere in sight. The city, I suspect, is too busy imagining the future, *creating* the future, to spare any bandwidth for the past. It is here though. It just requires some digging.

Pilgrims in search of Silicon Valley's roots typically head straight for 367 Addison Avenue. It's not the house that interests them but what's

behind it: a small garage with a green door. Here, in 1938, two young
Stanford graduates, Dave Packard and Bill Hewlett, spent hours experimenting, though that is probably overstating it. They were tinkering.
"They hammered away on projects such as a motor controller helping
the telescope at Lick observatory track objects better and a bowling alley
device that chirped when someone crossed the foul line," my guidebook,
Geek Silicon Valley, cheerfully informs me. Eventually, the duo happened
on a winning invention, an audio oscillator, used to test sound equipment.
I look up and see a small plaque, which confirms that I am standing on
hallowed ground: THE BIRTHPLACE OF THE WORLD'S FIRST HIGH-TECHNOLOGY
REGION: SILICON VALLEY. Like so much in the Valley, though, the sign is misleading. This is not the birthplace of Silicon Valley.

The true birthplace isn't far, though. I walk a few more blocks, past
charming little houses worth more than I'll earn in a lifetime, before stopping at what was once 913 Emerson Street. The house itself is gone. All
that remains is a small plaque, situated across from a dry cleaner's and
an auto repair shop. It informs me that this was the original site of the
Federal Telegraph Company. Despite its name, it was a radio company,
and a good one.

Radio was the digital technology of its day—new, magical, and brimming with the potential to change the world. If you were young and smart
and ambitious shortly before World War I, radio was where you wanted
to be. The fledgling industry received a huge boost in 1912, thanks to
the law of unintended consequences. After the sinking of the *Titanic* that
year, Congress passed a law requiring all ships to carry radios. As a port
city, San Francisco was perfectly suited to ride this new wave of interest
in radio technology.

At about the same time, Federal Telegraph hired a brilliant young
radio engineer named Lee de Forest, in what was perhaps the first, but
far from last, time the region poached talent from back East. De Forest
was hoping to rejuvenate a stalled career. He succeeded wildly, inventing, here on Emerson Street, the first vacuum-tube amplifier and oscillator, devices that shaped not only radio technology but also television and
all of electronics. De Forest was passionate about his work, relishing the

time he spent in this "Invisible Empire of the Air . . . intangible, yet solid as granite." I realize that statement could easily apply to the Silicon Valley of today. The Invisible Empire continues to expand its reach.

Radio wasn't only a business. It was a hobby, too. A culture of tinkering blossomed in the San Francisco Bay Area. Ham radio clubs proliferated, thus firmly establishing the cult of the amateur in the region. You can draw a straight line from the amateur radio clubs of the 1910s and '20s to the Homebrew Computer Club, which in the 1970s and '80s played such an important role in the development of the personal computer.

Palo Alto, a small town, was the unlikely hub of this radio revolution. Boasted the *Palo Alto Times*, "What Edison's Menlo Park is to the incandescent lamp, Palo Alto is to radio and the electronic arts." No one was more enthralled than a curious fourteen-year-old named Fred Terman. He was mesmerized by this new technology and the pioneers at Federal Telegraph, "literally a looming presence," writes his biographer Stewart Gillmor. "Four 50-foot poles strung with twelve miles of aluminum for 'secret' experiments now graced the company's new site." Danger signs were posted everywhere, and nothing piques a teenager's interest more than the forbidden. Terman spent every free minute hanging out near the company grounds and even managed to finagle a summer job. I'm reminded of a young Filippo Brunelleschi, walking past the domeless cathedral of Santa Maria del Fiore every day and wondering, "What if?" Did young Fred Terman harbor similar dreams?

Terman was a child of Stanford in more ways than one. Not only did he spend most of his eighty-two years here, but he was the son of Lewis Terman, a professor of psychology at the university and cocreator of a widely used IQ test, the Stanford-Binet Intelligence Scales. Lewis Terman believed it was crucial that educators recognize potential genius at an early age so that they could nurture it. "In Terman's view, nothing less than the future of civilization was at stake," notes Darrin McMahon in his brilliant history of genius. Terman was an American Galton, certain in his belief that genius was hereditary and that the job of educators was to identify those with the "right" genes.

In 1921, Lewis Terman launched a landmark study aimed at doing just that. He found some one thousand children with IQs of over 140 ("genius in the making"), then tracked them over many years. The "Termites," as they were known, performed well enough academically but produced little in the way of true genius. What's more, Terman's experiment failed to detect two future Nobel Prize winners, Luis Alvarez and William Shockley. "Their tested IQs failed to meet the cutoff of 140, and they were weeded out and discarded accordingly," explains McMahon.

Lewis Terman was smart, but like many smart men he had blind spots. He failed to realize that intelligence and creativity are only tangentially related, as are education and creativity. Higher education does not correlate with a greater likelihood of genius. Terman also failed to recognize that, as Paul Saffo, resident futurist of the Valley, told me over crepes one day, "you can be a really stupid genius."

I know it sounds absurd, but Saffo defended his claim by pointing out the apocryphal tale known as Egg of Columbus. In the story, Columbus returned from his voyage to America a hero, but some in Spain remained unimpressed with his feat.

"Anybody can sail across the ocean, just as you have done," one critic said over dinner. "It is the simplest thing in the world."

Columbus replied by reaching for an egg and challenging the dinner guests to make it stand on end. When none could do it, Columbus took the egg and broke the shell slightly. It stood easily. "It is the simplest thing in the world," he said. "Anybody can do it—after he has been shown how."

Young Fred Terman grew up in the shadow of his father's social experiment, and I can't help but wonder how it affected him. At the very least, he seemed determined to impress his father with his academic performance. He earned a pair of degrees at Stanford and soon established the first electronics lab west of the Mississippi. Later, as dean of Stanford's engineering school, he set out to attract the best and the brightest minds from the East Coast. Like the executives at Federal Telegraph, he poached shamelessly, choosing only the best. "It's better to have one seven-foot jumper on your team rather than any number of six-foot jumpers," he once wrote. His aim, he said, was to build "steeples of excellence."

Terman saw the world through an engineer's eyes. He believed in measurable results, metrics, long before it became fashionable. He was shy and would no doubt have found truth in that old joke about engineers: "How can you spot the extroverted engineer? He's the one staring at *your* shoes." Yet Terman pioneered what has since become a Silicon Valley trope: the heroic nerd.

Terman was an introvert who did a good impersonation of an extrovert. His forte was connecting people. He was the original networker, at a time when the word had not yet acquired the mercenary overtones it has today. "He did not 'network' for personal gain or to hook a juicy funding agency but rather saw his own job as expediting a circle of relationships," writes Gillmor.

One relationship he cemented was between two of his former students, Bill Hewlett and Dave Packard. He encouraged them to exploit the commercial potential of their device, the audio oscillator, and lent them $538 to help them get off the ground. That the country was in the midst of the Depression actually helped convince the two young graduates to take the leap. As Dave Packard would later explain, jobs were scarce, so why not start your own company?

Success came quickly. Their first big customer was Walt Disney Studios, which bought eight oscillators for the filming of *Fantasia*, marking the beginning of a collaboration between Silicon Valley and Hollywood, Pixar being the most obvious example of that partnership today.

Much is made of Stanford University's role in the birth of Silicon Valley, and deservedly so, but not for the reasons most believe. It was not because Stanford was a world-class university. At the time, it was not. Rather, what Stanford did under Fred Terman was redefine the role of the university. Terman demolished the walls that separated the academy from the "real world."

Stanford didn't have a lot going for it, but it had land. Lots of land. In 1951, Terman used some of that excess land to establish the Stanford Industrial Park (now the Stanford Research Park). At the time, it was a tremendously controversial decision. An industrial park? That wasn't what universities did, certainly not a university with Ivy League aspirations.

The project was a bit like Darwin's "fools' experiments." Terman didn't know exactly what he was doing, but he knew he was doing something different, and that's what mattered. In a practical move that would no doubt delight the Scots, the industrial park was designed so that, if the enterprise failed, it could be converted into a high school.

It didn't fail. Terman had the right idea at the right time. There was nothing else like it, and in the most unlikely of places, on Palo Alto's Page Mill Road, with horses grazing nearby. An Apollonian version of the industrial park. The park's first residents were the Varian brothers, sons of immigrants from Iceland and one of the Valley's early success stories.

Later, Terman established the Stanford Research Institute, which was tasked with "pursuing science for practical purposes [which] might not be fully compatible internally with the traditional role of the university." Terman created a sort of anti-university *within* a university. Clever. Very Scottish. Terman also established the Honors Cooperative Program, which enabled engineers and scientists to pursue advanced degrees at Stanford while still working full-time.

By now, the Cold War was in full frigidness, and Terman, unlike many of his counterparts on the East Coast, wasn't averse to accepting money from Uncle Sam, the mother of all early adopters. This profligate defense spending—mixing, ironically, with the counterculture movement that would soon sweep through the San Francisco Bay Area—midwifed Silicon Valley.

Fred Terman had something else going for him: the chip. Not the microchip (that was still years away) but the one on his shoulder. Stanford, as I said, was not the topflight university it is today. The region—and Stanford University in particular—had long been the subject of East Coast derision. When, in 1891, railroad baron and US senator Leland Stanford established the university, in honor of his son who'd died just before college age, the East Coast establishment wasn't exactly impressed. "There is about as much need for a new university in California as for an asylum for decayed sea captains in Switzerland," sniffed the *New York Mail and Express*.

Comments like that, which continued well into the twentieth century, no doubt irked Terman, but nothing irritated him more than to see a student move East after graduating. He envisioned Stanford as a magnet, the kind of place people fled to, not from. Today, the power of the chip, squarely planted on an ambitious shoulder, still animates Silicon Valley. One venture capitalist told me that when trying to decide whether to fund a start-up, he looks for the chip on the CEO's shoulder. The bigger the chip, the better.

Places can have chips, too. It dawns on me that most of the places of genius I've visited fit that bill: Athens outgunned by Sparta, Florence outgunned by Milan and outfunded by Venice. This was their motivation, part of it anyway, to strive for greatness. Edinburgh, likewise, desperately wanted to prove it was every bit as good as London or Paris; Calcutta every bit as good as the West. It's not only that underdogs try harder but also that they see better, thanks to their being outsiders.

Terman, despite his many accomplishments, and his legacy as "father of Silicon Valley," is not easy to get to know. One former Stanford student remembers him as "a kindly looking, somewhat rumpled man with glasses [who] always walked with a purpose, carrying files of paper. He never ambled." Others found him "harsh and humorless." Who was the real Fred Terman?

I head to the Silicon Valley Archives in hopes of finding out. I walk into a majestic room, brimming with wooden cabinets and history. A librarian hands me a large cardboard box, one of dozens of large boxes, for Fred Terman was, among other things, a prolific correspondent. This particular box contains letters from Terman's days at the Harvard Radio Research Laboratory. He had reluctantly left California to run the laboratory during World War II. Working secretly, with a budget bigger than for all of Stanford, the lab was tasked with finding ways to jam enemy radar. Terman and his team came up with an ingenious solution: deploying chaff, billions of tiny pieces of metal, which confused German and Japanese radar. It's credited with saving eight hundred Allied bomber aircraft and their crews.

I open one letter, yellowing and faded but still clearly legible. The war was raging, and Terman was overseeing a staff of 850, yet he found time to write to one C. K. Chang, a physics student at Stanford. "We should some day carry through those very long overdue plans to write up the work on heterodyne detection in the form of a paper," he begins, all engineering-like, before getting a bit more personal. "I feel rather badly about this. . . . You did an excellent piece of work here and should receive the credit which is coming to you." Other letters reveal a persistent streak, especially when it comes to Stanford's efforts to best the East Coast schools.

As I dig through Terman's correspondence, I find myself thinking of Dr. Barker in Florence and the letter from Galileo that she had stumbled upon; I now see what she means about the excitement you get from happening upon a letter, especially an ordinary one. It feels thrilling and vaguely dangerous, as if you were eavesdropping across the centuries.

I dig deeper into the box and find a newspaper clipping from April 1944, headlined "U.S. Plans to Train Foreign Engineers," and a handwritten note attached from Stanford president Donald Tresidder: "Do you know about this? Are we interested? What should we do, if so?" Terman's response is missing, but I'm sure it was assertive, followed up by action.

Toward the end of his life, Fred Terman wrote that he had no regrets: "If I had my life to live over again, I would play the same record." He died at age eighty-two in his campus home. Hundreds showed up at the Stanford Memorial Church to pay their respects. Delivering the eulogy, the university's president, Donald Kennedy, said that the most remarkable thing about Terman was his "capacity to think about the future." Not only to think about it, but to engineer it.

That all this was happening in California is no coincidence. The state was—and to an extent still is—a place one flees to, a refuge for jilted lovers, bankrupt businessmen, lost souls. As William Foster, of Stratus Computer, put it, "If you fail in Silicon Valley, your family won't know and your neighbors won't care."

California had another advantage. There wasn't much here. The state was "born modern," as historians like to say. It was settled late and therefore leapfrogged over the more established East Coast. Without a deeply entrenched culture on the ground, new arrivals simply made it up as they went along. It was a do-it-yourself adventure from the get-go.

Silicon Valley is the ultimate manifestation of the American flavor of genius, "not just thinking new thoughts and creating new things, but finding a use for them, and then using them to make a buck," writes historian Darrin McMahon.

If America possesses any resource in spades, it is optimism, and optimism, a certain amount anyway, is a prerequisite for genius. Despite the image of the brooding genius, creative scientists tend to be more optimistic than their less creative peers. One study found that optimistic employees are more creative than pessimistic ones. And you don't get any more optimistic than Silicon Valley.

"Brutally optimistic" is how one local put it. Anywhere else in the country, he explains, your new idea is met with an avalanche of reasons why it won't work; in Silicon Valley, it's met with a challenge. *Why don't you do it? What are you waiting for?* Brutal.

Like a Pixar movie or a Mozart symphony, all successful people and places operate on two levels simultaneously. There is the mythology of their success, and then there are the real reasons for it. Yes, there is some overlap, but only some. Silicon Valley is no exception to this rule; its mythology is as well polished as an Apple product launch.

The Silicon Valley myth goes something like this. Let's say we're talking about the development of a new app, one that enables users to access the creative genius of past greats with the simple tap of a finger. In our mythological Silicon Valley, the idea arises, fully formed, perfect in every aspect, in the mind of a sullen twenty-three-year-old wearing blue jeans and lounging on a beanbag chair. Said beanbag chair is located in an "incubator," a house occupied by other similarly sullen and brilliant twenty-three-year-olds. Coffee is involved.

The cadre of young geniuses immediately recognizes the brilliance of this new idea and huddle to brainstorm. Within minutes, they all agree on a name, Einstyn, and promptly celebrate. India Pale Ale is involved.

Our young genius then takes a meeting with a venture capitalist (also blue-jean clad, but accompanied by a neatly pressed dress shirt) who immediately recognizes the brilliance of Einstyn and writes a large check.

The venture capitalist, some thirty years older than our young genius, offers to impart his hard-earned wisdom. The young genius declines. He's going to do this his way, he says, follow his inner GPS. The venture capitalist nods approvingly. A launch party is held, attended by fit young people wearing jeans and expressions of smug superiority.

Our young genius rents office space in Palo Alto, next to a Tesla dealership, and not far from that holy of holies, Steve Jobs's old house. Within months, Einstyn is launched. It is met with . . . silence. Nobody seems to get it, leading our young genius to conclude that other people are idiots. Einstyn's burn rate, meanwhile, rivals that of an F-16 during takeoff. Soon, the venture capitalist pulls the plug on the enterprise. Our young genius, broke and out of work, is immediately hailed a hero, for, as we all know, Silicon Valley embraces failure.

A month later, back in the very same beanbag chair, our technokind comes up with another brilliant, fully formed idea: a GPS tracking device that enables people to find missing socks. He is calling it Scks. The venture capitalist loves it (loves it!) and writes another check, this one even larger than before.

It's a nice story, as pleasing to behold as the latest iProduct. Let's unscrew the back panel, though, and take a look inside. First of all, nothing good ever came from a beanbag chair. Nothing. I am speaking from personal experience. I sense the genius tale is problematic in other ways, too, though I'm not sure exactly how. Unlike our technokind, I am willing to admit when I need help. In an irony that would make a Janusian Scotsman smile, I turn to the Man with No Cell Phone.

Chuck Darrah, anthropologist and Silicon Valley native, arrives at the coffee shop in Mountain View in shorts and sandals and, true to his word, with no cell phone. "I don't want people to be able to reach me that easily," he says, as if it were the most obvious thing in the world, which, now that I think about it, it is.

In every other way, Chuck is about as Silicon Valley as you can get. He was born at Stanford Hospital, back when the region was best known as the prune capital of the United States. It produced orchards and dried fruits and not much else. For young Chuck, life in the Valley of Heart's

Delight, as it was known, was idyllic. Everything was a bit better than elsewhere. The fruit tasted better, the air was fresher. The walnuts were the size of grapefruits. "It was a very gentle place to grow up," he says, and I see by the look in his eyes he has left me, transported to another time, a better time. Eden before the microchip.

Chuck admits he never saw it coming. "One day, someone approached me and said, 'There's this new thing called silicon,' and I'm, like, 'What's silicon? That sounds like the stupidest gimmick in the world.' And he's like, 'Yeah, we're making chips for calculators,' and I'm like, 'What are you talking about, dude?' So, no, I didn't see it coming at all." Now, though, Chuck is the Margaret Mead of Silicon Valley, hacking through the overgrowth of US 101, studying the natives and their strange ways. He finds it endlessly fascinating.

We order coffee and find a table outside. We can do this because it is California and the weather today is perfect, just as it is every day. The light is almost Athenian in its brilliance, and I'm tempted to suggest, again, that climate might explain Silicon Valley. But I stop myself. It is never the weather, at least not only the weather.

The secret to Silicon Valley's success, he says, is not that it was the best but simply that it was the first. "First-starter advantage," it's called, and it explains a lot, not only about the Valley but all innovations. Consider your laptop keyboard. The top left letters spell QWERTY. Why? Is that the most efficient way of arranging the keys? Hardly. In fact, it is purposefully *inefficient*. The early typewriters jammed frequently, so designers arranged the keys in a way that would slow the typist and minimize the risk of jamming. Improved typewriters were no longer prone to jamming, but the QWERTY keyboard had already caught on. Typists got used to it and worked around the constraints it imposed. Typing schools taught it. So it stuck, even though it was not the "best" arrangement, just as the VHS video format bested Betamax, a clearly superior technology. Likewise, the Pilgrims settled in Massachusetts Bay and not Virginia, as they intended, simply because they got lost.

The point is, the "best" technology or idea doesn't always prevail. Sometimes chance and the law of unintended consequences win out.

More important is what happens *after* these forces have had their say. We adjust to the inefficient keyboard and our fingers fly. VHS works fine, until it is supplanted by DVDs and now streaming video. The Pilgrims endure the brutal New England winters and eventually thrive. It's the same way with places of genius. They may not be perfect or beautiful, but they challenge us in certain ways, and when we respond to these challenges in a bold and creative way, the foundation for a golden age is laid. But for that to happen, you have to get there first. This explains the Silicon Valley philosophy: better to get an imperfect product to market today than a perfect one tomorrow. As Steve Jobs once observed, when the lightbulb was invented, no one complained it was too dim.

First starters such as Silicon Valley become magnets, and once magnetized, an irresistible momentum takes hold. Again, creativity is contagious. Several studies have found that we are more creative when surrounded by creative coworkers, even if we don't interact directly with these colleagues. And recall that we get a creativity boost from merely watching "schema violations" (someone eating pancakes for dinner, for instance). Something about being in the presence of creativity inspires us to think more creatively ourselves.

I experience a bit of this contagion myself. After only a few days in the Valley, I begin to view the world differently. I begin to see possibilities that I didn't see back East. I find words such as *beta version* and *hackathon* rolling off my tongue fluently. I'm not the most entrepreneurial of souls, but here, basking in the California sunshine and fizzy optimism, I can see myself changing the world—and also becoming filthy rich in the process.

On my way to meet Chuck, I had spotted a moving van, parked outside a nondescript office building in Mountain View. The movers were busily carting off ergonomic chairs and Danish desks, no doubt discarding the carcass of some failed venture and making room for the next. Silicon Valley's most iconic symbol is not the iPhone or the microchip but the moving van.

This fluidity, says Chuck, is the key to understanding the Valley. Nothing stands still in Silicon Valley; the place has a kinetic energy—not unlike what I witnessed in Calcutta, but more directed. Facebook founder Mark

Zuckerberg's mantra, "Move fast and break things," has become part of the local mythology, even if he recently backed away from the "break things" part of that motto.

Look at the top ten firms in Silicon Valley, says Chuck. Every five or ten years, the list completely changes, with perhaps one or two exceptions. "There is incredible, incredible turnover," he says. This is not a new concept. I'm reminded of Florence and how the committee overseeing the famous Duomo, the Opera del Duomo, rotated its leadership every few months.

One of the biggest myths about Silicon Valley, says Chuck, is that people here take risks. It is a myth that is simultaneously true and untrue, a Janusian construction that would tickle a Scot. Chuck says Silicon Valley celebrates risk, yet at the same time "it has some of the best mechanisms for avoiding the consequences of risk in the world."

"Such as?"

"Just think about it. These entrepreneurs, we're told, deserve their money because of the risk they take. But you don't see people jumping off the tops of buildings here. They tend to land on their feet. They tend to land in places like this, drinking cappuccinos, because the risk is a peculiar kind of risk. Most of the people in high tech will admit if they lost their job, they would find another one. They might even find a better one."

"So they're working with a net?"

"Yes. A huge net. It's easier to take risk when you are insulated from it."

How different that is, I think, from the risk takers of Florence, where, as Dr. Barker, the art historian, told me, if you failed, "you destroyed yourself, you destroyed your family for generations."

I'm contemplating that sort of momentous risk, sipping my good coffee, gaping at the Google driverless cars that glide by, when the Man with No Cell Phone demolishes another Silicon Valley myth. Specifically, the myth that it is a hothouse of good ideas. It is not. I confess this surprises me. I always thought Silicon Valley's forte was the good idea.

"Bullshit," says Chuck, setting me straight. What makes Silicon Valley special is not the idea itself but what happens once the idea washes up here. The region Siliconizes ideas just as India Indianizes them. What comes out of the blender is recognizable but fundamentally different.

In Silicon Valley ideas aren't invented but are processed in faster and smarter ways than they are elsewhere. "If you have an idea, people will tell you where that idea fits in with the ecology of ideas that is operative," explains Chuck. "There are mechanisms in place, institutions set up, to bring together bright people." If Silicon Valley were a brain, it wouldn't be the frontal lobe or even a brain cell; it would be a synapse, a connector.

Silicon Valley is not about technology. Sure, the products are technological, but those are the ends, not the means. "People say they come here because it's a technology hub, but that is merely a way to legitimize the move," Chuck says. "The real reason people come here is that deal making happens here in different ways and it's possible to realize deals in different ways."

The Valley is good at absorbing new arrivals, and just as adept at spitting them out. "You can talk to people who have been here only a few weeks and they talk to you as if they've always been a part of Silicon Valley. It's an absolutely amazing place for taking people in and for releasing people, letting them go." Again, places of genius are colanders as well as magnets.

Another myth about Silicon Valley is that it is shallow. This one, says Chuck, happens to be true. Your average Valleyite knows a lot of people but not well, not deeply. This is precisely what makes the region so successful—not people's attachment to the place but their lack of attachment. "People can insert themselves into networks quickly and extract themselves equally easily, and that's what's magical about the place. It's not that people are saying, 'Silicon Valley do or die, I'll kill for Silicon Valley.' Quite the opposite."

In 1973, a young sociologist named Mark Granovetter wrote an academic paper that, over the years, has become the most cited paper in all of sociology (29,672 citations at last count). It's called "The Strength of Weak Ties." A short paper, a "fragment of a theory," he called it at the time, it is nonetheless fascinating for both its simplicity and its intriguing, counterintuitive thesis.

The title says it all. What we think of as weak ties—acquaintances, coworkers, etc.—are actually incredibly powerful. Likewise, what we think of as strong ties—close friends, family—are actually weak. In his paper, Granovetter concedes this doesn't appear to make sense but adds, teasingly, "Paradoxes are a welcome antidote to theories which explain everything all too neatly."

I'm captivated by this theory and suspect it goes a long way toward explaining the success of Silicon Valley. I'm determined to track down Granovetter, wherever he is, so you can imagine my delight when I discover that he is right here, in Palo Alto, a city where, like Calcutta, the possibility of coincidence is apparently greater than it is elsewhere.

The next morning, I find Granovetter at his Stanford office—one that would make Beethoven or Einstein proud. Stacks of paper rise from his desk like monuments built by some now-extinct civilization. Threatening to topple at any moment, they tower over the office's occupant, a compact man, quiet but not unfriendly.

I take a seat, craning my neck to see Granovetter behind the pylons of paper, and ask him about his fragment of a theory. How can weak ties be strong?

"You are more likely to learn something new from a weak tie," he tells me. This holds true for a number of reasons. A weak tie is more likely to come from a different background than you, thus the benefits of an immigrant society such as Vienna or Silicon Valley. (Today, 50 percent of all start-ups in Silicon Valley have at least one cofounder who was born outside the United States.) Also, we are more willing to offend someone with whom we have weak ties, and a willingness to offend is an important part of creativity.

Strong ties make us feel good, make us feel that we belong, but they also constrict our worldview. A group with strong ties is more likely to lapse into groupthink than one with weak ties.

Weak ties aren't always good, Granovetter explains. "If you are in a stable place where not much is happening and the main thing you need is support, then weak ties are not going to help you much." But in a place such as Silicon Valley weak ties are gold.

Think of weak ties as dots. As we've seen, the more dots at our disposal, the better. Each weak tie is a dot, and in fluid places all of these dots form a pipeline through which knowledge is transmitted and ideas processed.

The beauty of Granovetter's weak-ties theory is that it not only describes the process of Silicon Valley but also many of its products. What is Facebook, after all, but a supermarket of weak ties? Mark Zuckerberg didn't invent weak ties, but he did make them "a lot less expensive," says Granovetter.

Over the years, Granovetter's fragment of a theory has been put to the test by other social scientists, and it holds up. Jill Perry-Smith, a business professor at Emory University, studied an applied-research institute and found that those scientists with more weak ties, rather than a few close colleagues, were more creative. Other studies found similar results, leading one psychologist, Keith Sawyer, to conclude, a bit tongue-in-cheek perhaps, that "strong friendships aren't good for creativity."

I ask Granovetter about this, and he says that, while that may be true, both weak and strong ties have their advantages. And he wants to make one thing clear: he isn't advocating that we sever all strong ties. "I mean, my wife wouldn't like that."

I am sitting in a nondescript Starbucks (is there any other kind?) in a nondescript strip mall in Sunnyvale. It could be any strip mall in any suburb, but it isn't. Not if you know the history. If you were here in the early 1970s, you might notice two teenagers, long-haired slackers in jeans and military jackets, riding clunky ten-speeds en route to Owen Russell's Hobby Shop. There, they loaded up on wires, cables, motherboards, and alligator clips before cycling home. The slackers were Steve Jobs and Steve Wozniak, and they were buying parts to build the Apple One, one of the first personal computers.

"So the modern world starts here, in this thoroughly uninteresting strip mall," declares Michael Malone, with the sort of certainty I've come to expect in the Valley. Malone was a witness to this secret history. He grew up three blocks from Jobs and often saw the two Steves returning from the hobby shop and wondered what they were up to. He had assumed that the alligator clips were "roach clips," for smoking marijuana. In fact, the two Steves, who did smoke plenty of marijuana, were following a path of bold tinkering laid down by the likes of Lee de Forest and Fred Terman decades earlier.

Malone is a history nut in a place that, by all appearances, doesn't give a tweet about history. He's lived in the Valley since he was twelve years old, worked for Hewlett-Packard for a while, wrote a much-read column for the *San Jose Mercury News*, penned several biographies of key players in the region, and now enjoys the unofficial title of "professor emeritus of Silicon Valley."

I sense something different about Malone, then realize what it is. He's the only person I've seen here wearing a sports coat. A practical choice, he says, a bit defensively, a holdover from his newspaper days when he carried a reporter's notebook in the side pocket. In Silicon Valley, as in Scotland, even your fashion choices are justified on practical grounds.

Malone has an opinion, usually delivered in sailor's tongue, about everything, from his days picking cherries in the fields of Santa Clara County ("What a shitty job.") to the beautiful weather ("Weather is important. Everyone on the East Coast says it's not, but that's bullshit. It's completely important.") to the good life in the Valley ("Come on, why *wouldn't* you want to be here?").

When I push him about the real secret to Silicon Valley's success, he concedes, "There's a certain amount of luck in all this."

Let's examine the "lucky breaks" that came Silicon Valley's way, the various moving parts that had to click into place for this pleasant but otherwise unremarkable valley of orchards and dried prunes to transform itself into an economic juggernaut, and the closest thing we have to a modern Athens or Florence. The list is long. Beautiful weather. A tradition of tinkering, first with radios then with transistors and microchips. A brilliant and persistent professor and a university that backed his unorthodox approach. The Cold War and the buckets of government money it unleashed. The counterculture movement of the 1960s. All told, it was an incredible confluence of good fortune.

Not so fast, I can hear Dean Simonton say. It's one thing to be lucky and quite another to "exploit chance." Any one of Silicon Valley's "lucky breaks" might have been overlooked elsewhere.

"Come on," says Malone suddenly. "Let's go."

"Where are we going?"

"You'll see."

We hop into his pickup truck, which, given his sports jacket and professorial bearing, briefly causes a schema violation in my brain, but I recover nicely. We drive a few minutes, then stop at an intersection, the sort of California intersection where pedestrians dare not tread. But tread we do, hopping out of the pickup and standing there, with the cars whizzing by, their drivers eyeing us as if we were from Mars, or possibly the East Coast.

"Um, why are we standing in the middle of this intersection?"

"Let's say it's 1967."

"Okay, I'm with you, 1967. Can we go now?"

"And it's about five or six o'clock, on a weekday afternoon."

"Yes?"

"If you had been standing here, you would have seen a kid coming this way on his bicycle, heading home from Stevens Creek swim practice, and he would come up here and cut across to his home over here, and you'd see another kid, also on a bike, and you'd see a Mercedes blasting down Freemont Avenue, heading toward the Los Altos Country Club. The kid on the bike? Steve Wozniak, inventor of the personal computer. The other kid on the bike? Ted Hoff, the inventor of the microprocessor. The Mercedes guy? Robert Noyce, coinventor of the integrated circuit, founder of Fairchild and Intel. So you had the integrated circuit, the microprocessor, and the personal computer. How much money is that worth in the modern world? Ten trillion dollars. It defines the modern world."

"But it's only an intersection?"

"Exactly. What could be more Silicon Valley than an intersection next to a freeway in suburbia, and with geniuses crossing paths?"

Places, like artwork, can be too pretty. Their ornateness distracts from the serious purpose at hand. Silicon Valley doesn't have that problem. The region's main drag, El Camino Real, with its muffler shops, dry cleaners, and fast-food joints, could be anywhere in America. As we've seen, genius doesn't require paradise. Throughout the ages, many a genius has done his best work in shabby settings. Einstein, for one, wrote his general theory of relativity at the kitchen table in his dingy Berne apartment.

Genius doesn't need extraordinary settings because it sees the extra in the ordinary. The mundane, boring stuff is sometimes the most important. Consider "weak preferred stock." Admittedly not as sexy as the Apple Watch or Google's self-driving car, it is nonetheless one of the Valley's most important innovations, and crucial to its success. It created a whole new stock structure that helped make launching a new company more feasible. Boring but important.

Throughout my time in Silicon Valley, I keep having flashbacks. I keep thinking, "Wait, this isn't new at all. This is the way they did it in Athens or Florence, or Hangzhou." I don't say this aloud. Nobody wants to hear it. They're too caught up in the illusion that Silicon Valley was created ex nihilo, from nothing. Silicon Valley, in fact, is a Frankenstein place, assembled from bits and pieces of golden ages past and soldered together into something supposedly new.

Everywhere I look I detect echoes of these golden ages past. As in ancient Athens, people here are motivated by something other than personal gain. They are doing it not for themselves, at least not only for themselves, but to further their religion—making the world a better place through the transformative power of technology. A recent survey by the consulting firm Accenture found that people who work in Silicon Valley care more about what their peers think than do people who work elsewhere. They are deeply loyal workers. Their loyalty, though, is not to any particular company but to one another, and to the creed of technology.

Silicon Valley most closely resembles Edinburgh. This is no coincidence; America's founding fathers were deeply influenced by the Scottish Enlightenment. The geniuses of that day, as you recall, were not just thinkers but tinkers. They were men of action, guided by the Doctrine of Improvability. *There must be a better way.*

I'm excited about my meeting with the Man Who Can See around Corners. That's how Roger McNamee is known in some quarters of the Valley. A venture capitalist, musician, and friend and business partner of Bono's, he possesses the sort of elevated vision that is so essential when worshipping Hindu deities or funding start-ups.

I'm waiting in a small conference room on Menlo Park's famous Sand Hill Road, the Wall Street of the Valley, with its row of pleasant but perfectly ordinary offices, when Roger walks in. He looks just as I expected: blue jeans, T-shirt, woven bracelets, long hair. When discussing business practices, he is considerably more likely to quote Jerry Garcia than Michael Porter. Unlike the Man with No Cell Phone, the Man Who Can See around Corners owns several, which he places on the table, like talismans.

So far, so good. But you can imagine my disappointment when he promptly disabuses me of this seeing-around-corners stuff. "That's all bullshit," he says, deploying a word that I've heard more often than *microchip* since arriving here.

"Okay," I say. "So if you're not seeing around corners, or through walls, what is it that you do exactly?"

"I study history. I do real-time anthropology. Then I form hypotheses about what must come next in relative probability."

This is the way Roger really speaks. Like a tie-dyed Galton. Roger, I soon realize, personifies a certain Silicon Valley type: socially awkward, more comfortable with numbers than with people, but, paradoxically, also possessing rare insights into our social selves that elude more extroverted observers. The Valley, where the heroic nerd rules, is a great place for people like Roger McNamee.

I press him. What exactly do you *do*? How do you decide if an idea is worth backing or not?

"I'm open to the notion that the future is different from the past but not wedded to it."

I have another flashback. Again, to the Scottish Enlightenment, for those words could just as easily have come from the mouth of David Hume. Roger had just articulated Hume's empiricism, a school of philosophy, albeit with a California twist. Hume was open to the possibility that the future would be just like the past, but he wasn't wedded to it. Just because the sun rose in the sky yesterday, he said, doesn't mean it will tomorrow. David Hume would have made an excellent venture capitalist.

Roger, like that other Scottish invention Sherlock Holmes, takes a detective's approach to his job, focusing on motive and opportunity—especially opportunity, for that part of the equation, he says, "is grossly, grossly underweighted. You sit here and hear people say their success is based on their ability. The amount of self-deception here is amazing."

The way Roger sees it, places of genius such as Silicon Valley are all about creating critical mass—Martin Guttmann's phase transition—and two ways exist to do that, with space or with time. Timing matters. Extract Leonardo da Vinci from sixteenth-century Florence and plop him down in twenty-first-century Florence and he is no longer a genius but the inmate of a beautiful prison.

"All is flux," Heraclitus said, and this ancient Greek idea informs every aspect of life in the Valley, where an almost theological belief in fluidity has merged with a technological evangelism—or, as Roger puts it, "this notion that the world must change so it might as well be us in the driver's seat."

This sort of nervy optimism is helpful, but only if it's tempered with a keen understanding of timing. Technokinds arrive in Silicon Valley every day hoping, expecting, to be the next Mark Zuckerberg, forgetting that, as Roger tells me, "the Zuckerberg thing is over, and it might be another ten years before we get the next Zuckerberg. These things don't happen on demand, because in order for them to work the preconditions of societal acceptance of whatever it is you're doing has to be there."

Mozart could not have said it better. He knew that audience matters, and he owed his success, at least in part, to the highly appreciative audience he found in Vienna. The denizens of Silicon Valley (the smart ones at least) also recognize the importance of audience. Their audience, though, is not the royal court or music connoisseurs. It is the entire planet—anyone with an Internet connection and a few dollars of disposable income.

One of the more persistent myths of Silicon Valley is that it is wholly tradition-free, a place that exists in the near future, with no regard for the past. Consider this quote, though: "You can't really understand what is going on now unless you understand what came before." That statement could easily have been uttered by an ancient Greek, or a Chinese philosopher or perhaps an Enlightenment-era Scot.

Those are, however, the words of Steve Jobs. He was speaking about his relationship with Robert Noyce, father of the microchip. Jobs, not known as lacking in self-confidence, had reached out to Noyce for advice during Apple's early days. Years later, the Google founders would similarly turn to Jobs for guidance. When Mark Zuckerberg ran into trouble in the early days of Facebook, he turned to Roger McNamee for advice.

Every golden age has a mentor system, whether acknowledged or not. In incubators and start-ups across the Valley, high-tech versions of Verrocchio's workshop hum along. They are less dusty, with considerably fewer chickens and rabbits underfoot, but the principle is the same: older, wiser veterans relaying their knowledge to eager acolytes. Granted, these acolytes are less patient than Leonardo da Vinci, and few could stomach a decadelong apprenticeship, but they would certainly agree with Leonardo's maxim "The pupil who does not surpass his master is mediocre."

These technokinds may not know they are adhering to a tradition, but they are, even if that tradition is one of "disrupting" tradition. Culture is social DNA. It transmits traditions from one generation to the next, largely invisibly to us. We may not know which particular set of genes gave us blue eyes, but they're still blue. Likewise, we behave in certain ways because of this invisible social DNA.

A good example is open-plan offices. The evidence is now fairly clear that they don't work, that they squelch, rather than nurture, creativity. Yet walk into any start-up in the Valley and you'll find an open-plan office. Why? Because that's the way it's always been done.

Of course, appealing to tradition is no way to dislodge a big fat check from the well-manicured hands of a venture capitalist. You can't very well say, "My groundbreaking app is based on centuries of tradition." No, you must pretend that it is radically new and disruptive. Everyone in Silicon Valley plays this charade. The smart players, though, realize it is a charade.

Inevitably, our discussion veers to Silicon Valley's favorite topic: failure. I ask him about the truism that Silicon Valley embraces failure.

Yes, failure is part of the mix, he says, but it is a means, not an end. If you fail repeatedly, and in the same manner, you're an idiot, not a genius. The guiding principle for "successful failure" is the scientific method. "Scientific method is about failing until something works, right? It's about failing in a thoughtful and efficient manner. Failure can be a wonderful learning experience as long as it's in the aid of some continuing process." The important thing, he says, is to fail early. "You kill the ones that aren't working right away."

Here we run headfirst into what has become a Silicon Valley mantra: "Fail fast," and its offshoot, "Fail fast, fail better." While failing fast is a good idea—all geniuses through the ages have had this ability to cut their losses and move on—I think these slogans miss the mark. Fail better? What does that mean? You can't fail better; you can only fail different.

Charles Darwin, whose theories inform so much of Silicon Valley (we're all evolving!), would no doubt advise us to fail foolishly. His "fools' experiments" were designed to poke fate, on the off chance that today is not like yesterday and tomorrow is not like today. Darwin, like Silicon Valley, embraced possibility, not failure.

This approach to failure dovetails nicely with the Power of Constraints. The best ideas, Roger argues, are the ones that enter the world imperfect, broken. They require work, and through refinement, by failing foolishly over and over, eventually something better, something good, emerges. Silicon Valley's success is built on the carcasses of its failures. In the Valley, failure is fertilizer. Like all fertilizer, though, it must be used wisely by a skilled farmer, otherwise it is useless and smells bad.

As I said, little was actually invented in Silicon Valley. The transistor was invented in New Jersey, the cell phone in Illinois, the World Wide Web in Switzerland, venture capital in New York. Valleyites, like the ancient

Athenians, are tremendous moochers. What Plato said of the Greeks holds true for Silicon Valley. What they borrow (or steal) from foreigners they perfect. No, Silicon Valley is not the place where good ideas are born. It is the place where they learn to walk.

It is also a place where many ideas come to die. Every day, they are knocked off, mercilessly and systematically. This is the real genius of the Valley. Every golden age needs discerners, people gifted in the ability to distinguish good ideas from bad ones, beautiful music from workman-like, scientific breakthroughs from incremental advances, a sublime poem from a word salad. In Athens, that role was played by the polis, the citizens. In musical Vienna, it was the royal court and discerning listeners. In Florence, it was the patrons, especially the Medicis. Who are the Medicis of Silicon Valley?

There is no one answer to that question, but the venture capitalists, as well as so-called angel investors, probably come closest. It is not a perfect analogy—Roger scoffs at the notion—but in a world where cash determines which ideas are nourished and which are left to die on the vine, he who controls the cash controls much.

I like Roger. I like the way he talks like a scientist with a poetry problem. I like the way he looks at Silicon Valley with open eyes, and not rose-colored Google Glass. Is he a genius? I'm not sure, but he certainly has genius tendencies—the ability, for instance, to focus laserlike on a problem for longer than most of us would consider normal. Yet he also practices "defocused attention" and has many outside interests. He reads forty novels a year and plays in a band called Moonalice. "The novels help me understand others. The music helps me understand myself," he tells me before we say good-bye. I turn to leave, but stop to ask him one last question.

"Are you smart or lucky?"

Roger doesn't hesitate. "What fucking difference does it make?"

As I walk back to my car, I realize that his answer, delivered in colorful American vernacular, is actually a very Greek thing to say. Who are we, mere mortals, to say where the world of human agency ends and that of the gods begins?

Eugene, my late friend from Florence, would have liked Silicon Valley. Like a good piña colada, it gets the proportions right. It balances ruthless competition with a generous, and wise, collaboration. (One study found that people who have competed with each other are later able to collaborate better than those who had not once squared off.) It is simultaneously large and small—big enough to have a global impact yet small enough that people still use first names. It combines intrinsic and extrinsic motivation. *I'm doing this because I love it, and, oh, I'm also making boatloads of money.* It is a highly social place, but one where introverts rule. It is a place that is disrupting the world, but also a place that cares deeply what others think, what *you* think. It is a place where extraordinary leaps are made on a very ordinary stage. Whatever you can rightly say about Silicon Valley, the opposite is also true.

Myths are not necessarily bad. They serve a purpose. Myths inspire. A completely myth-free society would not be creative. Consider one of the most intractable of Silicon Valley myths: Moore's law. First observed by Gordon Moore, cofounder of Intel, it states that the processing power of microchips doubles every two years.

Moore's law is not a law at all. It is a social contract, a dare or, if you're feeling less generous, a whip. Yet by formulating it as a "law," as immutable as the law of gravity, Moore and his successors have transformed a possibility into an expectation, an inevitability. It is a neat magic trick, and Silicon Valley's greatest innovation.

Let's return to our young Silicon Valley "genius" and see how the process actually unfolds. Yes, he does live in an incubator, and, yes, coffee is involved. But the similarities end there. For starters, the Einstyn idea is not his, not his only. He stole it, Greek-style. But heeding the advice of Plato and Roger McNamee, he perfects the idea. None of this happens effortlessly. He struggles. His idea is revised, then revised again. He is racked by doubt, but, driven by some unnamed power, perhaps a chip on his shoulder, he persists. Alas, he fails. But he doesn't wallow in this failure. He observes it, noting exactly where and how he failed, and vows to fail differently next time. Eventually, he succeeds, but with an Einstyn that looks nothing like the original concept. At no point does a beanbag chair enter the picture.

Our young genius faces challenges that geniuses of the past did not. These challenges can best be explained by the observer effect, which states that it is impossible to separate the observation of an experiment from the results. The mere act of observing alters the outcome. This is exactly what is taking place in Silicon Valley today and what distinguishes it from past golden ages. In ancient Athens, pollsters weren't constantly gauging the public mood. In Renaissance Florence, they didn't stop people on the street and ask if they were very optimistic, a little optimistic, or not optimistic at all about the future. The experiment called Silicon Valley is affected every day by the observation of it. We are all active participants in its outcome. Every time you do a Google search or buy the latest iProduct, you are, in some small way, determining the course that Silicon Valley takes.

Unlike Athens or Florence, Silicon Valley is suffering from its golden-age hangover *right now*, while it's still glowing. The pressure to be the next Steve Jobs or Mark Zuckerberg is enormous. If a Stanford engineering student hasn't had an IPO by his junior year, he feels like a failure. Futurist Paul Saffo tells me he's been teaching a course at Stanford for ten years, and only recently did he have his first slacker student. "It was like, 'Wow, how refreshing.'"

Silicon Valley differs from other golden ages in one other important way. What it creates—digital technology in its many guises—also determines how and what the rest of us create. That was not true of, say, Renaissance Florence. The *Mona Lisa* is a sublime work of art, and it no doubt inspired many painters, then and now, but it did not alter the way a shopkeeper balanced his books or a prince ruled his territory. Digital technology, on the other hand, seeps into every nook and cranny of our lives. Never before in history has one place touched so many lives, for better or worse.

As we've seen, a golden age doesn't last long. A few decades, perhaps a half century or so, then it disappears as suddenly as it arrived. Places of genius are fragile. They are far easier to destroy than to build. Silicon Valley, by my estimation, is pushing a century, ancient in genius terms. It's been a good run, longer than that of any other place in the United States, with the possible exception of Hollywood. Is its time up? Might it go the way of Athens and Detroit?

That may seem far-fetched, given the heady ambience and robust share prices in the Valley, but in 1940 nobody in Detroit saw the end coming any more than Athenians did in 430 BC. Only the Viennese of 1900 sensed that the end was nigh ("a laboratory of world endings"), and this, ironically, inspired one last, dramatic surge of creative output. We can't sprint toward the finish line if we don't know where the finish line is or, worse, delude ourselves into believing that the race will go on forever.

I meet plenty of people in the Valley who pooh-pooh any talk of decline. They remind me that people have been predicting the demise of Silicon Valley since the 1970s, yet the region continues to—I hate to use this awful term but no other will suffice—*reinvent* itself. From ham radio to transistors to integrated circuits to the cloud, revolution begets revolution.

Yes, the Valley has proved nimble (in a fairly narrow way; pivoting from hardware to software isn't quite the same as pivoting from abstract art to theoretical physics), but it is not immune to the laws of nature. The sun doesn't rise in the west, and trees don't grow to the moon. Not even California redwoods.

Silicon Valley's continued success depends, ironically, not on some shiny new gizmo but on learning the lessons of history. Alas, there is no app for that, but there are some steps the Valley can take, and pitfalls it can avoid, if it is to beat the odds and live to an even riper old age.

Great civilizations rise to greatness for different reasons but collapse for essentially the same reason: arrogance. No civilization, no matter how great, is immune to this "creeping vanity," as professor of education Eugene Von Fange calls it. Here he is describing the decline of classical Athens, but his words could just as easily apply to any golden age that has begun to lose its bloom. "Soon, their sons, coddled in the use of all the great things their fathers and grandfathers had pioneered, became as helpless as newborn babes when faced with the harsh reality of an aggressive and changing world."

It doesn't take an Einstein to see signs of this creeping vanity in the Valley. Bling has reared its shiny head, and that is never a good sign. You'll recall that this was the case in Athens, too; the city's decline can be traced almost exactly to a concomitant rise in luxury, and a taste for gourmet food. When it comes to golden ages, bling is the canary in the coal mine.

Another sign that the Valley has lost its way is that it is beginning to confuse means and ends. The much-touted notion of disruption was once viewed as an outcome, a side effect of innovation. Now it has become an end in itself—witness the advent of the "disrupt conference." This is not good. Socrates didn't "disrupt" Athens for the heck of it. He had a purpose in mind, and that purpose was nothing less than wisdom.

There is no such thing as creativity in the abstract. Likewise, there is no such thing as innovation in the abstract. To describe yourself as an entrepreneur or a disrupter is as meaningless as describing yourself as an athlete or a thinker. Really? What sports do you play? What do you think about?

What jump-starts a golden age is not necessarily what keeps it going. The good ones manage to change fuel sources midstream. The Renaissance was initially powered by the recovered ancient texts, but the Humanists who discovered them soon generated their own ideas, their own intellectual momentum. Silicon Valley, if it is to survive, needs to find alternative energy sources, new ways of *being* creative and not simply new creative products.

It also needs to remember that small is not only beautiful, it's also creative. Girth is another form of complacency, and a particularly insidious one. Firms such as Apple and Google recognize this danger and, though they are now huge corporations, try to behave like the small start-ups they once were. They do this by decentralizing decision making, for instance, a move far more important than all the beanbag chairs in the world.

Along with smallness, it is essential that Silicon Valley remain fluid. It needs to keep those moving vans moving, the fertilizer flowing. This isn't easy, but Silicon Valley has one thing going for it: the region's product, information technology, is inherently diffuse. The nodes and networks of an IT system mirror the social networks of Silicon Valley—or perhaps it's the other way around; it doesn't matter. What does matter is that the Valley keep these networks flowing and churning like Class V rapids.

One more important lesson for Silicon Valley comes from an unlikely source. One day I wake to see Jack Ma staring at me. He has just taken his company, Alibaba, public on the New York Stock Exchange, and he's now worth not the $3 billion he was when I met him, but $26 billion. There is his smiley face splashed across home pages everywhere. Well done, Jack, I think, and silently calculate how much *guanxi* it would now take to land a meeting with him. All those zeros. My head hurts. Jack's prominence, though, reminds me that there is more than one way of being creative and of nurturing creative places.

Silicon Valley already looks toward Asia. Many of its products are manufactured there and, increasingly, sold there as well. On the streets of Mountain View, you see Asian faces, Asian restaurants, not to mention meditation centers and yoga studios. One lesson from the East that I think the Valley would do well to heed is that what goes up must come down, but eventually it will go up again. That is not the Western view. We believe that time flows like a river, and so we see decline as a one-way journey. Once you start to slip, there is no way to go but down. This worldview becomes a self-fulfilling prophecy, one in which decline begets only more decline. (Vienna being the exception that proves the rule.)

China and India remind us that it needn't be that way. If you view time as cyclical, then decline becomes reversible. This might seem like a subtle philosophical distinction, but it is not. China, for instance, has been up and down throughout its history partly because it believes there are ups and downs.

Silicon Valley raises another vexing problem: Is this the last great place? Might this be the end of the road for golden ages, the death not only of places of genius but of place itself? Certainly, the wizards of the Valley would have us believe this. Geography, they tell us, is so five minutes ago.

Thanks to the Internet and its digital handmaidens, you can live and work anywhere. Place has been rendered moot.

Isn't it interesting, though, that these prophets of a placeless future all live in one place? They eat at the same restaurants, drink their double lattes in the same cafés, ride their $10,000 bicycles on the same rolling country roads. The Vatican of Silicon Valley, the massive Google campus, is designed to facilitate face-to-face contact. Yahoo!, of all companies, recently announced it was eliminating telecommuting. They all know that, as futurist Paul Saffo puts it, "nothing propinqs like propinquity."

Geography is not dead. Place matters. It matters now more than ever. The proliferation of digital technology has made place more, not less, relevant. The more we skype and e-mail one another, the greater the desire for face-to-face contact. Air travel is more, not less, popular since the advent of digital technology. Ambitious young Chinese and Indian graduates, meanwhile, yearn to work in brick-and-mortar Silicon Valley, not some virtual knockoff. They've tasted the fruits of its harvest and want to take part in the growing. Every iPhone is a bread crumb leading to the promised land.

Perhaps Silicon Valley's greatest export is . . . Silicon Valley. City planners everywhere want to know what the secret sauce is, and they're willing to pay for it. A cottage industry of consultants has sprouted, and with their help dozens of places have attempted to replicate Silicon Valley, from England (Thames Valley) to Dubai (Silicon Oasis). With few exceptions, they have all failed. Why?

One reason is that they think Silicon Valley is a formula, forgetting that it is a culture, the product of a specific time and specific place. If they do recognize it as a culture, they try to transplant it into their own. Invariably, these attempts fail for the same reason many organ transplants do: donor and host are not compatible.

Perhaps the most important reason these Silicon Valley wannabes fail is simply because they're in too much of a hurry. Politicians want to see results while they're still in office, CEOs by the next quarter. That's not the way it works. Athens. Hangzhou. Florence. Edinburgh. They were all the result of long gestations, marked by painful complications (see Black Death and Persian Wars). Cities and nations attempting to replicate Silicon Valley think they need to create a frictionless place, when in fact friction and tension, certain amounts anyway, propel places of genius.

All of these efforts raise a larger question: Can we engineer a place of genius—not just a Silicon Valley but an Athens or a Florence? Or is that like trying to engineer a rainbow, or a happy family, a nice idea but wholly impractical? This is, I realize, the most vexing question I have encountered yet. Fortunately, answers lie only a few miles to the north in, of all places, a bakery.

EPILOGUE: BAKING
BREAD AND HANGING TEN

I BITE INTO THE BREAD. IT IS WARM AND CHEWY AND
moist. Pure—sorry, impure genius. Sourdough isn't unique to San Francisco; it was invented in ancient Egypt. Yet today San Francisco sourdough
is widely considered the best in the world. Why? The Boudin Bakery's
small museum at Fisherman's Wharf offers a few clues. For $3, you can
learn more about sourdough than you ever cared to know.

I learn that the company's founder, a young French baker named
Isidore Boudin, moved to San Francisco in 1849, at the height of the gold
rush. Isidore was an observant baker, with a keen understanding of "how
ambient conditions such as sea mist affect the leavening and baking process."

The museum offers an intriguing explanation for the primacy of San
Francisco sourdough. The bread is especially sensitive to the presence
of certain bacteria in the air. It depends on these microbes for its flavor.
San Francisco, the helpful placard explains, has a bacterium especially
well suited for baking sourdough. There it is, a rod-shaped little bugger
squirming under a microscope, named *Lactobacillus sanfranciscensis*.

It is a nice explanation, but misleading. To explain San Francisco sour-dough by the presence of a microbe is to fall into the Galton trap—that is, to attribute the bread's goodness to a single factor, and a biological one at that, just as Galton attributed all genius to the "right" genes. This explanation fails to consider all of the other factors that go into the making of a good loaf of sourdough: the innovative baking techniques of Isidore Boudin, the culture of bread-making that evolved in Gold Rush San Francisco, the miners who nourished that budding industry with their dollars, not to mention the inconvenient fact that New York and Paris also have plenty of interesting microbes, including, yes, *Lactobacillus sanfranciscensis*.

It's not only sourdough that befuddles us. Look out the window. Did your local weatherman get it right? Despite our many scientific accomplishments, we are still not good at forecasting weather more than a few days out. This is not because weather is completely random, like a roulette wheel in the sky. Weather systems behave rationally, but they do so as part of a "nonlinear dynamical system."

That's a mouthful, but essentially it means a system where two plus two doesn't always equal four. In a linear system, small inputs yield small outputs. Turn your steering wheel a smidge and the car veers right or left a smidge. In a nonlinear system, small inputs yield large, sometimes humongous, outputs. Turn your steering wheel a smidge and the car does a U-turn or your microwave goes on the fritz a few hours later.

The best-known example of this phenomenon is the butterfly effect. It describes a scenario in which the flapping wings of a butterfly in, say, Argentina weeks later affects the path and intensity of a hurricane off the coast of Bermuda. It sounds absurd, but it is not. Minuscule variations in the initial conditions of a phenomenon—such as the air disturbance caused by the flapping of a butterfly's wings—can snowball into much larger effects in a relatively short time. The problem, and the reason pop culture gets the butterfly effect so wrong, is that scientists find it extremely difficult, perhaps impossible, to predict exactly how this cascading chain of events will unfold. It is not the randomness of meteorological conditions that makes predicting the weather so difficult but their *interconnectedness*.

That sounds an awful lot like creativity, and especially collaborative creativity. When a jazz trio improvises, it produces something that none of the individual musicians could on their own. "Even if we knew everything there was to know about the mental makeup of each musician, we'd still have trouble predicting the emergence of the group's improvisation," says psychologist and jazz musician Keith Sawyer. The whole of the ensemble is greater than the sum of its parts. Now take that small ensemble and enlarge it into the size of an orchestra, then a small town, then, larger still, into a teeming city, such as Athens or Florence.

You see the problem. Golden ages are nonlinear systems, and these are extremely difficult, if not impossible, to predict. We can't explain them by homing in on any single factor. They are complex, interlocking systems, like the weather or a loaf of sourdough.

So while we can examine discrete parts of a golden age (tolerance, money, etc.), this doesn't enable us to predict where and when one will appear. Small inputs balloon into huge, and unexpected, outcomes, but we can't easily identify which small inputs matter the most. Just as not all butterflies produce a hurricane, not all outbreaks of bubonic plague produce a Renaissance.

Another mysterious aspect of creativity centers on what the great historian Arnold Toynbee called "challenge and response." All great human advancements, he believed, represented a creative response to a challenge. Makes sense. Why, though, do some people respond to personal tragedy—a debilitating illness, the death of a parent at a young age—by shutting down (or acting out), while others use these tragedies as fuel for bursts of creative genius? Likewise, why do some places respond to collective tragedies—an outbreak of plague, for instance—by turning inward, narrowing their gaze, while others expand their horizons and do great things? We don't know. This is why, I think, we can't invent a place of genius, any more than we can invent a sunny day.

That doesn't mean, though, that we should simply throw up our hands in surrender. We can prepare appropriately, by wearing sunglasses on a sunny day, carrying an umbrella on a rainy one. We can anticipate, too, by tracking approaching frontal systems, reading the sky, and riding the currents. That's what the geniuses I encountered in this book did so expertly. They were surfers. The surfer doesn't create the wave. She observes the wave, sees it, in the profound, Hindu sense of the word, and dances with it.

When a major storm batters a coastal town and evacuation warnings are issued, invariably local TV stations zoom in on a few crazy surfers determined to have the ride of their lives. Some, perhaps most, will wipe out spectacularly. But a few will ride the wave beautifully. Socrates. Shen Kuo. Adam Smith. Mozart. Freud. And, yes, Steve Jobs. Surfers all of them.

Our task is twofold: to improve our surfing skills, and also to increase the likelihood of good waves. Many people have tried to come up with a formula, a piña colada recipe, for places of genius. These almost always miss the mark. Too often they confuse the fruits of a creative place with the causes of one. One popular urbanist, for instance, has identified what he calls the "Three Ts" of creative cities: technology, talent, and tolerance. The first two—technology and talent—are *products* of creative places rather than causes, and technology is hardly a prerequisite for places of genius, witness ancient Athens and Renaissance Florence, two places that produced a mother lode of genius but little in the way of new technology. And while tolerance is certainly an attribute of creative places, it doesn't tell the whole story. Las Vegas is an extremely tolerant place but not an especially creative one.

A better set of attributes, I think, are—and I'll jump on the alliteration bandwagon here—the Three Ds: disorder, diversity, and discernment. Disorder, as we've seen, is necessary to shake up the status quo, to create a break in the air. Diversity, of both peoples and viewpoints, is needed to produce not only more dots but also *different kinds* of dots. Discernment is perhaps the most important, and overlooked, ingredient. Linus Pauling, the renowned chemist and two-time Nobel Prize winner, was once asked by a student how to come up with good ideas. It's easy, replied Pauling. "You have a lot of ideas and throw away the bad ones."

It is, of course, not so easy. There's a reason we've made a religion of genius, elevated these brilliant men and women to the realm of gods and goddesses. As an ancient Greek poet put it, "Before the gates of excellence, the high gods have placed much sweat. The sweat of labor often mingled with the sweat of pain."

We make creativity even more painful by clinging to unhelpful myths. In particular, the myth of the lone genius squanders our energies. Corporations spend huge sums of money on workshops designed to help employees "think more creatively," a noble ambition but one that will prove futile if the environment in which they work is not receptive to new ideas.

Clutching our shiny new iProducts, breathlessly awaiting the next Great Disruption, we consider ourselves thoroughly modern, but our beliefs about creativity are stuck in the nineteenth century. We're trapped in the Galton Box. We can't breathe in there. We need to break free. We need to begin thinking of creativity not as a genetic endowment, a gift, but as something that is earned—through hard work, yes, but also through the careful cultivation of favorable circumstances. We need to begin thinking of creativity not as a private indulgence but as a public good, part of the commons. We get the geniuses that we want and that we deserve.

Genius, like charity, begins at home. One reason I embarked on this colossal fools' experiment was not for my own stab at genius (too late for that) but for my nine-year-old daughter's. Family is the one sort of culture that we can actually mold. So mold I have. No, I have not converted my home into a raucous Athenian agora or a dusty Florentine *bottega*. I have not transformed the breakfast nook into a Viennese coffeehouse, or the living room into a Silicon Valley incubator. But I have learned some valuable lessons from my travels and done my best to apply them.

For starters, I provide a mix of intrinsic and extrinsic motivations. Sometimes, I throw up obstacles, owing to the Power of Constraints. Like Socrates, I play dumb, asking my daughter a lot of "obvious" questions. Like the poet-rulers of Hangzhou, I try to set an example by not only preaching creativity but practicing it as well. Like the Medicis, I assign her tasks that seem like a "bad fit." We occasionally hold an *adda*, that wonderfully aimless conversation, which nine-year-olds take to naturally. Sometimes, I introduce schema violations into the household, such as when I wore underwear on my head. I try to teach her the importance of remaining open to experience, even if that experience involves a green food. Our house is tolerant, but only up to a point. When she asks for a raise in her allowance, I point out, as Pericles did, that a little bit of money promotes creativity but too much squelches it. I encourage her to fail often and foolishly. I provide her with a (mostly) attentive audience.

I warn her of the dangers of complacency and have made it abundantly clear that under absolutely no circumstances is she to invade Sicily. Not even a little. I teach her the art of defocused attention, but not during homework time. I regularly demonstrate the importance of ignorance. We have a family routine, but one prone to spasms of chaos. We walk. We argue. We laugh. When she questions why, if education does not correlate directly with creative eminence, she still has to go to school, I tell her to ask her mother.

None of this has anything to do with genetics. I can hear old Galton harrumphing through the ages. Sorry, Francis, but ever since you coined that term *nature versus nurture*, we've energetically debated the relative merits of each. It's a silly argument, and unnecessary. Creativity doesn't happen "in here" or "out there" but in the spaces in between. Creativity is a *relationship*, one that unfolds at the intersection of person and place.

This intersection, like all such crossroads, is a dangerous, unforgiving place. You have to pay attention, slow down, and stay alert for the idiots out there. It's worth the risk, though, for the humble intersection, be it in ancient Athens or strip-mall Sunnyvale, is the true genius loci. The place where genius lives.

ACKNOWLEDGMENTS

You can't rush genius and, it turns out, you can't rush a book about genius either. That is a lesson I learned the hard way. Thankfully, I had help from many quarters—friends, family, and complete strangers.

Many people kindly provided me with a place to think and write: Sarah Ferguson, Art Cohn, Hans Staiger, Lisa Collins, and David and Abby Snoddy. I'm grateful to the Virginia Center for the Creative Arts, and especially its director of artistic services, Sheila Pleasants, for the many productive, and happy, residencies I spent there. I'm also indebted to Georgetown University's Mortara Center for International Studies, and its director, Kathleen McNamara, for providing me with that most valuable of gifts: a library card. Thanks, too, to Alex and Charles Karelis for having the good sense to launch, and maintain, the wonderful Writers Room DC.

Several people read early drafts of the manuscript and offered valuable suggestions: John Lister, Stefan Gunther, Manil Suri, Josh Horwitz, Barbara Brotman, and Chuck Berman. Alyson Wright diligently transcribed hours of interviews.

In researching this book, I relied heavily on what my late friend Laurey Masterton called The Golden Thread. People—sometimes friends but just as often strangers—generously offered an introduction or a suggestion that invariably led me to the right person in the right place at the right time. Some of these "golden threaders" appear in these pages, others do not. This latter category includes (but is by no means limited to) Joey Katona, Ross King, Yin Zi, Tom de Waal, Gerry Holmes, Tom Crampton, Alexandra Korey, Kimberly Bradley, Raju Narisetti, and Dan Moshavi. In Florence, David Battistella was exceedingly generous with his time and knowledge.

When discouragement reared its head, friends were quick to offer a kind word or a stiff drink, and often both. I'm grateful to Mark Landler, Angela Tung, Laura Blumenfeld, Steven Petrow, Martin Regg Cohn, Karen Mazurkewich, Steve LeVine, Nuri Nurlybayeva, Tracy Wahl, Jim Benning, Aliza Marcus, Andrew Apostolou, Jennifer Hanawald, and, in his own inimitable way, Warren Rabin. I am especially indebted to members of Writers Who Lunch, my informal, yet essential, support group: Maarten Troost, Florence Williams, Tim Zimmermann, David Grinspoon, Juliet Eilperin, and Josh Horwitz.

My agent, Sloan Harris, always has my back, keeps my nose to the grindstone, and isn't afraid to tell me when I have my head up my ass. At Simon & Schuster, several people worked tirelessly behind the scenes, including Megan Hogan, Jonathan Evans, and Sydney Tanigawa. They made this a better book, and for that I am grateful.

My editor, Jonathan Karp, maintains he is no genius. Don't believe him. I consider myself very fortunate indeed to have such a gifted hand guiding my sometimes shaky ship. My daughter, Sonya, was a tremendous inspiration, in ways large and small, intentional and otherwise. She patiently endured my absences, as well as my grumpy presences, when the words wouldn't flow.

It is no exaggeration to say I could not have written this book without the unfailing support of my wife, Sharon. She is my muse, my love. My genius loci is anywhere, so long as she is by my side.

Finally, it is with heavy heart that I thank Eugene Martinez. In the short time I knew him, he became a trusted guide and a friend. He is missed. This book is also dedicated to his memory.

SELECT BIBLIOGRAPHY

Albert, Robert S., and Mark A. Runco. *Theories of Creativity*. London: Sage, 1990.

Amabile, Teresa. *Creativity in Context: Update to the Social Psychology of Creativity*. Boulder, CO: Westview, 1996.

Anderson, David Emmanuel et. al., eds. *Handbook of Creative Cities*. Cheltenham, UK: Edward Elgar, 2011.

Arieti, Silvano. *Creativity: The Magic Synthesis*. New York: Basic Books, 1976.

Austin, James H. *Chase, Chance, and Creativity: The Lucky Art of Novelty*. New York: Columbia University Press, 1978.

Barron, Frank X. *No Rootless Flower: An Ecology of Creativity*. New York: Hampton Press, 1995.

Baxter, Stephen. *Ages in Chaos: James Hutton and the Discovery of Deep Time*. New York: Tom Doherty, 2003.

Bell, Clive. *Civilization*. London: Penguin, 1928.

Beller, Steven. *Vienna and the Jews, 1867–1938: A Cultural History*. Cambridge: Cambridge University Press, 1989.

Boorstin, Daniel. *The Creators*. New York: Random House, 1992.

Bramly, Serge. *Leonardo: The Artist and the Man*. London: Penguin, 1994.

Braunbehrens, Volkmar. *Mozart in Vienna: 1781–1791*. New York: Grove Weidenfeld, 1986.

Briggs, John, and David F. Peat. *Seven Life Lessons of Chaos: Spiritual Wisdom from the Science of Change.* New York: HarperCollins, 1999.

Broadie, Alexander. *The Scottish Enlightenment: The Historical Age of the Historical Nation.* Edinburgh: Birlinn, 2001.

———, ed. *The Cambridge Companion to the Scottish Enlightenment.* New York: Cambridge University Press, 2003.

Brucker, Gene. *Renaissance Florence.* Berkeley: University of California Press, 1983.

Buchan, James. *Capital of the Mind: How Edinburgh Changed the World.* Edinburgh: Birlinn, 2007.

Burckhardt, Jacob. *The Civilization of the Renaissance in Italy.* New York: Random House, 1954.

Burke, Janine. *The Sphinx on the Table: Sigmund Freud's Art Collection and the Development of Psychoanalysis.* New York: Walker & Company, 2006.

Campbell, Donald. *Edinburgh: A Cultural History.* Northampton, UK: Interlink Pub Group, 2008.

Chaudhuri, Amit, ed. *Memory's Gold: Writings on Calcutta.* New Delhi: Penguin Viking, 2008.

———. *On Tagore: Reading the Poet Today.* New Delhi: Penguin Books India, 2012.

Chaudhuri, Sukanta, ed. *Calcutta: The Living City, Volume 1: The Past.* New Delhi: Oxford University Press, 1991.

———, ed. *Rabindranath Tagore: Selected Poems.* New Delhi: Oxford University Press, 2004.

Chitnis, Arnand C. *The Scottish Enlightenment: A Social History.* London: Rowan & Littlefield, 1976.

Cronin, Vincent. *The Florentine Renaissance.* London: Pimlico, 1992.

Csikszentmihalyi, Mihaly. *Creativity: Flow and the Psychology of Discovery and Invention.* New York: Harper Perennial, 1996.

D'Angour, Armand. *The Greeks and the New: Novelty in Ancient Greek Imagination and Experience.* Cambridge: Cambridge University Press, 2011.

D'Epiro, Peter, and Mary Desmond Pinkowish. *Sprezzatura: 50 Ways Italian Genius Shaped the World.* New York: Anchor Books, 2001.

Dasgupta, Subrata, *Awakening: The Story of the Bengal Renaissance*. Noida: Random House India, 2011.

Deighton, Hilary J. *A Day in the Life of Ancient Athens*. London: Bristol Classical Press, 1995.

———. *The Renaissance*. New York: Simon & Schuster, 1953.

Durant, Will. *The Life of Greece*. New York: Simon & Schuster, 1939.

Dutta, Krishna. *Calcutta: A Cultural and Literary History*. Oxford: Signal Books, 2003.

——— and Andrew Robinson. *Tagore: The Myriad-Minded Man*. New York: Bloomsbury, 1995.

Ellis, Markman. *The Coffee House: A Cultural History*. London: Orion Books, 2004.

Eysenck, Hans. *Genius: The Natural History of Innovation*. Melbourne: Cambridge University Press, 1995.

Firestein, Stuart. *Ignorance: How It Drives Science*. New York: Oxford University Press, 2012.

Flacelière, Robert. *Daily Life in Greece at the Time of Pericles*. London: Macmillan, 1965.

Florida, Richard. *The Rise of the Creative Class*. New York: Basic Books, 2011.

———. *Extraordinary Minds*. New York: Basic Books, 1997.

Gardner, Howard. *Creating Minds: An Anatomy of Creativity Seen Through the Lives of Freud, Einstein, Picasso, Stravinsky, Eliot, Graham, and Gandhi*. New York: Basic Books, 1993.

———. *Mozart*. New York: Penguin, 1999.

Gay, Peter. *Freud: A Life for Our Time*. New York: W. W. Norton & Company, 1988.

Geddes, Patrick. *The Life and Works of Sir Jagadis C. Bose*. London: Longmans, Green, and Co., 1920.

Gernet, Jacques. *Daily Life in China on the Eve of the Mongolian Invasion: 1250–1276*. Stanford: Stanford University Press, 1962.

Gillmor, C. Stewart. *Fred Terman at Stanford: Building a Discipline, a University, and Silicon Valley*. Stanford: Stanford University Press, 2004.

Glasser, Edward. *Triumph of the City: How Our Greatest Invention Makes Us*

Richer, Smarter, Greener, Healthier, and Happier. New York: Penguin, 2011.

Goldthwaite, Richard A. *Wealth and the Demand for Art in Italy, 1300–1600.* Baltimore: The Johns Hopkins University Press, 1993.

Goody, Jack. *Renaissances: The One or the Many?* Cambridge: Cambridge University Press, 2010.

Gosling, David L. *Science and the Indian Tradition: When Einstein Met Tagore.* New York: Routledge, 2007.

Grudin, Robert. *The Grace of Great Things: Creativity and Innovation.* Boston: Houghton Mifflin, 1990.

Hall, Sir Peter. *Cities in Civilization.* New York: Random House, 1998.

Hamilton, Edith. *The Greek Way.* New York: W. W. Norton & Company, 1964.

Harding, Rosamond E. M. *An Anatomy of Inspiration.* New York: Routledge, 2012.

Herman, Arthur. *How the Scots Invented the Modern World.* New York: Crown, 2001.

Hibbard, Howard. *Michelangelo.* New York: Harper & Row, 1985.

Higgins, Charlotte. *It's All Greek to Me: From Homer to the Hippocratic Oath, How Ancient Greece Has Shaped Our World.* New York: HarperCollins, 2010.

Holland, John H. *Complexity: A Very Short Introduction.* New York: Oxford University Press, 2014.

Janik, Allan, and Stephen Toulmin. *Wittgenstein's Vienna.* Chicago: Ivan R. Dee, 1996.

Jardine, Lisa. *Worldly Goods: A New History of the Renaissance.* New York: W. W. Norton & Company, 1996.

———. *Socrates: A Man For Our Times.* New York: Penguin, 2011.

Johnson, Paul. *The Renaissance: A Short History.* New York: Random House, 2000.

Kaufman, James C. et. al., eds. *The Cambridge Handbook of Creativity.* New York: Cambridge University Press, 2010.

Kenney, Martin, ed. *Understanding Silicon Valley: The Anatomy of an Entrepreneurial Region.* Stanford: Stanford University Press, 2000.

King, Ross. *Brunelleschi's Dome: How a Renaissance Genius Reinvented Architecture*. New York: Bloomsbury, 2000.

Kitto, H. D. F. *The Greeks*. Piscataway, NJ: Transaction Publishers, 1951.

Kotkin, Joel. *The City: A Global History*. Oxford: Phoenix, 2006.

Kroeber, A. L. *Configurations of Culture Growth*. Berkeley: University of California Press, 1944.

Landry, Charles. *The Creative City: A Toolkit For Urban Innovators*. London: Earthscan Publications, 2000.

Landucci, Luca. *A Florentine Diary, 1450 to 1516*. Florence: Arno Press, 1969.

Lau, Sing et. al., eds. *Creativity: When East Meets West*. Singapore: World Scientific, 2004.

Levey, Michael: *Florence: A Portrait*. Cambridge, MA: Harvard University Press, 1996.

Lopez, Robert S. "Hard Times and Investment in Culture," in *The Renaissance: Six Essays*. New York: The Metropolitan Museum of Art, 1953.

Lubart, Todd I., and Robert J. Sternberg. *Defying The Crowd: Cultivating Creativity in a Culture of Conformity*. New York: The Free Press, 1995.

Lucas-Dubreton, Jean. *Daily Life in Florence in the Time of the Medici*. New York: Macmillan, 1961.

McCarthy, Mary. *The Stones of Florence*. New York: Harcourt, 1963.

McClelland, David C. *The Achieving Society*. New York: The Free Press, 1967.

McMahon, Darrin. *Divine Fury: A History of Genius*. New York: Basic Books, 2013.

Mitra, Peary Chand. *A Biographical Sketch of David Hare*. Calcutta: W. Newman & Co., 1877.

Morris, Edmund. *Beethoven: The Universal Composer*. New York: Harper-Collins, 2005.

Mote, F. W. *Imperial China 900–1800*. Cambridge, MA: Harvard University Press, 1999.

Mumford, Lewis. *The City in History*. New York: Harcourt, 1961.

Murray, Charles. *Human Accomplishment: The Pursuit of Excellence in the Arts and Sciences, 800 BC to 1950*. New York: HarperCollins, 2003.

Murray, Penelope, ed. *Genius: History of an Idea*. Hoboken, NJ: Wiley-Blackwell, 1991.

Musil, Robert. *The Man Without Qualities* (Vol. 1). New York: Vintage, 1996.

Nicholl, Charles. *Leonardo da Vinci: Flights of the Mind*. New York: Penguin, 2004.

Nuland, Sherwin B. *Leonardo da Vinci*. New York: Penguin, 2000.

Ochse, R. *Before the Gates of Excellence. The Determinants of Creative Genius*. Melbourne: Cambridge University Press, 1990.

Oldenburg, Ray. *The Great Good Place: Cafes, Coffee Shops, Bookstores, Bars, Hair Salons and Other Hangouts at the Heart of a Community*. New York: Marlowe & Company, 1989.

Parsons, Nicholas T. *Vienna: A Cultural and Literary History*. Oxford: Signal Books, 2008.

Paulus, Paul B., and Bernard A. Nijstad, eds. *Group Creativity: Innovation Through Collaboration*. New York: Oxford University Press, 2003.

Plumb, J. H. *The Italian Renaissance*. Boston: Houghton Mifflin, 1961.

Rao, Arun. *A History of Silicon Valley: The Greatest Creation of Wealth in the History of the Planet*. Palo Alto, CA: Omniware Group, 2013.

Repcheck, Jack. *The Man Who Found Time: James Hutton and the Discovery of the Earth's Antiquity*. New York: Basic Books, 2009.

Richards, Ruth, ed. *Everyday Creativity and New Views of Human Nature*. Washington, DC: American Psychological Association, 2007.

Roberts, Royston M. *Serendipity: Accidental Discoveries in Science*. Hoboken, NJ: John Wiley & Sons, 1989.

Robinson, Andrew. *Genius: A Very Short Introduction*. New York: Oxford University Press, 2011.

———. *Sudden Genius? The Gradual Path to Creative Breakthroughs*. New York: Oxford University Press, 2010.

Rogers, Perry M., ed. *Aspects of Western Civilization* (Vol. 1). Upper Saddle River, NJ: Prentice Hall, 2003.

Rothenberg, Albert. *The Emerging Goddess: The Creative Process in Art, Science, and Other Fields*. Chicago: University of Chicago Press, 1980.

Runco, Mark A. *Creativity: Theories and Themes: Research, Development, and Practice.* London: Elsevier, 2007.

——— and Steven R. Pritzker, eds. *Encyclopedia of Creativity* (Vols. 1 and 2). London: Harcourt, Brace & Company, 1999.

Sachs, Harvey. *The Ninth: Beethoven and the World in 1824.* New York: Random House, 2010.

Sawyer, Keith R. *Explaining Creativity: The Science of Human Innovation.* New York: Oxford University Press, 2012.

———. *Group Genius: The Creative Power of Collaboration.* New York: Basic Books, 2007.

Saxenian, AnnaLee. *Regional Advantage: Culture and Competition in Silicon Valley and Route 128.* Cambridge, MA: Harvard University Press, 1994.

Schorske, Carl E. *Fin-De-Siècle Vienna: Politics and Culture.* New York: Vintage Books, 1981.

———. *Genius 101.* New York: Springer, 2009.

Simonton, Dean Keith. *Creativity in Science: Chance, Logic, Genius, and Zeitgeist.* Cambridge: Cambridge University Press, 2004.

———. *Origins of Genius: Darwinian Perspectives on Creativity.* New York: Oxford University Press, 1999.

Singer, Irving. *Modes of Creativity: Philosophical Perspectives.* Cambridge, MA: MIT Press, 2011.

Smith, Leonard. *Chaos: A Very Short Introduction.* New York: Oxford University Press, 2007.

Som, Reba. *Rabindranath Tagore: The Singer and His Song.* New Delhi: Penguin Books India, 2009.

Spike, John T. *Young Michelangelo: The Path to the Sistine: A Biography.* New York: The Vendome Press, 2010.

Sternberg, Robert J., and Janet E. Davidson, eds. *The Nature of Insight.* Cambridge, MA: MIT Press, 1994.

Stokes, Patricia D. *Creativity from Constraints: The Psychology of Breakthrough.* New York: Springer, 2006.

———. *My Reminiscences.* New Delhi: Rupa & Co., 2008.

———. *Personality.* New Delhi: Rupa & Co., 2007.

————. *My Life in My Words*. New Delhi: Penguin Books India, 2006.

Tagore, Rabindranath. *Gitanjali*. New Delhi: Rupa & Co., 1992.

Thucydides. *History of the Peloponnesian War*. Translated by Rex Warner. London: Penguin, 1954.

Törnqvist, Gunnar. *The Geography of Creativity*. Cheltenham, UK: Edward Elgar, 2011.

Unger, Miles J. *Magnifico: The Brilliant Life and Violent Times of Lorenzo De' Medici*. New York: Simon & Schuster, 2008.

Vance, Ashlee. *Geek Silicon Valley*. Guilford, CT: The Globe Pequot Press, 2007.

Vasari, Giorgio. *The Lives of the Artists*. New York: Oxford University Press, 1991.

Walcot, Peter. *Envy and the Greeks: A Study in Human Behavior*. Warminster, UK: Aris & Phillips, 1978.

Waldrop, M. Mitchell. *Complexity: The Emerging Science at the Edge of Order and Chaos*. New York: Simon & Schuster, 1992.

Walker, Paul Robert. *The Feud That Sparked the Renaissance: How Brunelleschi and Ghiberti Changed the Art World*. New York: HarperCollins, 2002.

————. *Why Socrates Died: Dispelling the Myths*. New York: W. W. Norton & Company, 2009.

Waterfield, Robin. *Athens: From Ancient Ideal to Modern City*. New York: Basic Books, 2004.

Watson, Burton (translator). *Selected Poems of Su Tung-p'o*. Townsend, WA: Copper Canyon Press, 1994.

Watson, Peter. *Ideas: A History of Thought and Invention, From Fire to Freud*. New York: HarperCollins, 2005.

Weiner, Richard Paul. *Creativity and Beyond: Cultures, Values, and Change*. Albany: State University of New York, 2000.

Weisberg, Robert W. *Creativity: Beyond the Myth of Genius*. New York: W. H. Freeman and Company, 1993.

Wormald, Jenny. *Scotland: A History*. New York: Oxford University Press, 2005.

Yutang, Lin. *The Gay Genius: The Life and Times of Su Tungpo*. Beijing: Foreign Language Teaching and Research Press, 2009.

Zhang, Cong Ellen. *Transformative Journeys: Travel and Culture in Song China*. Honolulu: University of Hawai'i Press, 2011.

Zweig, Stefan. *The World of Yesterday*. Translated by Anthea Bell. London: Pushkin Press, 2011.

INDEX

ABOUT THE AUTHOR

ERIC WEINER is a philosophical traveler and recovering malcontent. His books include the *New York Times* bestseller *The Geography of Bliss* and *Man Seeks God*. A former foreign correspondent for NPR, his work has appeared in *The New York Times, Slate, Quartz, Los Angeles Times, Foreign Policy*, the BBC, *AFAR, The Best American Travel Writing*, and elsewhere. For some reason, he lives in the Washington, DC, area. Learn more at: www.EricWeinerBooks.com

CPSIA information can be obtained
at www.ICGtesting.com
Printed in the USA
LVHW011736290522
719821LV00001B/1

9 781451 691672